CW01237272

# DAY OF THE RANGERS

OSPREY
PUBLISHING

*"Energetically will I meet the enemies of my country. I shall defeat them on the field of battle for I am better trained and will fight with all my might. Surrender is not a Ranger word. I will never allow a fallen comrade to fall into the hands of the enemy, and under no circumstances will I ever embarrass my country."*

**5th stanza of the US Army Ranger Creed**

# LEIGH NEVILLE

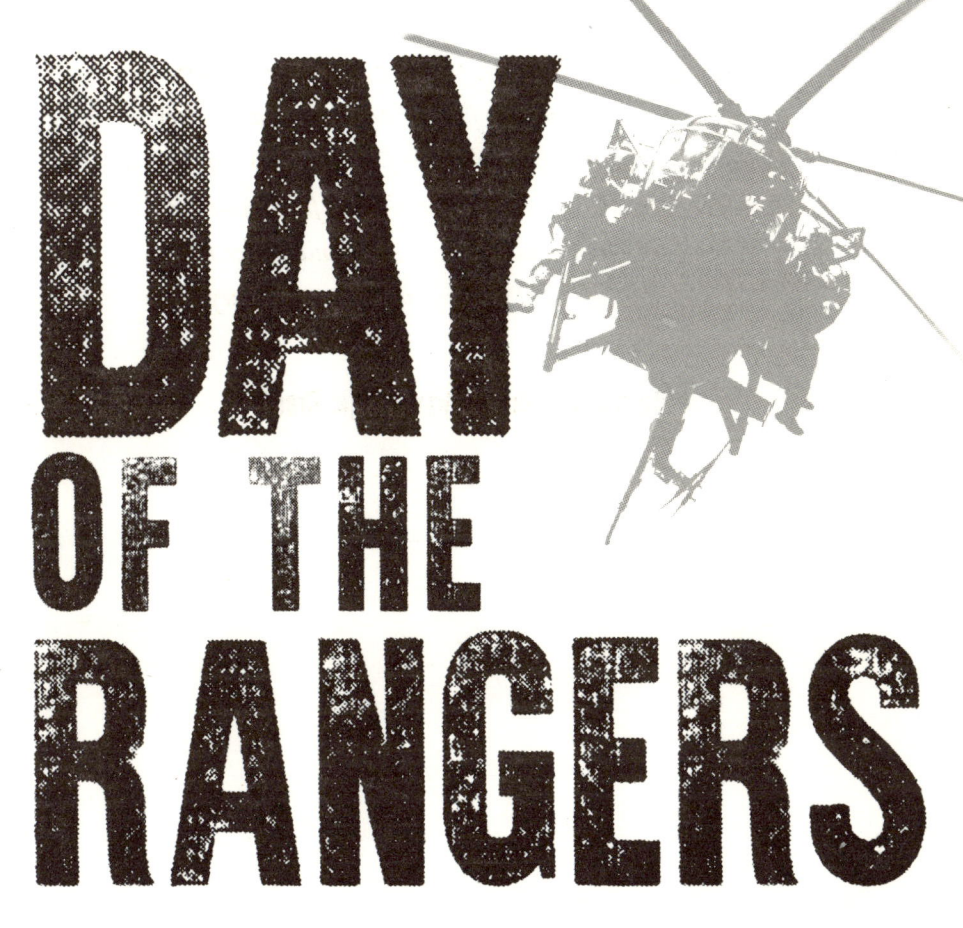

# DAY OF THE RANGERS

## THE BATTLE OF MOGADISHU 25 YEARS ON

# DEDICATION

To the fallen, their families, friends and units and to the men still suffering the visible and hidden wounds from the battle of Mogadishu.
"When you go home, tell them of us and say
For their tomorrow, we gave our today."

**1st Special Forces Operational Detachment-Delta (Airborne)**
Staff Sergeant Daniel Busch
Sergeant First Class Earl Fillmore
Master Sergeant Gary Gordon
Master Sergeant Tim Martin
Sergeant First Class Matt Rierson
Sergeant First Class Randy Shughart

**160th Special Operations Aviation Regiment (Airborne)**
Chief Warrant Officer Class 2 Donovan Briley
Staff Sergeant William Cleveland
Staff Sergeant Tommy Field
Chief Warrant Officer Class 4 Ray Frank
Chief Warrant Officer Class 3 Clifton Wolcott

**10th Mountain Division**
Sergeant Cornell Houston
Private First Class James Martin

**75th Ranger Regiment**
Corporal James Cavaco
Sergeant Casey Joyce
Private First Class Richard Kowalewski
Sergeant Dominick Pilla
Sergeant Lorenzo Ruiz
Corporal Jamie Smith

OSPREY PUBLISHING
Bloomsbury Publishing Plc
PO Box 883, Oxford, OX1 9PL, UK
1385 Broadway, 5th Floor, New York, NY 10018, USA
E-mail: info@ospreypublishing.com
www.ospreypublishing.com

OSPREY is a trademark of Osprey Publishing Ltd
First published in Great Britain in 2018
© Leigh Neville, 2018

Leigh Neville has asserted his right under the Copyright, Designs and Patents Act, 1988, to be identified as Author of this work.

For legal purposes the Acknowledgements on pp. 9–11 constitute an extension of this copyright page.

All rights reserved. No part of this publication may be reproduced or transmitted in any form or by any means, electronic or mechanical, including photocopying, recording, or any information storage or retrieval system, without prior permission in writing from the publishers.

A catalogue record for this book is available from the British Library.

ISBN: HB 9781472824257; eBook 9781472824271; ePDF 9781472824264; XML 9781472824288

18 19 20 21 22   10 9 8 7 6 5 4 3 2 1

Index by Zoe Ross
DiTomasso map by Bounford.com.
Bird's-eye-view by Alan Gilliland, © Osprey Publishing. Reproduced from RAID 31 *Operation Gothic Serpent*.
Originated by PDQ Digital Media Solutions, Bungay, UK
Printed and bound in Great Britain by CPI (Group) UK Ltd, Croydon CR0 4YY
Front cover: Main image courtesy of Leigh Neville

Osprey Publishing supports the Woodland Trust, the UK's leading woodland conservation charity. Between 2014 and 2018 our donations are being spent on their Centenary Woods project in the UK.

To find out more about our authors and books visit **www.ospreypublishing.com**. Here you will find extracts, author interviews, details of forthcoming events and the option to sign up for our newsletter.

# CONTENTS

Acknowledgments     9
Foreword     12
Dramatis Personae     15

**CHAPTER 1: Gothic Serpent**     20

**CHAPTER 2: The First Six**     41

**CHAPTER 3: Lucy**     79

**CHAPTER 4: Big Sky, Small Bullet**     123

**CHAPTER 5: "We Are Their Only Hope"**     160

**CHAPTER 6: "Ranger, Ranger. You Die Somalia"**     178

**CHAPTER 7: The Long Night**     206

**CHAPTER 8: The Mogadishu Mile**     **233**

**CHAPTER 9: Maalintii Rangers**     **251**

| | |
|---|---|
| Appendices | 286 |
| Glossary | 319 |
| Notes | 324 |
| References | 337 |
| Index | 346 |

# ACKNOWLEDGMENTS

This book would not exist without the pioneering efforts of journalist and author Mark Bowden. His account of the October 3–4 mission, *Black Hawk Down*, later filmed as a successful motion picture, was an invaluable resource and even greater inspiration. Later works by participants including Nightstalker pilot Mike Durant and co-author Steven Hartov's *In the Company of Heroes*, and *The Battle of Mogadishu* edited by former Ranger Matt Eversmann and Pararescueman Dan Schilling, were equally important. All three books are highly recommended to all readers.

The aim of this book is to complement Bowden's work. I have had the opportunity thanks to documents that have come to light over the past two decades and access to participants who are now more comfortable talking about the events of October 3, 1993, to provide new detail on the battle through the lens of military history. I have also tried to interview participants who didn't, for whatever reason, feature heavily in Bowden's book to hopefully provide a more rounded account and fill in some gaps, including a significant contribution from former members of Delta Force.

My greatest appreciation must go, in no particular order, to Mike Durant, Gerry Izzo, and Karl Maier, formerly of the 160th Special Operations Aviation Regiment; John Belman, Tom DiTomasso, Matt Eversmann, and Jeff Struecker, formerly of the 75th Ranger Regiment; and Norman Hooten, Gary Keeney, Paul Leonard, Michael Moser, Jim Smith, and Kelly Venden, formerly of the 1st Special Forces Operational Detachment-Delta. All of these gentlemen endured hours of personal interviews and rounds of no doubt annoying follow-up questions with both charm and good grace. Without them, this book simply could not have been written. A very special thanks must go to Matt Eversmann who kindly provided the Foreword to this book.

A number of other members of the Task Force Ranger units have requested anonymity, often due to their continued work in the field of special operations. To these gentlemen I give my profound thanks for their trust in agreeing to speak with me; I hope I have accurately portrayed their views and recollections. I am also deeply indebted to Tom Faust, James Lechner, Larry Perino, Lee Rysewyk, and Kurt Smith for the detailed first-person after-action reviews they wrote soon after the battle, which have proven an important historical resource.

As always, my thanks must also go to my wife, Jodi Fraser-Neville, and my editor, Kate Moore, for their support, patience, and encouragement. Others I must thank include Pete Panzeri and Mike Vining, both US Army veterans; author and journalist Sean Naylor; Bob Mitchell and the US Army Aviation Museum in Alabama; and Dr Nicole Suarez and the Airborne and Special Operations Museum in North Carolina. Both of the latter institutions include some incredible artifacts from the battle and the author strongly encourages readers to visit should they be in the area.

A note on naming conventions. In the case of personnel assigned to Delta I have made the decision upon consultation with a number of former members of the unit to only mention an operator's full name if I have received explicit permission from that operator. In all other cases, including for personnel attached to the Delta squadron, I have chosen to use their first name and the first initial of their surname only, in the interests of personal security.

Former Nightstalker Gerry Izzo sagely told me as I began this book that no matter how accurate I attempted to be, the story of the battle was like a jigsaw puzzle and that at the end there would still be some pieces missing. He was right. As with any historical narrative there are people and information I would have liked to have had access to but for various reasons did not.

All such missing parts, and the inevitable inaccuracies that have crept into the text, are my fault alone. Likewise there are many, many stories still to be told of this important battle. I have tried to tell some which are less well known and provide new perspectives on better-known events but ultimately this book still only provides a snapshot of that horrific 18-hour battle and its aftermath.

## ACKNOWLEDGMENTS

The book may also be viewed as slightly skewed toward the Nightstalker, Ranger, and Delta perspectives of the battle. This is purely a result of my contacts within those units and is no slight toward the Navy SEAL or Air Force Special Tactics personnel who performed so admirably and honorably on October 3 and 4. There is also, unfortunately, little depiction of the Somali perspective apart from a number of historical interview transcripts. Somalia remains an active warzone and access to participants, many of whom may have by now passed away, was impossible.

A final word about the *Black Hawk Down* film. There are several instances where the depiction of events in the movie was either fabricated or consolidated for dramatic effect. This is an understandable process and is common in Hollywood representations of historical events – it must be remembered that it was a blockbuster movie, not a ten-part documentary. Where such divergences from the historical record are identified, I've pointed them out in the hope of providing further insight for readers who have seen the film and wondered about particular scenes.

This should not be seen as a criticism of the film itself, which offered the public a surprisingly accurate account of most aspects of the battle and is well worth viewing if the reader has not done so. The extended version including commentary by Tom Matthews, Lee Van Arsdale, Danny McKnight, and Matt Eversmann is particularly recommended.

# FOREWORD

*"That he which hath no stomach to this fight,*
*Let him depart; his passport shall be made*
*And crowns for convoy put into his purse:*
*We would not die in that man's company"*

**Shakespeare's *Henry V*, Act IV, Scene III**

I had never read the play nor heard the famous words until Major General Bill Garrison, the commander of Task Force Ranger, delivered an extemporaneous version of the St Crispin's Day speech at the memorial service for our fallen comrades. We were still in country and he was the last to speak. I don't recall what any of the other officers said but I remember him and his speech. It was fitting. When I look back almost 25 years I can still remember standing in the formation with all the members of the Task Force. I can see the podium where the commanders gave their eulogies. I see the boots of the fallen on the makeshift stage, a rifle between them, dog tags hanging off the pistol grips and the headgear on top. Some memories I will never forget.

The deployment to Mogadishu was a scary time; it was chaotic, it was exciting, and of course it was sad; but all those feelings and emotions, while

# FOREWORD

very human, pale in comparison to the deep-rooted pride of being in the fight with this group of soldiers. I realized under the hot Mogadishu sun that we had the stomach for the fight. It was ugly. It was a brawl, but we, like the soldiers of King Henry, though outmanned and outgunned by a force estimated to number 10,000, stuck it out when everything went south. We stayed and we fought. The stories of those fights are extraordinary. Leigh Neville brings them to life in *Day of the Rangers: The Battle of Mogadishu 25 Years On.*

For many of the men from the 3rd Battalion, 75th Ranger Regiment this was the first combat deployment. The men from the other units, 1st Special Forces Operational Detachment-Delta and the Task Force 160th Special Operations Aviation Regiment, had more operational experience. It was in some regards an odd mix of talent, yet despite all that happened in the fight against Aideed's militia, this team of teams accounted for itself well. The lessons learned, both good and bad, impacted the way our forces have fought ever since. It may not have been textbook, but give credit to the men who "figured it out" on the battlefield. These stories deserve to be told and are very worthy of repeating.

It is hard to believe that the Battle of Mogadishu took place almost 25 years ago. The event on that day, October 3, 1993 has been called many things, some of them not all that nice. I still cringe when the newscasters or politicians recall "the disaster in Somalia." Or, even worse, "the debacle where American soldiers died on the streets of Mogadishu." In some regards I suppose it is true. It was a strategic failure. Our foreign policy changed overnight and it would haunt American policy for the next two and a half decades. It seems such a disservice to use words like those in the same breath as we honor the men who lost their limbs, spilled their blood, and made the sacrifice of sacrifices. Not a failure, any of them. Foreign policy is tough to understand and yet, in the end, when diplomacy does fail, they must turn to men like these to right a wrong. Aideed and his thug militia were bad men doing atrocious things and literally no other force in the world would go after him.

Eight years after this battle the United States itself was attacked and launched what has become the longest war in American history. For the past 17 years the stories from the battlefield have been everything from tragic to inspiring. We have a generation of citizens who have never known peace. I am hopeful that they will read this book. I wonder though, if we have learned the lessons from Mogadishu at the most senior level of politics. I am inclined to say no, we haven't, as witnessed by the 2016 battle for Mosul, again. We left Mogadishu in 1993 and 25 years later al-Shabaab occupies and kills with ease. Much like in Mosul, American forces in Somalia are walking through bloody sand. The politicians of the new millennium need to read these stories before they send America's sons and daughters to the four corners of the globe to fight. But politics is not for the soldier. The men of Task Force Ranger willingly said, "send me."

At the tactical level though, at the place where soldiers roam, these stories are a lens to the warrior DNA, the ethos that leads average men to do extraordinary things in the crucible. Leigh's investigation and follow up to Mark Bowden's *Black Hawk Down* is timely and well written. This isn't *Black Hawk Down* 2.0. It is another chance for incredible tales of valor to be told for the first time, as soldiers who did not have the opportunity to share their experience with Mark have the chance now.

For the past 25 years, war stories have become obviously more routine. But there is a common denominator and for a generation of warriors the similarities are profound. The faces and names of the heroic men and women who stand in harm's way change like the geography but their actions are very much the same. They put the needs of others first, they act courageously and they fulfill their duties, without exception. These are very much the stories from Task Force Ranger.

I retired in 2008 and ten years of business life has certainly made me softer than I was back then. Even though the acuteness of combat has faded I still know that war is ugly. Movies and TV shows make it look so sexy, but the reality of combat hurts. However, it is often necessary and because of this we need young men and women who are ready to stomach the fight and stand in the furnace. *Day of the Rangers* tells their story.

**Matt Eversmann**
West Palm Beach, FL

# DRAMATIS PERSONAE

**Mohamed Farah Aideed**, warlord of the Habr Gidr clan and target of Task Force Ranger. Killed in August 1996.
**Les Aspin**, US Secretary of Defense.
**Osman Atto**, Aideed's Finance Minister, targeted and captured by Task Force Ranger on September 21, 1993.
**Abdi Hassan Awale**, Aideed's Interior Minister, targeted and captured by Task Force Ranger on October 3, 1993.
**Sergeant John Belman**, 75th Rangers, Squad Leader, deployed on Super 68 CSAR.
**Staff Sergeant Ray Benjamin**, USAF Combat Controller, deployed on Super 63 C2 helicopter.
**Private First Class Anton Berendsen**, 75th Rangers, deployed with Chalk 4. Wounded in action at Chalk 4 blocking position.
**Private Todd Blackburn**, 75th Rangers, deployed with Chalk 4. Wounded in action after falling from fast rope.
**Colonel William "Jerry" Boykin**, Delta, Commander of Delta Force.
**Boutros Boutros-Ghali**, UN Secretary General.
**Staff Sergeant Jeff Bray**, USAF Combat Controller deployed with Assault Force. Passed away in October 2016.
**Chief Warrant Officer Class 2 Donovan Briley**, 160th SOAR, pilot of Super 61. Killed in action October 3, 1993 in the crash of Super 61.
**Staff Sergeant Daniel Busch**, Delta, member of 3 Troop (Sniper), deployed on Super 61. Killed in action October 3, 1993 after defending the Super 61 crash site.

**Corporal James Cavaco**, 75th Rangers, deployed on GRF #1. Killed in action October 3, 1993 whilst manning a heavy weapon during efforts to reach the Super 61 crash site.

**Staff Sergeant William Cleveland**, 160th SOAR, crew chief on Super 64. Killed in action October 3, 1993 after the crash of Super 64.

**Lieutenant Colonel Bill David**, 10th Mountain, Commander of 2-14 Infantry and Quick Reaction Force.

**Lieutenant Tom DiTomasso**, 75th Rangers, Commander 2nd Platoon, deployed on October 3 in command of Chalk 2.

**Staff Sergeant Ray Dowdy**, 160th SOAR, crew chief on Super 61. Wounded in action during Super 61 crash.

**General Wayne Downing**, Commander US Special Operations Command (SOCOM).

**Chief Warrant Officer 3 Michael Durant**, 160th SOAR, pilot Super 64. Shot down and captured on October 3, 1993.

**Major General Carl Ernst**, Commander US Forces, Somalia from October 15, 1993.

**Staff Sergeant Matt Eversmann**, 75th Rangers, Squad Leader, deployed on October 3 in command of Chalk 4.

**Master Sergeant Scott Fales**, USAF Special Tactics Pararescueman Jumper, deployed on Super 68 CSAR. Wounded in action at Super 61 crash site.

**Lieutenant Colonel James "Tommy" Faust**, JSOC, J-2 Cell.

**Staff Sergeant Tommy Field**, 160th SOAR, crew chief on Super 64. Killed in action October 3, 1993 after the crash of Super 64.

**Sergeant First Class Earl Fillmore**, Delta, member of 1 Troop, deployed with Assault Force. Killed in action October 3, 1993 during foot movement to Super 61 crash site.

**Chief Warrant Officer Class 4 Ray Frank**, 160th SOAR, crew chief on Super 64. Killed in action October 3, 1993 after the crash of Super 64.

**Major General William "Bill" Garrison**, Commander Joint Special Operations Command (JSOC) and Commander, Task Force Ranger.

**Chief Warrant Officer Class 3 Mike Goffena**, pilot Super 62. Passed away in February 1998.

**Private First Class Marcus Good**, 75th Rangers, medic assigned to Chalk 4.

**Master Sergeant Gary Gordon**, Delta, member of 3 Troop (Sniper), deployed on Super 62. Killed in action October 3, 1993 defending the Super 64 crash site.

## DRAMATIS PERSONAE

**Master Sergeant Jon Hale**, Delta, A-Team Leader, 1 Troop, deployed with Assault Force. Passed away in January 2016.

**Lieutenant Colonel Gary Harrell**, Delta, Commander of C-Squadron and deployed in Super 66 C2 helicopter as Ground Mission Commander on October 3.

**General Joseph Hoar**, Commander US Central Command (CENTCOM)

**Sergeant First Class Norman Hooten**, Delta, F-Team Leader, 2 Troop, deployed with Assault Force.

**Admiral Jonathan Howe**, United Nations Special Representative for Somalia.

**Chief Warrant Officer 3 (P) Gerry Izzo**, 160th SOAR, pilot Super 65.

**Chief Warrant Officer Dan Jollota**, 160th SOAR, pilot Super 68.

**Chief Warrant Officer Keith Jones**, 160th SOAR, co-pilot Star 41.

**Chief Warrant Officer Randy Jones**, 160th SOAR, pilot Barber 51.

**Sergeant Casey Joyce**, 75th Rangers, team leader, deployed with Chalk 4 blocking position. Killed in action October 3, 1993 during GRF #1 movement toward Super 61 crash site.

**Sergeant First Class Gary Keeney**, Delta, member of 1 Troop, deployed with Assault Force. Wounded in action on GRF #1 convoy.

**Private First Class Richard Kowalewski**, 75th Rangers, deployed on GRF #1. Killed in action October 3, 1993 during GRF #1 movement toward Super 61 crash site.

**Lieutenant James "Jim" Lechner**, 75th Rangers, B Company Fire Support Officer, deployed with Chalk 1. Wounded in action during foot movement to Super 61 crash site.

**Sergeant First Class Paul Leonard**, Delta, member of 1 Troop, deployed with Assault Force. Wounded in action on GRF #1 convoy.

**Chief Warrant Officer Karl Maier**, 160th SOAR, pilot Star 41.

**Doctor John "Rob" Marsh**, Delta, surgeon and commander of JSOC Joint Medical Augmentation Unit.

**Master Sergeant Tim "Griz" Martin**, Delta, member of 2 Troop, deployed with Assault Force. Killed in action October 3, 1993 during GRF #1 movement toward Super 61 crash site.

**Lieutenant Colonel Tom Matthews**, 160th SOAR, Commander 1st Battalion, 160th SOAR, deployed in Super 63 C2 helicopter as Air Mission Commander on October 3.

# DAY OF THE RANGERS

**Lieutenant Colonel Danny McKnight**, 75th Rangers, Commander 3rd Battalion, deployed to lead GRF #1 on October 3. Wounded in action on GRF #1 convoy.
**Colonel David "Dave" McKnight**, JSOC, J-2 Cell. Passed away in 1997.
**Staff Sergeant Jeff McLaughlin**, 75th Rangers, Forward Observer deployed with Chalk 4. Wounded in action at Chalk 4 blocking position.
**Captain Drew Meyerowich**, Commander of QRC, 2-14 Infantry.
**Captain Austin "Scottie" Miller**, Delta, Assault Force and Ground Force Commander, deployed with Assault Force.
**Major General Thomas Montgomery**, Deputy UN Force Commander and Commander US Forces, Somalia.
**Lieutenant Larry Moores**, 75th Rangers, Commander 3rd Platoon, deployed on October 3 with GRF #2 and Task Force David.
**Staff Sergeant Michael Moser**, Delta, member of 1 Troop, deployed with Assault Force. Wounded in action during foot movement to Super 61 crash site.
**Chief Warrant Officer Jeff Niklaus**, 160th SOAR, pilot of Super 67.
**Lieutenant Larry Perino**, 75th Rangers, Commander 1st Platoon, deployed on October 3 in command of Chalk 1.
**Sergeant Dominick Pilla**, 75th Rangers, deployed on GRF #1. Killed in action October 3, 1993 during GRF #1 MEDEVAC of wounded Ranger.
**General Colin Powell**, Chairman of the US Joint Chiefs of Staff.
**Sergeant Randy Ramaglia**, 75th Rangers, deployed with Chalk 3. Wounded in action during the "Mogadishu Mile."
**Sergeant First Class Matt Rierson**, Delta, C-Team Leader, 1 Troop, deployed with Assault Force. Killed in action October 6, 1993 in mortar strike on Task Force Ranger hangar.
**Major Herb Rodriguez**, 160th SOAR, co-pilot of Super 68.
**Technical Sergeant Pat Rogers**, USAF Combat Controller, deployed on Super 68 CSAR. Passed away in November 2001.
**Sergeant Lorenzo Ruiz**, 75th Rangers, deployed on GRF #1. Killed in action October 3, 1993 whilst manning a heavy weapon during efforts to reach the Super 61 crash site.
**Captain Lee Rysewyk**, 75th Rangers, Executive Officer, B Company.
**Omar Salad**, Aideed's principal political adviser, targeted and captured by Task Force Ranger on October 3, 1993.

# DRAMATIS PERSONAE

**Technical Sergeant Dan Schilling**, USAF Combat Controller, deployed with McKnight command element on GRF #1.

**Sergeant First Class Randy Shughart**, Delta, member of 3 Troop (Sniper), deployed on Super 62. Killed in action October 3, 1993 defending the Super 64 crash site.

**Corporal Jamie Smith**, 75th Rangers, deployed with Chalk 1 blocking position. Killed in action October 3, 1993 after foot movement to Super 61 crash site.

**Sergeant First Class Jim Smith**, Delta, member of 3 Troop (Sniper). Wounded in action defending the Super 61 crash site.

**Staff Sergeant Kurt Smith**, Delta, 2 Troop, deployed with Assault Force.

**Captain Mike Steele**, 75th Rangers, Commander B Company, deployed with Chalk 1 on October 3.

**Sergeant Jeff Struecker**, 75th Rangers, deployed on October 3 with GRF #1, led Blackburn MEDEVAC and returned to the city on GRF #2 and Task Force David.

**Sergeant Keni Thomas**, 75th Rangers, Squad Leader, deployed with Chalk 3.

**Lieutenant Colonel Lee Van Arsdale**, JSOC, deployed in command of Task Force Ranger element on GRF #2 and Task Force David.

**Sergeant First Class Kelly Venden**, Delta, deployed with A-Squadron to relieve C-Squadron after October 3.

**Staff Sergeant Charlie Warren**, 160th SOAR, crew chief on Super 61. Wounded in action during Super 61 crash.

**Sergeant Sean "Tim" Watson**, 75th Rangers, Squad Leader, deployed in command of Chalk 3.

**Captain Michael Whetstone**, Commander C-Company, 2-14th Infantry.

**Chief Warrant Officer Class 3 Clifton Wolcott**, 160th SOAR, pilot of Super 61. Killed in action October 3, 1993 in the crash of Super 61.

**Technical Sergeant Timothy Wilkinson**, USAF Special Tactics Pararescueman Jumper, deployed on Super 68 CSAR.

**Captain Jim Yacone**, 160th SOAR, co-pilot Super 62.

# CHAPTER 1

# GOTHIC SERPENT

*"If you think the National Rifle Association has a fixation regarding weapons, it's nothing compared to the Somalis. It is part of their manhood. And they learn how to use them. Like the Chechens, if there's nobody else to fight they fight amongst themselves. But if there's a foreigner who comes in, everybody is perfectly happy to fight him and fight even harder because he's from the outside."*

**Ambassador Robert Oakley, former Ambassador and Special Envoy for Somalia**

In 1993, the East African nation of Somalia was the very definition of a failed state. Situated on the Indian Ocean, Somalia had suffered years of civil war leading to the downfall of President Siad Barre. Barre had come to power in a military coup in 1969, installing himself as head of a socialist Supreme Revolutionary Council, aligning himself closely to the Soviet Union and brutally suppressing all dissent.

Somalia had only gained independence a scant nine years earlier. Before 1960, it had been two separate nations under United Nations trusteeship: British Somaliland and Italian Somaliland. The concept of a central government had always faced struggles in Somalia. Much like Afghanistan, the society was heavily clan-dominated. Six major clans had shared power whilst the country see-sawed through various iterations of colonial rule. Barre manipulated these clans, setting them against each other, outlawing some whilst bringing others into the fold to maintain his power base.

The beginning of the end for Barre was the disastrous conflict with Ethiopia in 1977 known as the Ogaden War, which saw the Somalis defeated largely due to their Soviet benefactors switching their support mid-flow to back the Ethiopians. Many in the Somali military lost faith in Barre in the aftermath and a failed coup ended in bloody reprisals and executions amongst the leaders of the clans responsible for the uprising.

This crackdown led to the eventual formation of the Somali National Movement (SNM), an insurgency based in the northwest of the country with the aim of overthrowing Barre's junta. The Somali leader sought to crush the SNM, establishing what he termed Mobile Military Courts to try suspected insurgents and sympathizers. These trials were perfunctory, typically ending in the execution of the unfortunate defendant. From these kangaroo courts, the Barre regime soon escalated to mass slaughter, attempting to literally wipe out the clans that made up the SNM.

The United States, which had stepped in as Barre's benefactor after the Soviets withdrew their sponsorship, also withdrew their support in the wake of this attempted genocide. With widespread international condemnation of the regime, clan-based militias emerged rivalling the SNM and attempting to wrestle control of regional centers from Barre's forces. The largest, the Italian-backed United Somali Congress (USC), was established in 1989 by the Hawiye Clan. This emergence of multiple armed rivals placed pressure on the increasingly fragile dictatorship of Barre.

After the USC conducted a major offensive against the capital Mogadishu in 1991, Barre saw the writing on the wall and fled the country in the time-honored fashion of the dictator. A factional war soon broke out within the USC itself as sub-clans vied for control. Former general Mohamed Farah Aideed, who had been sentenced to six years in jail by Barre, violently contested the USC's choice of president to replace Barre, Ali Mahdi Mohammed.

Aideed had been educated in Italy and served as Mogadishu's Chief of Police before attending military staff college in Russia. He progressed rapidly through the ranks in Barre's regime although, in the Stalinesque atmosphere, Aideed's popularity brought him under suspicion and he was imprisoned, only to be released to serve during the ill-fated Ogaden War. Following the defeat of Somali forces, Aideed served as Ambassador to India.

Aideed was from the Habr Gidr, a sub-clan of the powerful Hawiye. Mohammed was from another Hawiye sub-clan, the Abgaal. Arguments soon turned to violence and bitter fighting broke out between the factions in Mogadishu. In the power vacuum after the fall of Barre's regime, other clans who held territory outside of the capital soon joined the fighting that turned at least a fifth of the country's population into internally displaced refugees.

The civil war coupled with a crippling famine – itself a by-product of the war – and drought resulted in a burgeoning humanitarian crisis with more than two hundred thousand Somalis dying from malnutrition in 1992. Global television coverage spurred an international effort to relieve the suffering. Initially nongovernment agencies such as the International Committee of the Red Cross (ICRC) took on most of the task.

The United Nations Security Council established a number of resolutions which called for an arms embargo on all warring factions and an end to hostilities but lacked any scope for the deployment of international peacekeepers to enforce such measures. A token security force – UNOSOM or United Nations Operations in Somalia – was added in a later resolution to monitor an early UN-brokered ceasefire and ensure aid shipments were delivered to those in need. The UN were working toward an ambitious goal, the so-called "100-Day Action Programme for Accelerated Humanitarian Assistance," aiming to end the famine and subsequent humanitarian disaster in Somalia within months.

Whilst Aideed initially supported humanitarian efforts, or at least allowed them to proceed, the game changed on October 28, 1992. Aideed pronounced that the Pakistani battalion providing security for the UN operations in Mogadishu was no longer welcome. He also railed against what he saw as outside control of the airport. In reality, his position as powerbroker within Mogadishu was threatened by the arrival of the United Nations. Aideed's militias began firing mortars and artillery at both the airport and at cargo ships delivering the much-needed aid.

UNOSOM faltered in its efforts as most factions roundly ignored the ceasefire and Aideed stepped up his attacks. The United States under President George H. W. Bush offered to provide much-needed additional manpower, an offer readily accepted by the UN. The mission was known to US forces as Operation *Restore Hope*. Bush had recently heralded the arrival of a "New World Order" following the end of the Cold War and was keen to place the United States at the forefront of forging that new world. One official explained: "The intent is to allow the food deliveries to continue, to allow Somalia as a nation to kind of come together."[1]

The United Nations saw the US role as one of providing physical security for the humanitarian mission: "The United States has undertaken to take the lead in creating the secure environment which is an inescapable condition for the United Nations to provide humanitarian relief and promote national reconciliation and economic reconstruction, objectives which have from the outset been included in the various Security Council resolutions on Somalia."[2]

United States military forces first deployed to Somalia in numbers on December 9, 1992. Some readers may recall the images of Navy SEALs (SEa-Air-Land), their faces caked in camouflage cream, making a covert landing onto the beaches of Mogadishu, only to be met by the full glare of the world's press. Such press attention would continue to dog, and at times undermine, US military efforts in Somalia.

Aideed, a Machiavellian strategist of the first order, at first publicly supported the US efforts, hoping to drive a rift between the Americans and the United Nations. His Finance Minister and second-in-command, Osman Atto, produced leaflets extolling the US whilst decrying the UN. "USA is Friend – UN is Invader" read the leaflets.

The UN Secretary General, Boutros Boutros-Ghali, had supported Barre in his former role as Egypt's Foreign Minister and was particularly hated by Aideed, who believed that Boutros-Ghali had a secret agenda to undermine Aideed. Indeed Boutros-Ghali did nothing to dissuade Aideed of this opinion, arguing that only a complete disarmament of the clans, including the Habr Gidr, would solve the humanitarian crisis facing Somalia.

Aideed instead saw the chaos as a means to an end and positioned himself to become the kingpin of the Somali warlords, refusing to join the UN's negotiated solution with the other warlords, and continuing his war with the rival Abgaal as he felt the presidency was his right. The USC and Aideed maintained close relations with yet another armed militia, the Somali National Alliance (SNA) that also soon began attacks against UN forces, typically in the form of mortar harassment fires, sniping, and the laying of landmines.

Food distribution centers were still being hijacked by clan militias who stole the aid to re-sell on the black market or simply to deny relief to rival clans. Those who controlled the food, controlled Mogadishu. Security around the centers also became problematic with the distribution of aid resulting in food riots, which led to US Marines being deployed to guard the shipments. The militias, however, would simply wait for the Marines to leave for the night before seizing the shipments. A US State Department spokeswoman noted at the time: "The appalling and intolerable slaughter results from selfish attempts by clan-based factions to gain or maintain an advantage over one another."[3]

UNOSOM, and the US Operation *Restore Hope*, ended in May 1993 and both organizations transformed into UNOSOM II in May 1993 under the new American administration of President Bill Clinton. Under United Nations Security Council Resolution 814, signed by the UN Security Council on March 26, 1993, UNOSOM II was given an exceptionally broad mandate to secure humanitarian supplies and bring peace to Somalia, including the deployment of combat troops to actively target the troublesome warlords. In that month, the most brazen and brutal of attacks on United Nations forces occurred, one that would lead directly to the deployment of an American special operations task force to target Aideed.

On June 5, 1993, Pakistani peacekeepers had deployed to inspect one of the Authorized Weapons Storage Sites (AWSS), cantonment areas set up by the UN that held surrendered heavy weapons and technicals, the ubiquitous armed pick-up trucks. By chance, the AWSS was located near Aideed's radio station from which he transmitted self-serving Habr Gidr propaganda against the United Nations' presence. The Pakistanis found convincing evidence of significant numbers of missing technicals and of crew-served weapons including heavy machine guns and recoilless rifles. As the poorly equipped Pakistani troops returned to their base after the inspection, they were ambushed near an old cigarette factory deep in Habr Gidr territory. Their soft-skinned trucks offered little protection.

A US Army history detailed the ambush:

> A Pakistani escort unit ran headlong into an ambush on 21 October Road en-route to the stadium [the Pakistani forces were based at a former soccer stadium to the northeast of the city]. Delayed at hastily erected barricades, UNOSOM vehicles came under intense fire not only from small arms but also machine guns and rocket-propelled grenades ... Calls went out for reinforcements, but the relief column, in a scenario that foreshadowed the events of 3 and 4 October, immediately came under attack. In the ensuing chaos, Italian helicopters inadvertently sprayed fire at the very personnel they came to aid. At the same time, scattered roadblocks appeared around the city to hinder relief forces' movement, and additional ambushes ensued.[4]

Concurrently, another group of Pakistani soldiers detailed to provide security at a food distribution site on National Street, the main thoroughfare that bisected downtown Mogadishu from east to west and one of the only paved roads in the city, came under attack. American Major General Thomas Montgomery, then commander of all US forces in Somalia and Deputy UN Force Commander, commented:

> At one of those sites, Pakistanis ... were overwhelmed by women and kids, which was a typical way the Somali militia operated. They put women and children at the front and just sort of let the crowd press in, and they pressed in around them and then disarmed them and then there were shooters in the crowd and they shot a couple of them. A couple of them were literally taken apart by hand.[5]

A SEAL who was later assigned to Task Force Ranger remembered the event in graphic detail: "Aideed's people, including women and children, celebrated by dismembering, disemboweling, and skinning the Pakistanis." In all, some 23 Pakistani soldiers were killed in both incidents and more than 50 wounded.

Six were also captured during the ambush, one of whom later died whilst in captivity. Aideed believed that he could force the United Nations to withdraw from Mogadishu and thus eliminate the greatest threat to his power by inflicting casualties on the UN forces. Perhaps recalling the effect of press coverage of casualties during the Vietnam War, he knew that such mounting casualties would naturally play poorly in their home countries and lead to calls for disengagement and withdrawal from Somalia.[6]

Retired US Navy Admiral Jonathan Howe who served as Boutros-Ghali's Special Representative for Somalia, for all intents and purposes the face of the United Nations in Somalia, remarked:

> I don't think he liked the US being there. He opposed it until the last minute, and I don't think he liked the UN or any other international force being there. I don't think he liked what representative government would mean, because he didn't have the votes. I think this really meant a loss of power to him.
>
> My feeling is that [it was] probably the fact that the UN was actually starting to implement the Resolution 814 [nation building and power sharing within Somalia under UNOSOM II] and the Addis Ababa accords [to develop a representative government with all clans participating], even though he'd signed them.
>
> In the long term, representative government wasn't really in his interests because he was occupying a lot of territory that he'd gotten through guns, and he didn't have the vote nor did his clan have the votes in a totally representative national assembly. And so I think he saw this as a threat to his power probably, this whole international force. So he would be very happy to have all the international people pack up and leave. And I think he saw that striking a blow to the Pakistanis who had replaced the Americans in South Mogadishu, which was his territory, was a way to get the UN to leave.[7]

The response from the United Nations, however, was uncharacteristically fast and bold. On the following day, it passed Security Council Resolution 837 calling for Aideed to be held responsible for the attacks on the Pakistanis and allowing for military means to effect his capture:

> The UN Secretary of the Security Council went into emergency session. This had happened on a Saturday, and [by] Sunday New York time had passed

Resolution 837, which basically said three things: arrest the perpetrators of these crimes against the Pakistanis, disarm this city (obviously you've got way more weapons than you possibly anticipated because of all this shooting that went on against the Pakistanis), and put a stop to this vitriolic propaganda that is coming through various media means of the Somalis, obviously aimed at Aidid's [sic] radio station.[8]

A $25,000 reward was later placed on Aideed's head by Howe in the hope of incentivizing rivals to sell out the warlord to the United Nations. With the support of Boutros-Ghali, the Admiral believed that key to stopping the bloodshed and bringing about some kind of peace was the capture and trial of Aideed as a war criminal. Aideed and the Habr Gidr took the bounty as nothing short of a declaration of war on the Habr Gidr and immediately retorted with a tit-for-tat bounty of $1,000,000 for Howe's head announced via Radio Aideed.

It is important to note that at no time was Aideed targeted for assassination. Although clearly a significant thorn in the side of UNOSOM II and Boutros-Ghali, Security Council Resolution 837 called explicitly for the "arrest" rather than the targeted removal of the warlord. Aideed likely did not appreciate the difference with ground raids and airstrikes conducting missions against his clan infrastructure. Further events would only reinforce his belief that his nemesis, Boutros-Ghali, was carrying out a personal vendetta to eliminate him.

Four US Air Force AC-130 Spectre gunships based in Kenya were deployed to target Radio Aideed and an Osman Atto-owned workshop which built and repaired their technicals. The strikes caused some collateral damage to surrounding buildings and a number of civilian casualties that would return to haunt US forces in the months to follow. A Pentagon spokesperson claimed that the AC-130 strikes were "by any measure ... a very significant military setback for Aideed."[9]

On the following day, June 17, a multinational force of American, French, Italian, Moroccan, and Pakistani peacekeepers surrounded Aideed's headquarters compound and the homes of two of his chief lieutenants, attempting to capture the warlord and his cronies. Not surprisingly, and likely given advance warning of the impending operation by his network of spies and informers, Aideed managed to escape before the cordon was in place.

Somali militia and civilians flocked to the location. Combat soon escalated from random shots to a protracted firefight with Moroccan forces.

The close proximity of Somali militia to the Moroccans meant that circling American Cobra attack helicopters could not provide direct support without running the risk of inflicting friendly fire on their allies. Instead French armored vehicles engaged gunmen firing from the nearby Digfer Hospital with main gun rounds. Five United Nations military personnel were killed and some 46 were wounded. Both Somali militia and civilians were also killed in the exchange with some estimates placing the death toll at over a hundred.

Aideed cannily took to CNN to argue his case against the United Nations-sanctioned strikes and was shown visiting hospitals treating those claimed to have been wounded in the operations. An unnamed US official commented at the time: "The United Nations, having deprived Aideed of his voice, is now giving him an international stage to act on. He's always wanted to be the George Washington of his country, when in fact he is more like the Caligula."[10]

The June 17 operation also led to a fracturing of resolve amongst the multinational force with most of the partner nations refusing to again conduct operations in Aideed territory, inadvertently strengthening the warlord's position by creating "no-go zones" that Aideed could trumpet as a victory over the "imperialists" of the United Nations. Largely because of these "national caveats," by July the mission to capture Aideed had fallen to the in-country assets of the US Army's 10th Mountain Division and its 2-14 Infantry under the command of Lieutenant Colonel Bill David. The 2-14 manned the Quick Reaction Force (QRF) for the multinational forces, acting as a rescue force should a UN unit be ambushed or attacked. By this time, however, Aideed knew full well he was being actively hunted and had largely disappeared from radar; US officials called it "doing a Saddam Hussein."

The QRF maintained a significant standby force should Aideed surface. A US Army history noted its composition:

> "Team Attack" was comprised of one UH-60 [Black Hawk] helicopter with sniper[s] and three [Cobra] attack helicopters. "Team Snatch" was made up with the [infantry] scout platoon, two UH-60s, one UH-60 MEDEVAC [medical evacuation], and one EMT [Emergency Medical Technician] with surgeon. A rifle platoon and two UH-60s made up "Team Secure." Special Operations Forces initially provided the sniper and the "snatch" element, but handed over these taskings to the QRF.[11]

The concept of operations was for the QRF's "Team Secure" to land and establish blocking positions around the target location once Aideed's presence had been confirmed. "Team Snatch" would assault the location from the air and detain the targets whilst "Team Attack" would provide security overwatch from the air with its snipers and attack helicopters. "Team Attack" would also be responsible for stopping vehicle convoys containing Aideed. As we shall soon see, these mission templates would be used again in little-modified form by Task Force Ranger, the eventual special operations force (SOF) dispatched to capture Aideed. Unfortunately, intelligence gathering in Mogadishu would prove problematic in the extreme and the QRF could never confirm Aideed's location. The capture force was never launched.

On July 7 a half-dozen local United Nations workers who distributed a UN-funded newspaper were murdered, and as a result the US launched what many saw as a United Nations-sanctioned "decapitation strike" on July 12, attempting to kill the key leaders of the Habr Gidr in one targeted operation. Moderates who supported working with the international community and Aideed hardliners were meeting at the so-called Abdi House, owned by Abdi Hassan Awale, Aideed's Interior Minister and located in the center of Habr Gidr territory. As they sat down to debate the clan's response to United Nations-brokered peace initiatives, the first TOW (Tube-launched, Optically-tracked, Wire-guided) anti-tank guided missile struck the building.

Although the Americans denied the operation was an overt assassination attempt against Aideed, both the warlord's supporters and clan elders alike were killed by a fusillade of missiles and 20mm cannon fire launched from American Cobra attack helicopters that had encircled the Abdi House. "It was an armed helicopter attack with consequences we would pay for later," noted US Army Major General Carl Ernst who went on to command US forces in Somalia from October 15, 1993.[12]

The raid on the Abdi House on July 12 again played into Aideed's hands, increasing his stature amongst friend and foe alike. After a broadcast warning to those inside, the mixed aviation element of Cobras and OH-58 Kiowa reconnaissance helicopters began to bombard the building with missiles and cannon fire. In another mirror of future operations, the QRF landed ground forces by Black Hawk helicopter that stormed the compound, taking two prisoners, whilst a ground convoy in trucks and Humvees deployed in blocking positions around the building. Somali casualty numbers ranged (wildly dependent on source) from 20 to 73, some of whom, however, were undoubtedly noncombatants. These included the spiritual leader of the Habr Gidr, Sheikh Aden Mohamed.

The US operation received widespread criticism in the international press with statements from Aideed and his clan decrying the "wanton slaughter" of their fellows by the Americans. Now their ire was directed at US forces and any who were deemed to be in their employ. Four journalists covering the story of the July 12 attack were attacked and murdered by Aideed supporters near the Abdi House. The warlord and the SNA began to up the ante, specifically targeting US forces. On August 10, a command-detonated mine, an Improvised Explosive Device (IED) by today's definition, detonated under a US Army Military Police Humvee, killing four American servicemen. This would prove to be a turning point for American resolve.

A September 9 ambush of a combined Pakistani and US route-clearance mission resulted in further press condemnation after Cobras were forced to engage crowds with cannon and rocket fire to protect the encircled forces on the ground, inflicting numerous casualties including against civilians who flocked to watch the spectacle. Admiral Howe could see the method behind the attacks:

> We found what Aidid [sic] was doing, which was pretty clever, is that he was starting to increase the number of roadblocks and the number of ambushes that were occurring. We had a big incident that occurred in September where our people – the Pakistanis – were simply clearing a road, one of the primary access roads, and people fired [at them] from all sides. A favorite Aidid tactic was to bring women into the mix, so you have women and children in front; he even joked about this, it perplexes the soldier in terms of, "Well I can't shoot a woman, and I can't shoot children" and the gunmen are firing [from] behind [them] ...[13]

Only days later, the American QRF itself was ambushed after attempting to seize a stock of SNA crew-served heavy weapons. Only the timely arrival of ground reinforcements and Cobras overhead forestalled a tragedy and allowed the QRF to withdraw safely. Meanwhile, the White House was beginning to pressure the United Nations and Boutros-Ghali to instead pursue a negotiated settlement with Aideed and the Habr Gidr. At the same time, Admiral Howe was conversely using his every contact within the Pentagon and White House to request the deployment of elite US special operations forces to hunt down Aideed. This two-track strategy would end in disaster.

Major General Thomas Montgomery agreed with Howe: "I supported getting Special Forces for this operation; it didn't have to be our special operations forces, it could have been the British SAS."[14] In fact, according to one account, the Americans requested a team from 22 Special Air Service, Britain's own fabled Special Forces, to be deployed to snatch Aideed. The British went as far as deploying an SAS officer on a fact-finding mission to Somalia to gauge the chances of success for such a hazardous mission. The officer returned, stating that the mission was likely to fail as Aideed was already only too aware of the manhunt, and SAS units were consequently not deployed to Somalia.

By mid-August, however, the CIA's Chief of Station in Mogadishu was arguing that his agency could pinpoint Aideed and was adding to the call for the deployment of US special operations forces.[15] Howe, a longtime proponent of just such a measure, was adamant:

> One, it would help us if we had a chance of arresting Aidid [sic] [to do so] without a lot of [civilian] casualties. These [SOF] were the people that could do it for us.
>
> Secondly, it would add leverage that would make peaceful negotiations perhaps possible [with Aideed]. They [the QRF] just didn't have the troops that were trained to do that; unless he fell into our hands by some miracle, [they] weren't really capable of accomplishing that mission. That's why so very early on we asked for that kind of a force to have that capability, and also to deal with kidnapping which was a standard Somali way to dealing with things, to kidnap a relief worker or kidnap a UN person, and take them off and then hold them hostage. We wanted to have a response for that, so we asked very on early on, as early as the 8th of June, for that kind of capability to come to us.[16]

The then head of US Central Command (CENTCOM), General Joseph Hoar, with overall responsibility for US forces in the region disagreed fundamentally with Howe. Hoar was naturally wary of "mission creep" and further entangling US forces in the Somali quagmire. After noting the lack of actionable intelligence available on Aideed, he strongly doubted the prospects of such a force actually being able to capture Aideed. He predicted only a 25 percent chance of success, even with the deployment of US special operators.

Clinton's Secretary of Defense, Les Aspin, along with the outgoing Chairman of the Joint Chiefs of Staff, General Colin Powell, shared in Hoar's skepticism. Hoar was also skeptical of the CIA's claims that they could locate Aideed based on Somali human intelligence (HUMINT) sources: "My view was that these agents, who were being paid for information, would not finger Aideed because once they did and we snatched him, they would be out of a job."[17]

Powell was particularly concerned about "personalizing the conflict and getting deeper and deeper into ancient Somali clan rivalries."[18] A later 1995 report by the United States' Senate Committee on Armed Services agreed with his misgivings, adding that the decision "clearly put the US on one side in a civil war." Such an action would also further reinforce Aideed's stature amongst the Habr Gidr, the SNA, and the wider Mogadishu community in what Hoar reportedly called "unintended consequences." Aideed enjoyed widespread support. Even a rival clan elder commented at the time: "What we cannot agree to is to lose the rights for which we fought the previous regime. We don't want anyone to come and put his feet on top of our heads … As long as they say they want to arrest Aideed, we will fight."[19]

The requested deployment of special operations forces came at a time when the White House and Pentagon were attempting to actively reduce the US footprint in Somalia whilst trying to convince its reluctant United Nations allies to take on a greater share of the task. Senator John McCain articulated what many in the Senate and Congress believed: "the winds have blown us from a narrow well-defined humanitarian mission to taking sides in a prolonged hunt for a Somali warlord … we now seem to be on the edge of moving towards nation building."[20] This was in Hoar's view the very definition of "mission creep."

The Chairman of the Joint Chiefs was up against Boutros-Ghali and Howe, the Special Envoy for Somalia Robert Oakley, the United States Special Operations Command (SOCOM), and its component command, the Joint Special Operations Command (JSOC), who were all loudly lobbying for the mission. In the end Powell acquiesced to the request: "In late August, I reluctantly yielded to the repeated requests from the field and recommended to Aspin that we dispatch the Rangers and the Delta Force. It was a decision I would later regret," noted Powell in his memoir.[21] On August 22, Powell notified Hoar at CENTCOM and General Wayne Downing of SOCOM that "Secretary of Defense Les Aspin had authorized the mobilization and deployment of [JSOC] to support US efforts in Somalia."[22]

JSOC had not been resting on its laurels. The mission had been brewing for several months, time that the command used wisely by running joint training exercises with the component units likely to be called upon for any future task force. The mission had also grown in size over the preceding months. At first the Aideed capture mission was envisioned as capable of being conducted by a small element of two teams of operators totaling no more than a dozen from the Army's secretive Delta Force, who would carry out a low-profile capture and use the in-country QRF for transportation and security.

Delta Force or more correctly the 1st Special Forces Operational Detachment-Delta (SFOD) is the US Army's special mission unit (SMU), known within the special operations community as simply "the Unit." Delta had been formed in 1977 as a purely counterterrorist unit as a direct result of the 1972 Munich Massacre and following the wave of bombings and hijackings that had plagued Europe and the Middle East during the 1970s.

They were specialists in hostage and prisoner recovery, conducting such missions in Grenada and Panama, but had expanded to conduct covert reconnaissance and strike operations, often in what were termed non-permissive environments. They had deployed as part of Operation *Desert Storm* in 1991, hunting Iraqi Scud launchers in the Iraqi desert and, at the time of the Somalia mission, were also heavily deployed to Colombia, assisting the authorities in their manhunt for the notorious drug baron Pablo Escobar.

Delta was structured along the British SAS model, an organization its founder Colonel Charlie Beckwith had served with on secondment and much admired. In 1993, the unit had three squadrons of operators, a term invented by Beckwith to differentiate his men from the operatives of the CIA. These squadrons were supported by a number of other specialist units within the command. The Operational Support Troop, often known as F or Funny Troop, for instance conducted clandestine advance force operations, often undercover, and uniquely at the time included women operators.

Another element, the Combat Support squadron, housed the Unit's heavy breachers (tasked with breaking into heavily fortified locations such as nuclear bunkers or silos), Delta's military dog handlers and their Weapons of Mass Destruction specialists. Delta also had their own covert helicopter unit known as Echo Squadron and a Special Missions Cell based at SOCOM's Combat Developments Division to research and develop specialist weapons, equipment, and techniques for the operators.

At the lowest level, Delta teams were composed of between four and six operators depending on manpower levels, although a six-man team was the standard. Sergeant First Class Paul Leonard, who joined the unit in 1991, commented: "There were times we had four guys, other times we had six." The minimum for an assault team was four because that was the standard package carried on an MH-6 Little Bird, the nimble light helicopters that often ferried Delta operators to their targets, perched on external plank benches. There were three such teams to a troop, led by a troop sergeant major. Three of these troops – two of assaulters and one designated as snipers – along with a small headquarters element formed a squadron commanded by a colonel who had typically served as team and troop leader previously in his career.

Delta's A-Squadron initially received the call for the Somalia deployment. As more intelligence was received and the difficulty inherent in snatching Aideed became clear, the scope of the deployment grew. Sergeant First Class Norman "Norm" Hooten of C-Squadron remembered:

> That mission grew from one or two teams. A-Squadron had the mission and they gave the mission up because they couldn't take their whole squadron. They were on Aztec I think at the time [Aztec was the on-call Delta squadron originally tasked with aircraft hijackings but later encompassing all types of short-notice counterterrorism missions] and there was some other stuff going on at the time, missions that were developing over in northern Africa so they didn't want to split their squadron as it would make them ineffective for any other operation. So it went to Charlie 1 Troop of C-Squadron and it grew and grew until it was a whole squadron plus.

Kelly Venden, then a Sergeant First Class with Delta's A-Squadron, agreed: "Colonel [Gary] Harrell [then commander of C-Squadron] said, 'Hey we'll take it,' but he wanted to make sure it was the whole squadron and not a squadron minus." What was originally a deployment of a dozen operators or less had expanded into a troop and finally to a squadron. Some 50 Delta operators and support personnel were eventually earmarked for the mission.

As the Delta component expanded, elements from the Army's 75th Ranger Regiment were added to provide security around the target site and to crew the light vehicles that might be needed to extract the Delta contingent once they had completed their mission. When Lieutenant Colonel Danny McKnight, 3rd Battalion commander, was first notified of the upcoming deployment he hoped to take his entire battalion with him, a force of some 850 Rangers. Instead he was instructed to select just one company as his primary unit with an additional platoon drawn from another company as his theater reserve and to act as the Task Force's own QRF.

The Ranger Regiment, an elite parachute-capable light infantry unit with a storied history dating back to the French–Indian War, specialized in short-duration raids behind enemy lines and the opposed seizure of airfields, classic special operations tasks. At the time, the Regiment comprised three infantry battalions. Within each battalion were four companies: three rifle companies and a battalion headquarters company. Within these rifle companies, there were four rifle platoons. Each of these platoons was further divided into four squads: three rifle squads and one heavy weapons squad. These squads were finally broken down into the smallest tactical element: the fire team. There were two of these fire teams in each Ranger rifle squad, two teams of four soldiers and one squad leader.

After considering the abilities and length of service of key leadership personnel within the battalion, Colonel McKnight selected Bravo or B-Company under Captain Mike Steele as his primary maneuver element and a platoon from Alpha or A-Company as his reserve along with his own headquarters element. The Ranger contingent would initially number some 240 personnel.[23] They arrived at Fort Bragg, the home of Delta Force, on August 11 for build-up training with the other components of the task force: the operators of Delta, attached Air Force Special Tactics, and elements from the 1st Battalion of the 160th Special Operations Aviation Regiment (SOAR), widely known by their nickname "the Nightstalkers."

Ranger Lieutenant Tom DiTomasso recounted:

> Around the 10th of August, Captain Steele called all the Platoon Leaders and Platoon Sergeants into the company planning tent. We were told that we were deploying to Fort Bragg to rehearse with special mission units in preparation for a real-world mission. The mission was classified, and the cover story would be an Emergency Deployment Readiness Exercise (EDRE). We were not to discuss anything about the exercise until we reached Fort Bragg.[24]

According to a book McKnight later wrote, the Task Force trained solely to effect the capture of Aideed. Killing the warlord would undoubtedly have been the simpler course of action; however, as noted previously, United Nation Security Council Resolution 837 was clear that capture, rather than assassination, was the objective. The training at Fort Bragg saw the development of a template approach to targeting Aideed that unconsciously resembled those being planned by the QRF in Somalia. The Task Force worked on the two most likely scenarios; assaulting a building where Aideed was present, perhaps for a meeting, or halting a vehicle convoy carrying the warlord. Both were bread-and-butter missions to Delta.

Staff Sergeant Kurt Smith with F-Team, 2 Troop of Delta's C-Squadron confirmed:

> The training was realistic, challenging, and almost exclusively live-fire (at least for the main effort). When it wasn't live-fire, there was ample support from outside units providing noncombatants to test our ability to manage hostile crowds with non-lethal munitions. Our operation was based on a template plan that would apply to any scenario encountered. The two scenarios we focused on were the convoy takedown and the stronghold takedown.
>
> We conducted these types of rehearsals for approximately ten days before the National Command Authority seemingly lost interest in deploying the TF [task force]. This was not unusual. We frequently "spun up" and began mission rehearsals for a lot of missions that would never take place. If a mission had the slightest chance of happening, we would conduct rehearsals for it. Most of these missions never took place, but it all chalked up to good training.[25]

Indeed after more than a week of intensive drills, it appeared that the Somali mission would join that same fated category.

The bad news was delivered by General Wayne Downing himself amid much internal frustration during a Friday evening meal for the task force at Delta's compound. The mission was officially "scrubbed." "[The] TF was dissolved, the Rangers returned to Fort Bliss for a scheduled deployment, and the rest of us went home for the weekend," added Smith. When the Rangers arrived at Fort Bliss the next day, Colonel McKnight was informed, however, that circumstances had changed and the mission was now on. An advance party from JSOC would fly out to Somalia immediately to begin preparations for the deployment of the task force.

Those circumstances had been the August 21 ambush of the US Military Police Humvee in Mogadishu. The National Command Authority made a hasty about-turn and Aideed had been elevated to JSOC's public enemy number one. The elite operators soon received confirmation. It was a normal weekend morning for Kurt Smith:

> It was Sunday morning, August 22, 1993, at approximately 0900. I was on my way to church when my pager began to vibrate. I looked at the display; I recognized the coded message that directed the squadron to proceed to work for training.
>
> I immediately turned around. When I arrived at work, the first person I saw was Tom S. He told me a deployment order had been signed. A notice on the chalkboard confirmed what he had said. We would leave Wednesday, but, until then, we would resume our mission rehearsals. I proceeded to my team room to prepare my kit.[26]

The operators had to conduct one final act that many, with the unit's relaxed grooming standards allowing beards and longer-than-regulation hair, resented: "Squadron members were giving themselves last minute high-and-tight haircuts in the latrine. The haircuts were required for us to blend in with other TF members." As Delta was at the time and still is officially a classified unit, the haircuts were intended to help disguise their presence amongst the larger Ranger contingent, all of whom would sport the distinctive Army buzz cuts.

Whilst the task force components had been training and anxiously waiting for the order to deploy, three separate force packages had been proposed by JSOC and presented by General Downing. The decision on exactly what and how many to send to Somalia to hunt Aideed rested with Central Command, the Joint Chiefs of Staff, and ultimately Secretary of Defense Les Aspin who would make the final decision. Each of the three options was given a nickname. The largest was the so-called "Cadillac" option which included a full Ranger battalion and attached AC-130H gunships. The medium-size option was named "Oldsmobile" and reduced the number of Rangers to a company. The final package, the smallest and the one eventually chosen, was known as "Volkswagen."

The political leadership was adamant that they wanted to keep the numbers of deploying special operators as small as possible. They feared increasing the American footprint at a time when they were strategically attempting to disentangle American forces from Somalia. The fact that a diplomatic solution was also being pursued may have also contributed to the requirement to minimize the force posture, as a large force might spook the negotiating parties. Downing also commented that realistically "the numbers were driven by the aircraft load. We were to be deployed with five C-141s and two C-5s. There is some logic to that."[27]

The "Volkswagen" package consisted of Delta's C-Squadron along with personnel from their Operational Support Troop; the majority of B-Company of the 3rd Battalion of the Rangers plus the attached platoon from A-Company; a small contingent of Air Force Combat Controllers and Pararescue Jumpers from the 24th Special Tactics Squadron; and a four-man team of snipers from the Navy's SEAL Team 6. Providing aviation lift and close air support would be elements of the 1st Battalion of the 160th SOAR deploying with a range of MH-60L Black Hawks, MH-6J Little Birds, and AH-6J attack helicopters.

The lack of AC-130 Spectre gunship support in the "Volkswagen" package would become an ongoing controversy for many years after, with most participants believing that their inclusion would have saved lives. It is also important that none of the three options included any organic armored vehicles, another controversy that remains hotly debated to this day. In fact, apart from a number of lightly armored Humvees that Delta managed to borrow from Army Special Forces Groups based at Fort Bragg in advance of the deployment, neither of the principal ground units deploying held any armored vehicles of any type on their table of organization and equipment, nor did either unit routinely train with such vehicles.

The selection of the "Volkswagen" option was unfortunately not the final cut to the task force. A scant 24 hours prior their deployment, the Ranger platoon from A-Company was stripped from the force package as the Pentagon again trimmed the size of the force. Colonel McKnight's reserve was gone. If anything went wrong in Mogadishu, the Rangers now lacked their own QRF and would have to depend on the 10th Mountain and United Nations units.

General Hoar implied later that the platoon was cut as he believed it would be "employed for local security – a job I definitely would not allow them to do." Hoar argued that "local security was outside our mission and was in the areas under allied responsibility."[28] Whatever Hoar's feelings on the matter, as we will see, the task force would feel compelled to conduct local force-protection measures to reduce the threat from Somali mortars, a job that they felt the United Nations garrison forces were simply incapable of doing.

Once the force package and deployment were finally agreed, the task force was formally named Task Force Ranger. The operation itself was called Operation *Caustic Brimstone* during training but was changed to Operation *Gothic Serpent* once the actual mission was authorized. In overall command was a cigar-chomping Texan Major General, William F. "Bill" Garrison.

At the time of the *Gothic Serpent* deployment, Garrison was head of JSOC. Previously, Garrison had led the Operations Squadron of the shadowy Intelligence Support Activity in the mid-1980s and had been the commander of Delta between 1985 and 1989, although his operational experience in special operations extended as far back as the Vietnam War where he served with the infamous Phoenix Program, targeting enemy leadership personnel.

Colonel William G "Jerry" Boykin was second-in-command under Garrison as the then-current commander of Delta. Under Boykin were the three operational commanders responsible for their respective units: Lieutenant Colonel Danny McKnight, battalion commander of 3rd Battalion, 75th Ranger Regiment; Lieutenant Colonel Gary Harrell, squadron commander of Delta's C - or Charlie Squadron; and Lieutenant Colonel Tom Matthews, battalion commander of 1st Battalion, 160th SOAR.

On the ground, the Delta assault element would be led by a Delta Captain whilst the Rangers reported to the Bravo Company commander, Captain Mike Steele. The Delta Captain was also the official Ground Force Commander. Theoretically equal in rank, the friction of battle would cause significant challenges between these two positions and between Delta and the Ranger company commander.

The objectives of Task Force Ranger were deceptively simple on paper at least: "The special operations forces had the mission to capture General Mohammed Farah Aideed and designated others, and to turn over captives to UNOSOM forces."[29] Major General Garrison succinctly outlined his concept of operations based on those objectives: "When directed, deploy to Mogadishu, Somalia; conduct operations to capture General Aideed and/or designated others. The aviation task force must be prepared to conduct two primary courses of action: moving convoy and strong point assault. Success is defined as the live capture of General Aideed and designated individuals and recovery to the designated transload point; safely and without fratricide."[30]

Kurt Smith recalled that there were three distinct stages:

> The operation would be conducted in three phases: phase one consisted of a train-up period, deployment, and preparation for combat operations; phase two consisted of the search for Aideed and operations conducted specifically to capture him; and phase three consisted of the dismantlization [sic] of Aideed's infrastructure through the meticulous and methodical capture of the top personalities in Aideed's organization.[31]

The advance party consisting of Garrison and a senior representative from each of the three primary units arrived in Mogadishu on August 22. The main body of Task Force Ranger followed on August 25. Garrison met with General Montgomery to explain their purpose and to emplace liaisons within his headquarters, Colonel John Vines with Montgomery and Major Craig Nixon with the 10th Mountain who comprised the QRF.

Aviators from the 160th SOAR met with their fellow pilots from the 10th Aviation Brigade to begin to understand the environment of Mogadishu. By the end of August, all 441 members of Task Force Ranger were dispatched to Somalia and were soon ready for their first missions to begin.

Ranger Lieutenant Tom DiTomasso later recalled: "This excitement was a new feeling, mixed with both adrenalin and fear. As a platoon leader, I often wondered what it would be like to take my platoon into combat, to do something real. Later, I would learn to be more careful of what I wished for."[32]

# CHAPTER 2

# THE FIRST SIX

*"There is no question that we lost strategic surprise when we moved the force in the country, therefore we had to maintain tactical surprise."*

Major General William Garrison, Commander Task Force Ranger

By August 28, the Task Force had settled into their new home and were now, in Garrison's words, "fully mission capable." Their home for at least the next three months was a rundown aircraft hangar on the edge of Mogadishu's equally rundown international airport. A disused concrete building opposite would become their Joint Operations Center (JOC) as well as housing the various intelligence collection entities working for the Task Force.

The hangar was open to both the airfield and to the outskirts of Mogadishu, a scant 50 meters from the JOC Building. First priority went to establishing some form of defenses. Using whatever was handy, the Rangers placed shipping containers to form a defensive wall to shield them from prying eyes and stray bullets from the continual internecine firefights occurring just beyond the wire. Sandbagged fighting positions with overhead cover were built, and an access control point established by the Rangers.

It was evident that Task Force Ranger would have to provide its own security after all, despite General Hoar's pronouncements to the contrary that such security would be provided by the United Nations. What little security there was appeared to the men of Task Force Ranger to be wholly inadequate. Major General Garrison made an immediate request for reinforcements in the form of the missing platoon from Alpha Company that McKnight had been forced to cut. Predictably, given the prevailing political climate around the deployment, the request was denied.

The poor security environment around the hangar was underlined several nights later when a United Nations sentry position nearby was taken under fire by unknown assailants. The UN soldiers, likely Egyptians, did not return fire as incredibly they had been issued with no live ammunition. Instead, a small element of Rangers posting security at the hangar itself maneuvered against the gunmen and a number were shot and killed before the survivors beat a hasty retreat. Even this incident did nothing to convince Washington to grant Garrison's request.

The Task Force lived a spartan existence in the hangar. Each man only had a folding bed in his respective unit area and each kept his weapons and equipment next to his bed. There were neither curtains nor internal walls. The aviators, because of safety rules regarding flying, moved into a number of air-conditioned trailers. A TV room was eventually established by one of the operators with a VCR to watch movies, and boardgames provided some relief from boredom.

The living conditions in the hangar were made worse each time it rained. As the airfield was located at the base of the higher ground upon which most of Mogadishu sat, the rain would head downhill, bringing with it all manner of refuse including human sewage which regularly overran portions of the hangar. That was not the only sewage-related issue to blight the Task Force. During the early days of the deployment, the entire 441 members of the Task Force were forced to use just half a dozen Port-A-Loos which consistently overflowed. The rat-infested hangar was also overrun with pigeons which provided some sport for the Delta operators who attempted to shoot them down with BB guns imported from the States.

Task Force personnel would conduct physical training or marksmanship sessions at a makeshift small-arms range they had established at the nearby beach. The Task Force also spent time on a makeshift volleyball court. "We played a lot of volleyball in the afternoons to pass the time. When intelligence would come down that might turn into a mission, these became known as 'pants alerts' because it meant we needed to change from our PT uniform to fatigue trousers and boots in case the intelligence resulted in a mission," noted Kurt Smith.[1]

Delta Sergeant First Class Gary Keeney, known by his unit nickname of "Greedy," remembered: "There was a volleyball net outside the hangar and we sometimes played every day. If we weren't on a mission, if we weren't planning, if we weren't PTing or doing maintenance, you could catch me out on the volleyball court!"

Although the sea beyond the volleyball court looked inviting, the Task Force members were warned about unseen perils. A rumor spread that a Russian firm had once run an abattoir near the beach, throwing their off-cuts into the sea. This attracted sharks who had continued to frequent the area ever since, long after the departure of the Russians. Despite this, some members of the multinational forces braved the waters, leading to at least one death by shark attack: "A shark attack happened while we were there. A soldier from another Coalition force got bit by a shark and it happened in the exact same little cove that me and a couple of other guys were swimming at. I never went back in that water after that!" recalled Keeney.

Training was constant, whether shooting, first aid, and radio procedures or room clearance. Exercises were held to rehearse the actions to be taken in the event of a downed aircraft so that every soldier, airman or sailor knew the basic drills to be followed in such an event. Delta operators passed on the finer points of close quarter battle (CQB) shooting to the young Rangers and explained how to breach and clear an enemy-held structure.

Delta also planned for assaults against targets that might prove to be possible locations of Aideed and his lieutenants. Keeney explained:

> Each team was tasked to plan contingency operations if something happened that led us to certain sites or venues or locations in the city. C-Team's mission [for example] was the Digfer Hospital. Matt Rierson was given the mission of how the squadron would assault the Digfer Hospital. We spent a lot of time and effort planning that. Of course we never went there but we planned for it.

Other training sessions were run by the Delta surgeon, Doctor John "Rob" Marsh. These were termed "goat labs" after the Army Special Forces practice of conducting practical first aid on live animals. In Somalia, goats were purchased from locals and flown to a secure location where the unfortunate animals were shot. Delta and SEAL operators had to administer lifesaving first aid on the goats. The goats were then given back to the locals for food, a useful hearts and minds activity along with providing the most realistic first aid training possible to the operators.

Along with the goat labs, Delta and the small SEAL Team 6 contingent would conduct what amounted to hunting safaris from the air. Snipers would perch on the bench seats of a pair of MH-6s and hunt a range of African game which was brought back to the hangar for impromptu barbecues. Along with providing a welcome break from military rations and the limited fresh food available, it allowed the snipers to practise their skills in engaging moving targets from the air, something which would prove critical in later operations.

The Task Force also began what were known as "signature flights." Their aim was to desensitize the population of Mogadishu, and Aideed himself, to the presence of their helicopters over the city. The Task Force planners knew that launching an armada of special operations helicopters would be a sure sign of an impending mission, so the signature flights were an attempt to both normalize their prescence and confuse the enemy. Lieutenant Colonel James "Tommy" Faust, the Operations Officer of the JSOC J-2 [intelligence] Cell noted: "TF Ranger randomly launched missions for training and rehearsal at all times of the day and night. We could not protect our launches but the idea was to put the challenge on the surveillance to determine if it was a real launch or not."[2] It had the added benefit of getting the aircrews of the 160th SOAR and their passengers used to the norms of the city and its inhabitants.

Kurt Smith recalled his first briefing on the rules of engagement for these flights:

> Norm [Hooten] briefed the team on the rules of engagement (ROE) for the signature flights. He briefed, "If you see a technical vehicle in the open, you're cleared hot. If you see anyone with a weapon, you're cleared hot. If you have any doubt in your mind whatsoever …" I nodded my head, already knowing the rest. We were conditioned never to fire at anything unless we were absolutely sure of the threat. Norm continued, "… you're cleared hot." My eyes widened as I digested this clear departure from normal procedures. It was a simple and welcome adjustment, however.[3]

Knowing they were likely under surveillance by Aideed loyalists, the Task Force began deception operations, as Garrison explained:

> Once each day we loaded the entire force and went out and did something. Once each night that we were there, we loaded the entire force up and went out and did something. There was no way that anyone, and we assumed that they were watching us, could tell when we loaded up as to whether or not we were going out to conduct a mission.[4]

Major General Garrison was right. A Somali militia commander later stated:

> We knew that immediately after their arrival because we were in all the places where they would have arrived, say in the port, airport, the American compound, some people of us were always there, and the minute they arrived we knew that they were there. And after a very short [time] their own radios announced the arrival of these Special Forces.[5]

Their target was doing everything in his power to avoid detection including "moving every two hours, changing his means of travel, wearing disguises, sleeping at a different location each night."[6] He had also stopped appearing at the regular SNA rallies as these were obvious targets for the Task Force.

The Rangers had also started patrolling within the immediate vicinity to increase the security envelope around the hangar. "We did 42 total missions while we were there, mostly dismounted patrols ... the first night we were there my whole platoon went out and did a dismounted patrol through Mogadishu. We had [enemy] contact that very first night," explained Lieutenant DiTomasso. Ranger Staff Sergeant Matt Eversmann remembered these early patrols: "We conducted foot patrols out into the city at night. As I understood it the idea was [as a] presence patrol, go out and let the bad guys know that we're here and by the same token let the good people of Mogadishu know that the good guys were there." These patrols met with much heated resistance once the practice became known to the Pentagon.

General Downing commented:

> General Garrison wanted to get out and do active patrolling and do more for force protection. The JCS [Joint Chiefs of Staff] found out and went ballistic. They said that we were not there to do that, do not send out patrols. That is the mission of UNOSOM and the QRF. General Montgomery would say they had the situation in hand – the Egyptians had the force protection mission for the airfield ... The Joint Staff was concerned that the Task Force would get away from its mission. Garrison wanted the Rangers to conduct ambushes and to patrol adjacent to the airfield. Hoar and I talked about it. This provoked a firestorm – it was not a minor issue. It was not a negotiable issue. Powell was concerned about mission creep. People were very emotional during this time.[7]

The Task Force were also concerned about operational security (OPSEC). OPSEC is a vitally important consideration for any special operations unit. Special operations forces are trained to operate covertly and maintain the vital strategic and tactical element of surprise. Disguising or concealing the true nature of a deployment is a typical measure to maintain this operational security requirement. In Task Force Ranger's case their efforts were compromised early by the release of the name of the task force in the international press, even before the deploying elements touched down in Somalia.

Naming the task force after its largest component unit was in hindsight a questionable decision. This has led to similar task forces operating during the Global War on Terror to adopt far less evocative and far more confusing numerical identifiers that conceal their true role and purpose. Task Force Ranger also tried their level best to conceal the presence of the Delta element within their ranks, again with little apparent success.

Incredibly media outlets affiliated with the Knight-Ridder news service were soon publicly reporting that Task Force Ranger included "about two dozen of the Army's top-secret Delta Force commandos."[8] The fact that this information was sourced to "Pentagon officials" is equally troubling: at best it may have been a crude attempt at a psychological warfare operation to instil fear in their quarry; at worst it was an incredibly dangerous breach of operational security.

One anonymous source quoted by the newspapers even declared: "We're not going to come right out and say we're trying to nab him but if the opportunity presents itself, having Delta there gives us a better chance."[9] In late September, however, the same news service was reporting efforts to dampen such aggressive notions, adding that the US administration were now attempting to politically isolate Aideed. They even quoted Marine Lieutenant General Robert Johnston, former commander of US forces in Somalia: "If you end up fighting him, you play to his strong suit."[10]

The members of Task Force Ranger recognized the on-the-ground effect of this press speculation. The Executive Officer of the Ranger's Bravo Company, Captain Lee Rysewyk, commented:

> The press had a major impact on the outcome of TF Ranger's mission. Before the force even deployed, the news of the day described how the US was sending 400 elite Rangers to Somalia to hunt for fugitive warlord Aideed. CNN waited on the airfield tarmac for the Rangers. This only telegraphed our mission to Aideed and set TF Ranger up for failure by sending Aideed into deep reclusion. It was no wonder that intelligence reports rarely pinpointed Aideed.[11]

As noted, there were two main plans to capture Aideed. Ranger Lieutenant James "Jim" Lechner, the Fire Support Officer attached to Captain Steele's command element and responsible for managing air support from the AH-6 Little Birds, described the "Building Assault" template in detail and is worth quoting at length, particularly as he spells out the exact package later employed on October 3:

The assault element was made up of special operations personnel and would be inserted directly on top of the target's location. Once on the ground the assault element would have the responsibility for the capture and security of targeted personnel referred to as Precious Cargo (PC). The assault element would conduct the actual entry and clearing of buildings or vehicles where the PCs were located.[12]

Two to four AH-6Js, the armed attack helicopter variant of the Little Bird, would arrive just before the MH-6s that would deliver the assaulters to scout the target location, looking for potential threats including RPGs [anti-tank grenade launcher] or anti-aircraft guns. Although unarmored, the AH-6s, known colloquially as "Guns," were heavily armed with six-barrel 7.62mm miniguns and unguided 2.75-inch rocket pods.

Lechner's explanation continues:

Assisting the assault element in this mission was the security element. It was made up of two reduced strength Ranger platoons, broken down into four separate elements or "chalks," which would surround the target, landing by fast rope, and form a perimeter of blocking positions (BPs). The mission of the Rangers was primarily to prevent any outside interference with the assault element and secondarily to seal off the target area so no one could escape.[13]

The term "chalk" dated back to Operation *Overlord* and the D-Day invasion of France during World War II. Airborne troops were assigned to a specific aircraft that had its identification number noted in chalk on the side of the plane or glider. The paratroopers were then divided into groups based on this chalk number. The Rangers continued the use of the term in Somalia to easily identify who was assigned to which helicopter. Whilst the chalks fast-roped in, the Ranger Ground Reaction Force or GRF would drive toward the target. As Lechner further explains:

Bravo Company would also provide the vehicular ground force made up of a platoon-sized element of ... HMMWVs, armed with .50-caliber machine guns, and Mark 19 automatic grenade launchers. Immediately, upon the launch of the assault force, the vehicles would race from the airport to the target location and would reinforce the perimeter. Once our intelligence provided us a target, the recon birds would be used to pinpoint the target's location and lead the airborne assault force to the landing zone (LZ). This was critical as the LZ was generally right on top of target among buildings or vehicles in the streets.

The lift birds carried the assault force to the target, then inserted them, generally by fast rope. After the insertion, the majority of the lift birds would fly a safe distance away and take up an orbit to wait for the call to extract the assault force. Some of the helicopters would remain over the target and support the assault force on the ground. The helicopters consisted of two birds carrying snipers who would provide precise fires to interdict Somalis approaching the perimeter. The snipers would be assisted in this by the doorgunners of these helicopters.

In addition to the sniper birds, four helicopter gunships would provide heavier firepower if needed. A Command and Control bird and one other lift bird carrying a Search and Rescue (SAR) team would also remain overhead. The SAR team was made up of medics and rescue personnel and was a contingency in case of a downed helicopter.[14]

The "Vehicular Convoy Intercept" template was primarily a Delta-led option. Once a targeted individual was identified moving in a vehicle convoy, the Task Force would launch with either MH-6 Little Birds or Black Hawks carrying Delta snipers in the lead, supported by a pair of armed AH-6 attack helicopters should close air support prove necessary. The snipers would engage the vehicle from the air using M249 squad automatic weapons (SAWs) or their sniper rifles, aiming for the engine block to immobilize the vehicle. If this did not stop the vehicle, the driver would subsequently be engaged.

Operators would then land and capture the targeted individual. Typically, the Ranger chalks would stand by in Black Hawks overhead to act as a cut-off force or to reinforce the operators should the target escape into a building. Both mission templates could be modified as needed, often on the fly. For instance, in some circumstances the assault force would be extracted by helicopter from roofs or from the street outside a target location. At other times, a Ranger vehicle convoy would drive into the target area to extract the operators.

In all scenarios, a number of helicopter-borne elements were ever present. High above was the C2 or Command and Control Black Hawk, callsign Super 63, piloted by Chief Warrant Officer Class 4 Stu Kaufman and Chief

Warrant Officer Class 3 Mark Bergamo. This carried the Air Mission Commander, Colonel Tom Matthews, and the Ground Mission Commander, Colonel Gary Harrell. Super 63 was also equipped to carry out emergency MEDEVACs in extremis, although finding a large enough landing zone in the urban sprawl of Mogadishu would prove challenging.

Along with the C2 Black Hawk, another MH-60L carried Task Force Ranger's insurance policy, the Combat-Search-And-Rescue or CSAR team. "We had seven Rangers, five Delta, two Pararescue and one CCT [Combat Controller] and we had an abundance of rank – we had two Delta Sergeant Majors and a Delta Captain," explained Ranger Sergeant John Belman, assigned to the CSAR element's security team. "It was a very senior team. I wasn't in my usual team leader or squad leader role on that team."

Amongst the five Delta operators on the CSAR element was Captain Bill C, who would later command C-Squadron during the Iraq invasion, C-Squadron Sergeant Major Tommy C, Sergeant Major Rick W from the sniper troop (also known as 3 Troop), Sergeant First Class Bob M, a highly trained special forces medic, and the C-Squadron EOD (Explosives Ordnance Disposal) technician, Luke V. The EOD technician was a mainstay in all Delta squadrons, available to make safe bombs or IEDs located during the course of raids or to destroy targets with explosives. One of Luke V's chief roles on the CSAR team was to plant demolition charges on a downed helicopter to deny it to the enemy. Belman added:

> Captain Bill C was in command, the senior person on the team. In the CSAR unit we all worked very well together even though effectively you had three different units reporting to three different chains of command. One of the Delta Sergeant Majors would have taken over if Bill C went down. Medically it was the PJs [Pararescueman Jumper] and Bob M in the lead – I'd had EMT training and everyone had had some form of [first aid] training. That was one of the lessons learned coming out of Somalia – to have more of that.

Three Air Force Special Tactics personnel were assigned to the CSAR team. Amongst them was the hugely experienced Air Force Master Sergeant Scott Fales. Fales had passed selection to become a Pararescueman Jumper or PJ back in 1980 and had participated in Operation *Just Cause* in Panama, jumping in to the airfield at Torios-Tacuman to position infrared strobes for the main air-landing force. A decade after qualifying as a PJ, Fales was selected into the 24th Special Tactics Squadron that supported JSOC operations. His first deployment was Operation *Desert Storm* where he was involved in the extraction of compromised Special Forces teams caught far behind enemy lines.[15]

The second PJ on the team was also a Panama veteran, Technical Sergeant Timothy Wilkinson, as was their CCT, Technical Sergeant Pat Rogers. All three airmen would be key to the events at the first crash site on October 3. The PJs carried a full suite of trauma kits to provide emergency first aid and were specially trained to rescue trapped aircrew.

In fact, Task Force Ranger included almost a dozen members of Air Force Special Tactics with CCTs spread amongst all elements, including Technical Sergeant Dan Schilling who accompanied Ranger battalion commander Colonel Danny McKnight on the GRF. Combat Controller Staff Sergeant Ray Benjamin would be stationed with the Task Force command element in the C2 aircraft.

Staff Sergeant Jeff Bray was assigned to the Delta assault force and would ride in with the operators. Bray replaced Master Sergeant Dave Schnoor who would only serve on the first three Task Force Ranger missions as he had to return to the United States on emergency compassionate leave. The role of these CCTs was to manage air support requests from the teams they were embedded with and to deconflict the airspace over the target to minimize the risk of collisions or friendly fire – it was a daunting task with up to 16 aircraft overhead at any one time. Each CCT carried a number of radios allowing them to communicate directly with the Little Bird and Black Hawk pilots or the C2 helicopter.

As previously noted, the Ground Force Commander as well as the Assault Force Commander was Delta Captain Austin "Scottie" Miller. The Ranger chalks were commanded by Captain Mike Steele. Colonel Danny McKnight led the Ranger ground reaction force convoy. The command relationship on the ground may not have been crystal clear to Steele and it led to command difficulties on the eventual October 3 mission.

Norm Hooten explained:

> Scott Miller was the Ground Force Commander. It was clear as day to everyone that the Delta Force Assault Force Commander was the Ground Force Commander. That's the way it had been on every single mission. There

was no change to the command structure. I'm not sure if Captain Steele would say different but if he does, he's wrong. Scott Miller up until a few days before had been the Operations Officer. Bennett S had been the Ground Force Commander and Bennett S's father got sick and Bennett went home so Scott was put in charge temporarily until Bennett got back.

Whilst the close confines of their living arrangements naturally led to the occasional disagreement, all three units maintained a generally close relationship. The pilots of the 160th SOAR and the Delta operators had long experience working with each other and had an especially tight bond. Many of the Rangers were very young and by their own admission inexperienced in combat. Many were also understandably hesitant about their first real-world mission, although they tried to cover this with Ranger bravado. The young Rangers naturally looked up to the older Delta operators who exuded an irreverent air to army norms. Delta strongly encouraged individual initiative and rank was largely shunned with deference only to those with the most experience.

This did not sit well with the Ranger company commander. Steele, by all accounts a very dyed-in-the-wool army traditionalist, saw this as a negative and did his utmost to keep the two units apart, fearful of the influence of the operators. He also put a stop to some of the positive cross-pollination between the two units. Operators conducted classes in advanced CQB shooting and room clearance for the Rangers that would have no doubt helped them during the events of October 3, but Steele tried to stop the training sessions. Some Rangers snuck out after dark to attend secret training sessions with the Delta operators to avoid Steele's wrath.

The Ranger captain was by all accounts a divisive individual. Most members of Delta and the 160th SOAR who had contact with Steele typically described him in almost uniformly negative terms. Some questioned his handling of the case of a 7th Special Forces Group soldier attached to the Ranger battalion as a Direct Support Special Operations Medic. He publicly argued with Steele over the tactical sense of briefing his Rangers after they had left the relative safety of the base as opposed to prior to the mission. As a result he was blacklisted by Steele and sent back to the United States the next day.

The individual concerned, then-Staff Sergeant Stan Goff, has his own colourful story. He was in fact a former Delta operator who had been kicked out of the unit in 1986 for alleged sexual improprieties. Whilst deployed to El Salvador, he was alleged to have had improper relations with a woman in the residence of the US Ambassador. He transferred to the 7th Special Forces Group after the incident. Despite leaving Delta under a dark cloud, Goff was a very experienced operator, and medic, who had conducted operations with Delta in Central America. Some viewed Steele's treatment of Goff as yet another example of Steele's poor command decisions.

Delta Staff Sergeant Mike Moser remarked: "As a general rule, I tried to avoid mixing with the Ranger folks as much as possible since I realized we were a major disruption [or] distraction to their internal chain of command." This seems to have been true for most of his fellow operators. The Rangers saw Delta wearing whatever they wanted, carrying whatever modified weapons and equipment they felt were best suited for a specific task and exhibiting a general lack of adherence to regimented army doctrine, the polar opposite of their company commander. Some of this attitude undoubtedly began to rub off on the more impressionable Rangers.

Hooten added:

> When you're dealing with operators, you're dealing with a pretty irreverent bunch of guys. I think he saw that as some sort of disrespect. His tactics didn't work with 30-year-old men who'd been around a while. We couldn't give a damn about Captain Steele as he was not involved in our life.
>
> He had a lot of young Rangers looking up to the Delta operators and he thought, "Hey, these guys are usurping my authority," I guess, and he felt like he was losing control of his guys. He'd come over and say [to his Rangers], "Get back to your own section, don't talk to those guys," or they'd want to come train with us and he wouldn't want them to train with us. I think he was a little bit intimidated to be honest with you.

The relationship between Steele and Delta was captured in both the book and film *Black Hawk Down*. Some, including Colonel Danny McKnight in his memoir, felt that the difficulties have been overstated: "It may be somewhat correct relating to some very specific situations, but by no means correct in the normal day-to-day environment."[16] He goes on to pinpoint the origin of the alleged discontent to one particular member of Delta, most likely then-Sergeant First Class Paul H, team leader of E-Team. Paul H, who declined to be interviewed for this book, spoke to Mark Bowden and formed a major part of his re-telling of Delta's role in the *Gothic Serpent* missions. He was scathing of Steele and of the performance of some of his Rangers.[17]

Ranger Sergeant Keni Thomas gave his own account of the issues between Steele and some members of Delta and perhaps strikes at the heart of the issue. He quoted Steele telling him:

> You know, Sergeant Thomas, it's not that I don't respect how good they are at what they do. I get that. But what you have to understand is that these men are seasoned NCOs [non-commissioned officers] with years of experience. You know why our training has to stay so basic? It's because we have privates who are new and inexperienced soldiers coming into the regiment. It's our job to get them up to combat speed quickly and efficiently. We have to keep it simple.[18]

Thomas further noted that "It's not that Mike Steele disliked the men of Delta or believed them to be 'undisciplined cowboys' as the movie portrayed. He respected their level of training and expertise. But their methods were not our methods. For command and control purposes, he could not afford to mix the two."[19]

The two units had often served alongside each other but never on the same objective. The Rangers would typically provide the perimeter security whilst the operators would conduct the actual assault. On October 3 both units were forced into operating alongside and intermixed with each other, something that neither had trained for nor anticipated. Arguably Steele had his soldiers' best interests at heart. He was visibly shocked and saddened for instance at the casualties from October 3.

One example of Steele's fractious relationship with Delta has now become a celebrated internet meme and even a tee-shirt design after it was first detailed in Bowden's book and film, the infamous "This is my safety" line. In the movie, actor Eric Bana playing Norm "Hoot" Gibson, a character based on a number of operators but most obviously Sergeant First Class Norman Hooten, is stopped in the hangar by Jason Isaacs playing the role of Captain Steele. Isaacs' character notes that Gibson's weapon is not on safe. In response, Gibson holds up his trigger finger and states disparagingly, "This is my safety, sir."

Norm Hooten explained that Bowden and the screen writers had conflated two separate incidents:

There's a little bit of truth to it. The story is that he came up to me in the cafeteria and he said, "Hey, put your weapon on safe." We would clear our weapons and drop the hammer on it which when you drop the hammer on a carbine you can't put it on safe, it won't go on safe. The bolt is forward and the magazine is out, the tension's off the sear. It's a way for us to tell a weapon is clear at night for example without looking at it – if it won't go on safe I know it's clear.

He said, "put your weapon on safe." I said, "It's clear," and he goes, "Put it on safe." I said, "You put it on safe – because the gun is clear, it won't go on safe." I said, "Don't worry about it, I got it." That was it. Later on that night, some of the Rangers were doing a skit and in the skit they did the finger thing [also seen in the film being performed by Ranger Sergeant Dominick Pilla, played by Danny Hoch].

They did that because we'd been out teaching them CQB that same day and I told them, "The gun has got a safety on it but your primary safety is your finger and that's the only one connected to your brain so use that one as your primary safe." So they took that and they combined it with that incident in the chow hall and it went down in the movie as that's the way it happened. I got a kick out of it.

Despite whatever difficulties existed between Steele and Delta, they still had a job to do and that job depended upon timely, accurate, and actionable intelligence. From the start, the struggle for "ground truth" was an uphill battle. The US Army history of operations in Somalia notes "The task would prove extraordinarily difficult, for Aideed had gone underground after the AC-130 air raids and ground assaults on his strongholds in June and July."[20]

US Army Major Timothy M Karcher documented these difficulties in *Understanding the Victory Disease*:

During the preceding months, the US Joint Special Operations Command had sent two different reconnaissance parties to Mogadishu to determine the feasibility of capturing Aidid [sic] and to gain an initial intelligence assessment. The initial reconnaissance party reported that the capture of Aidid was possible, due to his very public movements. However, by July, Aidid had significantly curtailed his public appearances due to his increasingly hostile stance toward the UN, thus the likelihood of capturing him became quite remote.[21]

The members of Task Force Ranger, somewhat divorced from the cloak and dagger world of intelligence collection and targeting, remained optimistic. "We found out that starting this operation was going to be difficult as there was no real intelligence network established at the time, at least as far as I was privy to. But I had no worries. After all, we were well-armed, well-equipped Rangers and this enemy was living in the Stone Age. That was my thoughts on the Somalis," explained Matt Eversmann.

CIA veteran Jack Kassinger noted that even before the arrival of Task Force Ranger, CIA assets had been deployed to Somalia to support the US humanitarian mission: "The first teams into Somalia were CIA/DO [Directorate of Operations]/SAD [Special Activities Division] paramilitary personnel with elements of JSOC. They conducted very high risk, advanced force operations prior to the entry of the follow-on forces. The first casualty of Operation *Restore Hope* was a CIA officer, Larry F, who was assigned to one of these teams."[22] Larry F was Sergeant Major Lawrence Freedman, a former Delta operator who was killed in a landmine strike on November 22, 1992 in Bardera, southwest Somalia.

An impressive array of intelligence assets were deployed in support of Task Force Ranger in an attempt to provide actionable intelligence that would lead to the capture of Aideed. The JSOC J-2 or "intelligence shop" was headed by the late Colonel David "Dave" McKnight (with no relation to the Ranger battalion commander, Danny McKnight). Dave McKnight worked with both his own JSOC analysts and elements from the CIA and a covert Army unit that specialized in signals intelligence (SIGINT), then known as the Office of Military Support, which we will return to later in this chapter.

HUMINT remained largely the domain of the CIA. An American commander, Major General Carl Ernst, mentioned the inherent difficulties of deploying undercover CIA or army personnel on the streets of Mogadishu: "Intelligence collection was complicated because we didn't look like them. It is how we appear, the way we walk and talk and so it's very difficult to break into a society that's clan by culture, and then its sub-clan and they know everybody."[23] Instead the Task Force and CIA relied upon locally recruited sources whose loyalty and basic competence, particularly in tradecraft, was always in question.

Professor James Howcroft, Director of the Program on Terrorism and Security Studies at the George C. Marshall Center and a 30-year Marine Corps Intelligence veteran, later explained some of these unique difficulties:

Just like SIGINT, it takes time to set up HUMINT networks in a new city. HUMINT professionals need time to understand the ethnic/tribal makeup and power dynamics of the city, which will have an effect on who reports on whom and how reliable that reporting will be.

It will be tough to ascertain the reliability and truthfulness of local population reporting – after all, it is your actions that are bringing death and destruction to their neighborhoods, putting their families at risk and causing them to flee. They don't know yet if you are going to win or how long you will be around. Talking to you compromises their families.[24]

The CIA eventually recruited a Somali warlord who offered to lead them to Aideed, for a price. A veteran CIA officer who had previously acted as the warlord's handler, known by the codename of Condor, was flown in to manage the source. Crucially, Condor was both a very experienced intelligence hand with a field career dating back to Vietnam and he was African-American, a trait which allowed him somewhat of a better chance of blending in with the Somalis, at least from a distance or in a vehicle. Condor's job was to get his warlord in close proximity to Aideed to allow independent verification of Aideed's location before a strike could be launched.[25]

The Office of Technical Services at the CIA's Langley headquarters had developed a solution befitting the mythical Q-Branch of James Bond fame – an ivory-handled walking stick containing a hidden homing beacon that would silently transmit its location to aircraft overhead. The CIA's plan was for the warlord to give the walking stick to Aideed as a gift. With any luck, Aideed would keep the walking stick which would lead the CIA, and ultimately Task Force Ranger, directly to his location. Before the gift was delivered to Aideed, however, fate played its brutal hand. The warlord shot himself in the head with a revolver playing a drunken game of Russian roulette. The CIA were back to square one.

Condor volunteered to instead employ the warlord's men in two local units of spotters, Team One and Team Two, and send them out into the city to track down Aideed. The plan was agreed by Langley and Garrison, and Condor was moved to a rented safe house accompanied by the four SEALs from Task Force Ranger. The SEAL snipers were to provide security for the safe house which was subsequently codenamed Pasha. It was located in the Lido district of northern Mogadishu, named from the Italian for beach.

Along with functioning as a base of operations for Condor's locally recruited surveillance teams, Pasha was also the home of a team of Army and CIA SIGINT specialists.

The SEALs kept watch from the flat roof with their sniper rifles. Should an informant be followed, they were under orders to engage whoever was tailing the asset. The operators established procedures for an emergency escape should the safe house come under concerted attack. The SIGINT gear would be carried out in rucksacks and whatever couldn't be carried would be denied to the enemy by the use of thermite grenades. The SEALs ensured all personnel maintained a "bug-out bag" ready for just such an eventuality. Thankfully it was never required, although the SEALs did their bit for neighborhood security by engaging and killing three gunmen trying to break into a neighboring house.[26]

Despite the risks, CIA operatives did go out on the ground in an attempt to pinpoint Aideed themselves. One CIA officer codenamed Leopard attempted to meet a local Somali source who said he was willing to sell out Aideed in exchange for the $25,000 in reward money offered by Admiral Howe after the murder of the Pakistani peacekeepers in late June. Instead, Leopard was led into an ambush and severely wounded. He was lucky to escape with his life: his team's vehicle, an unmarked and unarmored Isuzu Trooper, had been hit some 49 times.

The CIA and SIGINT elements stationed at Pasha were under increasing threat. A CIA source told them that Aideed's militia knew the makes of their vehicles and how they were armed, and knew that Condor was a CIA officer. A CNN film crew were ambushed, according to SEAL Howard Wasdin, because the Habr Gidr mistook them for the CIA team and their SEAL minders. An interpreter and four local security officers were killed in the incident.[27]

When news reached the CIA on September 11 that Pasha had indeed been compromised and Aideed was planning to directly attack the safehouse, Garrison ordered the Americans to leave. They drove to the Pakistani-controlled soccer stadium to the north of the city and were flown out immediately by helicopters from the 160th SOAR. The CIA's local Somali assets continued their mission, infiltrating Habr Gidr and SNA gatherings and searching for the scent of Aideed.

Garrison was growing tired of the antics of some of the local sources recruited and funded by the CIA.

Generally [the local asset] appears to believe that a second-hand report from an individual who is not a member of the team should be sufficient to constitute current intelligence. I do not. Furthermore when a team member is reporting something that is totally different from what our helicopters are seeing (which we watch here back at the JOC), I naturally weigh the launch decision toward what we actually see versus what is being reported.[28]

Known to be working alongside the J-2 Cell and the CIA were the operatives of the US Army's Office of Military Support (OMS). The OMS had operated under a bewildering variety of titles and codenames, many referring to the Special Access Program designations in which the unit was routinely hidden. Originally called the Intelligence Support Activity (ISA), the unit was also known to Delta at the time of the Mogadishu operation as Centra Spike. Their involvement in *Gothic Serpent* was perhaps facilitated by Dave McKnight who was their former Operations Officer. Garrison himself had also served in the unit.

The CIA had embedded an operative within Task Force Ranger to work directly with Garrison to ensure the smooth flow of intelligence between the CIA and JSOC. This operative, with the codename of Buffalo, had flown in with Task Force Ranger and had even shaven his head to blend in with the Rangers. Garrison also placed one of his own JSOC intelligence officers, codenamed Gringo II, within the CIA station to coordinate activities between the Agency and his own J-2 Cell. This officer was likely from the OMS, a unit he later commanded.

Lieutenant Colonel James "Tommy" Faust, the second-in-command and Operations Officer of the JSOC J-2 Cell, mentioned "several airborne SIGINT platforms based out of country and supporting TFR [Task Force Ranger]."[29] These were more than likely OMS teams, as a similar mission was then ongoing in Colombia in support of the hunt for Escobar. In fact, a number of these assets were redirected from that effort to support Garrison. Faust also noted the addition of a "SIGINT Research & Development capability"[30] that mirrors what little is known of OMS capabilities.

There is scant open-source information available on OMS and even those within the SOF community are often ignorant as to its actual role. US Navy Admiral Harry Harris, former head of Special Operations Command in the Pacific, jokingly commented in 2016: "The Office of

Military Support doesn't sound very 'hooah' so I had some folks tell me what it actually does – and all I can tell you is that it does some 'hooah-ingly' interesting things."[31]

The unit was organized into troops as per the Delta model and had an Operations along with a Mission Support and SIGINT Squadron. It is from the latter squadron that the aerial SIGINT teams supporting Task Force Ranger were likely drawn. OMS operated its own highly modified civilian prop aircraft, typically Beechcraft 300s and 350s. Their mission in Somalia was to scan the airwaves for mentions of Aideed or his chief supporters, hoping that one would slip up and lead Task Force Ranger to their target. Some personnel from the OMS's Operations Squadron may have also deployed on the ground as sources mention three women operatives from the unit being present in Mogadishu, although there may have been confusion with Delta's F-Troop.

Alongside the SIGINT intercept efforts of the OMS, a range of other aerial intelligence-gathering platforms flew in support of the Aideed mission. These ranged from Army reconnaissance helicopters equipped with video cameras to a once secret Navy reconnaissance aircraft and "a quiet, manned surveillance aircraft"[32] controlled by the CIA.

The non-classified reconnaissance helicopter assets present were OH-58D Kiowas from Task Force Raven which were drawn from the US Army's Task Force 2-25. Raven had temporarily detached, or "chopped," their Fort Hood-based aircraft to Task Force Ranger for the duration of the mission. The OH-58D's unique mast-mounted optics and Forward-Looking-Infrared laser (FLIR) could be downlinked directly to Garrison's JOC, although the technology was still very much in its infancy. Little Bird pilot Chief Warrant Officer Karl Maier explained that "[It] was very, very primitive back in those days. They had one video feed there on a small screen but most of it was sitting around a table with a radio in the middle of it, listening to the radio. [They] are so different now."

Despite this, the video technology gave the chain of command a unique perspective on the battlespace during the *Gothic Serpent* missions. This would be the first time in history that a land battle would be observed by its commanders in real time via airborne cameras, a first that would lead directly to the development of the far more advanced camera systems employed on today's Predator and Reaper unmanned aerial vehicles.

There has been some question over whether Delta's own covert air wing was also deployed to Somalia. The unit, known as Echo Squadron, was rumored to operate unmarked versions of the MH-6 Little Bird outfitted with cameras and sensors to conduct surveillance in preparation for Delta assaults. Author and historian Sean Naylor has stated that the deployment of Echo Squadron to Mogadishu was confirmed to him by sources within JSOC but the author has been unable to independently verify this.[33]

A curious entry in the Task Force Ranger operations log notes "Recce launch (2 x H-530 & 1 x OH-58D)" indicating the use of two commercial Hughes 530s, which are similar to the Little Bird type airframe. All other sources, including veterans from both Delta and the 160th SOAR, only note the presence of the OH-58Ds. A minor mystery we will perhaps never solve.

An aircraft that has been confirmed to have been flying over Mogadishu during the hunt for Aideed was a specialist variant of the US Navy's P-3 Orion surveillance and search aircraft. Although a number of accounts claimed this was a standard specification P-3, records indicate that it was in fact a classified model known as a Reef Point. Reef Point was the codename for a specialist variant of the P-3 flown by the Navy's Special Projects Patrol Squadron, who conceal their aircraft within the regular Orion fleet. Today known as Iron Clad, the Reef Point was a specially equipped covert surveillance aircraft carrying telescopic infrared video cameras that could beam a wide-angle view of the action, in colour, directly to Garrison's JOC.

A Schweizer RG-8 spy aircraft was also overhead with its own FLIR and video equipment fitted. The Schweizer was a unique two-man design which would throttle back its engines once over a target location and glide almost soundlessly whilst recording and transmitting intelligence data from a suite of cameras. The RG-8 was likely flown by Air Branch of the CIA's Special Activities Division. All of these surveillance aircraft were involved in establishing patterns of movement and looking for changes to that pattern that could indicate the presence of a high-value target like Aideed or one of his key lieutenants.

One of the best leads developed in early September came from a CIA asset who managed to give Aideed's daughter a cell phone which was immediately intercepted by the OMS. Through the intercepts, the CIA learned where Aideed had allegedly been staying the previous night and the Navy Reef Point was launched to track his vehicle convoy as he left the residence. Unfortunately he managed to escape detection in the teeming masses of downtown Mogadishu.

There were valid concerns that Aideed might well have been receiving tip-offs about the Task Force's intentions from at least one of their multinational partners in UNOSOM II. Early on in the deployment, questions were raised over Italian colonial links to the clans, including Aideed's Habr Gidr. Certainly Italy had a lengthy history with Somalia. The country had been an Italian colony until early in World War II. After the war, the Italians became trustees for the country under the United Nations. Even after independence in 1960, the connections with Italy remained strong. Indeed Aideed himself had been educated in Rome and once served in the Italian-administered colonial police.

Even the United Nations eventually became suspicious of Italian intentions. General Montgomery noted, "They [the Italians] felt they had a special relationship with the Somalis." Historian Kenneth Allard makes mention of backroom deals between the Italians and Aideed: "the commander of the Italian contingent went so far as to open separate negotiations with the fugitive warlord Mohammed Aideed – apparently with the full approval of his home government."[34]

These suspicions of Italian complicity even led to embarrassment for Task Force Ranger. During a visit to the Italian contingent's headquarters on September 14, the J-2 head, Colonel Dave McKnight, was informed by his escorting Ranger detachment that Aideed had just been seen leaving the very same Italian compound. This resulted in the launch of an assault force in a case of mistaken identity that will be examined later in this chapter.

A Somali militia leader was quoted years later confirming the relationship between Aideed and the Italians, saying: "I'm not sure of any agreement as such but we were on friendly terms with the Italians. We understood that the Italians were not happy about the Americans operating so much force on us."[35]

Along with the constant struggle for intelligence and worries about Italian duplicity, the physical terrain of Mogadishu made upcoming operations difficult, particularly for ground forces. The city was criss-crossed by narrow alleys and dirt roads that had largely developed organically, catering to local needs, rather than by any conventional form of city planning. From the air, the city resembled a traditional grid pattern but once on the ground, that illusion quickly disappeared.

Many of the roads, nearly all unpaved, were extensively pot-holed and covered in all manner of debris – perfect grounds for the laying of landmines such as the one that had killed the American Military Police patrol on August 10, leading to the deployment of Task Force Ranger. It also slowed traffic into choke points that could be easily ambushed. Once ambushed on the narrow streets, it would be difficult for any vehicles, let alone large military Humvees or trucks, to turn around or maneuver. Once a vehicle was immobilized, a convoy could easily be halted and forced to reverse out under fire. For aircraft, the situation was little better. Wires from illegal electricity connections hung above and across the roads making fast roping dangerous and limiting the availability of helicopter landing zones, particularly ones large enough to accommodate a Black Hawk.

Buildings in Mogadishu were a mix of styles and heights but most were formed around a central courtyard and were typically a single to two stories in height. These were joined by rough thatch huts and aluminum shanties that had been constructed as shelter for the millions of internally displaced people who had flooded Mogadishu since the famine began. This confusion of structures made for ideal concealment: "they could fire through doors or windows even when closed and pop out into an alley or street to shoot rocket-propelled grenades, with little chance of being hit because of their short exposure time," wrote Ranger Captain Lee Rysewyk.[36]

Despite these difficulties, Task Force Ranger finally launched on its first mission on August 30. There had been numerous false starts: "Perhaps two or three times a day, the TF senior leadership would mull over some intelligence received about Aideed's whereabouts. Each time, the TF would spin up, and sometimes launch, only to be called back and the mission scrubbed," noted Kurt Smith. "Sometimes we would just turn one of these scrubbed missions into a signature flight since the whole task force was on the aircraft and kitted up anyway."[37]

In fact, Task Force Ranger "spun up" perhaps as many as 35 to 40 times prior to October 3, only to have the mission aborted, typically down to the poor quality of actionable intelligence. Garrison decided that they needed to start hitting targets in an effort to flush out Aideed. He also wanted to demonstrate that the SNA mortaring of the hangar would not go unpunished.

Garrison would not be intimidated by the SNA. The militia had begun their regular mortar bombardments from the first night of Task Force Ranger's arrival and, although largely inaccurate, it continued every night like clockwork.

Their first operation targeted a building known as the Lig Ligato Compound, codenamed Objective Flute, located on a road called Via Lenin, just north of the K-4 Traffic Circle and near to the Parade Reviewing Stand, a regular venue for rallies held by Aideed and the SNA. According to the CIA's assessment the location was a known "hang-out" for SNA leaders and the warlord had been seen frequenting it in the past. UNOSOM II provided additional late intelligence that a second adjacent building was also "Aideed associated" and a possible source of command and control for the nightly mortar attacks. This second location was added to the target set.

As the official history explained: "that night [August 30] at 19:27, mortar rounds rocked the TF Ranger compound. The attack by Aideed's followers lasted about 30 minutes, and a total of nine rounds landed at the airport, injuring four TF Ranger personnel. TF Ranger responded by launching an assault at 0309 on 30 August."[38] This first mission would be conducted purely by air with the 160th SOAR delivering and extracting the assault force upon completion of the operation.

Objective Flute was deep within Habr Gidr-controlled territory. Task Force Ranger reconnaissance aircraft monitoring the target during the night reported that it appeared that there was significant activity inside and the buildings were illuminated in the early morning darkness as much of Mogadishu slept. Garrison was confident enough in the CIA targeting and what his own reconnaissance assets were seeing to launch a helicopter assault force at 03:09 that morning.

Delta snipers shot out the security lights around the compound from their orbiting helicopters as the assaulters fast-roped to the ground. Moving swiftly, they gained entry into the buildings using breaching charges and shotguns. Nine inhabitants were detained and flexi-cuffed, blindfolded, and flown to a detention center before being released once their identities were confirmed. To the surprise of Task Force Ranger, the detainees were a mix of Westerners and local Somalis, all employed by the United Nations.

The SOCOM history continued: "The assault force cleared the Lig Ligato house and an adjacent building, both of which were on the UNOSOM priority target list. This operation was conducted professionally and on short notice. The assault force detained nine people who turned out to be UN employees. They also took weapons, drugs, communications gear, and other items from the buildings. The UN employees were not supposed to be there."[39]

There were questions raised of racketeering, particularly after it emerged that the employees had been previously ordered from the site by UNOSOM. Later intelligence indicated that the second building was in fact owned by Osman Atto, a key associate of Aideed and number two in the SNA organization, but leased to the United Nations as additional office space during the day.

This last point was missed by much of the following media frenzy. Headlines in the international press mocked the results of the operation: "Can Delta farce now get it right?" screamed one. Others spoke of a supposed "keystone cops" approach. Although the accusations of the press were at best uninformed, Dave McKnight at the Task Force Ranger J-2 Cell conceded, "we placed too much credence in (these sources) and failed to adequately confirm the target."[40] Kurt Smith remembered: "The next day, newspaper clippings posted at the JOC read 'Delta Farce Strikes Again' and similar headlines. It's frustrating to read things like that, especially written by someone who clearly has no understanding of how difficult it is to do our job."[41]

Despite the "dry hole," the operation itself had gone like clockwork. After the assaulters had completed their mission, 160th SOAR helicopters had landed in a nearby schoolyard and exfiltrated the operators and their detainees. There were some reports of light small-arms fire directed toward the helicopters as they had arrived, but this would not prove to be unusual in Mogadishu. As one Nightstalker pilot recalled to the author, "They shot at us every day!"

Colonel Danny McKnight's Rangers, idling nearby in the standby Ranger GRF should ground extraction be required, spotted what they thought, through night-vision devices, might be a gunman with an RPG on a nearby rooftop. The Rangers held their fire as they couldn't positively identify their target as the rules of engagement stipulated and the figure was later identified as a CNN cameraman. The resultant footage of Delta fast roping into the target aired on the international networks the next day.

Garrison immediately received pressure from the chain of command due to the press coverage of the raid. Lee Rysewyk wrote that they "now felt considerable restraint to go on [a] mission."[42] Furthermore there was now a "checklist of precursors" imposed by Hoar that would have to be followed before Task Force Ranger could launch. Garrison would now have to inform and clear targets through Montgomery, Hoar, and UNOSOM.

Garrison explained the decision-making behind the Lig Ligato operation in later testimony to the House Select Committee hearing:

> I launched the first raid because the mortar attacks were the first time that the majority of our troops were ever in combat. I didn't want them to develop a "bunker mentality" and I knew how important it was to get my guys up and operating.
>
> So I went to UNOSOM headquarters and said give me your number one target that Aideed had reportedly been at within the last 24 hours. It was the Lig Ligato house. We launched on that target. After the first raid, General Hoar gave me specific guidance that I had to have current, actionable intelligence, i.e. I had to know the guy was actually at the target – it had to be verified. That is why we spun-up more than 40 times but only conducted seven raids.[43]

September 5 saw the CIA receive intelligence from one of their local assets that Aideed would be visiting his aunt's home that night. The source even provided a drawing of the internals of the house itself and the CIA thought the tip was solid enough to launch. Garrison declined to launch, probably on the basis of the information coming from a single source, particularly in light of the criticism following the Lig Ligato operation. Garrison was likely referencing this mission when he later said: "One time, we had intelligence that Aideed went into a building and wasn't seen coming out. We launched reconnaissance helos but there was nothing to see associated with Aideed, i.e. no extra guards. I was fairly confident he was there, but we did not launch because of our guidance."[44]

The next target would be the former Russian Embassy, otherwise known as the Military Compound, on the night of September 6. This target was again located north of the K-4 and near the Reviewing Stand. Delta inserted by a mix of MH-6s and Black Hawks whilst the Rangers fast-roped in to establish their blocking positions to isolate the objective from outside interference. Again this would be a helicopter-borne operation but with

McKnight's GRF standing by in the vicinity in case of difficulties. Smith remembered:

> One night we received intelligence that Aideed was attending a meeting at an old Russian compound in the city. We launched as usual and lined up on the compound. I sat on the front left side of our MH-6. Norm [Hooten] sat next to me on the rear seat. As we were on approach into the compound, I viewed through my NODs [night observation device] the AH-6s lift up high, level off, then turn down on their gunruns.[45]

The AH-6s had seen militia in the immediate vicinity of the objective and had engaged them with their miniguns before the gunmen could harass the assault force. As the MH-6s landed, one of the operators spotted more gunmen and fired his SAW in their direction to warn them off. The assaulters breached and cleared a number of buildings and initially captured some 30 people, although there was no sign of Aideed. According to a number of sources, he had been present only a short time earlier. Tommy Faust mentioned: "We were off by one building and Aideed barely escaped. I do not know if [it] was caused by the source [a member of the CIA's local surveillance teams] or our interpretation [of the source's directions]."[46]

The assaulters and their 17 eventual detainees, including two Tier 3 Habr Gidr leadership targets and a number of assault rifles and machine guns, were extracted by helicopter without incident. The Rangers in the GRF saw for the first time Somalis setting alight stacks of old automobile tires around the target location. It would also be the first mission on which the Rangers would receive direct enemy small-arms fire.

The nine-Humvee GRF was engaged by AK47 and RPG fire as they waited for the assaulters to complete their part of the mission, inflicting minor wounds to two Rangers: Specialist Steve Anderson was hit in the leg by an RPG fragment and another, the turret gunner on McKnight's own Humvee, Sergeant Mike Pringle, was struck in the helmet by an AK round. The Kevlar luckily stopped the bullet but part of it broke off and inflicted a nasty graze.

The Ranger GRF returned fire against the militiamen that engaged them near the Reviewing Stand. Orbiting AH-6s were called in to provide close air support and a dismounted operation cleared out the gunmen. Paul Leonard remarked: "[After] the first two or three missions we did notice that they were getting quicker to responding to where we were going."

After the Somali combatants were suppressed, the Ranger GRF began to receive what could only have been friendly fire from one of the small US outstations known as Sword Base located to the northwest. Indeed, upon their return to the hangar at least one .50-caliber hole from a US heavy machine gun was discovered in the door of a Ranger Humvee. Luckily no one had been hit by the undisciplined fire.

The next operation occurred on September 14 and again caused significant embarrassment to Garrison and Task Force Ranger. As mentioned earlier, relations with the Italian contingent had deteriorated amid growing suspicions that they were passing information to Aideed. Whilst visiting his opposite number in Italian intelligence at their compound, the Ranger security element for Colonel Dave McKnight, led by Staff Sergeant John Burns, spotted an individual whom they thought was Aideed. His behaviour, seemingly quickly spirited away upon the arrival of the Americans, only increased that belief.

McKnight reported the sighting to the JOC and an OH-58D was launched to trail the suspect vehicle, a brown Land Rover. The helicopter's camera apparently confirmed the Rangers' sighting and the assault package was launched against the building where the Land Rover eventually stopped. Again the mission template was a helicopter insertion and extraction with the GRF convoy standing by. No enemy fire was received upon approach, particularly unusual for a daylight mission. The reason for this would soon become painfully clear.

At 13:00 the assaulters stormed a building in northern Mogadishu and detained the suspect individual and 38 other Somalis. The individual wasn't Aideed but General Ahmed Jilao, another former police chief from the Barre regime. The other detainees were members of the Abgaal Clan who were violently opposed to Aideed and were vocal supporters of UNOSOM. The location of the target should have indicated that it would have been an unlikely place for Aideed to hide out, deep in rival Abgaal territory in the north of the city far from the Habr Gidr enclaves to the south. Jilao and his clan members were soon released.

Three days later, on September 17, Task Force Ranger conducted an operation to silence the warlord's personal propaganda station, Radio

Aideed. Although it normally only transmitted for three hours each evening, it had become a thorn in the side of UNOSOM and was added to the target list as an Aideed infrastructure target. The J-2 Cell had improvised a direction-finding kit to narrow down the exact location of the pirate radio station.

Tommy Faust explained that his men rather ingeniously "wrapped WD-1 telephone wire around a broomstick as an antenna, attached it to a signal strength test receiver and put the assembly in a helicopter. The helicopter was cued by direction-finding assets into the general area and then used the fabricated antenna and receiver to find an aural null. This refined the location down to a building and what looked to be an antenna."[47]

Instead of helicopters, this time Task Force Ranger used the Ranger GRF to approach the target. Kurt Smith remarked:

> The convoy was a collection of turret and cargo Humvees. F-Team was on a turret Humvee, the last in the order of movement in and the first out. Since navigation was difficult throughout the city, the lead vehicle received help from a command and control aircraft hovering high above. The aircraft would designate the route with an IR [infrared] laser so that the lead vehicle would know where to make the appropriate turns. Upon arrival at the objective, the mission went similarly to the others thus far. The execution went well, but we didn't find what we were looking for.[48]

An SNA militiaman was engaged and killed by a member of Delta's E-Team as they cleared the area but no trace of the radio station could be found. One civilian was also wounded during the assault. The antenna that had been spotted later turned out to be a "derelict light pole" according to Faust. A significant portent was the rapid arrival of masses of Somali civilians, some armed. Kurt Smith recounted:

> After the search was complete, we began our exfiltration. MH-60s were hovering around the objective, providing air support with 7.62mm miniguns. This created a beacon by which to draw crowds on this night. As we began our exfil, many Somalis had begun converging on the objective area. War is a spectator sport to Somalis. Even if the area is dangerous for spectators, they still want to come watch.[49]

The GRF spotted a number of gunmen during their exfiltration from the objective. "On one of the missions, we did a convoy of vehicles in and on the way out. A couple guys made the mistake of looking [down from] a two- or three-story building with guns. I told the Ranger behind the .50 cal to engage them. The .50 cal ripped through the cinder block making it look like it was exploding," recounted Paul Leonard, a member of C-Team. Other militia were spotted down an alleyway by Kurt Smith. He engaged them with his SAW which alerted the other Humvee gunners to the Somalis' presence, and recalled:

> Almost immediately, the Ground Force Commander, Captain Ben S, was on the radio. "Looks like we're taking some fire from the left side." With that, I looked back and saw every turret in the convoy turn its weapons in that direction. Each Humvee was alternately equipped with a MK19 40mm automatic grenade launcher or a M2 .50-caliber machine gun. Every vehicle's occupants on the left side fired down the alleyway as they passed. The explosions from the grenades and tracer fire from crew-served weapons made it appear like a 4th of July celebration through my NODs.[50]

Tommy Faust confirmed that Task Force Ranger later used "helicopter gun cameras"[51] to watch SNA personnel erect the actual antenna for Radio Aideed just across the street from the targeted location. The Task Force had been within meters of striking the right location. Garrison was informed and the radio station kept on the target list.

During the post-mission "hot wash" or debrief following this mission, Colonel Boykin, the then commander of Delta, decided to hold an impromptu prayer session for the armed militiaman killed during the operation. This decision was met by much bewilderment from the operators present. Boykin's evangelical Christian beliefs would later impact on his career after he conducted a presentation in which he displayed aerial photos of Mogadishu taken on October 3 and bizarrely reportedly claimed there was a demonic presence visible in the smoke over the city.[52]

Another little-known operation was also conducted by Task Force Ranger during September. Civilian employees at the airport had been discovered to be acting as forward observers for Aideed's mortar strikes. The American SIGINT capability meant that voiceprints could be taken from recordings of radio intercepts guiding in the mortar rounds and compared to those of the ostensibly civilian airport workers. When they matched, the J-2 Cell knew they had identified the culprits. A security operation in late September resulted in the temporary capture of one of these spotters. The mortar attacks continued, unfortunately, but that particular spotter never reappeared on the radio net.

After the death of their main HUMINT source from Russian roulette, the CIA and J-2 Cell now conferred with the 10th Mountain QRF's J-2 unit, requesting a list of Aideed's top half dozen key lieutenants. This was phase three of Garrison's plan. Phase one had been to establish Task Force Ranger and make it ready for immediate operations. This phase had officially concluded on August 28. In phase two, Task Force Ranger had targeted Aideed directly to no avail. Now, with phase three, Garrison was going after the warlord's henchmen, aiming to isolate Aideed by targeting his immediate supporters, a group termed the "Tier One Leadership." There was also the distinct possibility that one of his lieutenants would give up Aideed's location under tactical questioning.

Back in the United States, White House opinion had turned increasingly toward a negotiated solution to the "Aideed problem." Diplomatic overtures were now being made to the warlord by representatives of the US government through Habr Gidr intermediaries. At his address at the United Nations General Assembly in September, President Clinton, however, made no mention of any such a change in policy. Incredibly, these diplomatic efforts were never directly communicated to Garrison, Montgomery, or the Task Force Ranger leadership. Les Aspin was later directly quoted as claiming: "The Pentagon's understanding of the policy was to move to more diplomatic efforts but snatch Aideed on the side, if you can."[53]

Interviewed years later, General Thomas Montgomery tellingly explained:

> There had been a recommendation to re-think new ways to maybe engage the Somali faction leaders, Aideed specifically. I knew that recommendation had been made, but not even the Ambassador knew that anybody had taken it under consideration or advisement back here ... You may recall the President said something about the fact they'd kind of made a decision in Washington to take a different course. And he was appalled at the news – well, I think we were appalled at the news – that somebody had decided to take a different

course and yet we were continuing our operations. Here [in Mogadishu] we had no new orders or new guidelines.

But apparently the President's remarks were about maybe they were deciding to take a different course ... But nothing had ever been communicated to the field. I wish if that was the case, that whenever somebody had made that decision back there [in the US], [they] had told the military chain of command to cease and desist in this effort to bring Aideed to justice.[54]

Garrison, as the head of JSOC, was astute enough, however, to understand this dimension and knew that the longer his units struck "dry holes," the more the political willpower supporting the mission would ebb away – he needed a success. Public approval of the mission in the US was also flagging badly as the situation in Mogadishu degenerated. All of the political indicators pointed to a phased but speedy US withdrawal and handover to the United Nations. Congress had recently passed a resolution which would require specific Congressional approval after a November 15 deadline to maintain US forces, including Task Force Ranger, in Somalia.

The wider US effort under Montgomery was increasingly concerned about the roadblocks that Aideed's militias had been using to block and channel American and United Nations forces and that were beginning to be seen during Task Force Ranger operations. Tanks would have been able to easily clear such obstructions. Armored vehicles were possessed by several of their United Nations partners including the Pakistanis and the Italians but Montgomery was uneasy relying upon them.

He was particularly concerned that under the convoluted United Nations command structure there would be delays or even the potential for a contributing nation to flatly refuse to support his forces with their armor, particularly following the June 17 operation which had seen Habr Gidr territory declared off-limits to many of the UN contributing nations. Instead, he wanted American armor under his direct command. Montgomery made his initial request for four M1A1 Abrams main battle tanks and 14 M2A2 Bradley infantry fighting vehicles on September 14, a request that was denied by Hoar and Aspin again citing the aim of minimizing, and in fact reducing, the overall US footprint.

The first opportunity to strike at an Aideed leadership target was early on September 18. Osman Atto, Aideed's financier and a top target on the Tier

One list, had been spotted. One of the CIA's local assets signalled, under the watchful eye of a pair of SEAL snipers stationed atop a water tower at the Pakistani-controlled soccer stadium, that Atto had arrived at one of his numerous places of business, a garage and mechanical workshop which built and repaired technicals and heavy vehicles for the Habr Gidr.

Aerial surveillance confirmed the target's presence at around 08:15 that morning and the Task Force launched by helicopter on another daylight operation. To avoid establishing a pattern, this time the GRF would conduct a ground extraction of the assault force whilst any detainees would be transported directly from the objective by Little Bird back to the hangar. When the assaulters arrived on the objective and breached into the garage a mere 30 minutes later, they apprehended suspects with ties to Atto, but the principal target and his bodyguards had fled. Apparently Atto had quickly changed clothes and fled at the first sign of trouble.

The operators also discovered and released a local national who had been chained to a nearby tree, apparently a member of a rival clan taken hostage. A press photographer who strayed too close to the target was warned back with flashbangs thrown by a sniper on board Super 61. Three gunmen, including one armed with an RPG, were shot and killed by the SEAL snipers providing overwatch during the mission.

On this raid, the Task Force had received significantly more small-arms and RPG fire directed at their helicopters. A report authored by US Military Intelligence Major Roger Sangvic would highlight the standard Somali response to these Task Force Ranger incursions, mirroring Kurt Smith's comments: "Any mission gathered hundreds of curious, bored onlookers who had nothing better to do. Sniping would soon pick up, many times coming from crowds or behind women or children. This would escalate to more bold actions and even an RPG or two."[55]

The Task Force did not have to wait long for a second shot at Osman Atto. On September 21, the JOC was alerted to a possible sighting. Team One, one of the locally recruited CIA surveillance cells, had established contact with an associate of Atto's who was willing to sell him out. A hasty plan was concocted, again using the infamous CIA walking stick with the implanted beacon.

The walking stick was handed to the contact who was scheduled to meet with Atto later that day. Team One trailed the car carrying the contact and the walking stick as it headed to the presumed meeting destination. Instead, one of the Team One spotters spied Atto in the car with their contact when it stopped for petrol. The information was immediately transmitted to the CIA and from there to Garrison's JOC. It was decided to launch an interdiction using the second of the standard templates, the Vehicle Intercept.

This mission was entirely conducted by Delta, with the Rangers aboard Black Hawks in a holding pattern nearby in case Atto managed to escape the intercept. Operators on Little Birds caught up to Atto's Fiat and the engine block was engaged by sniper and minigun fire from one of the Black Hawks. The reality differed from the film in which there were several vehicles shown in the convoy and Atto's is disabled by precision fire from a sniper's CAR15. Delta Sergeant First Class Jim Smith was the sniper who took the actual shots and noted that it wasn't just his CAR15 that was fired: "I shot the engine block of his vehicle to stop the vehicle. I initially engaged it with my CAR15 and then the minigun on my side of the bird opened up." The vehicle was allegedly hit more than 50 times.

One of the Little Birds almost landed on top of the car. Atto's driver/bodyguard attempted to engage the operators with an AK47 but was intentionally shot in the leg and disabled. Atto ran from the car as the helicopters landed and disappeared into a nearby building, the assaulters in hot pursuit. Paul Leonard, on one of the Little Birds, recalled: "After the car was disabled, several men including Osman Atto ran in to a nearby house to hide. I believe E-Team rounded up all the guys from the car and were sitting on a covered deck and Captain Miller told C-Team to guard the prisoners. Gary Keeney started to ask each one of them their names."

Leonard's fellow C-Team member Gary Keeney was indeed the operator who made the positive identification of the Task Force's first high-value target capture. He recounted:

> The vehicle with Osman Atto was shot and immobilized by another team from one of the helos. We then landed and assaulted the building that we thought we saw them go into. The first building was a dry hole and then we're getting reports that they might've squirted to the next building so we ran to the next building.
>
> I distinctly remember C-Team entered that building first and we entered into basically a living room area. We froze down that first big room and E-Team kinda flowed through us and we could see through a small [internal]

window – the type of window you would pass food through from a kitchen – bad guys in that kitchen area type room, [with] no weapons.

E-Team's lined up to enter that room and they threw a flashbang in, and I could see these guys all huddled together, [then] boom, the banger went off and E-Team entered and secured those guys. As they pushed them out of the room, I positively ID'd Osman Atto. We had studied the photos – we had Aideed and all of his lieutenants in photos. They're [E-Team] moving them out of the room for C-Team to take possession of them and control them as prisoners. When I see Atto, I grabbed him and put his back up against the wall, made sure he's got no weapons on him and I looked him in the eyes and I asked him "What's your name?." He didn't respond and I said "What's your fucking name?" and he said "Osman Atto" and I looked over at my team leader Matt Rierson and said "We have jackpot, this is Osman Atto."

When he [Matt Rierson] called it in, you could sort of feel the excitement, like "we'd finally got one of these guys we were here to get, we were accomplishing the mission." C-Team were then given the task of bringing him back immediately. So then of course we flex-tied him and then went straight to the roof, an MH-6 landed, we threw him in and we flew back to the airfield and brought Osman Atto in.

Paul Leonard added that the intelligence imagery didn't exactly match the reality: "As C-Team pulled him to the roof up three flights of stairs with my rifle muzzle up his ass, trying to get him to move fast. The picture we had of Osman Atto made him look like a smaller guy. But in actuality he was over 6 foot tall and 200 plus pounds."

Outside on the streets, the situation was heating up. Ranger Lieutenant James Lechner in Super 64 could see the Somalis starting to encircle the target. He recalled:

The Somalis ... were probing the perimeter in small groups of two and three. Farther out, large mobs could be seen forming, summoned by the SNA's crude but effective alarm system of burning tires in the streets around the target. Although I could see few weapons in the crowds, they were obviously agitated and converging cautiously on the target building.

Both the remaining sniper bird and the gunships were now firing in support of the assaulters as they extracted from the rooftop. I was convinced that if they had remained on the ground much longer they would have required our assistance to extract. As it was, a number of gunmen had been engaged as they probed the perimeter and at least 15 enemy casualties were inflicted by the assaulters and aircraft. [56]

Post-operation analysis also confirmed that the Somalis had launched at least 15 RPG rockets at the helicopters during the operation.

Norm Hooten summed up the mission succinctly: "We shot the engine block and shot the driver. We attacked the convoy, engaged it, and they ran into a building. We landed the aircraft and went into the building and captured him." Despite the increase in the ferocity of the Somali response, the Task Force were buoyed by their first big capture of one of Aideed's key people. Days later, however, an incident that should have rung all kinds of alarm bells within Task Force Ranger occurred.

On September 25, a QRF Black Hawk, callsign Courage 53, was struck by an RPG whilst flying over the city. The helicopter was engulfed in flames and crash landed. It was only by great skill and bravery that the pilots managed to land the helicopter in one piece. The three crew chiefs in the rear were incinerated in the fire and both pilots were badly burnt. One fended off advancing Somalis with his 9mm Beretta service pistol whilst they awaited rescue. A friendly Somali civilian led them to a nearby United Arab Emirates United Nations patrol before Lieutenant Colonel Bill David's Quick Reaction Company arrived several minutes later and conducted a near-perfect downed aircraft recovery operation, in an operation that would somewhat foreshadow the events of October 3.

Although the Black Hawk crew chiefs had perished in the fire, the news passed around Task Force Ranger that their burnt bodies had been further mutilated in a similar fashion to the Pakistani peacekeepers back in June, although this seems to have been incorrect as the QRF recovered what little remains existed before withdrawing from the crash site. Super 65 Black Hawk pilot Chief Warrant Officer 3 (P) Gerry Izzo mentioned that in Somalia: "My greatest fear was being captured, being crippled, or being killed – in that order."

Courage 53 had been flying very low at rooftop level on a moonless night, even though it was moving at an estimated 120 to 130 knots. The QRF had received intelligence that the SNA might be planning to shoot down a helicopter. It was implicitly recognized by Aideed that the helicopters were the Achilles heel of the Americans, as downing one would draw rescue forces who could then be ambushed. Gerry Izzo explained that the downing of the QRF helicopter "really was the silver bullet, a lucky shot. It was nighttime and I think one guy flung a rocket, an RPG, at him. The Somalis took a different attitude I'm sure: 'Oh look we can really shoot down helicopters with these things.'"

Tommy Faust in the J-2 Cell later felt that the downing of the 10th Mountain Black Hawk was an omen Task Force Ranger failed to recognize and militate against. He asked a 160th SOAR pilot his opinion of their vulnerability. The response was that the Nightstalkers had discussed the downing in some detail and: "In their opinion, the shoot down was lucky, i.e., 'big sky, little bullet.'" The unnamed pilot also felt that the 160th SOAR's tactics and techniques would help guard against such an eventuality:

> TFR aircraft ... flew rapidly random and irregular flight profiles. He also said that 10th Division pilots were good, but they had less flight time and experience than TFR pilots did. The combination of experience and better tactics minimized the RPG threat to TFR aircraft.
>
> This appeared to be the consensus assessment of the September 25 shoot down. We did not correlate the Black Hawk loss and the number of RPGs available in Mogadishu. We did not view this event from the Somali perspective: successfully shooting down a helicopter with a RPG added a potential TTP [Tactics, Techniques, and Processes] to the SNA.[57]

A SOCOM after-action report on the *Gothic Serpent* deployment recorded:

> During August and September 1993 TF Ranger conducted six missions into Mogadishu. These six missions were tactical successes, and the cumulative effect of these missions was to impair Aideed's movement and to undermine his authority. In each case, the assault and blocking forces landed with no or only minimal opposition, seized their objectives, searched them, detained suspects, and departed the area. Although Aideed had eluded apprehension, his key lieutenants were vulnerable, and the capture of Osman Atto had proven TF Ranger's capability to strike in the heart of the SNA stronghold.[58]

Indeed, of the target list of Aideed and 49 of his Tier 1 clan members in the Habr Gidr, 26 had actually been captured during these first six operations – Task Force Ranger were rolling up the warlord's network.

Despite this, some within Task Force Ranger were becoming uneasy at what they saw as the increasing speed of the response from the Somali militia; they were getting faster and shooting was happening earlier on nearly every mission. "Somewhere around halfway through our deployment the Habr Gidr militia started to fire a lot of RPGs into the air and they are clearly taking shots at our helicopters but we always had this 'big sky, little bullet' theory," recalled Ranger Sergeant Jeff Struecker.

Gerry Izzo had seen the steady increase in ground fire from the air in Super 65:

> I was noticing the missions were getting hotter and hotter. Looking back, maybe I should have been a little more adamant about my misgivings but we were having success, mission after mission, at this point. Each mission that we did we would take a little more gunfire earlier and earlier and somewhere around the fourth or fifth mission I mentioned to [veteran 160th SOAR pilot of Super 61] Cliff Wolcott; "You know I think they're catching onto what we're doing."
>
> Not that I was clairvoyant or anything but I just noticed they were getting a little bit more organized. I remember when I mentioned it to Cliff, and he was eating French C-rations, and he just looked at me and said "Well, I don't know any other way to do this" so I acquiesced to his experience.

Karl Maier added: "We could tell that the guys on the ground were getting smarter because we were doing the same thing over and over."

Colonel Boykin later wrote in his memoir that despite the increasing opposition from the militias he believed that they were getting closer to capturing Aideed through the systematic targeting of his key lieutenants:

> Did our risks go up with each operation? Yes, I personally felt our risks were going up as the enemy was figuring out how to stop us, but we always achieved surprise on the target. It did become a matter of concern over time, but I did not believe that our chances of success were going down. I believed they were increasing because we were destroying Aideed's infrastructure, which should force him out into the open.[59]

# CHAPTER 3

# LUCY

*"There was debris and dust from every helicopter around us. You couldn't see the building – the building was only at the edge of the rotors! As the bird lifted off you could already hear small-arms fire. On the other missions the fire didn't start until the exfil and it was unusual that you would receive any fire early on. We were already exchanging fire before we got into the house."*

Master Sergeant Norman "Norm" Hooten, F-Team, 2 Troop, C-Squadron

After the success of the Atto capture operation, Task Force Ranger continued to "aggressively prosecute" the target list of Aideed's lieutenants. On September 24, they came close to launching against Colonel Abdi Hassan Awale (otherwise known as Abdi Qeydid), a close Aideed aide and his Minister of the Interior. CIA intelligence indicted that Awale was intending to visit his favorite tea-house that day but the target was never confirmed by aerial surveillance and the mission was scrubbed.

The CIA's locally recruited surveillance teams hit the jackpot on the morning of October 3. The CIA had established Team Three led by a former SNA leader with a grudge to bear against Aideed and who was willing to sell him out for the right price. He arrived that morning at the CIA compound with startling news – Awale and Omar Salad Elmi, Aideed's principal political adviser, were meeting that afternoon.

The asset believed Aideed might even be at the meeting and there was a good chance other individuals from his inner circle could be present, making it a tempting target. Tommy Faust recalled: "A HUMINT source reported that Salad … was to attend a meeting at a specific house in the Habr Gedir section of town. The specific location was unknown but it was assessed to be close to the Olympic Hotel."[1] In fact, Salad had been sighted earlier that morning at an SNA rally at the Reviewing Stand on Via Lenin, north of the K-4 Traffic Circle, but had disappeared before Task Force Ranger could launch.

The Olympic Hotel was a famous local landmark on one of the city's main thoroughfares, Hawlwadig Road, which ran north to south past the Olympic. It was located near to the notorious Bakara Market to the northwest. The Bakara Market and surrounding streets were central Habr Gidr territory. This was the area that the multinational forces had refused to enter again after the abortive raid on Aideed's headquarters compound on June 17.

Any incursion would likely result in large numbers of SNA militias opposing the operation. Adding to the potential difficulties was the Sheik Aden Adere Compound just to the east of the Bakara that served as a logistics base for jihadists. The J-2 Cell had received intelligence that some 200 foreign jihadists, mostly from Sudan, had arrived a week earlier and would likely reinforce the SNA from the Compound.

Bill Garrison was aware of the dangerous nature of the Bakara Market: "If we go into the vicinity of the Bakara Market, there's no question we'll win the gunfight. But we might lose the war," he noted in a memo.[2] Tommy Faust agreed: "A direct action mission near the Olympic Hotel and surrounding area was the Mogadishu equivalent of bombing downtown Hanoi in daylight during the Viet Nam War."[3]

Garrison estimated that his units had perhaps 30 minutes in which to accomplish their mission and exfiltrate before the SNA began to respond in significant numbers. Any longer and Task Force Ranger ran the very real risk of being swarmed: "I knew that the closer we got to the Bakara Market, the faster we had to get in and get out. The bad guys' reaction time was well known."[4]

Tom DiTomasso confirmed that the reputation of the Bakara was known even amongst the Rangers: "The target was east of the Bakara Market which we knew was really bad."[5] Delta Captain Scott Miller recalled: "3 October was a Sunday, which was traditionally a down day for the task force. The idea was a quick in, secure the target, then quick out."[6]

**1459 HOURS:** SOURCE CONFIRMED ON TARGET. RECCE [RECONNAISSANCE HELICOPTERS] MANEUVERING TO PROVIDE VIDEO OF BOTH SIDES OF BUILDING. RECCE ADVISES THIS AREA HAS REPORTED NUMEROUS SMALL-ARMS FIRE IN RECENT PAST. AIRCREWS/GROUND FORCES BRIEF MISSION.*

The plan was relatively straightforward. The CIA source was to drive his vehicle to the site of the meeting and park outside. He would then open the hood (bonnet) of his car in a prearranged signal for the Task Force Ranger helicopters and spy plane observing high above to confirm the exact target building for the assault force.

The source was becoming increasingly nervous about the numbers of SNA gunmen around the building and stopped short until, after a number of false starts, he was finally convinced by his handlers to stop outside the correct building. The large numbers of gunmen also indicated that at least some high-value targets were likely present at the location but how many was still unknown. The source quickly exited his vehicle and gave the prearranged signal. The surveillance helicopters confirmed the signal and added that they could see Omar Salad Elmi's yellow Volkswagen parked inside the compound.

Another daylight mission was risky but the target was both time-sensitive and of enough importance to outweigh Task Force Ranger's natural reluctance

---

\*   From Task Force Ranger JOC Timeline – see Appendix 3.

to operate in the daytime. Norm Hooten, team leader of F-Team, explained: "The mission that day was to capture key leaders of his executive staff. We had all of his executive staff at one meeting which was very rare. Usually you get one or two but to have [maybe] 10–12 key leaders in one spot ... was just something we couldn't turn down."[7]

Super 64 pilot Chief Warrant Officer 3 Mike Durant said:

> We could tell this was not going to be quite as straightforward as any of the others. The city was dangerous at any time, and this was in a particularly bad part of town. It was also daytime, and we couldn't land the Black Hawks anywhere close to the target. So we knew there were some intricacies to this one that were going to make it more of a challenge.[8]

A mission to capture Salad and Awale was finally launched. "We got spun-up three times already that day so we were getting tired of it: 'when's this thing going to happen?' So we were up and down all day and we were napping [that afternoon] when all of a sudden 'let's go, we're going'," explained Paul Leonard.

The Rangers were playing volleyball whilst one squad had been dispatched on the regular "water run" to pick up fresh water for the Task Force Ranger base. The aircrews of the Black Hawks were due to conduct some training with their Direct Action Penetrator variant, an armed gunship kit that could be bolted onto a standard MH-60L. "We were in fact planning a range event to go shoot the DAPs when the October 3 mission unfolded," said Mike Durant. Ranger First Sergeant Glenn Harris emerged from the JOC to advise the Rangers of the upcoming mission, shouting "Get it on!"

At around 14:30, the Delta team leaders, Ranger chalk leaders and the aircrews convened for a quick orders group to explain Bill Garrison's concept of operations. Using the Building Assault template, Delta would insert on the roads directly outside the target building using a combination of MH-6 Little Birds and MH-60 Black Hawks. If the Little Birds could land they would, otherwise the teams would fast-rope in. The larger Black Hawks had no room to land and thus their assigned operators would be forced to deploy by fast-ropes. The assaulters would then breach into the objective and, after overcoming any resistance, detain and round up all suspect personnel.

Whilst the operators were storming the objective, the following four Black Hawks would hover over each corner of the block in which the target building was located and fast-rope in their cargo of Ranger chalks. Tom DiTomasso recalled:

> The initial assault came in with four Little Birds and two Black Hawks who brought in the primary assault force and then probably 20 seconds later the four Black Hawks come in at all four corners of the intersection, near simultaneously, to drop off the blocking positions, their job was to contain the enemy from running away from the target area and to isolate the target area from external influences – two different things: keep people in and keep people out.
>
> At approximately 15:23, the commander gave the order to execute the mission. The chalk leaders quickly briefed their team leaders as they loaded the helicopters. Everyone was very sharp by this time and knew exactly what we had to do on the ground [because of their experience on previous missions]. As I passed around the diagram of the objective for the Rangers to study, I discussed with the pilots exactly where we needed to be inserted.

The Ranger chalks were then briefed by their squad and platoon leaders. The Ranger leadership had each received an 8"x10" black and white aerial photograph taken by a surveillance aircraft over the target location. On the photo were marked the location of the target, their insertion points, and their intended blocking positions, all using the Olympic Hotel as a landmark. Matt Eversmann confirmed: "All the reference points for me were structures, I didn't know the street names."

The objective itself was one block north of the distinctive five-story Olympic Hotel. Facing onto Hawlwadig Road, the L-shaped target building had two floors at the front facing the road, and three at the rear with a small attached courtyard typical of most Somali structures to the south. The entire block in which the target building nestled was surrounded by an 8- to 10-foot-high stone wall. A gate led into the courtyard in an alley running west to east along the short end of the L.

The Rangers were advised that this would be a fast-rope insertion, meaning that two braided ropes would be dropped from either side of the Black Hawks once they were over their assigned insertion points. The Rangers, using heavy gloves to protect their hands from the friction, would then slide down the ropes to the ground. Fast-roping was only used if a suitable landing zone for the helicopters could not be identified.

Mogadishu was full of dangers that made such a landing difficult, chief amongst them an array of electricity wires strung up in a haphazard fashion on nearly every street. These and the incredible amounts of debris on the ground made fast roping the only option in many cases. A typical urban fast-rope was 20 to 30 feet in height but on this occasion, due to the amount of wires and telegraph poles in the target area, some of the Rangers would be fast-roping from between 40 and 60 feet in height as the helicopters simply could not safely descend any lower, the longest fast ropes they had yet encountered in Mogadishu.

It took a considerable amount of practice to find the optimum placement for every Ranger in relation to the fast ropes that were bolted to the center of the helicopter's rear cargo bay. The bench seats and the usual long-range fuel tanks had been removed from the Black Hawks to fit all of the Rangers and their equipment in. Even with the seats and tanks gone it was a tight fit. The Rangers needed to ensure that the fast-rope process was completed as efficiently as possible to minimize the period of time their Black Hawk spent hovering exposed over the city. The big helicopters were "bullet magnets," as one 160th SOAR aviator explained, and their greatest defense was their ability to get in and out quickly.

The Ranger squads were divided up into chalks typically composed of elements of two rifle squads along with an attached machine-gun team with a senior NCO or platoon leader as commander. There were four such chalks assigned to the October 3 mission drawn from the 1st and 2nd platoons of Bravo Company. Chalks 1 and 3 were from Lieutenant Larry Perino's 1st Platoon whilst chalks 2 and 4 were from Lieutenant Tom DiTomasso's 2nd Platoon.

Each chalk was supported by a Radio Telephone Operator (RTO) to provide communications and a Fire Support Officer (FSO), or Forward Observer (FO), to manage close air support from the AH-6s and sniper Black Hawks orbiting overhead. Each chalk also included a designated medic or at the very least a Ranger trained in advanced combat lifesaver techniques. In total, each chalk numbered between 12 and 15 Rangers dependent on how under-strength the squads were; one of the rifle squads assigned to Chalk 3, for example, was only five men strong to begin with.

Chalk 4 under Sergeant Matt Eversmann is a good illustrative example of the structure of the chalks. He recalled: "I was normally in charge of a Ranger squad of nine people but on this day, however, I was in charge of 13 Rangers, a composite of soldiers assigned to one aircraft. James Telscher and Casey Joyce were my two team leaders, young sergeants, both E5s."

He had the two senior Rangers as fire team leaders, Sergeants Jim Telscher and Casey Joyce; a two-man M60 machine-gun team in the form of Specialist Kevin Snodgrass and Private First Class Todd Blackburn; a pair of SAW gunners, Specialists Dave Diemer and Adalberto Rodriguez; and a pair of grenadiers, Privates First Class Marcus Good and Anton Berendsen. Completing the chalk were Eversmann's RTO Specialist Jason Moore and his FO, Staff Sergeant Jeff McLaughlin.

Along with his role as a grenadier, Private First Class Marcus Good served as the chalk medic. Eversmann explained:

> Marc Good was an infantryman, a young Private First Class, who had been trained as an EMT [emergency medical technician] through the Army, he'd done the Advanced Lifesaving Course prior to deployment so that our platoon medic was with Tom DiTomasso. Marc Good was our assigned medic on Chalk 4 even though by trade he was an infantry guy. He did an incredible job.

The principal firepower of each of these chalks lay with their single 7.62mm M60 medium machine gun and their two 5.56mm M249 squad automatic weapons or SAWs. Supplementing the incredible suppressive fire of the M60 and SAWs were two M203 single-shot grenade launchers that could deliver 40mm high-explosive projectiles out to some 400 meters. These M203s were mounted under the barrel of the standard 5.56mm M16A2 assault rifle. Every other Ranger was issued with either the M16A2 rifle or a carbine version known as the CAR15. Along with fragmentation and smoke hand grenades, each Ranger also carried flashbang stun grenades and non-lethal Stinger riot grenades filled with plastic pellets to disperse civilian mobs.

Each chalk had a geographic responsibility around the objective. Chalk 1 was under the command of Lieutenant Perino and was tasked with the southeastern blocking position. Captain Mike Steele and his company command element were also attached to Perino's Chalk 1. Chalk 2 under Lieutenant DiTomasso would manage the northeast corner whilst Sergeant Tim Watson's Chalk 3 was diagonally opposite DiTomasso at the southwest, directly outside the target building. Sergeant Eversmann's Chalk 4 completed the square at the northwest corner on Hawlwadig Road.

Once the Rangers had deployed via the fast ropes, the plan called for the Black Hawks to leave the immediate vicinity and fly holding patterns several kilometers away in case they were required. "Air extraction was not the primary plan this day so we were a contingency asset at that point which included possible extraction by air as a backup," explained Mike Durant. Flight lead for the MH-6 Little Birds, Karl Maier, confirmed that his crews were also ready for such a contingency: "We could've picked them up off the roof, it wouldn't have been a problem – that's one of the things the Little Bird is really great for."

**1527 HOURS**: ASSAULT FORCE ROUTE PASSED TO RECCE; BARBER FLIGHT WILL HAVE ROCKETS – NO PREPLANNED FIRES AT THIS TIME. CONVOY ROUTE (K4 – NATIONAL – OLYMPIC) 9 X HMMWV & 3 X 5 TONS: WILL DEPART WHEN HELO FORCE DEPARTS AIRFIELD.

The extraction or exfiltration plan as it was known to Task Force Ranger was to be by ground. Several minutes after the helicopters lifted off from the airfield, the Ranger GRF convoy would leave the gate and head toward a holding location southwest of the objective, near the Olympic Hotel. The GRF was tasked with extracting both the assault force and their prisoners along with the Rangers from their respective blocking positions.

There were 12 vehicles in all – nine Humvees and three five-ton cargo trucks – carrying a total of some 56 Rangers and attached personnel. The Humvees included two open-back M998 cargo variants, and the other seven were regular M1025 or "turtleback" models. All of the Humvees had just a week earlier been fitted with armored floor pads to improve crew survivability in the event of a mine strike. None featured any form of gun-shield or turret for the gunner, leaving the weapons crews dangerously exposed.

Some of the M1025s were fitted with ballistic glass and armored doors courtesy of Delta but others lacked doors altogether. Some had also been modified in the field, taking the rear hatch off to facilitate firing behind the vehicle. Along with the Humvees were three M923A2 five-ton cargo trucks that had been reinforced with sandbags to provide some rudimentary level of protection to passengers. The M932A2s would arrive empty, tasked with moving the prisoners and the majority of the Rangers back to the airfield.

Colonel Danny McKnight would command the GRF with Air Force Combat Controller Technical Sergeant Dan Schilling acting as his FO. Ranger Sergeant Jeff Struecker commanded the lead Humvee with a fire team of Rangers and would act as the primary navigator for the convoy. Struecker noted:

> It wasn't common for McKnight to go out with the Humvees. Lieutenant [Larry] Moores and one of the squads went out across the city to pick up resupplies – that was pretty much a daily occurrence. If you were not on a mission, maybe you'd be on a resupply and miss the mission.
>
> I did supply convoys fairly regularly and we [also] did a number of patrols through the city to not demonstrate a standard template of how we did operations – I was [in] the first Humvees in all of those – but really my responsibility was to memorize the maps – it was a kind of tourist map of sorts and then there was a very thorough satellite image. My responsibility was to memorize the major points of travel in the city.

Many of the young Rangers had no experience operating Humvees or in operating in a vehicle convoy. The Rangers were a light infantry unit and at the time had no Humvees on their organic table of organization. "Part of my job was to teach my men how to drive Humvees, how to drive under night-vision goggles, most of them didn't have any experience with vehicle-mounted weapons systems. Some of that we did in the city and some of that we did in a little training area outside the city," explained Struecker.

Those Rangers with experience with crew-served weapons like the .50cal M2 Browning heavy machine gun or 40mm Mark 19 automatic grenade launcher crewed those mounted on the Humvees. Struecker added: "The Ranger company had three rifle platoons and there was technically a fourth platoon, the weapons platoon. That weapons platoon would be spread across the two rifle platoons that went in by helicopter and my platoon on the Humvees and a lot of those guys ended up using the heavy weapons systems on those Humvees."

A second Humvee manned by Rangers and commanded by Ranger Sergeant Danny Mitchell followed Struecker. Third in the column was another Ranger Humvee carrying McKnight and Dan Schilling along with FO Staff Sergeant Bill Powell, an interpreter, and two Rangers; McKnight's

RTO Specialist Joe Harosky who was driving the Humvee and Sergeant Mike Pringle manning the .50cal. Dan Schilling, as well as acting in his assigned role of Combat Controller, managed communications for McKnight with the C2 helicopter overhead and was a team medic for the vehicle.

In the fourth Humvee, an M998 cargo variant with an open back and no armor, were the four SEAL Team 6 snipers along with two Delta operators, Sergeant John M, a sniper from 3 Troop, and Master Sergeant Tim "Griz" Martin, the squadron's Master Breacher who had transferred across from B-Squadron. A Ranger manned the .50cal on the "Cutvee," as the SEALs christened their vehicle. Their role was different in that they were tasked not to wait at the holding area along with the rest of the GRF but to proceed immediately to the target building and reinforce the assaulters. The three five-ton trucks and five more Humvees, all manned by Rangers, followed the SEAL and Delta vehicle.

If McKnight's ground convoy ran into trouble or was delayed, as on previous missions the Black Hawks might be called upon to conduct an in-extremis extraction. Indeed, Delta were concerned that the operators might have completed the capture portion of the mission before the ground convoy had a chance to arrive, particularly if it faced opposition or road blocks.

Mike Moser on B-Team recalled: "We would intentionally mix things up between missions, partly to keep the Somalis guessing about our TTPs as best we could. We preferred the air exfil option so long as things were generally quiet." Fellow operator Norm Hooten agreed: "We always had redundancy in our exfil plan. We had options to leave via helo, vehicle and, as a last resort, afoot."

If such an emergency option was needed on October 3, it would have been fraught with its own unique challenges. A Delta officer noted there was an antenna tower on the roof of the target building that Delta would have to destroy with demolition charges before helicopters could land on the roof. Gerry Izzo mentioned that, although the infiltration and exfiltration plans often differed, on October 3 "it was always infil by helo, exfil by truck and Humvee. There was no way to land on a roof or in a vacant lot with a Black Hawk to get everyone out."

As the Rangers and operators boarded their respective aircraft, Bill Garrison personally visited each helicopter to wish the units well, something he had not done before. Matt Eversmann was on his first mission as chalk leader and was feeling understandably nervous:

Firstly, for me it was the first time being in charge on an actual mission. Second of all, I was on the headset with the pilots and believe it or not I'd never done that before. I'm sitting at the airfield and put on the headset and they were on the common frequency so everybody's talking at once and finally one of the crew chiefs reaches over and sort of punches me on the arm and says, "Hey, the pilot's talking to you." I was like, "Holy smokes man, I didn't even know he was talking to me!" so this is a kinda new experience for me in this particular situation being chalk leader.

To the relief of Lieutenant Lechner, the Fire Support Officer who had been requesting their use for some time, the AH-6 Little Bird attack helicopters had now been loaded with 2.75-inch rocket pods in addition to their standard miniguns, another first for Task Force Ranger. The seven-tube 2.75-inch rocket pods were loaded with high-explosive warheads, not the fletchette variant the 160th SOAR sometimes trained with. Although superb in the anti-personnel role, the area of effect of the 2200 steel fletchettes in each rocket was highly dangerous to both friendly personnel and civilians caught in their beaten zone (the likely impact area of munitions). The high-explosive rockets, while still packing a significant punch, were more limited in their effect.

### 1532 HOURS: HELO ASSAULT FORCE LAUNCHES.

At 15:32 local time the codeword "Irene" was transmitted to all stations, the signal for launch. With the AH-6s in the lead, the 16-helicopter armada lifted into the air. Matt Eversmann recalls: "The helicopters en-masse take off from the airfield, fly out over the ocean to the south, come out over the desert, we're going to do a big clockwise loop and the approach from the north. As I recall, it was only a short flight, it was only three or four minutes from take-off to insertion." The whole package flew past their intended target in an effort to deceive the Somalis of their intentions before turning as one and heading for the objective.

Each aircraft was identified by a callsign followed by an aircraft number. The armed Little Birds operated under the callsign Barber, their unarmed brethren in the MH-6s were Star, whilst the Black Hawks were designated Super as their callsign identifier. Karl Maier explained that the callsigns held no special significance and changed regularly between operations: "They're randomly assigned … computer generated. We fortunately got some good ones that trip. I've been on trips where my callsign was 'Wimpy'!"

As the Task Force approached their objective, the codeword "Lucy" was transmitted at 15:37, the signal for the assault to begin. The two AH-6 Little Birds swept down to overfly the target building to ensure there were no immediate threats like antiaircraft cannon, machine guns, or RPG teams visible that could target the helicopters carrying the operators and the Rangers.

As the AH-6s – Barber 51 flown by Chief Warrant Officer Randy Jones and Chief Warrant Officer Hal Ward and Barber 52 flown by Chief Warrant Officer Larry Kulsrud and Chief Warrant Officer Tony Rinderer – approached the target, one of the OH-58D surveillance helicopters spotted a Somali machine-gun team near the objective, but they disappeared inside a building before the Little Birds could engage them.

Craning their necks to spot any potential threats, the AH-6s screamed over the target and swung away into a low orbit. Following on their heels were the four MH-6 Little Birds led by Star 41, piloted by Chief Warrant Officer Karl Maier and Chief Warrant Officer Keith Jones. The MH-6s were unarmed and instead carried what the 160th SOAR referred to as "people pods"; folding external bench seats attached to either side of the airframe with two Delta operators sitting on either side. Along with the pods, each MH-6 was equipped with a fast-rope system should the Little Birds fail to locate a suitable landing zone.

**1542 HOURS:** HELO ASSAULT COMMENCES ON TARGET/EXACT TARGET BUILDING UNKNOWN/CITY BLOCK WILL BE CLEARED.

Perched upon the "people pods" of Star 41 were four members of B-Team. Michael Moser, one of the newest members of the squadron at the time, remembered: "At the time of the train-up, C-1-B [C-Squadron, 1 Troop, B-Team] consisted of five people; it was decided to detach one of us to another element, one of the Blackhawk loads, since the Little Bird load was maxed out with four assaulters."

Karl Maier in Star 41 was busy trying to identify landmarks:

> I had to navigate from photos, so I would pick prominent points, like on that particular day I picked the [Olympic] hotel as a reference as it stuck up above

everything. I knew I had to turn a few streets short of that. Actually Cliff [Wolcott in Super 61] was in front of me to the left and he stopped short, he stopped at the wrong intersection. My co-pilot Keith was like, "Do I turn here?" and I was like, "No, he's in the wrong place." It's not easy to do in a city like that, it's a ramshackle city, everything looks the same – it was not easy to navigate in that environment. He [Wolcott] picked one block short, realized when I passed him I think and moved forward and got his people in the right place.

With the MH-6s we land them right at the front or back door. The guys from where I landed probably walked three steps and he was at the door.

Mike Moser remembers a short fast-rope from Star 41 into the alley directly to the south of the objective: "We had an uneventful infil, approaching along the axis of flight, then turning left to settle into an alley, boxing in the target. The alley was too narrow to accommodate the MH, [we hovered] approximately two to three feet off the alley's dirt floor with his rotors humming one to two feet off the alley walls as we roped down."

Karl Maier said that he could hear small-arms fire already at this point:

I didn't see any RPGs then – lot of the times you can't see those in the daytime but you can hear them going by. Didn't get a whole bunch then that I remember, although I was kinda focused on making sure we got to the right target building. I did notice a lot of small-arms fire. In that place, everybody had a gun and every time we went out, it didn't matter if we were going to do a mission or we were just flying around, we got shot at so that was nothing new. It was just another day.

Behind Star 41 was Star 42 carrying C-Team. "Five members of a six-man team were deployed [on October 3]. Four of us were assigned to an MH-6 Little Bird, that was Matt Rierson, myself, Paul Leonard, and Mike F," explained Gary Keeney. The team's fifth member, Steve C, a Special Forces combat medic, was assigned to the Delta element on one of the trailing Black Hawks, Super 61. "On the Little Bird I sat front right on the outside pod, Mike F was behind me and on the opposite side of Mike was Matt Rierson, the team leader, so he could lean into the aircraft and talk to the pilot from his headset. Paul Leonard was directly opposite me on that left hand side."

**1543 HOURS:** SUPER 61 REPORTS GROUND FORCE HITTING THE GROUND; RECCE IS PROVIDING FLIGHT FOLLOWING INSTRUCTIONS TO GROUND FORCE.

The dust clouds caused by the rotor wash of the helicopters made navigation particularly difficult. The brownout only increased as the following Little Birds and Black Hawks arrived. "Chalk 3, Star 43, had to do a go-around [because of the dust]. I was flight lead but even I was enveloped in dust. Chalk 2 had it even worse and by the time Chalk 3 got in there he couldn't see anything so he did a go-around," explained Maier. Super 64 pilot Mike Durant also recalled Star 43 not locating its insertion point: "One Little Bird had to go around, because the dust was pretty bad in this particular part of the city. They couldn't see their landing area and they circled around, but again, it's a contingency that's planned for, so no real big deal."[9]

Kurt Smith aboard Star 44, the last of the Little Birds to arrive, recalled:

> I fought back my usual anxiety as the formation of aircraft circled the city to line up on Hawlwadig Road. As we descended into the objective area, I scanned for targets on the ground with my SAW. Somalis were running everywhere as the dust began to form from the aircraft rotorwash.
>
> In time, I could see nothing. I wasn't sure if the aircraft was going to land or hover in place, so I stowed my SAW in the back of the aircraft and secured the fast rope, getting ready to throw it out. The brownout was so thick I could barely see ten feet in front of me.[10]

Indeed in video footage from the surveillance helicopters, the Little Birds all but disappeared into the colossal dust clouds kicked up by their rotor wash.

Star 42 also landed in the alley to the south of the objective and its team of operators took off swiftly heading for the objective. "The first Little Bird coming in with B-Team took a left and went a little further down the road due to the dust cloud. C-Team, the second Little Bird, landed right in front of the target building. E and F-Team were right behind in the other two Little Birds respectively," remembered Paul Leonard.

Leading the entry into the target building was Sergeant First Class Matt Rierson, a 33-year-old veteran operator who had previously served with B-Company of 2nd Battalion, 75th Rangers. Rierson was the team leader of

C-Team. His men raced through the outer courtyard door and headed for the main door into the objective.

As Star 44 carrying Norm Hooten's F-Team descended, its main rotor struck a telephone pole. Hooten explained:

> Everyone hangs their own power poles in Somalia – there's no official power company so somebody had put a pole outside of their little hut and we clipped the top of it going in. When that happened the bird went into a hover so instead of going directly in … normally Little Birds go in directly and land very quickly, [but] this bird's kinda stopped its descent.

Based on past experience, Hooten assumed the aircraft could not find a clear landing zone so immediately deployed the fast rope: "I remember the dust that had been kicked up from the lead birds going in was so bad that we couldn't even see the ground. I thought we were roping, so I threw the rope and stepped off and I was on the ground. It was a two-foot fast rope!"[11]

Hooten continued:

> There was debris and dust from every helicopter around us. You couldn't see the building – the building was only at the edge of the rotors. As the bird lifted off you could already hear small-arms fire. On the other missions the fire didn't start until the exfil and it was unusual that you would receive any fire early on. We were already exchanging fire before we got into the house. You could hear the [Ranger] machine guns at the blocking positions exchanging fire on the perimeter.

Hooten's F-Team had landed further up on Hawlwadig Road north of the target building.

By comparison, Moser on Sergeant First Class John B's B-Team didn't remember much incoming enemy fire at first: "I do not recall any small-arms fire … my impression was that it grew, sporadically at first, shortly after we began clearing our building. There may have been some engagements on the periphery, whether from our snipers, or the Ranger security folks." His team proceeded to conduct an entry upon a secondary structure next to the meeting site: "Once on the ground, the B-Team objective was to clear a single-story building adjacent to the primary target building while the bulk of the assault element entered the primary structure."

Star 43 landed its operators on Hawlwadig Road on the western side of the objective moments later. E-Team led by Sergeant First Class Paul H initially breached into the wrong building, making entry on a warehouse. Realizing their mistake, E-Team quickly moved with F-Team to the courtyard that Rierson's C-Team had already breached and swept into the target building.

Hooten's F-Team had also landed short of their objective, almost two blocks north of the target building, but got off the street as quickly as possible: "We moved directly into a building that was some sort of crude store. There were empty glass soda bottles in plastic crates stacked in the corner of the room. We ordered the Somalis to get down using the internationally recognized hand and arm signal: pointed rifle and an open palm lowered in a rapid downward motion," one of F-Team's operators later wrote.[12]

Gary Keeney on C-Team noted:

> The [target] building itself was on a corner and when the four Little Birds landed in the street, we were the second in the order of movement. We kinda landed like an L-shape. We landed on the corner. Everything's browned out but we were the closest ones right there by that entrance courtyard so C-Team was essentially the first ones to get to the courtyard door and enter the building.

Each operator on the four-man teams on the Little Birds had a specific role. Along with the team leader, the assault teams included the team medic, known as an 18D in reference to the military occupational specialty code of Special Forces medic; the grenadier carrying the M203 grenade launcher; and the specially trained and equipped breacher who carried a shotgun for ballistic breaching of doors and pre-configured explosive charges for "loopholing" or "mouseholing" through walls or reinforced doors.

No breaching was required on the objective on October 3 as both the external courtyard door and the main door to the target building were inexplicably unlocked. Paul Leonard recalled:

> It seemed like a long time before another team came up behind us. There were several people trying to come down the stairs. But we were blocking the

entrance. Once E-Team arrived, C-Team went up three stories of stairs. C-team entered the building first. The first room to the right, which only had curtain for door cover, and Gary Keeney and I cleared the room and found the guy we were looking for that day, probably Salad. He was trying to take his pants off and change into the local garment. I threw him to the floor in the main room. I vaguely remember a very large women running at me when I did this and [another operator] Scott S knocking her to the ground.

The Somalis within the target building gave up immediately as the operators made entry. The Somalis were happy to fire away at Task Force Ranger from a distance but once faced with operators at close quarters breaching into their building they quickly surrendered. Smith remembered:

I never had to shoot anyone or heard of anyone shooting a Somali inside a building on the assault.

It took us [F-Team] several minutes to move to the target building. We had been set down at least a block away. As we moved to the target building, I could hear the first reports of the distinctive sonic crack made by bullets passing nearby. The bullets could be passing next to my ear or 50 feet away. It's impossible to tell, especially when wearing earplugs, except that the bullets are definitely out there. We finally turned the corner to the target building and proceeded inside. We were the last assault team into the building, having been dropped off the farthest from the objective. We moved up to the second floor and joined the assault in progress.[13]

As the assaulters started to search and secure the prisoners, the two Black Hawks carrying the remainder of the assault force came to a hover north of the objective on Hawlwadig and began fast-roping to the ground. A-Team along with Staff Sergeant Jeff Bray (their attached Air Force Combat Controller) and Captain Scott Miller's command team descended from Super 61, nicknamed "Thunderstruck".

Behind them came G-Team from Super 62, nicknamed "Black Widow." G-Team at the time had a full complement of six operators so wasn't one of the original assault teams as they had too many operators for an MH-6: "They weren't super happy about that one," Hooten laughed. "Everyone wants to be on a Little Bird going in!"

Once the operators roped to the ground, the two Black Hawks cut the ropes and ascended into what was known as a "low CAP" or combat air patrol. Super 61 carried four snipers from 3 Troop, the squadron's recce/sniper troop, whilst Super 62 carried three, all of whom would stay on board after the insertion.

The two helicopters would then conduct aerial sniper support over the objective at a typical height of around 150 feet to allow the snipers to take their shots targeting RPG gunners and militia leaders. The doorgunners were also able to fire their miniguns should suppressive fire be required. Tom DiTomasso explained:

> We'd been using two Black Hawks for airborne security and surveillance locally around the target. On board those two helicopters were US Army SMU [special mission unit] snipers. If they needed to shoot from the helicopter they could; they provided critical airborne situational awareness with the capability to employ precision marksmanship fire as required.

Above the two sniper helicopters was Super 63 carrying the command and control or C2 element who would manage the battle from the air. Inside Super 63 was the Air Mission Commander, Lieutenant Colonel Tom Matthews; the Ground Mission Commander, Lieutenant Colonel Gary Harrell; and Staff Sergeant Ray Benjamin, their assigned Air Force Combat Controller.

Also orbiting nearby was Super 68, nicknamed "Razor's Edge," flown by Chief Warrant Officer Dan Jollota and Major Herb Rodriguez. On board Super 68 was the specialist Combat-Search-and-Rescue or CSAR team who would fast-rope in should the unthinkable occur and a helicopter was shot down over the city.

Directly behind Super 61 and 62 were the Black Hawks carrying the Ranger chalks. In the film and book *Black Hawk Down*, much is made of the numerous fires lit using burning tires and identified as signals by the SNA that the Americans were approaching. As they flew toward the objective on October 3, Mike Durant in the lead Black Hawk, Super 64 nicknamed "Venom," didn't "recall a noticeable difference" in the amount of fires that were burning below in the city.

Both Durant and Gerry Izzo in Super 65 confirmed that neither saw anything that they considered out of the ordinary on their approach to the target and certainly nothing to the scale of that shown in the movie. Izzo explained:

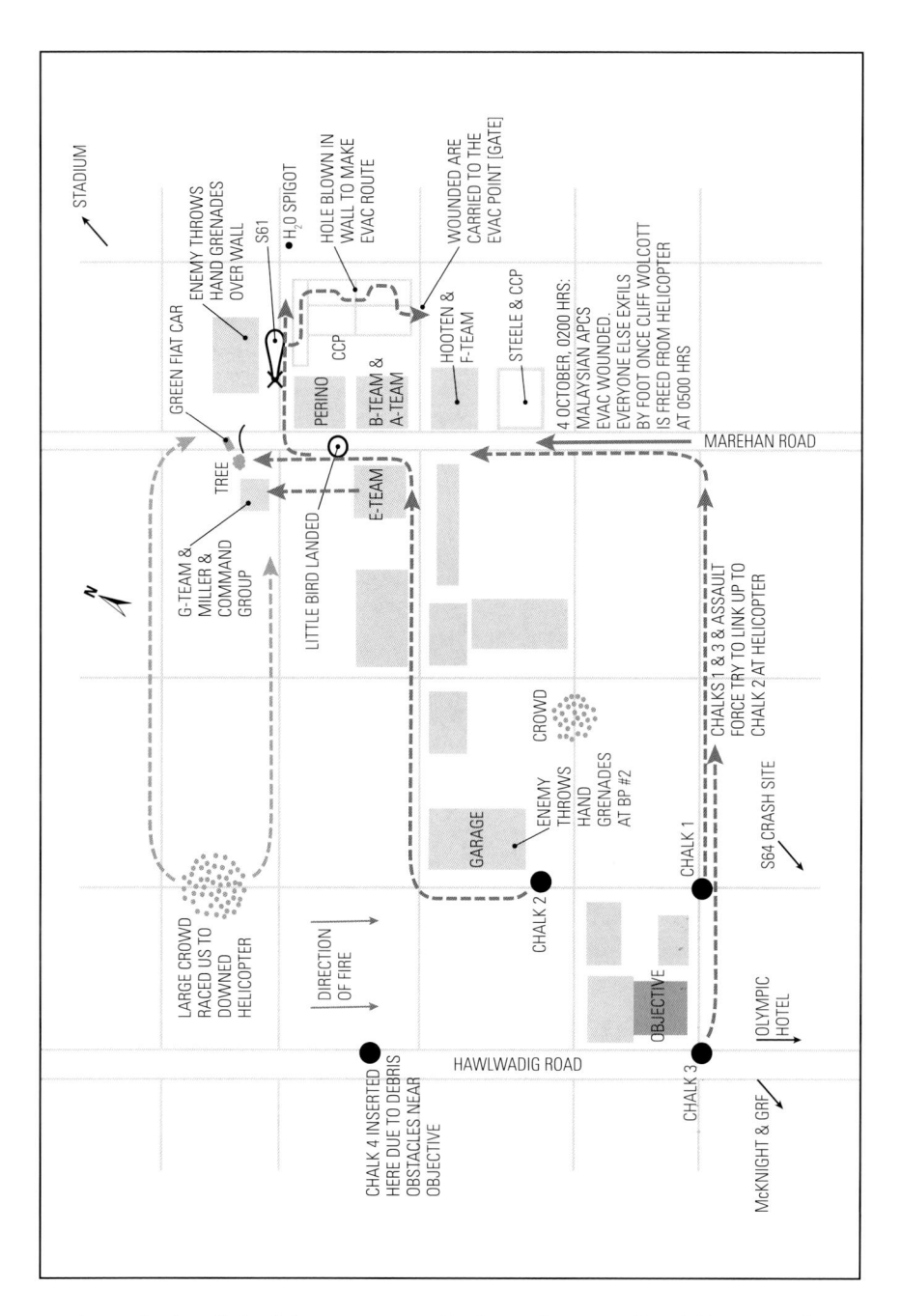

A reproduction of a hand-drawn map created by Ranger Lieutenant Tom DiTomasso in the aftermath of the battle and with some additional information added on subsequently.

21 OCTOBER ROAD

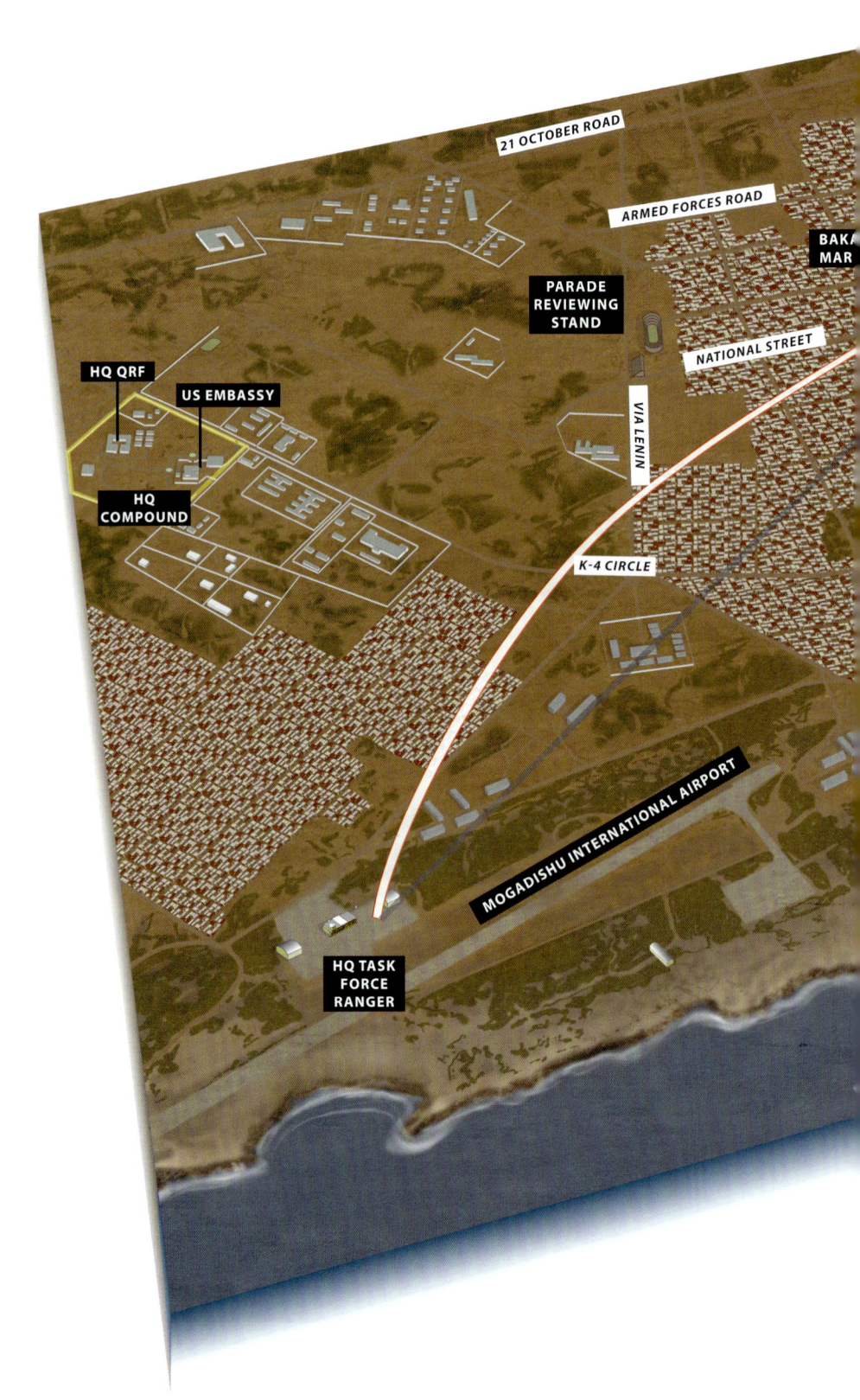

ARMED FORCES ROAD

BAKA
MAR

PARADE REVIEWING STAND

NATIONAL STREET

HQ QRF

US EMBASSY

VIA LENIN

HQ COMPOUND

K-4 CIRCLE

MOGADISHU INTERNATIONAL AIRPORT

HQ TASK FORCE RANGER

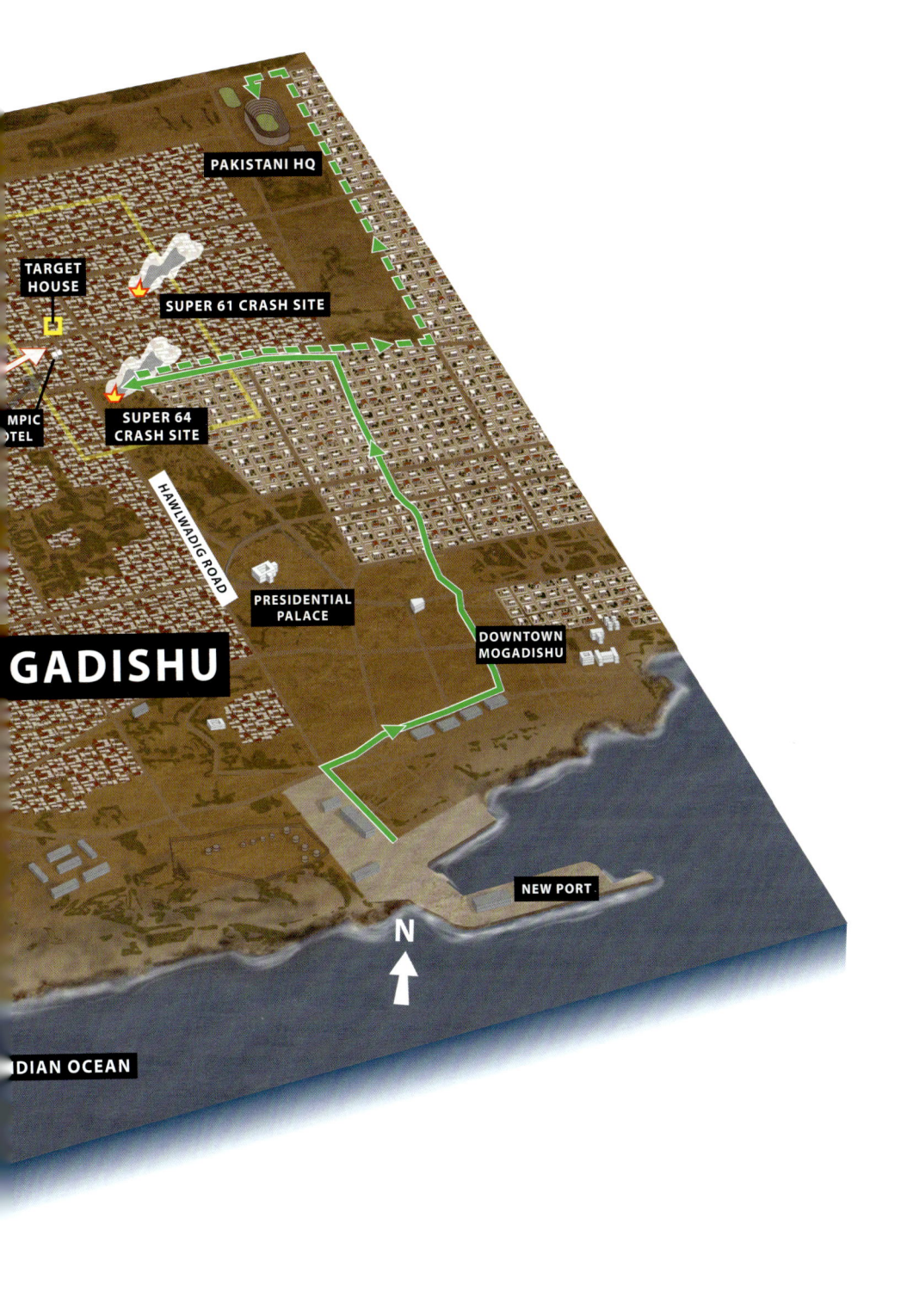

Bird's eye view showing the routes taken by Task Force Ranger from headquarters and the QRF from New Port.

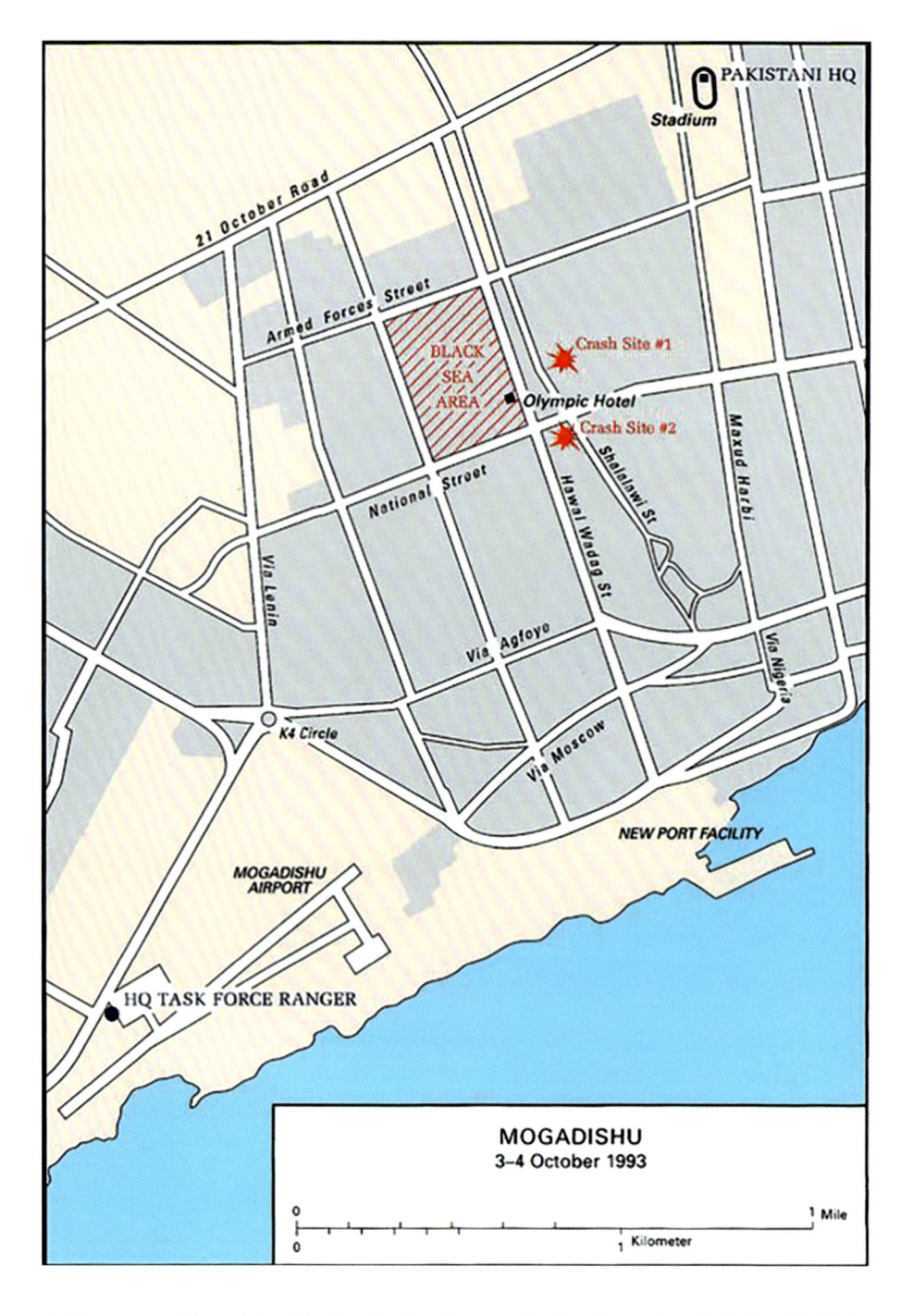

US Army map of the vicinity of the October 3 battle, noting key locations such as the K-4 Traffic Circle and Hawlwadig Road. (Courtesy US Army)

1st Flight Platoon, Company D, 1st Battalion, 160th SOAR posing in front of Super 62. Three of the aviators in this picture were tragically killed in action on October 3, 1993. (Courtesy Gerry Izzo)

Super 65 conducting a practice mission prior to October 3 flown by Captain Richard Williams and Chief Warrant Officer 3 (P) Gerry Izzo. (Courtesy Gerry Izzo)

Super 64 (photo taken from Super 65) en route to a target prior to October 3. Note the Rangers sitting in the doors. (Courtesy Gerry Izzo)

Super 65 flown by Gerry Izzo and Richard Williams on a "signature flight" above Mogadishu. Members of Tom DiTomasso's Chalk 2 are visible in the cargo area, legs dangling over the side. (ALEXANDER JOE/AFP/Getty Images)

The Super 65 flight crew: Staff Sergeant Pat Powers, Chief Warrant Officer 3 (P) Gerry Izzo, Captain Richard "Trey" Williams, Staff Sergeant Foy Fields. Note the MP5A3 submachine gun carried by Fields. Crews were issued both the MP5A3 and the MP5K, whilst crew chiefs often carried M16A2s stored in the cargo area. (Courtesy Gerry Izzo)

A number of unidentified Task Force Ranger personnel with a 160th MH-60 at Mogadishu International Airport on August 28, 1993. Unfortunately the image is too poor in resolution to make out the aircraft number of the Black Hawk. (ALEXANDER JOE/AFP/Getty Images)

Photo taken from Super 64 looking aft at Black Hawks Super 65, 66, and 67 during a prior mission over the outskirts of Mogadishu. (Courtesy Gerry Izzo)

A group shot of C-Squadron and supporting elements at the hangar. A range of small arms are on display including 7.62mm M14 battle rifles, 12 gauge Remington 870 shotguns, CAR15s mounted with Master Key shotguns, M249 SAWs with collapsible stocks, and CAR15s mounting M203 grenade launchers. (Courtesy Paul Leonard)

3 Troop from C-Squadron in the hangar at the airfield. 3 Troop comprised the squadron's snipers and reconnaissance specialists and was typically manned by the most experienced operators. Visible amongst the operators are Gary Gordon and Randy Shughart (back row second and third from the left) and Dan Busch (kneeling to the left). Jim Smith can be seen to Busch's right. (Courtesy Paul Leonard)

It wasn't that really thick black smoke like they did in the movie – the main thing that we noticed was that when the assault force went in, they threw up a tremendous amount of dust and that was the thing that was limiting our visibility.

Truthfully I don't think they had those fires going until after the battle started. When I saw that in the movie I was sitting there going, "Huh, must've missed that!" You do get a little tunnel vision when you're scared but I would have seen all of that smoke! When the assault group went in, the Little Birds they get in and they get out very, very quickly and on this particular day they had a little difficulty getting in, they threw up so much dust that one aircraft had to go around and come back in. So that delayed their assault.

With the blocking force, you want to come in right on the heels of the assault force, but you got to let them get in and get out. So while all of this was going on, Mike [Durant] brought us to a hover a quarter mile short of the objective area. We were in a box formation so Mike was in front of me, I was behind him, the number three aircraft was 90 degrees out Mike's right side, and the number four aircraft was right behind him. We were approaching the target in a box formation so that we could put our Rangers in on the four corners. So as we came to a hover, we started throwing up a tremendous amount of dust and finally when we got the radio call that the assault Little Birds had come out, then we moved forward and we flew out of our dust cloud into the clear and then we plunged into the dust from the assault.

As we were groping along, from block to block, all of us had a photocopy of an overhead photograph of the objective area so that we all knew what our insertion point was going to look like. Mine was like a little sidewalk café with a white fence around it – as we got closer and closer I could start to hear a lot of gunfire, I could hear rounds snapping past the aircraft. At first I was thinking, "Oh, this is our guys really letting them have it," but they were shooting at us.

My co-pilot said, "Is this it? Is this the intersection?" and I said no, there's no fence, there's no patio, we're going to keep going. While we were doing this, I couldn't see Mike in the aircraft in front of me because of the dust. I had two concerns; one, I didn't want to ram him from behind and the other was I didn't want to put my guys in short either, I wanted to put them in the right spot.

Aircraft collisions between special operations helicopters are a very real risk in these types of operations. 160th SOAR aircrew had lost their lives training for similar missions, as had Allied SOF. In fact two Australian Army Black Hawks would collide in midair during a nighttime exercise only three years later in October 1996 resulting in the deaths of some 18 soldiers, most from the Special Air Service Regiment. Izzo, Durant, and the other pilots were all acutely aware of the danger posed by collisions and strived to maintain their distances, even in close-to-zero visibility.

All of the aircraft had begun taking ground fire on their approach but most of the aircrew and passengers were unaware of the amount of RPGs being launched against them as the dust rose up around them. The brownouts obscured almost everything. Mike Durant confirmed that the brownout concealed the RPGs spiraling skyward, plus "the fact that most often they were firing after we went by" meant that he wasn't aware of the number of RPGs being launched. Tom DiTomasso distinctly remembers the ground fire, however: "As we were making that approach the helicopters were all being shot at."

A Somali militia leader saw the helicopters arrive: "We saw the aircrafts flying over us. As soon as we saw them flying over us, we starting firing at them immediately because they were flying on a very low level. They responded to the fire and troops from two aircrafts descended into the house." The SNA had developed an ingenious method for remaining hidden from the helicopters:

> Each of those militia men was taking cover from the aircrafts in the manner which we're accustomed to take cover from the aircrafts. The easiest way to take cover from an aircraft is to have a piece of sheet over the person and he fires from under the sheet of cloth. If necessary, two small boys or two women [are] used to stretch the piece of cloth over the militia men.[14]

The Black Hawks continued to edge forward, peering through the dust to try to identify their insertion points. In the rear, nervous Rangers watched for the signal from the crew chiefs to throw the fast ropes out the doors. Ranger Sergeant Keni Thomas noted in his memoir: "Super 66 stayed over Hawlwadig Road, one of the only paved main roads in the city. Across from me, a block over to the east, I could see the other Black Hawks slow down and begin creeping above the street just like we were doing."[15]

Super 66, nicknamed "Gunslinger" and piloted by Chief Warrant Officer Stan Wood and Chief Warrant Officer Gary Fuller, finally flared over Chalk 3's assigned insertion point and the crew chiefs shouted "Ropes!" With that, the Rangers hurled the three-inch-thick ropes from the open doors. In the other Black Hawks, an identical process was being followed as the Rangers leapt out into midair, grabbed onto the rope and descended quickly to the ground.

Sergeant First Class Sean "Tim" Watson's Chalk 3 successfully inserted into the southeast corner of the target block, directly outside the objective. Already they too could hear enemy gunfire. Chalk 3 followed their well-rehearsed drills and quickly established overwatch positions to cover the western and southern approaches to the intersection. To their east at another intersection, Chalk 1, led by Lieutenant Larry Perino and accompanied by Captain Steele's command element, had landed and were also taking enemy fire.

In "Heavy Metal," Super 65, Izzo brought the aircraft to a careful hover. He explained:

I called "Ropes" and all the while I could hear rounds cracking past the aircraft. They sound exactly like pneumatic nail guns – a very sharp crack like that. Normally I would get down to about 20 or 30 feet and as I was trying to come down lower both of my crew chiefs said, "Whoa, whoa, don't come any lower." There was a wire or a cable or something beneath us that I couldn't see that they could.

Tom [DiTomasso] would sit on the center console and I would reach around and squeeze his arm or pat him on the back and I'd say, you know, "Be careful Tom." He always said he would wait until he got that "Go get 'em" before taking his headset off. He got superstitious about it. So Tom, just before he went out the door, said, "I heard a double explosion" and I thought it was somebody blowing a door on a building. One of my gunners said "That was close. They just fired an RPG at us."

It missed us and detonated about 75 feet behind us. The two explosions I'd heard; the first was the launch and the second was when it exploded. What saved our bacon I think was four 20,000-pound helicopters blowing up a hurricane of dust and sand and the guy probably couldn't see, probably couldn't breathe ... I wouldn't be surprised if he just pointed in the general direction with his eyes closed and fired. He was very close, certainly within a block of us.

As Tom was fast-roping down he said it felt like someone snapped a wet towel onto his face, the shockwave and the concussion hit him [from another RPG]. When he got on the ground he thought we were going to come crashing down on top of his head! He looked up and saw us hightailing it out of there and thought, "Okay, they got away."

Not surprisingly the Rangers felt very vulnerable whilst they were on the aircraft. Conversely the pilots naturally felt more secure whilst the Rangers were on board, "because if we got shot down, I have 15 Rangers around me," explained Izzo.

Although the helicopters were by now receiving significant RPG and small-arms fire, the dust also had the effect of making return fire from their doorgunners difficult. With the large numbers of Somali civilians on the ground, target identification was equally problematic: "My gunners never had a clear shot, never fired a shot. They maintained good fire control and fire discipline. I was very proud of them because they could have just started hosing up and down the streets," added Izzo, continuing:

I had to come up about 20 feet to come out of the dust and Mike and Ray were already out on their way [to the holding area to the north] and I looked over at my co-pilot Captain [Richard "Trey"] Williams and I said,"I think we're wearing out our welcome here!" They would take pot shots at us but that was most definitely the first time they were shooting at us on the way in. I was very, very lucky that throughout the whole operation, I didn't take a single hit on the aircraft. It was just luck.

Tom DiTomasso on board Izzo's Super 65 recounted:

We approached the objective from the north. As we got closer, I was again amazed at how the pilots could navigate and avoid obstacles as they "flared hard" to stop on a dime. They put us exactly where they said they would. Gerry [Izzo], Trey [Williams], and the crew of Super 65 were great to work with. Absolute professionals. I could hear explosions that sounded rather close and I fought to swallow my heart again. Small-arms fire cracked overhead as the helicopter, Super 65, "pulled away." As we were fast-roping in I could hear rounds going off, I could hear explosions ... We were a good half block away from the target building. There was no shooting going on at the target building, all of the shooting was occurring outside at the blocking positions.

His chalk established their overwatch positions: "Staff Sergeant [Ed] Yurek's team was oriented east and Staff Sergeant [Steven] Lycopolus's oriented north with Specialist [Shawn] Nelson and his M60 crew. Both elements of Chalk 2 emplaced their chase teams, consisting of two riflemen, on the inside corners of the intersection facing the objective."

DiTomasso's men almost immediately found themselves in a vicious close-quarters fight at the northeast corner of the objective. DiTomasso recounted:

> A bunch of enemy drivers and bodyguards were throwing hand grenades over a wall from a [parking] garage – we had literally fast-roped in outside this garage. I think they were the drivers to the folks that were at the enemy meeting we were attacking.
>
> Chalk 2 consisted of 15 Rangers. Six on one team with Staff Sergeant Yurek, and six with Staff Sergeant Lycopolus. The last three were me, my Radio Telephone Operator (RTO) Specialist Jason Coleman, and my Forward Observer (FO) Specialist Joe Thomas. Joe was with Staff Sergeant Yurek's team positioned to the north and saw the enemy throwing grenades over the wall on top of us. Some exploded and some didn't. He screamed at me, "They're in there!" as he pointed to the garage.
>
> At that time, myself, Specialist Coleman, Sergeant Struzik, and Staff Sergeant Lycopolus were closest to the open gate. We needed to go into the garage to fight those guys. We moved across the street and stacked near the half-open gate. It all happened very fast. I took out a fragmentation grenade; pulled the pin; let the spoon go; counted "1000, 2000, 3000"; and threw it through the gate. As soon as it exploded, we moved through the gate and scanned our sectors. We cleared the lot, killed two, and captured two.

DiTomasso attributes this early success to the extra training they had received from the operators, often conducted covertly without the knowledge of Captain Steele. DiTomasso disclosed:

> Days earlier, we sneaked out of the hangar and met Norm and Kyle, SMU operators that bunked adjacent to me in the hangar, for training. They told us

to meet them down on the beach at night, where they would show us how to tactically enter a room and move inside structures, something we did not do a lot of in the Rangers at that time. This training saved our lives.

To the northwest, Super 66 with Matt Eversmann's Chalk 4 was now approaching their insertion point. Eversmann recounted:

As we were going in, we came to a very abrupt halt on the approach. The pilot gave us a time warning and about 30 seconds out we start getting really into that focus: "Hey this is really going to happen here very shortly." So the helicopter comes to a stop and the pilot says "I can't see shit," those were his words and I'm thinking, "What does he mean?" I look out the window and we're in the middle of this sandstorm, it really was like going into a sandstorm. You don't have to be an expert to think, "That's not a great situation to be in."

We're pretty low and we know the enemy has rocket-propelled grenades so this is not a good place to be and I remember that sort of anxiety jumping out of me: "Holy smokes, we need to get on the ground!" The pilot is trying to maneuver the aircraft and I guess wait for the brownout to settle and there was some confusion whether we could advance or not.

Eventually the ropes get thrown and the pilot says, "I'm putting you in here, but you're about three blocks short of your insertion point so when you get on the ground, go three blocks in the direction of flight and you'll be in the right spot. There was some discussion about "Can we continue to move even with the ropes physically outside the aircraft?" which clearly is a safety hazard. I think it was just bad luck.

The pilot's focused on avoiding the brownout, the crew chiefs are looking for an enemy threat, the Rangers are looking at the crew chiefs, and it's, "The ropes are tossed and now we're stuck where we are." My assumption would be that the crew chief told us to do it [throw the ropes] but I don't remember. I didn't think it was a bad deal. On the first mission on helicopters, we were inserted in the wrong spot [too] and my chalk went into the wrong spot. It's combat, it happens.

Warned to expect a long fast-rope of some 40 feet, the reality was even worse. "We knew it was going to be about a 40-foot fast rope, after the fact I was told it was closer to 60 feet. That's a long way down," said Eversmann.

The enemy gunfire was already increasing as the assault helicopters lifted out. Co-pilot Captain Jim Yacone in Super 62 said: "We started receiving enemy fire almost immediately after the insertion. We had no idea we would receive that volume of fire."[16] "The Somalis came to the sound of the gunfire. They kind of got used to our tactics so they knew to just wait until the helicopters leave and then they can converge on whoever they dropped in," agreed Maier.

After depositing their Rangers, the Black Hawks flew to the north of the city to establish a holding pattern. Gerry Izzo explained the plan:

> There was a road called 21 October Road, south of that was the city and north of that was desert. We were in a racetrack pattern north of the city and it was wide open country so nobody was going to sneak up on us. We were holding there, out of the gunships' way, out of the P-3's way, we were keeping ourselves deconflicted, a mile, maybe a mile and a half away. We were a backup contingency, maybe if a truck gets ambushed on the way back and shot up, maybe we can land at an intersection and pick guys up, that kind of thing. Plan was to stay flexible and be ready for anything.

The MH-6s flew instead directly to Sword Base where they waited, rotors spinning, should an emergency extraction or MEDEVAC be required.

On the ground at the objective, Delta already had their prisoners secured. "We started clearing and it was over with within a minute," said Norm Hooten. In fact the Delta assaulters had captured 24 Somalis including their two primary targets from Aideed's clan, Omar Salad and Abdi Hasan Awale. The Ground Force Commander, Captain Scott Miller, radioed Gary Harrell in the C2 Black Hawk: "Hey, boss, I think we've got the guys you sent us in for." Hooten's F-Team then moved to the rooftop to join E-Team in providing overwatch security for the loading of the prisoners.

**1550 HOURS: SUPER 61 REPORTS FRIENDLIES ON ROOF OF TARGET BUILDING.**

Paul H, the E-Team leader, had led his men straight up to the roof only to be fired upon by at least one AK47-armed Somali gunman from an adjacent rooftop. As two of his operators returned fire, the team leader warned his men to avoid exposing their profile to other rooftops and potentially other enemy.

Unfortunately a Ranger M60 gun team, most likely from Chalk 2, mistook them for hostiles and opened fire.

"When F-Team made it to the rooftop, the members of E-Team were already there. They were taking cover behind the raised wall on the roof in an effort to protect themselves from fires from one of the Ranger blocking positions," said Kurt Smith. Paul H contacted the Assault Force Commander and requested Miller to contact Captain Steele and order all Ranger callsigns to cease fire on the target building. "That happened before I got to the roof but I remember [one of the operators] telling me to keep my head down as one of the blocking positions was firing up at the roof," recalled Norm Hooten with F-Team.

Staff Sergeant Jeff Bray, the only one of the Combat Controllers directly attached to the Delta assault element, provided security outside the objective whilst the operators "policed up" (a term meaning to secure and organize) their prisoners. As the amount of incoming fire increased, Bray, using his callsign Kilo 64 Charlie, called in an AH-6 to provide overhead cover at the target house. He was also one of the first to fire his weapon when a Somali charged at him, firing his AK47 from the hip. Bray swiftly shot and killed the man.

**1545 HOURS: GROUND REACTION FORCE AT PREPLANNED HOLD POINT.**

Whilst Delta secured the objective, Colonel McKnight's GRF was waiting around the corner in an alleyway just south of the Olympic Hotel. It had taken less than 10 minutes to drive from the hangar to the Olympic. "I roll in as the operation initiates and I lead the Humvees into the target building. I make a turn one block too early, everybody else peeled off and goes straight to the target building and it takes me about 30 seconds to catch up," recalled Jeff Struecker in the lead Humvee.

The GRF had experienced light small-arms fire and already taken a casualty as they headed northeast toward the K-4 Traffic Circle. Delta operator "Griz" Martin administered first aid to SEAL Chief John G, known as "Little Big Man" to the SEALs, who had suffered a minor but painful wound when an AK round shattered the Randall combat knife he carried at his waist. The SEAL hoped that the manufacturer would be keen on a product endorsement upon his return to the States, but reportedly Randall showed no interest.[17]

# LUCY

**1553 HOURS: RPG/SMALL-ARMS FIRES REPORTED 1 BLOCK EAST NEXT TO GREEN WATER TANK; GROUND REACTION FORCE MOVES TO EFFECT LINK-UP.**

Once they arrived in the area of the objective, the convoy pulled up to await the order to drive forward and load the prisoners from the target building. Struecker reported: "We staged about a block away from the target building waiting for the all clear to roll up and put the bad guys on [the trucks]." Unbeknown to the assaulters and the waiting GRF, the Rangers had suffered their first casualty.

"Everything changed for Chalk 4 after take-off. We were short of our location by at least 100 meters. We had to insert there due to the brownout conditions, the resulting concern regarding collisions with other aircraft, and incoming enemy fire. The pilot told me and I acknowledged it. It had happened before and we had a contingency worked for it," said Matt Eversmann.

The young sergeant had been the last out of the helicopter because of his position in the aircraft: "There's the pilot and co-pilot up front and then the two crew chiefs who are also the doorgunners behind them and then there's a seat in between and that's where the chalk leader sat." After his last man grabbed the rope and disappeared into the dust, Eversmann took his turn. When he landed on the ground, he was confronted by his worst fear:

> I got to the bottom of the rope and I saw this body of a Ranger lying on the ground and Rangers administering aid. By the time I got to the bottom [of the rope], I just assumed, "Holy Mackerel, this guy's been shot," and we're in a firefight and I'm in charge and I haven't even gotten here yet! I don't believe we were taking fire right then but I do recall thinking he'd been shot because he was bleeding all over the place. I asked one of the guys working on him where he got shot and the answer was, "He didn't get shot, he fell." Like, how do you process that one? It's the last thing that you would think from a casualty perspective. Someone's just fallen 60-plus feet from an aircraft, but there we are.

Each Ranger chalk carried a collapsible litter (stretcher) to enable them to move seriously wounded casualties. Unlike what may be portrayed in Hollywood, moving a critically wounded soldier typically requires four men and is exhausting over anything further than short distances. It is obviously exponentially more difficult under enemy fire.

Marc Good, Chalk 4's medic, was working to stabilize the injured soldier, Private First Class Todd Blackburn. "One of the Delta teams [likely E-Team] that preceded us onto the target had been inserted in the wrong spot so the initial aid administered to Todd Blackburn was Marcus Good and one of the Delta guys who were on their way to the target," said Eversmann.

Each Delta troop had an assigned Direct Support Special Forces Medic along with the medics within each team. The Special Forces Medics were trained to an exceptionally high level, completing a minimum of 12 months of advanced medical training. Exceeding the capabilities of a civilian paramedic, the Special Forces Medics were even capable of conducting field surgery if required. Each carried a distinctive pack of medical supplies along with their weapons and other battlefield equipment.

A second Delta medic assigned to the assault force, Sergeant First Class Bart B, immediately moved to assist fellow Delta medic Kurt S and Ranger medic Good in administering an intravenous drip to the fallen Ranger. Blackburn had "a closed head injury with a Glasgow Coma Score of approximately 6 [the Glasgow Coma Score is a method of evaluating the consciousness of a casualty who has likely suffered a traumatic brain injury – 5 is classed as 'Severe', the most dangerous category], a skull fracture, multiple rib fractures, fractures of the femur and humerus, and he had a retroperitoneal hematoma"[18] although thankfully there was no immediate evidence of internal bleeding. Bart B later wrote: "Good, the Ranger medic, was trying to start an IV when I got there. I looked at Blackburn, and he was already starting to posture. Initial survey [examination] – he had an airway and was breathing, no gross bleeding, but he was in the middle of an intersection."[19]

Blackburn, lying in the middle of the road, was at significant risk from the increasing enemy small-arms fire. Bart B recounted his actions as he arrived on the scene;

> The Somalis were starting to move in, so we moved him out of the intersection and behind a vehicle. I told Good to put a C-collar on Blackburn and put in a J-tube, while I finished the IV. We waited for a vehicle, which never came. There was no choice but to move him to the vehicles, so I grabbed his vest under the upper back and tried to support his head/neck as well as possible on my forearms while we moved him.[20]

The Rangers and the two Delta medics carried him gently off the street, taking care to "keep his neck straight."

Medic Kurt S was clear that the casualty needed immediate evacuation. Matt Eversmann and his RTO tried to raise Captain Steele or Lieutenant DiTomasso on the radio net to inform them of the casualty but neither of their radios were working properly. Eversmann remembered checking the radios was part of their standard operating procedure;

> The last thing we did we did before getting onto the aircraft with your radioman was a radio check. We knew that it worked when we left the airfield. By the time we got on the ground, [Specialist] Jason Moore, who was my radio operator, said, "I can't get comms" and I'm like, "Well, that sucks" … It was a combination of the buildings, the helicopters … at this particular moment it wasn't working.
>
> I've got a backup handheld and that's really not working [either]. I remember eventually getting in touch with [Lieutenant] Larry Perino who was a platoon leader at one of the blocking positions with Captain Steele and I remember him telling me, "Hey, calm down" and I remember thinking, "Holy shit, what do you mean calm down – I've got a kid who's about to die, we're in the wrong spot, and now we're taking fire – you know, maybe give me a little bit of help here!"
>
> Eventually what does happen is that my Fire Support [Staff] Sergeant Jeff McLaughlin – he's got his own radio – and he's able to transmit the predicament we're in with the commander that we've got an immediate litter casualty and he needs evacuation.

Eversmann told his men to carry Blackburn toward the target building on the litter. The folding litter was deployed and Ranger Sergeants Casey Joyce and Jeff McLaughlin carried the unconscious soldier away from the intersection, heading south on Hawlwadig: "They put that kid on the litter and off they go," remembered Eversmann. The weight of incoming fire forced the two Rangers to stop to return fire a number of times as they made their way to the objective.

Bart B dashed over to McKnight and Combat Controller Dan Schilling who were located outside the target building and updated them on Blackburn's status. Schilling immediately passed on the details over the radio command net to Gary Harrell, above in the C2 Black Hawk. Harrell then passed the critical information on to Doctor John "Rob" Marsh back at the airfield so that he could prepare his field trauma team for the impending arrival of the casualty. Bart B continued:

"When we got to the vehicles, I told … McKnight the serious condition Blackburn was in, and explained that we did not have the equipment or place to deal with such a casualty. The target area was still under our control at that time, so the decision was then made to evacuate him back to the airfield."[21]

**1613 HOURS: MCKNIGHT REPORTS ONE CRITICAL WIA [FRIENDLY WOUNDED IN ACTION] WILL EVACUATE BY GROUND ASAP [AS SOON AS POSSIBLE]; HELOS WILL PROVIDE GUNS AS REQUIRED. GRF #1 AT BUILDING #1 FOR EXFIL.**

McKnight later wrote: "Based on the medical recommendation, I quickly decided to conduct a casualty evacuation of Blackburn. I radioed the Operations Center to inform them of what was about to take place; the response was roger and that an AH-6 Little Bird would provide air cover during the evacuation. This had to be a vehicular evacuation as the enemy fire was far too intense to bring a helicopter down into the streets."[22] Soon Struecker's vehicle was summoned forward: "Immediately we've got a casualty – Todd Blackburn – and we're tasked to take him back to the base and drop him off."

Tom DiTomasso recalled learning of the casualty:

> Specialist Coleman reported to me that he heard Chalk 4, Sergeant Eversmann, report a litter urgent casualty. At the same time, I noticed that I could not see Eversmann's team from my position. This was a standard visual link-up that all the chalk leaders conducted to ensure that we had mutually supporting blocking positions. Eversmann reported that due to obstacles he inserted 100 meters short of his planned position.
>
> When Blackburn fell, I moved four of my men north so we could make visual contact with Eversmann. He and I waved to each other, they were evacuating Blackburn and everything was good to go. We took a casualty – we train for that and we expect it. We're realists and we know there is a very good chance it could happen.

Blackburn to this day remembers very little: "Sometimes bits and pieces come through, but that's about all." His memories end with the Black Hawk hovering over the intersection with the dust clouds obscuring the ground. The last thing he remembers is the sound of Somali small-arms fire.[23] What exactly happened to cause the fall is still unknown. "Todd doesn't even know. A lot of people think he might have got hit right when he was about to grab that rope [and it] bounced him off, maybe the bird leveled off and he missed the rope, maybe halfway something happened," said Private First Class Anton Berendsen, an M203 grenadier in Eversmann's Chalk 4.[24]

Super 64 pilot Mike Durant remarks in his book that he feels that the pilot of Super 67 with Chalk 4 on board may have become disoriented by the brownout, noting, "this was his first encounter with the 'brown monster' … The dust cloud was more than a hundred feet high, and he [the pilot of Super 67] felt his way down into it like a wader tiptoeing into cold lake water. He deployed his ropes too early …"[25]

He also notes that the pilot had been flying Super 63, the C2 platform, and had only recently taken over a spot in the assault lift formation. Mike Durant confirmed his belief to the author: "I was not on the aircraft obviously, so what I think happened is second-hand information, but I do believe the crew actions led to Todd's mishap." Gerry Izzo recounted that even the aircrew was unsure exactly what occurred: "At the time I couldn't even see 67 [because of the brownout]. They were a block or two short. Nearest I ever heard from the crew was that Blackburn missed the rope."

Matt Eversmann is in perhaps the best position to comment definitively on the incident:

> What I recall as I took off my headset to put on my goggles, the strap that holds the goggles on broke so my goggles were worthless. I'm kneeling in the belly of the aircraft and as I'm putting on my helmet, because I couldn't wear my helmet flying in because I had the headset on, I remember the helicopter keeling over a couple of degrees off of its horizontal axis. Enough that I remember putting my hand down to keep me from losing my balance. Eventually I grabbed the fast rope and started to slide down.
>
> Piecing it together afterwards that was about the time that Blackburn lost control [of the rope] when the helicopter keeled over and then righted itself. Could I say empirically that's what did it? Well no, but I'm guessing that's probably right where it happened. The thought was that as soon as the Ranger that preceded you, as soon as his head got below the deck [of the helicopter],

the next guy would go. The next guy saw Blackburn grab the rope and go, he grabbed the rope, the helicopter tilted and boom.

Chief Warrant Officer Jeff Niklaus was the pilot of Super 67 nicknamed "Texas Express." He could not be reached for an interview for this book but explained in a 2013 video testimony that, although he could not see the other aircraft around him, he "knew where I was going. A few blocks north of the Olympic Hotel there was a white, two story building … with a little patio area with an antennae sitting there. That was my target."[26] He recounts that his crew chiefs told him to stop as the fast ropes had landed on power lines – the pilot was apparently unaware that the ropes had been dropped although Niklaus is somewhat unclear on this point.

Whatever the ultimate cause, Chalk 4 were inserted at least 100 meters short of their blocking position and they immediately suffered a non-combat-related casualty after Blackburn fell approximately 70 feet to the road below. According to a later medical report, he would have been traveling at around 50 miles per hour when he hit the ground.

Jeff Struecker was assigned the task of leading a three-Humvee convoy back to the airfield with Blackburn. He explained:

> Colonel McKnight rode in on the Humvees with me and didn't know exactly where Blackburn was so told me to go up to Captain Steele's position [on foot] and get exactly where Blackburn was from Captain Steele, which I did, and then send my Humvees back to get Blackburn, put Blackburn in a cargo Humvee in the middle and then put the rest of my squad in two Humvees right behind them.

Because of the urgent nature of Blackburn's injuries, Struecker said, "I was tasked to take Blackburn back before we got the all clear signal [from the objective]. I drove my two Humvees and the cargo Humvee up into the middle of it and we started to get it on [began firing] from the Humvees because the blocking positions down the street were taking some pretty intense fire."

In fact McKnight's GRF had been taking enemy fire as they waited for the signal to move and most of his Rangers had dismounted to return fire. Struecker recounted:

Humvees were easy targets – I referred to them as "bullet magnets." It wasn't uncommon for us to take a little small-arms fire [on earlier missions] but it was very, very inaccurate. On that day it was heavier small-arms fire than normal and more accurate small-arms fire than normal and that was from the moment we got close to the target building.

There's a definite ping when it goes to your left and to your right. There's a sound like slapping a tight metal wire with a piece of steel – like a suspension bridge, if you hit the wire on a suspension bridge it makes a very distinctive sound – that's the sound a bullet makes right as it passes over the top of your head. The louder that sound, the closer it is.

The three-vehicle convoy would be led by Struecker with his Humvee mounting a .50 cal. Driving an open-back cargo Humvee carrying Blackburn was Delta Master Sergeant Chuck E. Delta operator John M and a SEAL rode along with him as did the Ranger Medic Marcus Good. "It was basically a driver and a couple of guys in the back working on Blackburn while he was on an Israeli litter, trying to keep him alive." The third vehicle was commanded by Ranger Sergeant Danny Mitchell with an Mk19 mounted on the roof. An AH-6 was assigned to provide air cover for the convoy.

Struecker continued:

The route that I take is down along an alleyway next to the target building and then down Hawlwadig Road down to the port and then over to our base. We're getting shot at down Hawlwadig Road – we did get shot at just trying to get Blackburn on the litter into the Humvee. People are just having a field day shooting at these three Humvees …

At this point we are getting hit from 360 degrees, from dozens of different weapons and most of them from 20 or 30 feet away. RPGs going both sides of the road, people are lobbing hand grenades off of rooftops at us, and heavy and light small arms.

All three crew-served weapons on the Humvees were returning fire along with the passengers, who were firing as best they could out of the windows of the Humvees. Jeff Struecker explained how the vehicles had been optimized as firing platforms:

We had modified the Humvees to take the back hatch off, we took the back doors off and put a bomb plate between the gunner/driver compartment and the back of the Humvee. [Sergeant] Dominick Pilla and [Specialist] Tim Moynihan were sitting in the back, [they] were in the back hatch and Moynihan's got the rear of the Humvee [with an M16] and Pilla's got the right side [with his M60] because the guy on the .50 [Paulson] is manning the left side. There's no hatch but we put some sandbags in there to give some protection but we wanted to have as much field of fire as we can.

In the crescendo of small-arms fire, Sergeant Dominick Pilla was fatally shot soon after leaving the objective. Task Force Ranger had suffered their first death on the October 3 operation. "Dominick Pilla was killed within a minute of turning the corner onto National Street. He was wearing a ballistic helmet but he was shot just above his right eye, probably from a heavy weapons system [PKM] from the looks of the wound," recounted Struecker. It was obvious to the Rangers that Pilla had been killed instantly. Struecker continued:

[Platoon Sergeant] Bob Gallagher calls me up to get a status. Our SOP [standard operating procedure] at the time was "If I'm in a fight, don't bother me, I'll call you back when I get a chance" and he called me in the fight of my life. He was calling me again and again and finally to get him off my back, and to be honest I never should have said anything over the radio, I said "It's Pilla, he's dead." There's 14 conversations going on over that radio net and when I said "Pilla's dead," total silence for about 30 seconds.

Struecker regrets naming the casualty over the radio: "We had what we referred to as line numbers and technically I should have given his line number over the radio. I was not authorized to give his real name. I did that just to get my boss off my back. To this day, Danny McKnight reminds me 'Jeff, we had line numbers for a reason.'"

The three-Humvee evacuation convoy was receiving little support from the air. Struecker said:

The Little Birds are pretty much committed to the guys who are on foot or McKnight's convoy. The snipers on the Black Hawk are taking shots when they see them but they're flying big circles around the city, they'll pass over our head about every three minutes and take a shot but basically there is no support from the air at this point.

Struecker recounted that even when the firing decreased as they neared the port facility controlled by the United Nations ("The port just equalled not getting shot at"), a new problem emerged: "It was feeding time and the United Nations had a food distribution site on National Street – I didn't know that – so at one point the road had 10,000 people in front of us and the only way to part the crowd was to fire my .50 cal right across the top of their heads."

"There's roadblocks but not roadblocks set up to stop this three-vehicle convoy, the roadblocks are there to channel the traffic the way the warlords want the traffic to go." Struecker was forced to deploy concussion and flashbang grenades to clear the crowds out from in front of his convoy. All three Humvees had sustained significant damage; "the Humvees are shot to pieces even before we get down to the port," and at least three of his Rangers had by now been wounded by enemy gunfire and RPG fragments.

As they finally neared the New Port, Struecker's Humvee had to ram a pick-up truck that refused to pull out of their way. Eventually the battered convoy arrived at the port, out of Habr Gidr territory, and immediately headed for the airfield. Struecker had radioed ahead to alert the medical unit and the shot-up Humvees were met by Doc Marsh and his team. As Marsh treated the wounded, the two Delta operators along with the SEAL sniper began resupplying themselves with ammunition, in anticipation of returning to the battle.

At the blocking positions back at the target building, the situation was worsening. Matt Eversmann remembered:

> They were throwing everything at us. We got it all. What we realized after the battle was that Aideed's militiamen and all the other bad guys with guns came around to the west of the target building and started to move in and were generally moving from the northwest toward our target. So where Chalk 4 was, and I don't want to say "Gosh, we took all of the fire," but we took a massive amount of fire in a very short order of time.
>
> We wound up taking fire from three directions – the north, the west, and the east – almost immediately. That sound of RPGs going off is just one that

you don't forget. I remember at the point that Blackburn was getting evacuated, we're fighting guys who are 25 meters away.

Eversmann's chalk was already a man down and was missing Joyce and McLaughlin who had accompanied Blackburn to Struecker's Humvees. Eversmann was relieved when they returned, running up Hawlwadig. "Casey Joyce got back and said they'd got him [Blackburn] on a vehicle and he'd been evacuated. Clearly we couldn't land a helicopter because of all the fire we're under now so we do the next best thing." Eversmann remembered:

> [Sergeants] Telscher and Joyce, to their credit, great young Rangers, they were fighting tooth and nail with the enemy from three directions. It's a testament to their tenacity and their courage that I didn't even have to give them any guidance. They were following the rules of engagement immediately. It was really reassuring to know that that was the quality of young soldiers – they'd never been in battle before although we had been in a firefight on one of the [earlier] missions [the September 6/7 raid on the former Russian Embassy compound] so everyone knew that they could do their job in a crucible. It was a tremendous psychological advantage, certainly for me.
>
> I remember thinking "Holy shit, there are a lot of bad guys and there's a lot of fire going on."

Eversmann even joined the fray himself, firing his M16A2: "Historically when you read books about battles … leaders fight with their radio but not with their weapon. Unfortunately we were at the point that we all gotta shoot. That was an interesting experience, the guy who should be leading and organizing this fight is now kneeling behind a vehicle shooting at bad guys."

It was later established that the majority of Somali reinforcements were entering the battlespace from the north and were running directly into Chalk 4's blocking position in the process. This accounted for the incredible amount of enemy small-arms and RPG fire encountered at the northwest blocking position. A Somali militia fighter later noted: "Immediately afterwards all the people in the neighborhood took their guns and participated in the fight because the area was one of the largest markets in Mogadishu, and there were many people having their properties there."[27]

Matt Eversmann's Rangers were deployed at either side of the intersection, using whatever sparse cover they could while they returned fire at the growing numbers of Somali militia. Eversmann said:

> Cover for me was behind a car, some crappy old Somali car, right next to a building. The other guys were behind vehicles or wherever you could make yourself small enough to have something metal or brick in front of you.
>
> They [the Rangers] put a lot of lead down against a lot of bad guys to allow us to accomplish the commander's intent which was not to let bad guys in to influence the objective where the Delta guys are capturing the targets. It is a testament to the intensity of training we had done and I know that sounds like a Ranger TV ad but it really was true. Something kicked in and the only answer is training.
>
> We [were] always making sure that you're only shooting at bad guys. This isn't just a free-for-all, you can't just shoot at every window, every door or every corner. This was, granted, a large volume of fire being returned at the bad guys, but I'll go to my grave saying that one thing we did well [was that] we followed the rules of engagement in Chalk 4- empirically.

With the incredible weight of incoming enemy fire, casualties to Chalk 4 were only a matter of time. Private Anton Berendsen was the first to be hit. He recalled in an interview:

> I put my selector switch to semi, and I had a bead on him [a Somali gunman] and I knew if he popped his head out again I would take him. And it so happened he didn't do that again, what he did was, instead of peeking out, he darted out through the alleyway and as he was turning I just remember him slowly going like this, it was almost like a slow motion … he just started firing rapidly, automatic AK47, and at that point I remember it was like dust, like somebody had just taken some dust and hit it at your face. I remember looking at him, and I saw blood on my nose, and I remember looking at my shoulder.[28]

Matt Eversmann recounted the shooting and the incredible tenacity of his young grenadier:

Berendsen takes one in the arm. Thankfully not a deadly wound, it didn't hit a bone. He was still able to engage the enemy. He was a grenadier and I remember I was trying to put a bandage right over his arm just to stop the bleeding and he was sitting on the ground behind this vehicle and he's fumbling around with his grenade tube, he's got an M203 and I'm like, "What the fuck are you doing?" Another of these surreal moments.

He was trying to place an HE round into the tube of his grenade launcher and he couldn't do it one-handed. So while the other guy's working on him, I put the round into the tube, close it and hand the weapon to him. He's sitting on the ground with this 203 balanced on his leg and there's a bad guy about a block away on this corner of a building, like an aluminum shed attached to the corner of this building, and the bad guy keeps putting his weapon out and shooting toward us. Berendsen puts this HE round right on the corner. Unbelievable, absolutely a gold medal shot – one-handed while he's getting bandaged up!

It's difficult to ascertain the exact order of the casualties so many years after the fact but Sergeant Scott Galentine, M60 gunner Specialist Kevin Snodgrass, and Eversmann's Forward Observer, McLaughlin, were all hit in a very short space of time after Berendsen. Eversmann remembered the details of each of the wounds:

I saw Scott Galentine right across the street from me get shot right in the thumb. I watched it explode like a tomato and to his credit, he didn't panic. He just ran across the street to me with his thumb dangling off. I remember just putting his thumb back in place and saying "Scott, hold it while we bandage it." You're in that mode, wrap a gauze around it, tie it in close and put him behind cover.

Snodgrass had been shot in the thigh, a round skips off the ground I suspect [under the car he was using for cover], thankfully it doesn't hit an artery, didn't hit his femur so [we] stop the bleeding and work on evac. Jeff [McLaughlin] I think he got shot in the hand as I recall.

Including Blackburn, Chalk 4 had now suffered five casualties within the first several minutes of the operation. Eversmann added:

To this day, people ask, "When did you start losing your hearing?" and I'm like, "October 3rd, 1993!" I wear hearing aids today. It was so loud. When we were in the blocking position and one of the Black Hawks went across right above us and just opened up with the miniguns. It was so loud the molars in your teeth hurt!

Despite the enemy fire directed toward the blocking positions, the aircrews in the Black Hawks were showing considerable restraint. Super 64 Pilot Mike Durant recalled:

So, we're having a heck of a time sorting out where everybody is. We've got these miniguns that'll fire over 4000 rounds a minute. We don't want to just go crazy, hosing down the countryside until we know where all the friendlies are. So, in the end, we never fired a round. And I don't regret that at all. We never had sufficient understanding of the tactical situation to do it. I armed the crew chief's guns, but we all talked about how we weren't going to shoot until we all agreed we had it all figured out, because there were just too many friendlies down there.[29]

At Sergeant Tim Watson's position immediately southwest of the objective and north of Eversmann's Chalk 4, the amount of enemy fire was still relatively sporadic. Chalk 3's SAW and M60 gunners would regularly engage individual gunmen who darted out of alleyways to empty a magazine in the direction of the blocking position. Large crowds had gathered at each of the main junctions but were largely staying at least a block back, content to watch the spectacle. Gunmen used the cover of the crowds to spray bursts at the Rangers, knowing that they would be protected by the Americans' adherence to their rules of engagement.

Some of these bullets struck home. Sergeant Keni Thomas was one of Watson's team leaders and was up against the wall outside of the target location when he was hit twice, miraculously surviving both gunshots. One round struck a magazine pouch and was stopped by one of his M16 magazines whilst another also struck a magazine pouch but exited only to strike his RBA's (Ranger Board Armour) trauma plate.

Lieutenant Larry Perino, co-located with Captain Steele and Chalk 1 at the southeast blocking position, later wrote that he experienced a similar phenomenon:

At my position, small crowds of Somalis had begun to form. The crowd was mostly men and women, curious to find out who had just landed in their neighborhood. We cleared them out of the way by gesturing and throwing flashbang grenades.

Gradually, the direct fire around the area began to increase. Shortly after scattering the curiosity seekers, my blocking position began to receive sporadic fire from the south and west. I diverted my attention from the radio and concentrated on the fight at hand. No one in my chalk could identify exactly where the fire was coming from, but I could see that the AH-6 Little Bird helicopters were engaging enemy targets to the south with their 7.62-caliber miniguns.

The situation became even more intense when a woman stepped out into the street south of our location and began walking toward us with her arms outstretched. Behind the woman was a man with an AK47, apparently using her as a human shield. Private First Class [Brian] Heard cried out, "I can see him. Right behind her. He's got an AK" ... Heard fired a long burst from his M60 machine gun, killing the two Somalis.

A couple of minutes later, several children walked out and began pointing out our locations. Not wanting to take any chances, I placed several well-aimed shots at the feet of the children and sent them running for cover. Bullets began cracking over our heads from the east, and my other M60 gunner, Specialist [Mike] Hawley, fired in the general direction of the enemy fire. Another burst of fire impacted mere feet from Specialist Hawley, but he still continued to engage enemy targets down the street.

By this time, almost everyone in my chalk began to engage armed Somalis as they ran out into the streets. Somalis were firing RPGs at us and the helicopters overhead from every direction. Out of the corner of my eye, I spotted a woman carrying an RPG across the street about 150 meters away. I aimed my CAR15 and fired three rounds. The first shot was behind her, but the next two found their mark, and the woman fell down in a heap.[30]

Chalk 1 had also suffered their first casualty when Sergeant Aaron Williamson was struck in a finger on his right hand. He ignored the wound and kept shooting. Williamson would join a unique club, the small number of the Rangers who would suffer more than one gunshot wound that day but thankfully survive the ordeal. One of the Ranger team leaders in Chalk 3, Staff Sergeant Doug Boren, had also been hit by a round that grazed his neck. All of the Ranger blocking positions apart from Chalk 2 now had wounded.

At DiTomasso's position, the fire was also increasing. They too encountered the militia using human shields. Unwilling initially to engage the gunmen hiding behind civilians, they instead used flashbang grenades to frighten the civilians away. They also shot at least one militiaman who stood in the street firing west at Eversmann's Chalk 4, unaware of the Rangers to his southeast. Eventually the mobs began to advance toward their position and the Rangers were forced to engage the crowds. An AH-6 added its minigun fire to the fusillade.

An SNA militia leader later commented:

While I was going to the battle I had a radio. I spoke to Aidid [sic] and asked them for permission to go into the war and I was given the permission, and then we started it. And when I was given the order to fight, I immediately took 30 militia into the place. I sent the car back and it brought more from other adjacent places.

I didn't come from the direction of Olympic Hotel, but I came from the direction of that road which is known as the 30 Road. Then we immediately called women in the neighborhood to spread sheets above us. They did so, and we started firing at the Americans. While we were engaged in the fight with those Americans who descended from the plane, we were informed that there were reinforcements coming for the Americans. Then we immediately started to erect barricades for the convoys. When those convoy arrived we started fighting them.[31]

**1602 HOURS:** LTC MCKNIGHT REPORTS 9 X PC [PRECIOUS CARGO – PRISONERS] WITH POSSIBLE PRINCIPAL CAPTURED.

Finally, some 27 minutes after the first assaulters leapt from their Little Birds, the codeword "Laurie" was broadcast to all stations, indicating that the prisoners were ready to be loaded onto the GRF before returning to the Task Force Ranger base. According to an account by Dan Schilling, there had been some confusion that had delayed the link-up between McKnight's GRF and the Delta assaulters with their prisoners, with each group seemingly waiting for the other.[32] Schilling dismounted to find out what the hold-up was. He was acutely aware that they were nearing the end of the 30-minute "honeymoon period" before significant Somali resistance could be expected.

Gary Keeney recounted:

When we went back out into the courtyard and we had all the prisoners secure, 24 total out of that house, C-Team was given the mission to secure [the] prisoners and take them back to the airfield. We're all back out in the courtyard, there's the metal gate that's separating the assault force from the street. We can hear some sporadic firing going around in the city around us. What we could hear and hear over the radio was something we hadn't seen before in any of the [previous] missions.

Mike Moser from B-Team recalled:

During this time I was employed with several other guys trying to load our cargo – the various detainees obtained in the target – into the back of a truck in the alley outside the courtyard. This is the interval at which I recall a growing volume of fire – most noticeable as I made forays in to the street to load the trucks. It seemed the vehicle column attracted a lot of attention.

Paul Leonard from C-Team added: "We were taking a lot of fire already. Bullets were coming in the window. When we were going back down the stairs I said 'This is going to be a nightmare as people are shooting at us already.'"

**1558 HOURS: RPG REPORTED HIT 5-TON – ONE WIA (GUNSHOT TO LEG) AND VEHICLE DISABLED.**

The Somalis had also begun to launch RPGs down toward the stationary GRF. Approximately five minutes after McKnight's convoy had pulled onto Hawlwadig, an RPG struck a five-ton truck, immobilizing it and wounding Ranger Staff Sergeant Dave Wilson in both legs. Ranger Private Clay Othic returned fire at the RPG gunner with the .50 cal on his Humvee only to be hit himself moments later in his right forearm. The disabled five-ton would later be destroyed by a Delta operator with a thermite grenade to deny it, and any remaining sensitive items or ammunition, to the enemy.

"I saw the burning five-ton truck and tires when we went out to load the bad guys onto the convoy," recalled another operator. The tires were the Somali version of smoke signals – the smoke served as a target indicator for everyone in the capital who wanted to join the battle. They also served another purpose, as they would make it increasingly difficult for the helicopter crews and the orbiting P-3 and CIA spy aircraft to see what was happening on the ground. "The black smoke you could see for six or seven blocks. It was a signal to say 'This is where you need to go if you want to kill Americans,'" noted Jeff Struecker.

Gary Keeney was stewarding the prisoners to the two surviving trucks. He remembered:

> As we left that courtyard we could see that some of the Rangers were engaging and I believe this was nearly the same time as Paul H's team (E-Team) was up on the roof and they received some friendly fire by some Rangers. We moved out of that courtyard into the street and there was firing going on out in the street. We moved out into the intersection, almost where we landed at, there's a lot of rounds cracking in the air all around us. As we're getting the prisoners in the five-ton truck, and of course they're flexi-tied so they can't get into the truck and some of them were fat and out of shape and wearing sandals, so we had to physically get these guys on the truck.

**1604 HOURS:** ALL FORCES TO BEGIN COLLAPSING TO BUILDING #1 FOR LINK UP AND GROUND EXFIL OF ALL FORCES AND PC. WILL USE BUILDING #1 ROOF PZ [PICKUP ZONE] IF REQUIRED.

Keeney continued his account:

> As we got them in, we loaded up one of the Rangers on a stretcher [and he] ended up in the truck with us. I think an RPG hit a wall and he took some fragmentation or some concrete hit his leg. I remember sitting in that truck and the convoy's not moving. We're completely exposed and in the street where bullets are cracking past our head – we needed to get moving.

SEAL Howard Wasdin, who had been providing overwatch down an alleyway opposite the target building, was hit by a ricochet that struck him in the back of the left knee. Schilling, fellow SEAL Homer N, and a Delta medic dragged him to cover around the corner to the GRF's vehicles. Ranger Staff Sergeant Bill Powell, the Forward Observer on McKnight's vehicle, was hit moments later, again by ricochets from the same alley. Powell staggered over to the Humvee and collapsed inside, where Schilling treated his wounds.

As the last of the prisoners were loaded on board the two remaining five-ton trucks, both marked with bright orange VS-17 panels to identify them from the air, a total of six Delta operators climbed in to guard the Somalis. Paul Leonard was one of them:

> Scott Miller told Matt [Rierson] to take C-Team and two snipers and all prisoners by convoy back to the airport. Lieutenant Colonel McKnight was in charge of the convoy. It was C-Team plus two people assigned to us from the Sniper Troop, [Sergeant First Class] Alex S and [Sergeant First Class] Joe V on that five-ton. [Delta operator] Griz Martin was with the SEAL Team guys [on the cargo Humvee].
>
> There were two Humvees in front of us that had a .50 cal and an Mk19, then there was us [in the truck with the prisoners]. I think Grizwold [Tim "Griz" Martin] was in there; it was a crazy-looking Humvee that was wide open and no doors [the modified cargo Humvee] and then they had two more Humvees with a .50 cal and an Mk19.

At approximately 16:20, just as the Ground Reaction Force finally prepared to leave the objective and head back to base with the prisoners, the voice of Ranger Specialist Mike Kurth, the RTO with Tim Watson's Chalk 3, broke through on the command net with a message that would forever alter the course of the battle: "All stations be advised – we have a bird down, we have a Black Hawk down."[33]

# CHAPTER 4

# BIG SKY, SMALL BULLET

*"61 and 62 were making left-hand turns, they were 180 degrees apart, they were orbiting the objective area, their snipers were engaging people and the doorgunners were engaging people. Cliff [Wolcott, pilot of Super 61] called after about 10 or 15 minutes and said 'We're taking a lot of fire down here, let's hurry up and get these guys on the trucks.' There's only so long you stay over an area in daylight in an urban environment."*

Chief Warrant Officer 3 (P) Gerry Izzo, Super 65

### 1610 HOURS: SUPER 61 REPORTS RPG BURST OVER TARGET; LOCATION OF FIRES PASSED TO BARBER [AH-6]

Super 61 had been providing fire support from the air since the start of the mission. Along with the two crew chiefs manning the miniguns, Staff Sergeants Ray Dowdy and Charlie Warren, the helicopter carried a four-man sniper element from Delta. Sergeant First Class Jim Smith was the Sniper Team Leader. With him were Sergeant First Class Steve D, a Special Forces Medic from the Sniper Troop, Staff Sergeant Dan Busch and Sergeant First Class Jim M.

Most of the snipers were armed with suppressed CAR15 carbines with red dot sights. "I was using a CAR15 5.56mm carbine with an Aimpoint optic. I also had an M21 7.62mm rifle with Leupold Ultra 10 power scope. I had the M21 if I got dropped off on a rooftop to support with long-range fire. Dan [Busch] chose a SAW so we would have light machine-gun capability if we needed it," explained Jim Smith.

The role of the aerial sniper teams in both Super 61 and 62 was to "provide precision fire if and when needed by the ground forces. We were in a counter-clockwise orbit around the target building," explained Smith. When targeting an individual on the ground, the snipers would fire a volley of aimed shots to ensure they hit: "It was not that difficult to fire while we were in an orbit but accuracy was gained by the shooter firing a high volume of fire at the target. Several fast well-aimed shots."

Along with sniping and minigun fire, the Black Hawks could help disperse the mobs by another tactic, "The rotor wash was a by-product of getting the helicopter in to get good observation on the crowd and potentially provide sniper marksmanship fire. The brownout from the rotor wash would disperse the crowds – it's very uncomfortable to stand under helicopter rotor wash if you don't have any eye protection," said Tom DiTomasso. The snipers also attempted to disperse the Somali mobs with non-lethal munitions, as Gerry Izzo recalled: "They were throwing flashbangs out to get people to move back."

One of the crew chiefs on Super 61 had spotted an RPG gunner under the helicopter but couldn't engage the Somali as he had emptied his minigun and was reloading. Delta sniper Jim Smith recalled: "The door gunner on my side, Charlie [Warren], went dry on ammo on the minigun. I leaned my body out the open door and by holding on with one hand so I could see directly below the helo. I then shot the RPG gunner directly below the helicopter." This scene is misrepresented in both the *Black Hawk Down* film and book, showing it leading directly to the later downing of Super 61. In fact, as Jim Smith confirmed, it had occurred some time before.

The Fire Support Officer and FOs on the ground attached to the assault and Ranger chalks were requesting fire support from both the AH-6s and the sniper Black Hawks. It was whilst trying to support Chalk 1 that Super 61 was struck by an RPG, an event that would dramatically alter the course of the battle. Lieutenant Lechner wrote:

> ... my position was attempting to identify a gunman who was sniping at us. I let my FO control the mission thinking he may be after the same target I was. The sniper bird [Super 61] was unable to identify the gunman but made a number of passes firing its doorguns in the general vicinity.
>
> After the first pass I contacted the pilot, Warrant Officer Clifton Wolcott, and added my target information. On subsequent passes the gunman was not found, so we ended the mission and directed the pilot to resume his orbit. However, about a minute later the sniper bird reappeared flying south to north in front of our position. Suddenly, the aircraft swung hard to the right and I thought for a moment that the pilot was attempting to get a better position to fire from. I soon realized something was wrong when I observed that the tail rotor had stopped spinning and the aircraft began to spin unsteadily ... the aircraft had come in to take one final look [for the gunman] and had been hit by an RPG.[1]

**1620 HOURS:** SUPER 61 SHOT DOWN BY RPG – SOMALIS APPROACHING CRASH SITE. GRG SHEET 24, 16.2/0.7, UTM NH 36142685. GROUND REACTION FORCE 1 MOVING TO SECURE CRASH SITE. SURVIVORS CLIMBING OUT OF WRECKAGE – AIRCRAFT IS NOT ON FIRE. ASSAULT FORCE PERSONNEL (APPROX. 7) SECURING THE POSITION. REPORT: AREA SECURE FOR MH-6 ELEMENT TO EFFECT EXFIL OF CASUALTIES (2 X KIA, 2 X WIA).

It appears Super 61 may have in fact been on its way to support Lieutenant Tom DiTomasso's Chalk 2 after being unable to identify the gunman harassing Chalk 1. DiTomasso recounted:

> Specialist Thomas, my Forward Observer, was calling Super 61 to help disperse the large crowd to our north. The Black Hawk was coming in from our northeast

when a rocket-propelled grenade hit it. The aircraft spiraled down and crashed approximately four hundred meters away. Specialist Thomas, seeing the whole thing, yelled to Specialist Coleman [DiTomasso's RTO], who, in turn, told me that a "Bird had gone down."[2]

The RPG had struck Super 61's tail rotor assembly, shredding it and sending the helicopter into a violent spin, smoke pouring from its tail boom. Jim Smith, the Sniper Team Leader inside the rear cargo area of the Black Hawk, remembered that there was "no warning with the exception of feeling the helicopter shudder and shake and start spinning out of control." Chief Warrant Officer Cliff "Elvis" Wolcott made one last fateful transmission as his helicopter began to spiral toward the ground: "61 going down."

Several of the snipers managed to spreadeagle themselves on the floor, bracing for the inevitable impact. Smith almost fell from the wildly spinning aircraft and at one point both his legs and most of his body were outside the Black Hawk as it spun toward the ground. He explained:

> Back then we didn't use safety harnesses. We had an A7A strap (nylon cargo strap) rigged across the open door just to keep us from falling out. I was almost slung out of the helicopter while it was spinning out of control. The strap luckily caught my armpit while my body was completely outside of the bird. I then pulled myself back in and scooted behind the crew chief/doorgunner's seat. I then reached up as high as possible on the pipe framework of the doorgunner's seat and I made a radio call that Super 61 had been hit and was going down.

The pilots valiantly attempted to shut the engines down to reduce the spin and slow their descent but the aircraft was at a low altitude and hit the ground hard. Matthews in the C2 helicopter recalled: "The nose went into a wall that was reinforced with another wall on the other side. The tail boom knocked down the wall behind it. The cockpit did not break through that wall because it was reinforced. So it crushed that cockpit."[3]

Boykin in the JOC "saw Cliff Wolcott's Black Hawk, nose over and twist out of control … the helo did several complete pancake rotations, sickeningly slow. Then the Black Hawk simply slid out of the sky, snagged the roof edge of a building and keeled over into an alley."[4]

## BIG SKY, SMALL BULLET

**1622 HOURS:** REPORT: LARGE CROWD OF SOMALIS APPROACHING CRASH SITE.

Moments later, as the dust cloud from the crash began to settle, Matthews transmitted the fateful message from the C2 helicopter: "We got a Black Hawk going down, we got a Black Hawk going down. We got a Black Hawk crashed in the city. 61, 61 down." Chief Warrant Officers Cliff "Elvis" Wolcott and Donovan "Bull" Briley had been killed instantly as the nose of the MH-60 impacted with the wall to the southern side of the helicopter, crushing the cockpit in around them. Miraculously, both the crew chiefs and the four snipers on board had survived the impact, although most sustained injuries from the crash.

The helicopter was down in an alleyway running from east to west several blocks northeast of the objective with the cockpit facing toward the east and its broken tail to the west. The main rotor assembly had sheared off on impact but the helicopter was largely in one piece, a testimony to the skill of the pilots and the aircraft's design. Super 61 ended up lying on its left hand side against a retaining wall on the southern edge of the alley, most of which had collapsed from the impact.

At the objective, a number of operators and Rangers witnessed the RPG strike and Super 61 spinning toward the ground. One of the assaulters, who requested anonymity in his interview with the author, remembered, "It was shot overhead, we heard it, looked up and watched it crash to our north."[5] Norm Hooten on the roof of the target building recounted: "I was on the east side of the building and saw it start to spin so I didn't see the impact of the RPG, I saw the aircraft lose control and crash. We could not see the aircraft once it crashed because of all of the rooftops. It was a little further away than we thought."

"We were getting ready to leave – I get the word 'Prepare for exfil' right when the bird got shot down," said Tom DiTomasso at the northeast blocking position. One of the Chalk 3 Rangers with Tim Watson, Private First Class David Floyd, who only moments earlier had fired his SAW for the first time in combat, actually saw the RPG hit the helicopter. He stated, "Super 61 was flying overhead, giving covering fire. And that's when I noticed the RPG or saw the RPG hit him in the tail boom."

His sergeant, Randy Ramaglia, added:

It's like it never came out of the turn. It just continued to go, go and go. And it was like slow motion. I just remember that bird just spinning out of control. Seeing that get shot down, it was, like, "Wait a minute." You know, "this isn't … it's not supposed to work like this." You know, "we're Americans … we're the ones dictating the game here."[6]

Super 64 Pilot Mike Durant remarked: "Once Super 61 went down … That was the game-changer."

**1624 HOURS: MH-6 HAS LANDED AT CRASH SITE – SUPER 62 PROVIDING COVER – RPG GUNNER REPORTED IN TARGET AREA – BARBER [AH-6] INBOUND.**

Amongst the first to react to the crash was Karl Maier in Star 41. After they had inserted their assaulters around the objective, the MH-6s had lifted out of the battlespace and flew in formation to a holding location north of the city. Maier explained:

The whole city is like six by 12 kilometers so it's pretty small. On the north side of the city we had a logistics base called Sword Base and they had a bunch of SeaLand [Conex] containers stacked up. I found we could land my flight on top of the SeaLand containers and I could see out over the city. That's where we were after we did the infil.

His Little Birds waited with rotors spinning: "All I had to do is pull pitch and I can get into the air right away." The MH-6s stood by in case they were needed to extract the assaulters and their prisoners. They were also standing by for other contingencies. Maier continued:

If they needed a quick CASEVAC [casualty evacuation] then we could do that, we don't have any [flight] medics with us though so we're not the primary on that.

I heard the call first. Super 61 and 62 were both doing that mission. I heard the call that Super 61 got hit and was going down. So I looked over in that direction and I saw him spinning and I saw him go down but he disappeared beneath the level of the buildings. I knew about where he was and he was maybe a mile away from me. So I immediately took off and started heading toward there.

It's just an intuitive reaction. I started heading in there, and I've got to be honest with you, I thought my whole flight came with me. I think they started to but as I got closer to the downed aircraft, Colonel Matthews called me and said I could not go in there. I guess he didn't want to risk another one. I hadn't found the aircraft yet. I was flying around looking for it frantically and I was stalling for time. Finally I came back [to Matthews] and said, "I'm already there." I admit that I said that and I wasn't yet. So he came back and said, "Okay, only one" or something like that. I think that's about the time that the rest of my flight turned back and we were by ourselves.

At the target building, immediate preparations were made to move to the crash site on foot. Kurt Smith was briefed by his team leader Norm Hooten: "Norm briefed the team 'A helo has crashed; we need to go secure the site.' 'Where's it at?' I asked. Norm gestured to the northeast, 'Over there somewhere.' I knew better than to ask for more details. They simply weren't available and weren't of immediate importance anyway. We excelled at adapting to the unknown."

Gary Keeney explained:

Once that bird went down, it wasn't long before Scottie Miller turned to Matt Rierson and said "Matt, you and C-Team are going to take these 24 prisoners, with two snipers [from 3 Troop], and you're going to get in the convoy and take these guys back to the airfield. The rest of us are going to move by foot to that crash site and secure that crash site." That's almost word for word.

Gerry Izzo recalled: "We were wracking our brains saying 'Can they get to a vacant lot, can they get to a rooftop, and we'll land and get them out of there?' They knew that the area was too hot to bring helicopters in."

"Sergeant Joe Thomas, my Forward Observer, he was talking to Super 61 when they got shot down. He was bringing them in to observe a large crowd that was building to the north of our position. When the bird got hit and spiraled down and crashed, the crowd saw it too and began running toward the bird," Tom DiTomasso remembered.

The Wescam Ball on the OH-58D helicopters transmitted a live video feed to Bill Garrison and the JOC. On it they saw two of the Delta snipers on board, Sergeant First Class Jim Smith and Staff Sergeant Dan Busch, somehow managed to extricate themselves from the wreckage. Matthews in the C2 helicopter saw "a guy crawl out of the wreckage of Super 61, one of the operators who was in the back, and take up a defensive fighting position at the corner of the building to protect that crash site. And that happened within probably 30 seconds of the crash."[7]

In the crippled Super 61, Jim Smith came to, concussed but thinking of his priorities:

> My main concern is that we were immediately receiving enemy fire. Dan left the wreckage almost immediately and I wanted to get out of the wreckage to assist him with protecting our mates still in the wreckage. There initially was an exchange between Jim M and myself concerning if he was okay and coherent as he received a severe head injury. Initially Jim M was a bit incoherent for possibly 8 to 10 seconds and then he regained full consciousness and got busy directing actions on the ground.

Staff Sergeant Dan Busch, who served as a Ranger with Bravo Company before passing Delta's Operator Selection Course, was first out of the wreck and immediately opened fire with his SAW on the Somalis who were already surging toward the crash site. Busch knew from his training that his shooting was critical in those first few moments to slow the enemy's advance and give the CSAR team overhead in Super 68 the chance to insert into and secure the crash site.

Busch and Jim Smith moved a short distance to the intersection west of the crash site to better engage the Somalis swarming toward Super 61: "Initially Dan and myself, and a bit later [Sergeant First Class] Steve D set up a defensive perimeter. Dan's actions saved all of our lives with his quick reactions and putting himself in harm's way to protect our lives as we initially sorted out the aftermath of the crash."

Smith was soon engaging targets: "I shot initially the two that Dan had engaged and then another four …" After firing at a number of enemy with his SAW, Dan Busch was hit in the stomach below his body armor and collapsed against a wall. Delta Medic Sergeant First Class Bob M later recounted: "One of the survivors engaged the Somalis rapidly, took well-aimed shots, and killed perhaps 10 of them before he went down, mortally wounded, hit in the pelvis and abdomen."[8]

Boykin was watching from the JOC: "One West-cam [sic] monitor showed the alley. I saw two men crawl out of the wreckage, stumbling and disoriented. Gunfire immediately pinned them against the wreckage. I saw Delta operator Dan Busch firing back. Somalis fell dead in the alley but not before one of them shot Busch. He grabbed his belly and slumped into the street."[9] "Dan received one gunshot wound, which I did not witness, to the pelvic region and was unconscious when I got to him. Dan was lying in a small defilade so I left him there until a time I could recover him. Dan was out of harm's way so to speak," remembered Jim Smith.

Smith then had his own close brush with friendly fire:

Our sister helicopter [Super 62] almost killed me with minigun fire. A friend was on the gun and he saw Dan lying in the street. He saw my rifle sticking out from around the corner of a wall and started to fire at me with the minigun. I remembered hearing the buzz of the minigun and having ceiling tiles rain down on my head. Later in the hospital, my mate told me that he almost killed me. At that point I had forgotten about it. During the arc of travel of the helicopter he saw it was my rifle and me and when he identified that it was I, he got off the trigger immediately.

Moments later Smith was hit by enemy fire:

I was shot a few minutes into the event, as I was the only person defending the crash site because Dan was [now] injured and unconscious. An assailant who came from the front of the helicopter and fired an extended burst from an AK on full auto and hit me with one shot. I received only one gunshot wound to the left shoulder. I then shot him.

Sergeant First Class Steve D had also by now emerged from the wreckage despite suffering a concussion and severe back compression injuries. Smith remembered Steve D moving to him to treat his gunshot wound:

After I was shot, I saw Steve and he checked my shoulder wound and then took up a security position. [Along with his CAR15] I was carrying an M21 semi-auto rifle [but] I did not use it but Steve used it as his 5.56mm ammo ran low. After the crash, it was in the wreckage and later Steve retrieved it and used it – he was holding the rifle by the pistol grip as the stock was broken off.

At this point, Karl Maier's Little Bird, Star 41, appeared overhead and immediately landed. Maier explained:

We flew over it [Super 61], I think we did one circle around it and then landed really quickly with our tail rotor just barely into the intersection. We landed in a street that was perpendicular to the one that they crashed in. I couldn't see the aircraft after we landed but it was to my left rear.

I did see that two guys had gotten out of that crash and they were taking blocking positions on the corners so they were to my right rear [Busch and Smith] and there was one other guy who was left rear and I kept waving at him – his face was swollen and bloody. I tried to get him to come to the aircraft and he just shook his head no, he wasn't coming because he pointed behind him and tapped his head which meant there were still people back there. So he wasn't coming.

The man with the swollen face was Sergeant First Class Jim M, the third Delta sniper on board Super 61. Jim Smith recalled: "I did not see Jim M outside the helo. I think he was trying to get the crew chiefs out of the wreckage and checking on the pilots." Although severely wounded, Jim M would stay at the crash site to protect the helicopter until the Rangers and CSAR element could arrive to secure the location. "He stayed and was part of the siege all night. He was a brave guy, he was obviously hurt but he stayed there," said Maier.

"They're hurting but they're moving and shooting. I can't say enough about those guys. They are real professionals – I've never worked with anyone quite like them. They were doing what they needed to do, trying to secure the crash site." Star 41 had taken fire upon their approach and now that they were on the ground, that fire increased although much of it was thankfully woefully inaccurate. Maier continued:

We were taking a lot of fire, they were sticking their heads over walls and around corners. You know you've seen when a non-professional combatant picks his rifle up and sticks it over his head and just starts spraying? I mean there was a lot of that going on. All I had was my MP5 [submachine gun], I was returning fire when I could see them but we're basically sitting on the ground waiting for somebody to come to the aircraft. It was starting to look like that wasn't going to happen and I was getting ready to make a decision.

I shot a couple of guys that ran around the left front of me. The first guy, he came around the corner, he's probably 50 meters from me, he's got his rifle, it's an AK and it's down by his waist and he just pulls the trigger and starts waving it around. I literally closed my eyes and when he ran out of bullets I was like, "Okay, I'm okay" and I shot him. It was pretty scary.

Maier was typically self-deprecating about his own marksmanship: "The MP5 was doing the job. I went through a lot of ammunition – I'm not a good infantry guy so I went through a lot of bullets!"

Each of the MH-6s typically carried a Delta-modified M249 SAW in the rear that was used by the assaulters. Once the operators dismounted from the pods, the SAW was left behind with the aircrew who could employ it in an emergency such as the one Maier and Jones now faced. Maier explained:

> It was in the cargo compartment and I have to admit I forgot it was back there! Later on I thought about it and was like, "What was I thinking? I could've grabbed the SAW!"
>
> I said to [co-pilot] Keith, "Where are they at?" and he turns around and goes "Okay, one of them [Busch] has got shot and is laying in the intersection" and he [Keith Jones] said to me, "I need to get out, can I get out?" I said, "Well, if you have to, but hurry up!" So he got out and he ran back there. In the meantime Dan Busch is shot and Jim Smith had picked Dan up and was carrying him on his shoulder toward the aircraft and then he got shot.

A medical report later noted that "Sergeant Jim Smith was shot through the meaty part of his left shoulder (under his Kevlar vest)."[10] Despite being hit, Smith managed to struggle toward Star 41 with the semi-conscious Busch. Keith Jones was outside the aircraft firing his 9mm M9 Beretta pistol at the converging Somalis. Maier recalled watching Jones trading fire with the Somalis:

> He was like James Bond running around out there! As a matter of fact, at one point he came back to the aircraft and we traded ammo – I was using a lot of

the MP5 magazines and he needed more pistol ammo so we traded. As we were doing that we just looked at each other and laughed as if to say, "What are we doing!"

Colonel Matthews in the C2 Black Hawk was all the while urgently calling upon Maier to get Star 41 out of the danger zone. Maier recounted:

I said to him, "I can't, my co-pilot is not in the aircraft and I'm not leaving without him." He just said "Oh"! I guess he was up high in the C2 bird and he could see the crowds converging and by this time Keith is out of the aircraft, I'm already in a gunfight out of the cockpit with some guys around the corner and he's telling me I've gotta get out of there.

Smith was struggling with Busch:

As the Little Bird landed, I ran out and got Dan and dragged him to the bird. Initially I dragged him two-handed with me traveling backward. But I was receiving fire so I had to shoot an assailant down the street and then I dragged him with one hand and then shot my rifle with the other hand. Once at the Little Bird, I attempted to load him but I could not with his bodyweight, his equipment, and my wounded shoulder and I dropped him just short of the door.

Jim Smith knew via his Motorola radio that a Ranger ground element were inbound to their location and decided to hold on to assist with defending the perimeter until they arrived: "I waited to exfil to the hospital with Dan until the Rangers were at our location. Dan was loaded and I was outside the bird until the Rangers arrived. There were no other severely wounded that needed to be extracted."

Maier reported:

Keith got Dan in the back and then Jim in the back and we could get them out of there. When we got him [Dan] in the back, he didn't look good. I was really worried about him. As soon as I saw him I was thinking we had to get him over to the MASH. Unfortunately Dan didn't make it but Jim did.

Tom DiTomasso's Chalk 2 were the closest to the crash site and the young Lieutenant had immediately contacted Captain Steele to request permission to move toward Super 61. Steele still didn't have communications with Eversmann's Chalk 4 due to ongoing problems with their radios and was likely concerned to keep the blocking positions in place until they could all move as a group toward the crash site.

After some discussion Steele agreed with DiTomasso's compromise. He would split his chalk in two, leaving one in place to hold down the northeast blocking position while he personally led the other half to the crash site. DiTomasso related:

> By this time, Staff Sergeant Yurek had come over to my position. I told him to keep his team at the blocking position. I took Specialist Nelson's M60 team and Staff Sergeant Lycopolus's team, a total of eight men, and started moving toward the crash site. As we started running, I noticed that the crowd to our north had also seen the crash. They were paralleling our movement with the same intent: to get to the crash site first.

Chalk 2 took off at speed, moving first north and then turning right, to the east, past the parking lot that they had cleared earlier. They ran through a gauntlet of enemy fire from all directions for three city blocks until they finally broke through to Marehan Road to approach the crash site. DiTomasso was faced by an unexpected sight. He recounted:

> It seemed like every window and door had a weapon firing from it. As we made the last turn, I was shocked to see that a Little Bird had landed in the street just behind the downed helicopter. Bullets were popping off the walls and ground from every direction. As I stumbled over two dead bodies, I could see one pilot firing his weapon from inside the cockpit, while steadying the aircraft with one hand on the joystick. He was pointing his weapon in our direction, until he realized it was us. I tapped my head to question the headcount, a typical Ranger hand and arm signal; he shook his head no ... To me this meant that he didn't have all the men from the crash site. I saw him put two men on the helicopter. Years later, Karl told me that he didn't know what the arm and hand signal meant, so that's why he shook his head!

Maier was just as surprised by DiTomasso's arrival. He said:

> By this stage I think we were [on the ground] just shy of ten minutes, somewhere between seven and ten minutes. I couldn't believe it was that long. It seemed like an hour! Everything seems to slow down and you get very focused. While all this was all going on, I had been shooting at guys who ran around the corner shooting at me. I'm leaning out the door shooting back and forth at these guys and then looked to my right and there's Lieutenant DiTomasso coming around the other corner!

The arrival of Chalk 2 almost ended in friendly fire. No one had informed Star 41 that the Rangers were on their way and the sudden appearance of DiTomasso and his men surprised Maier, so much so that, spotting movement out of the corner of his eye, he brought up his MP5 ready to fire:

> I hadn't had any trouble out of that corner [the right side or southwest] yet so I wheeled around and was just about to shoot him through the right windshield when I recognized the Kevlar [helmet]. He put his hands up, his eyes got really big because he knew what had been about to happen! He tapped his helmet to ask me for a head count [as Maier later realized] so I shrugged and pointed to my left rear to give him the direction. I was really glad to see them, I'll tell you that!
>
> So we loaded up Jim and Dan and we pulled out and we were supposed to bring them back to the JMAU [Joint Medical Augmentation Unit, JSOC's field surgical unit run by Doc Marsh] but when I saw Dan I made the decision I was going to take him to the hospital over at the UN compound because they had a true MASH there. So we went over there and landed and the docs came out, and Keith got out and helped get Dan and Jim out. The Colonel in charge came over to me and said, "What's going on?" I said, "It's gonna get busy."

The courage shown by Maier and Jones was remarkable. Mike Durant indicated that it was entirely Maier's call to go in and stay so long on the ground: "He was Pilot in Command of his aircraft and it's his discretion to do what he believes is right in a situation like that. I have always felt that Karl's actions that day were at least worthy of consideration for the Congressional Medal of Honor."

**1631 HOURS:** MH-6 EXFIL 2 X WIA FROM CRASH.

DiTomasso continued:

> When that Little Bird took off, we ran underneath it and one of the crew chiefs [likely Charlie Warren] was standing in the middle of the street with his hands over his face and his face was all bloody and the Somalis were beating him with sticks. We pushed all of the Somalis off that guy, grabbed on to him, and we moved him to the crash site.
>
> The other crew chief was sitting against a wall and it appeared he had a back injury. Somalis were running all over the helicopter. The two pilots were still inside the helicopter and [the body of] Cliff Wolcott was trapped. We pulled [the body of] Donovan Briley [the co-pilot] out. Initially we were just fighting the Somalis, trying to get them off the helicopter.

Whilst his men secured the site, DiTomasso radioed Staff Sergeant Yurek commanding the remainder of his team back at the blocking position to move up and link up at the crash site, following the same route they took. At the objective, the assault force was making plans to join DiTomasso's men at the crash. A Delta operator explained: "Through contingency training we knew that we would move on foot to that crash site and secure the dead and wounded, we knew what these Somalia fighters would do to their bodies so that was a focus."

**1626 HOURS:** GRF #1 WILL MOVE TO CRASH SITE WITH ASSAULT FORCE AND PC; MOVE TO CRASH SITE #1 APPROXIMATELY 1635. PC EN-ROUTE BACK TO TF RANGER COMPOUND VIA 5 TON WITH HMMWV SECURITY. QRF ASSISTANCE REQUESTED; QRF TO REPORT TO TF RANGER COMPOUND TO LINK-UP.

Back at the objective, Mike Moser was still loading the trucks. He said:

> I do not recall precisely how I learned of Super 61, I believe I got word through the Assault frequency [radio] I'm pretty sure that was broadcast, however, in the moments following the clearing of the target, most of us were collected in a courtyard and there was considerable face-to-face communication between the team leaders/Ground Force Commander [Miller] as they

definitively established the situation and formulated a plan to move towards the crash site.

During this time I was employed with several other guys trying to load our cargo – the various detainees obtained in the target [known by the brevity codeword Precious Cargo] – into the back of a truck in the alley outside the courtyard. It was during this period that I definitely was aware of 61 and the proposed foot movement toward its location. The vehicle convoy, which included the truck into which I just loaded the detainees, would attempt to move to the same location via a separate route. In relatively short order we began to move into the alleys toward 61. This is the interval at which I recall a growing volume of fire, most noticeable as I made forays in to the street to load the trucks. It seemed the vehicle column attracted a lot of attention.

Delta Captain Scott Miller issued clear orders to his men: "Okay, we're moving. Find the crash and secure it." Another operator noted: "Scott M [Miller] was the squadron operations officer at the time and was acting as the Ground Force Commander. He organized the assault force and got it moving east down the road toward the crash."

Norm Hooten, at the time a five-year veteran of Delta, noted:

We rehearsed prior to going to Mogadishu ... and one of the things that happened during our rehearsal was we had an aircraft go down ... and that's where we came up with the plan that we would move on foot to that crash site immediately. Not in vehicles as we couldn't move through the tight streets in vehicles.

We [Delta] understood the plan. Delta had crashed a helicopter on every operation I'd ever been on! The original mission in Iran [Operation *Eagle Claw*], they crashed birds. Crashed birds in Grenada. We crashed one in Panama. Crashed them in the Gulf War, crashed them in Somalia, so we'd gotten used to sending recovery teams and SAR birds. It wasn't something that was new to us because unfortunately we're famous for crashing helos!

The inevitable Clausewitzian friction or fog of war that features in some way or another in every battle now made its first untimely appearance. After Tom DiTomasso moved off with half of his chalk toward the crash site he expected the closest blocking position, Chalk 4 under Sergeant Matt Eversmann to their immediate north, to move parallel toward Super 61 with Chalk 2. DiTomasso explained the procedure:

> The intent is that we would all move together, providing mutual support for each position. Think of a box with north being up. At the lower right hand corner you have Chalk 1, with Lieutenant Perino and Captain Steele. At the top right hand corner you have Chalk 2 where I was. At the top left hand corner you have Chalk 4, with Eversmann. And the lower left hand corner is Chalk 3 with Sergeant First Class Sean T Watson.
>
> If you imagine that entire box moving to the right, or east, that's how we rehearsed it and that's what I expected to happen. Chalk 2 went to the crash site, we went to the east, to the crash site, racing the crowd. I expected Chalk 4 to follow because before I left I got on the radio with Sergeant Eversmann and said, "Do you see me? I'm running down this road" and he said, "Roger." We were all under a lot of enemy fire. I know Colonel McKnight and Staff Sergeant Eversmann did everything they could to get to the crash site, it just didn't work.

Sergeant Eversmann's Chalk 4 were with little doubt receiving the lion's share of the enemy fire and by this stage had multiple wounded. Enemy from three separate directions were trying to suppress them, particularly from the north, which was as noted the major enemy reinforcement route. Eversmann recalled how he became aware of the downing of Super 61:

> Picture two Rangers behind a vehicle facing to the east. [Specialist] Dave Diemer is my SAW gunner, he's engaging to the east, I'm kneeling right next to him behind this vehicle and Dave turned to me and says, "A Black Hawk just crashed." I didn't hear anything on the radio, knew nothing about it.
>
> I looked down toward the east, it was too far for me to absolutely say, "That's a helicopter" but I just remember this big pile of rubble. I remember I could see a black helmet that far away – somebody was there. I said, "Hey, there's bad guys in between us so you've really got to check your fire, you know we don't want to have fratricide [friendly fire] here."
>
> The problem was first of all I've got enemy between my position and the target [the crash site] so running right down this alleyway is kinda suicide so [my] second thought is, "How do we bypass around there?" I remember

talking to Jim Telscher and asking him how much demo, C4 [plastic explosive], he had because the thought was maybe we could punch through, maybe we could get there by going through a house and blowing through some courtyards. Unfortunately he only had very limited demo. Maybe we could go north a block and go east a couple of blocks and come that way. That whole idea of how're we going to move without going full frontal right into the fray with bad guys, I'm trying to figure that out when [Colonel] Danny McKnight pulls up.

DiTomasso recalled the confusion, noting that McKnight intended to move the entire GRF along with Eversmann's Chalk to the crash site:

Colonel McKnight, the battalion commander, happened to be with the vehicles that day because the platoon leader [Lieutenant Larry Moores] for that platoon was on a Convoy Escort Patrol when the mission came into the JOC. That's why he was not with the vehicles on the initial insertion. When the first bird got shot down, Colonel McKnight was there with Matt Eversmann and Colonel McKnight made the decision to load Chalk 4 onto the Humvees and five-ton trucks instead of moving by foot.

Eversmann added:

McKnight pulls up with his convoy and Dan Schilling's with him. They're picking up our fast ropes that are still lying there and picking up our wounded guys too. I remember saying, "Hey sir, we're moving to the crash site right down there, to the east down this alley," and his words, and I can't remember verbatim, are "Well, we're going to the crash site too, jump on board and we'll drive over there." I'm like, "Okay, that's the battalion commander, that makes sense, he's got comms with everybody."

At the time, and it's not true, but I assumed that Mogadishu, like any other city, would be on a grid. Go up a block, turn right, go two blocks then turn right and we'll be right there. I didn't think for even a second [that] we wouldn't be able to do that. So we loaded everyone onto their convoy and started that movement towards the crash site. The assumption was, for me, the battalion commander's here and I go with the boss. I didn't think at the time, "Well, shit, driving down this alleyway with bad guys on both sides is probably a bad idea too," so the idea of getting on his vehicles to head over there made perfect sense. Plus being down to six guys.

With Chalk 4 now on board McKnight's GRF, the remainder of the blocking positions and the assaulters moved on foot toward the crash site after first collapsing their perimeter around the objective. Their route would take them directly east from the objective. Norm Hooten's F-Team led off. He recounted:

> C-Team, Matt Rierson's team, had been designated to escort the prisoners back to base so we split the assault force. We sent one team [C-Team] back with the prisoners and the rest of us to the crash site. It was F-Team, E-Team, B-Team and Alpha [A] Team. G-Team were with Scottie Miller but they were moving with us. We were going down the street with F-Team on the right front and Echo Team was on the left.

They headed four to five blocks east before reaching Marehan Road. At the intersection, they turned to the left and headed north up Marehan toward the crash. Hooten remembered the weight of enemy fire as they crossed intersections which had become 'fatal funnels':

> Captain Steele and a blocking position [Chalk 1] was in the center and behind us was Earl Fillmore's team, Alpha Team, and [then] B-Team. There was a pretty heavy engagement moving up that street and we were doing fire and maneuver – shooting and moving but getting directions at the same time from the helo that was trying to guide us in to the aircraft. Every time we crossed an intersection we'd see them and shoot. They were shooting around corners, they'd run to the sound of the gunfire, get to an intersection and dump their magazine. All of them were converging on that one point [the crash site].

Fellow F-Team member Kurt Smith detailed the foot movement:

> We moved in a column formation on both sides of the street. We took advantage of cover as best as we could while moving down the street, but we took casualties anyway. We could hear the sonic crack of bullets passing down the street but very rarely could we see the actual shooters. Many times the Somalis would simply stick their weapon around the corner and fire off a

magazine in our general direction without aiming. I saw a Ranger across the street get hit and go down. It was frustrating because there appeared to be nothing to shoot at, no known enemy positions to suppress.

At the same time, the second half of DiTomasso's Chalk 2 under Sergeant Yurek were moving on foot following the same route as DiTomasso had used minutes earlier. They braved the shooting gallery of the big alley next to the parking lot to emerge onto Marehan Road and quickly linked up with DiTomasso who was by now crouched behind a green Fiat car with his RTO.

In a significant departure from reality in the *Black Hawk Down* film, two members of Chalk 2, M60 gunner Specialist Shawn Nelson and SAW gunner Specialist Lance Twombly, were shown in an almost comedic sequence afraid that they have been unintentionally left behind and moving through the city by themselves toward the crash site. This simply did not occur. In fact, Nelson left with DiTomasso in the original group and Twombly moved with Yurek and the remainder of Chalk 2 after receiving the order from DiTomasso.

### 1628 HOURS: SUPER 68 (SAR) INFILS AT CRASH – SUPER 68 HIT BY RPG – REQUIRE RTB [RETURN TO BASE] ASAP

Above the crash site, Super 68, "Razor's Edge," piloted by Chief Warrant Officer Dan Jollota and Major Herb Rodriguez, was inbound to the crash site. The first the CSAR team knew of the crash was when the pilots passed a chalkboard back to the team inscribed with the simple yet chilling message "61 DOWN." "We knew that if we were going to be on the ground at all, it was going to be a bad situation, and we knew that the mission automatically would change if a helicopter got shot down. I went in knowing things were going to be ugly and things were going to be bad," Ranger Sergeant John Belman recalled.[11] In a sad irony, Super 61 had been used as the simulated crashed aircraft in a CSAR exercise run by Task Force Ranger just a week before the October 3 mission.

The CSAR helicopter was filled to the brim with 15 heavily laden personnel drawn from Delta, the Rangers and Air Force Special Tactics. The large number of personnel on Super 68 meant that some useful equipment had to be left behind: "There wasn't enough room on the Black Hawk for the Quickie Saw and all of that kit. We just didn't have room," said Belman.

A more compact version was developed after Mogadishu with a range of cutting tools that could be more easily fast roped into a location.

One of the Pararescueman Jumpers, Master Sergeant Scott Fales, later said:

> Normally when you assess a crash site, one of our tactics is to turn hard over the top of the site and look down on top of it to see exactly what you have and then come back and set up on an approach and either land or fast rope to the crash. In this particular case, brownout was very bad, the enemy situation was very bad, enemy fire was very high, to include lots of RPGs being fired at the helicopter in the sky, so it was made clear we were only going to have one attempt. So we basically flew straight to the relative vicinity of the crash site.[12]

As they flared over the crash site, Belman remembered: "A Delta guy on one side and a Ranger on the other deployed the ropes. I was one of the last people off the helicopter and so I was crammed in the middle." The first man leapt onto the fast rope and descended to the crash site just under eight minutes after Super 61 went down.

As the CSAR personnel fast roped to the ground, they experienced significant ground fire directed toward the hovering helicopter. Moments later, an RPG hit the helicopter. Air Force Pararescueman Jumper Technical Sergeant Tim Wilkinson was actually on the right-hand-side rope, sliding to the ground when the RPG struck. DiTomasso explained what happened from surveillance footage he later watched:

> There is video footage that was taken by an airborne platform of that infiltration and you can see Super 68 come in, you see them flare, you see the guys going out on the ropes, and you can see RPG and machine-gun fire hit the helicopter. The helicopter gets hit in the back, in the tail section, and lurches up with Rangers still on the ropes.
>
> You can see the helmet of the crew chief and he's probably screaming on the microphone, "You've got guys on the ropes." The helicopter lurches up like it needs to get out of there and then it settles back down really quickly, the rest of the Rangers go out and then the crew chief pulls a lever on the Black Hawk that releases the ropes.

Super 68's pilot Jollota remembered:

An RPG has a very unique sound. There was no doubt in my mind I had been hit by something pretty heavy. Fear took over, so I immediately took in power and I was getting out of there. My crew chief in the back saved the Rangers' lives. He screamed at me, "Sir, you've got to stop. We've got Rangers on the ropes." These poor guys were hanging on to the fast ropes for dear life as I picked this thing up to a hover. The crew chief talked me back down into the hover hole. We got those Rangers off and we took off.[13]

DiTomasso and his chalk were right under the CSAR Black Hawk when it arrived:

It was (both) a horrifying and pleasant surprise. I knew that the CSAR element was up there in Super 68 but I didn't know they were coming. At the time we were distracted by all of the enemy combatants at the crash site and I was standing on the corner right near the bird [Super 61] and all of a sudden I couldn't breathe – literally could not take a breath. I thought I was going to pass out. It was all brownout around us and I didn't realize at the time but the CSAR helicopter was fast roping right on top of us.

Literally I'm on my hands and knees trying to take a breath and I see soldiers running out of the (dust) cloud toward me and they fall down. And another one falls down. Four guys out of the CSAR helicopter, as they fast roped down the ropes – they were getting shot and falling down right in front of me. So now you have these 15 plus the 15 that were there (Chalk 2) and you have the two pilots deceased, the two crew chiefs who were wounded, and four more wounded from the CSAR element.

As the CSAR team roped in, the assault force was fighting its way block by block toward the crash site. Mike Moser of B-Team recounted:

A-Team was just ahead of us, taking the right side of the alley. I believe the teams from C-2 [Charlie Squadron's 2 Troop] were on the left side. There was a moderate amount of shooting early on – some incoming, judging from flying brick chips and even a small piece of RPG shrapnel or a secondary wall chip which struck my left arm following a nearby impact.

Some of the fire was suppressive, as we crossed alley junctions. The alleys formed long empty canyons, featureless walls occasionally punctuated with metal doors usually leading into courtyards and some windows [and] upper housing structures. I saw Somalis here and there, poking out of doorways up the alleys. Mostly [I] noticed the increased cadence of supersonic cracks as one of us would scoot across an exposed gap.

I recall basically an L-shaped movement to the 61 site; a few blocks this way, then a left turn and we knew we were approaching the site. Shortly following this left turn, more Somalis became visible far up the alley – approximately 100 meters or so [away], one of whom I saw was holding an AK as he bobbled between two points of cover looking across the alley. This met my criteria for bad guy [as] up until this time I had seen few Somalis actually holding weapons, and in my mind I was still in surgical mode [firing only at clearly armed individuals with hostile intent].

Although there were a number of our guys to my front, it was a clear shot and in fact, the only one I ever took during the whole day. [Sergeant First Class] Earl [Fillmore on A-Team], who was a few feet to my front immediately turned to admonish me, saying, "Hey, there's Rangers up there." I smiled back and reassured him that I wasn't in danger of hitting our own folks. A few seconds after this, we were again on our feet and moving.

Kurt Smith of F-Team recalled:

At the corner of the intersection, the enemy fire began to increase. [Sergeant First Class] Greg A engaged targets with his M203 at the intersection, and the column turned north. As we moved north up the street, it was clear we were getting near the crash site. I could see Rangers and operators down the street at an intersection ahead and could clearly see Somali militiamen further beyond. I took up a kneeling firing position and engaged targets down the street. At this point, I could see women and children intermingled with the militiamen, making target acquisition difficult. We continued to move north toward the crash site when enemy fire began impacting close around us.[14]

By this point, the level of incoming fire was heavy and only increasing. Another Delta operator made this assessment: "The guys we were fighting were not well trained [but] there were just a whole lot of them. They were not real good with their guns or other gear but had a lot of ammo and kept shooting." Norm Hooten explained that often targets were appearing at very close range: "You're within a doorway away or over a brick wall ... within 10 feet. So it's very, very close and very personal."[15]

Further up Marehan Road, the CSAR team were by now on the ground and establishing security around the crash site. Belman remembered:

> We hit the ground, get our stuff together and then you're moving toward this courtyard because we're trying to move up the street whilst staying off the street. We clear a couple of rooms. In one building there was some women and children in there, we just kind of left them alone and moved on because we weren't staying there. So we moved up the road and hung a left toward where the actual crash site was. Tom's [DiTomasso] guys got there just before us.

Moments after descending from the fast rope, PJ Fales was hit. He recalled: "As we collected at the crash the enemy zeroed in on our location and steady rifle fire increased and while all of that was happening I was hit in the leg." The AK round had struck him in the back of his left leg.[16]

Belman continued:

> The first indication of enemy fire was I saw Scott Fales limping and he's bleeding but it wasn't really registering that he'd just been shot. Then I saw Jim M, a Delta guy who'd been in the crash and his face was pretty badly damaged was sitting against a wall and then I clued in that there was a ton of fire going on. I became acutely aware of bullets all over the place and that lasted until the evening when we could get inside the buildings adjacent to the crash.

Fales managed to limp into cover with the assistance of two of the Rangers and treated his own wound. The highly experienced Fales saw the first signs of shock setting in and quickly administered an IV on himself whilst still providing covering fire with his GAU-5 carbine. Meanwhile Wilkinson headed to the helicopter. He encountered one of the crew chiefs, Staff Sergeant Charlie Warren, whom DiTomasso had earlier saved from the Somali civilians, in a stunned and concussed state. He asked C-Squadron's EOD technician to escort Warren over to the casualty collection point [CCP] that Delta medic Bob M had established near the tail of Super 61.

One of the other Delta snipers that had been on board Super 61, Jim M, although suffering from a serious head wound inflicted during the crash, was working to free the dead pilot. Wilkinson confirmed that both pilots were deceased and with the assistance of Belman, managed to cut free the body of the co-pilot, Donovan "Bull" Briley. Wilkinson then instructed Belman to move the wounded Delta sniper to the CCP so his head wound could be assessed and treated.

Tom DiTomasso had established the initial defensive positions using his Ranger chalk and these were reinforced by Belman's security element. "As the CSAR team started treating the casualties from the crash, I linked up and positioned Sergeant Yurek's team on the southwestern side of the crash. I also sent Specialist Gould's M60 crew, which traveled with Sergeant Yurek, to the northeast with Staff Sergeant Lycopolus," commented DiTomasso.

"This alleyway really isn't very large. On my side you basically had a four-way intersection [with Marehan Road heading north and south]. You had Rangers at the far side of the alleyway pointed north, west and south. The CSAR team trained so well together … we just flowed into our responsibilities," said Belman. "Out in front was some folks from DiTomasso's team – [Specialist] Shawn Nelson, [Specialist John] Stebbins was there, [Specialist John] Waddell …"

Belman continued: "My [own] defensive position was right at the end of the helicopter, under the tail, facing the alley. Right next to me was Tom DiTomasso, [DiTomasso's RTO] Jason Coleman, and [Air Force Combat Controller] Pat Rogers. [Delta Captain and commander of the CSAR element] Bill C was there, moving in and around the crash." Ranger Sergeant Alan Barton and Specialist Shawn Nelson covered the north-south axis of the intersection with Marehan Road. C-Squadron Sergeant Major Tommy C and Sergeant Major Rick W from 3 Troop established defensive positions near the cockpit.

Belman noted that "the volume of fire was extremely high," and growing as more Somalis surrounded the crash site. "Women and children were screaming and running at us from all directions. Some of them had weapons, and some did not. The weapons ranged from machine guns to small knives and machetes," said DiTomasso.

Crew chief Sergeant Ray Dowdy was still alive and trapped in his seat on the left side of the helicopter. Wilkinson managed to dig him out of the rubble and cut him free. As he was dragging the wounded crew chief from the wreckage, the PJ was struck in the face and lower arm by steel fragments from incoming gunfire striking the Black Hawk. The crew chief was also wounded again before Wilkinson could get him to cover, losing the top of two fingers to a Somali bullet.

At Delta medic Bob M's suggestion, Belman then began pulling the Kevlar ballistic lining from the aircraft in an effort to improve their position. The lining might not stop the bullets and RPG fragments but it might have slowed them down. Belman positioned the Kevlar sheets to help shield the CCP from fire as much as possible. Bob M later mentioned:

> In hindsight, this could have been avoided by moving the wounded directly into a building. We had anticipated a fairly rapid extraction by vehicle and had planned to establish the CCP in relation to the downed AC [aircraft] so the wounded could be easily loaded. The CCP was in a fairly open spot. By the time we figured out we were going to be there for a while, it was difficult to move casualties without being exposed to fire.
>
> When we tried to move the wounded into a house, we took more casualties. We ended up waiting until dusk to move. The lesson learned was to establish the CCP in the most secure and accessible area ASAP and delay all but immediate lifesaving treatment until you get there. A generic location can be planned ... but look for a better spot when you get there.[17]

DiTomasso agreed:

> Every time someone tried to pick up a litter, he drew fire. It was as if the enemy could see our every move. One soldier and I tried to pick up one end of a litter when a bullet pierced through the soldier's right rear hip, knocking him over. The decision was made that we would wait until dark to move the casualties inside the building.

"Every time we tried to move someone, somebody else would get shot. We had 19 wounded there at one point," added Belman.

Bart B, another Delta medic, detailed how they even tried using tin sheets to drag casualties to safety;

At the first crash site, I do know of one instance where a group of people on one side of an alley tried to push a piece of tin roofing across to the other side to pull a wounded soldier back across the alley. The plan was to tie a rope to the tin sheet, push it across the alley, the group on that side would load the casualty onto the tin, and the other side would then pull him across the danger area. The empty tin was shot up on the way across – needless to say, that plan didn't work.[18]

Wilkinson explained that, although wounded, his fellow PJ Fales was not out of the fight: "As we carried folks back to the triage point, Scott [Fales] positioned himself at the tail of the aircraft and was setting up and providing cover down the alleyways and up the street, and we would put the casualties behind him." Even when told the arrival of McKnight's convoy was imminent, Fales refused to be placed on a stretcher. "No, I'm not getting on the litter. I'll shoot from here." Eventually he relented under considerable protest.[19]

When hand grenades were posted over a wall by the encircling Somalis, Fales saw the danger and threw himself onto two wounded Rangers to shield them from the blast. Incredibly, the fragmentation missed all three. Fales later managed to escape his stretcher [he had been tied to it to force him to try and stay under cover] and rejoined the fight. "I'd fire a few rounds to push them back, then put my rifle across my lap and turn around to do my medical duties."[20]

Despite the incredibly difficult conditions under heavy enemy fire "the level of first aid performed at the crash site was extraordinary because nobody died of their wounds at the crash site. I believe the two pilots were killed on impact of the crash," noted DiTomasso.

Whilst the CSAR team and the Rangers of Chalk 2 held down the crash site, the assaulters and other blocking positions were fighting their way to them and were by now heading up Marehan Road toward the intersection. Norm Hooten remembered: "[In terms of] true cover there was only the recesses of the doors and little piles of debris" to take shelter behind. The majority of the enemy fire was directed from the north down Marehan Road and from the west and east into the alleyway where Super 61 lay.

Hooten recalled:

We bypassed the street we were supposed to turn to the north and as we went past it we got the call [from the helicopter], "You're going too far." We had to stop to figure out what they were saying and we realized that we'd gone about half a block on. At that point, the line of march changed. So we [F-Team] ended up second in line on that side of the street. So that put Jon Hale's team in the lead and that's when Earl Fillmore got shot. It was a fatal hit, he didn't fall, he just collapsed.

I remember Earl turning around. I was standing next to [Staff Sergeant] Michael Moser and [Sergeant First Class] Chris F and we were kinda down behind this pile of rubble between a tree and maybe about a meter away from the external wall of a house. We were hunkered down and I could see Earl stopped at the intersection on one knee up against a house on the corner. There was probably only five meters between my team and Earl's team so we were in close trail formation.

That's when Earl got hit and that one burst of fire that hit Earl Fillmore actually hit Mike Moser in the arm as well. When Earl got hit we all returned fire immediately and as we were returning fire Mike got hit through his right forearm. Chris F and I picked him up [Mike] to move him inside and Chris got hit in the back but his body armor stopped it. John B [team leader of B-Team] and another guy recovered Earl so they were dragging Earl and we were dragging Mike.

Mike Moser remembered being hit: "Within several yards, that nasty 'crack-crack-crack' sound erupted again, and I was struck in the right elbow. Kinda surprising how painful that was – put me on my back instantly. I spent a few seconds or so wondering if I'd regain the use of my right arm as my teammate wrapped some Kerlix [bandage] around my boo-boo [wound]."

Moser added:

It was only after he [Chris F] was struck in the back by another burst that I realized there were bigger concerns than my little elbow ... That burst was the one I assume killed Earl [but] I do not know this. Shortly, Norm [Hooten] and my team leader [John B] hustled us up and directed us all through a set of doors opening into a courtyard. Upon standing up, I looked over and saw Earl in the street, obviously gone.

The round had struck Earl Fillmore, the medic from A-Team, in the head, easily penetrating the plastic ProTec helmet he wore and killing him instantly.

He was at the time the youngest soldier to ever pass Delta selection and was widely respected within the unit. "He was a fearless and tenacious combat medic," said Delta medic Bob M later, "he kept his medic skills intact so he could not only fight his way out of a tight spot, but he could take care of his injured comrades."[21]

Hooten said that he:

> finished dragging Mike in [after Chris F was hit] and went back to get Chris and we're talking maybe two meters – we had almost had Mike in the door when Chris got hit. Chris was on his back and obviously in a lot of pain. They fired another burst and I lay down next to him and said, "Where are you hit?" and he said, "I'm hit in the back." I felt around under his vest looking for the wound and I felt the round. It was still hot. So the round was sticking through the inside of his vest. So I said, "Hey, your vest stopped it" – it looked like the round had hit a wall and ricocheted. He was a lucky guy.

Kurt Smith tried to hold Chris F down while the operators "isolated and exposed the wound under his body armor. On his lower back side, where his kidneys would be, there was a five-inch diameter area where it appeared the skin had been burned off like a giant blister. Whatever hit him did not penetrate the soft portion of the body armor. His armor saved him quite a bit of pain."[22] Moser added: "My teammate who caught the round in the back was okay – turned out it was likely a rabbit round – skipped off a wall – and was pretty spent. His soft body armor stopped it."

"When B-Team got hit, that's when we started to do entries. Moving from house to house, either internally or externally. We were doing bounding overwatch and actually doing entries on the rooms. Some of the doors didn't require [explosive breaching] charges, we could just kick them open," said Norm Hooten. All the while they were under continual heavy fire. "There was quite a bit of RPG fire, most of it going down the street – it wasn't very effective, they'd just point it around a corner and shoot. Sometimes you'd see them skipping off the ground and think, 'Oh man, here it comes'. They weren't good with the RPGs but they had a lot of them."

The operators were by now perhaps a block short of the crash site and, with several wounded, quickly established their own casualty collection point in a Somali house. Smith recounted:

Earl Fillmore and Mike M [Moser] went down. Norm directed me to enter and clear the building next to us and establish a casualty collection point. I entered the building. Greg A followed me in. There was a family inside the building. After ensuring they had no weapons I instructed them to sit in the back corner of a room and be quiet.[23]

"Within the courtyard, we estimated we were still short of the crash site by some 50 to 100 meters. So, this courtyard position was what grew into a larger CCP," explained Moser. Although seriously wounded himself, Moser:

> tried to assist Bart B with rigging an IV using my one arm. A few unwounded guys naturally cleared the residence of any threat, and aside from a very unlucky Somali family, no enemy were found. The family was flex-tied and sequestered, the immediate room secured. It was here in this room adjacent to the courtyard that I spent the remainder of the event. At some point I distributed my unused ammo to my TL [team leader]. He told me to remain here, but the bulk of the assault force was continuing on toward the site. The CCP population continued to grow with Rangers.

Hooten added:

> At this point we had John B and Jon Hale and their guys in one of the buildings and then we had my team and Moser and a couple of casualties in the building next to it. Captain Steele and his crew had come up and they were right where we had been hit. We were exchanging fire from building to building by this stage.

Ranger Sergeant Keni Thomas with Watson's Chalk 3 braved the street to run back to Steele to request a medical evacuation for Fillmore. In a still controversial move, Steele asked Thomas whether the casualty was "one of ours?," undoubtedly meaning the Rangers and underscoring the tension between Steele and the operators. Thomas replied that the casualty was Delta. With the area considered too hot for an evacuation by helicopter, their only hope lay with McKnight's convoy.[24] Sergeant Watson continued to attempt to reach the GRF and arrange a ground evacuation, with no success. No one knew exactly where McKnight's convoy was.

The other Ranger chalks were still some distance behind further down the street from the operators and were taking a tremendous amount of fire. "We moved forward until we reached the intersection, and, immediately, we were suppressed by intense enemy fire. We quickly returned fire and continued to move. With Somalis shooting at us from every direction, it seemed as if we had run into a wall of lead. We began to bound from wall to wall and low crawl to any available cover," recalled Lieutenant Perino in a written statement.[25]

His statement continues:

> I briefly paused outside of a courtyard with Sergeant [Mike] Goodale and tried to call Lieutenant Tom DiTomasso … on the radio to get him to guide us to his location at the crash site. He answered me, but I couldn't understand him due to all of the weapons fire around us. As I began to move down the street, a hail of bullets landed where I had been kneeling. One of those bullets hit Sergeant Goodale. He began yelling, "I'm hit! I'm hit."
>
> I looked down and saw a pool of blood gathering underneath him. Surprisingly, his wound did not seem to be too bad, so I immediately grabbed him under the arms and dragged him into the courtyard. Almost immediately, one of our medics ran into the courtyard and began to administer first aid. I checked with the medic who assured me the wound wasn't serious, so I headed out into the street and linked up with my lead element. Up the street, I saw two American soldiers about a block ahead. I figured that they were either with the Combat-Search-and-Rescue element or from Lieutenant DiTomasso's chalk.[26]

In the temporary CCP, Hooten's operators were looking to continue moving up to the crash site. "Bart B was seated across from me, Norm and others [were] manning the doorway keeping us safe and evaluating whether we could continue to move further up the street once the threat was reduced. Several other wounded were collected there as well, including Goodale, one of the Ranger kids who was shot in the ass – about which we had many laughs," said Moser.

Steele and his command element had stopped in the street and established a temporary command post [CP] near the tree where the Delta operators had been hit. Steele, Lechner, and their RTO Sergeant Chris Atwater were attempting to call in close air support from the AH-6s. Atwater's UHF radio was receiving interference from the emergency beacon on Super 61 and Lechner had to rely upon his FM radio to make contact with the pilots. They had placed bright orange VS-17 panels on the ground to mark their position from the air and Lechner vectored in Barber 52, who conducted two quick passes to establish the location of friendly forces before swinging back in and engaging targets north up Marehan Road with his miniguns.

Hooten tried to warn Steele and his headquarters element that they were in a kill zone but despite Hooten's warnings, Steele refused to move his CP into one of the buildings to either side of the street. Hooten explained:

> Captain Steele and [Lieutenant] Jim Lechner stopped at the same debris pile that Chris, Mike Moser, and I had hunkered down [behind], I remember looking out and telling Captain Steele, "You've got to move." A couple of guys [Somalis] popped up over a wall and dumped a mag on them and hit Jim Lechner in the leg and a Ranger RTO [Atwater] was shot as well. Lechner was very severely wounded. I remember seeing bone fragments on the ground when they went out to get him. He was bleeding profusely.

Mike Moser heard the firing that struck Lechner and watched Bart B leap into immediate action:

> Shortly another burst or two sent a round through the open doorway and into the wall above Bart's head, as Jim Lechner, who was still out in the street at this time, was also hit. Bart ran out to assist him, and we all withdrew deeper into the residence. Jim's calf was shattered badly – bullets do nasty things to bone – and he was in a great deal of pain.

Hooten, Smith, and an A-Team operator, Dan N, ran out to provide covering fire as Bart B dragged Lechner into cover.

The incident would provoke some controversy in the "hot-wash" debrief after the battle as a number of operators felt that Steele should have moved out into the street immediately and recovered Lechner instead of racing for the cover of the doorway. By Ranger accounts, Steele reportedly did turn around to head back out as soon as he made cover but the Delta medic had already reached Lechner and was bringing him in off the street.

Further ahead, Lieutenant Perino's chalk were now nearing the crash site. He recounted:

> As the first man in my lead element was crossing a small alleyway, a large volley of fire from the west erupted, but luckily, he was able to dive out of the way and crawl to safety. The next few Rangers crossed and established covering positions for the rest of the element to cross. I waited for the signal from the man ahead of me and then sprinted across the alleyway. I got halfway across when bullets began kicking up the dirt at my feet. The man covering me, Corporal James [Jamie] Smith, fired a 40mm high-explosive round from his M203 grenade launcher toward the unknown assailant, and the enemy fire ceased by the time I finished crossing.[27]

Perino successfully linked up with Chalk 2 and the CSAR element and soon began to distribute their Rangers to reinforce the perimeter around the downed helicopter. Enemy fire was now increasing from the west as Somalis who had converged on the objective were heading toward the crash site. Perino's statement further recounts:

> The Somalis began volley firing RPGs at our location, and bullets ricocheted off the walls over our heads. My M60 machine gunners and M249 squad automatic weapon gunners were engaging enemy targets of opportunity and met with some success. The moment any Somali with a weapon popped out, he was killed. Our M203 grenade launchers were also very effective neutralizing Somalis firing at us from the windows of buildings.[28]

After taking cover behind a set of stairs leading into a courtyard, Perino attempted to engage a number of gunmen that had narrowly missed him when his grenadier, Corporal Jamie Smith, was hit. "I yelled at the men behind me to help move Corporal Smith and that I needed a medic immediately. We dragged Corporal Smith up the stairs where I had been taking cover moments before and moved him into a small courtyard." Perino continued:

> A medic [Delta medic Kurt S] arrived at my location almost immediately and began to treat Corporal Smith. I radioed Captain Steele that I had another casualty and was down to ten men. I left the courtyard and ran into Staff

Sergeant Elliott. I told him that Corporal Smith was wounded and that a medic was treating him in the courtyard behind me. Corporal Smith had two IVs running, and another soldier had two hands buried in Smith's inner thigh, attempting to stop the bleeding. Smith was not doing too well: the bullet had severed his femoral artery, and the wound was too high on the leg to apply a tourniquet. The only way to stop the bleeding was by direct pressure.[29]

Whilst the medics worked to save Corporal Smith's life, the Rangers established security as best they could. Captain Steele and most of the wounded moved into the building with Hooten's operators. There were now several disparate groups in the vicinity of the crash site: Steele and his Rangers furthest away to the south with Hooten's men; elements of A-Team and B-Team in the next building up who were still trying to make their way further up the street; Perino's chalk in a building at the end of the alleyway leading to Super 61 with the critically wounded Corporal Smith; Ground Force Commander Miller and G-Team opposite the intersection; and the combined force of DiTomasso's Chalk 2 and the CSAR around the helicopter itself.

Tom DiTomasso commented:

Chalks 1 and 3 and the rest of the assault force made the move east and north. That's when Corporal Jamie Smith got hit and that whole foot patrol stopped. It was like hitting a wall of lead because the crowds to their north at the crash site were shooting through the crash site and it was like grazing fire further down the road as Chalk 1 and 3 approached.

At the crash site, the heavy firefight continued. Belman recalled: "It's hard to convey just how much fire there really was. It was basically non-stop from almost every direction before nightfall and then things tapered off a little in terms of getting direct fire." There also appeared to be at least some primitive organization to the SNA: "I think there was some level of command and control," explained DiTomasso. "They weren't stupid. Some of them were experienced fighters but I think part of their demise was that they adopted kamikaze tactics. We literally had people running at us and just firing away with no cover at all. They would just run down the street – part of it was, because it was Sunday, they were all high on Khat."

Khat was a narcotic that was widely popular amongst the Somalis. Chewed, it provides an amphetamine-like effect that can lead to hyperactivity. It would typically be consumed in the early to mid-afternoon. The arrival of Task Force Ranger was unfortunate in that the battle commenced during the peak of this cycle.

"It seemed like everybody had a gun. There were children and women running around the crash site carrying AKs, there were women running around with baskets of RPG rounds … They just kept attacking," remarked DiTomasso. "We had individuals who were spotting – that alleyway we were in extended for a long period to the west," said Belman. "There's a rise in the road so if you were a Somali trying to shoot at us, you wouldn't necessarily be able to see where we were. So they did have people who were pointing and spotting; I think there may have been some heavy weapons and RPG folks who were benefiting from that spotting."

The rules of engagement were understood in the main but individual Rangers clarified with their leadership or Delta operators around the circumstances of particular targets such as women carrying RPG rounds or the unarmed civilians acting as spotters. Belman recounted the difficulty engaging unarmed individuals who nonetheless were participating in offensive action against the Rangers:

> That was the only time, there was a definite pause as the person didn't seem to have a weapon. There was definitely pointing, spotting, those kinds of activities that a person just trying to get the hell out of the way wouldn't be doing. Nobody, including the Delta guys, had faced anything like what was going on. Some guys had been in Panama, some had been in Grenada, some of the Delta guys had been involved in other small stuff, but no one on the ground that day had been in real, heavy combat before.

Hooten remembered that, unlike in the movie, Aideed's technicals did not feature heavily in the fight. "We saw some technicals early on but they didn't play a big part in the battle. They wouldn't have survived very long in that environment. Any time you got the [AH-6] gun birds out, they'd disappear pretty quickly." Aideed wasn't about to lose his vaunted technicals. In Somalia, the number of technicals under a warlord's control directly equated to that warlord's influence and power. In any case, the AH-6s would have made short work of any technicals that threatened the crash site.

"The Somalis were definitely trying to kill us. Whether they were actually trying to organize an assault to overrun us, that I don't know, but they were certainly trying to get into positions to shoot at us. I'd see people sticking their heads out of windows, sticking their weapons around corners, kind of bobbing in and out and then firing at us," commented Belman. "It was difficult to tell between an RPG explosion and a hand grenade explosion. At the other side of the helicopter [at the cockpit end], they had grenades being thrown over a wall. I could hear them going off but I couldn't see it."

The Rangers and operators were returning the enemy fire. Belman added:

> It was not a free-for-all but you're also laying down suppressive fire. If you're taking fire from a certain area you're going to shoot at that certain area to prevent that guy from shooting at you. I went in with a basic load of 210 [5.56mm] rounds so seven [30 round] magazines and went through that relatively quickly. We resupplied from people getting wounded. The ammunition became a concern very early on.

Rangers were still being hit and PJ Wilkinson would respond without a second thought. He repeatedly braved the incoming fire from all directions to attend to the wounded Rangers. Each time, he leapt to his feet and cried, "Cover me!" before darting out with his medic's bag. Steele later commented that "These trips across the open street were at the peak of the battle when enemy fire was at its most intense. We were receiving intense and accurate small-arms fire. His repeated acts of heroism saved the lives of at least four soldiers."[30]

The CSAR element eventually used pre-made breaching charges to blow holes through intervening walls to strongpoint their location, with the aim of moving the CCP out of the alleyway and into a building where it could be better protected from fire. Belman carried C4 plastic explosive with him for this very task, as did the EOD technician. He explained: "We had moved our casualties into these adjacent buildings that we had connected by blowing holes in the walls."

The Kevlar pads from the helicopter they had been using as makeshift cover around the CCP under the tail of Super 61 proved to be somewhat less than optimal protection as Belman remembered:

A guy named John Waddell [a Ranger Specialist from Chalk 2], a good friend of mine who'd been a team leader for me, ended up taking up my position. He was a SAW gunner. He looked at one of the Kevlar pads we had taken from the Black Hawk and [had] propped up in front of me and he told me afterwards that the thing was pretty much completely perforated by bullets except for where I was. My outline non-perforated, the rest like Swiss cheese!

Overhead, the Barber callsigns ran continuous gunruns on targets around the alley guided in by the forward observer, Specialist Joe Thomas. "They're doing runs and the brass is falling on us and it felt like maybe 20 or 30 meters out in front of us tops. They're in close for sure," said Belman. Despite this, they still believed the McKnight ground convoy would be approaching any minute, they would load everyone into the vehicles, and with the AH-6s flying top-cover, return to the airfield. The next radio transmission would change that plan: "I think it was Pat Rogers, the CCT, who was right next to me, and a good friend of mine, just going, 'Shit, another bird's down.'"

# CHAPTER 5

# "WE ARE THEIR ONLY HOPE"

*"I heard something odd and looked skyward to see a Black Hawk overfly us at approximately 75 to 100 feet above ground level. The tail rotor had been damaged and the fin was dangling. The bird remained airborne and continued in the direction of the airport beyond my sight."*

Staff Sergeant Michael "Mike" Moser, B-Team, 1 Troop, C-Squadron

## "WE ARE THEIR ONLY HOPE"

**1641 HOURS: SUPER 64 IS DOWN – RPG; GRID 36402625, SUPER 62 FAST-ROPES 2 X SNIPERS ON SITE. JOC DIRECTS ASSAULT FORCE ASSIST ASAP. REPORTS: LARGE CROWD MOVING TOWARD SECOND CRASH SITE.**

After Super 61 had been downed by the RPG, Colonel Tom Matthews in the C2 helicopter requested Super 64, piloted by Chief Warrant Officer Class 3 Mike Durant and Chief Warrant Officer Class 4 Ray Frank, to take on their "low CAP" over the battlespace. Super 64 left the holding area to take up an overhead position and provide fire support for the ground forces with its miniguns.

Mike Durant later remembered:

> Well, he [Matthews] calls me to replace 61 and we go around the target maybe three times. And the reason we're doing that is No. 1, to keep moving. No. 2 is to figure out where everybody is, because nobody is where we put them at this point, and they're all trying to move because the order has been given for everyone to consolidate around the crash site.[1]

Durant was aware of the RPG threat and actively trying to negate it as much as possible:

> It's always a threat. I think we understand that much more so now than we did then. But even then, we viewed it as a threat. The problem with that weapon is that there's not a whole lot you can do about it. You have to use cover and concealment and that's about it. We were told they didn't have all that many of them ... which turned out to be false.[2]

Gerry Izzo testified to the seemingly never-ending number of RPGs: "We were getting volleys of RPGs fired at us. It was like flying through a shotgun blast." Colonel Matthews later confirmed that about 200 RPGs were fired at the aircraft on October 3. Using the Black Hawks for fire support over an urban environment during daylight with such a heavy concentration of RPGs may not in hindsight have been the appropriate tactic. Izzo for instance now believed: "[It was a] poor tactic for the daytime. We got away with it at night, but not a good idea in daylight."

Others still maintain that the tactics had relevance. An operator on the assault force who had inserted from Super 61 stated: "I think it was a good plan, but they may have stayed in position too long." Asked whether he thought it was a valid tactic for daytime operations, he noted: "Yes it is, but for limited time and mission specific."

The Somali RPG warheads themselves may have increased the risk to the helicopters. The book *Black Hawk Down* was the first to claim that the RPG warheads used by the Somalis had been "replaced with timing devices to make them explode in midair."[3] Unfortunately there is no source provided for the claim. This idea of specially modified RPG rounds has become received wisdom, although no actual documented evidence seems to exist to definitively support this contention.

Most RPG warheads have a self-destruct mechanism that detonates at 920 meters or around four and a half seconds after the warhead has been fired from the launcher. This means that when fired into the sky at passing helicopters, an airburst effect will be caused as the warhead spews lethal fragments upon its self-destruction at 920 meters.

In conversations with both Task Force Ranger veterans and various EOD personnel with years of experience in Iraq and Afghanistan, including a question posed on my behalf by a former Delta EOD Chief to a group of military and federal law enforcement EOD operators, the author is yet to find anything concrete that indicates the RPG warheads in Mogadishu were in fact modified. "We kinda thought it a little odd that they'd modified the self-destruct feature of the rockets, but we never got any kind of definitive word on that," said Gerry Izzo. Karl Maier had not heard of the modification and believes that the warheads were detonating at their normal self-destruction distance.

One would expect, should such a technique have proven so successful in Mogadishu, that it would have been exported to insurgents in Iraq for example who faced American helicopters in similar urban environments, but according to the EOD experts this hasn't occurred. This is not to say ad hoc field modification of RPG warheads does not occur. Videos from Chechen insurgents in Syria show how to remove the self-destruct mechanism, for instance, but not how to modify it to detonate at different distances.

Most RPG warheads encountered in Somalia were the PG-7 or later variants of the same round, which were designed primarily for engaging armored vehicles and thus to penetrate first and foremost rather than to fragment like the OG-7 anti-personnel warhead. This makes the fragmentation effects of the PG-7 type relatively limited, although of course a near-miss can still be catastrophic to a thin-skinned helicopter.

US Army historian Lester Grau wrote about the Afghan mujahideen tactics during the 1980s, but notes no modification of the warhead itself:

> Should the helicopters be flying further away, it was better to wait until the helicopter was 700–800 meters away and then fire, trying to catch the helicopter with the explosion of the round's self-destruction at 920 meters distance. Chances of hitting a helicopter at this range by the self-destruct mechanism were very limited, but they served to discourage reconnaissance helicopters and air assault landings …[4]

Mark Bowden also mentions the SNA digging pits to channel the lethal backblast of the RPG when fired at elevation against an aerial target. Again this has been difficult to verify but seems like a reasonable field expedient measure. According to Vietnam Special Forces veteran and historian Gordon Rottman, however, examples of RPG-7s have been recovered in Afghanistan fitted with "small steel plates welded to the bottom rim of the blast defector to direct the blast slightly upward for firing at aircraft," so the use of such blast pits is a possibility.[5]

It has also been hinted that the militia received instruction from Sudanese jihadists and indeed there may have been some ad hoc training of SNA elements, specifically for engaging helicopters with the RPG. "Yes, I remember a few of us in the flight saw what looked like some instruction going on. I have no idea where the people were from though," recalled Karl Maier, detailing an incident where a number of militia were observed with RPGs pointing toward the sky during a signature flight prior to October 3.

Whatever the case, as Durant's Super 64 orbited above the crash site it was struck by an RPG as they passed the Olympic Hotel. "I was flying the helicopter and it felt like a speed bump, like when you're going too fast in a parking lot. It hit the tail, just below the tail rotor, and it blew the gearbox apart. The tail rotor didn't leave the aircraft immediately, but it decided to go pretty quickly, and when it did … we started to spin violently," recalled Durant. "I heard a rapidly accelerating whine, an unearthly, building scream, and then the tail rotor assembly completely disintegrated into vapor with an earsplitting bang." Durant continued:[6]

We were in a flat spin and the only way to stop it is to shut the engines off. And when you do that you're not much better off. You have more control but you no longer have engine power, so we hit the ground in a partially powered spin, a spinning flat condition, and the only reason any of us survived is we landed on the wheels.[7]

From the Task Force Ranger radio logs, the pilot of Super 62, Chief Warrant Officer Class 3 Mike Goffena, asked Durant; "64, are you ok?" after he was hit by the RPG. He was answered by a quick "Roger" from Durant. Moments later, as the tail rotor fell apart and the aircraft began its terrifying spin, the pilot declared "Going in hard, going down. Ray! 64 is going down. 64 is down." The aircraft spun an estimated 15 to 20 times from an initial height of some 70 feet in the air. Super 64, nicknamed "Venom" by one of its crew chiefs, Tommy Field, had crashed some 800 meters southwest of the Super 61 crash site.

Durant had managed to keep Super 64 upright as it crashed into a shanty village on the ground and the stricken helicopter landed on its belly, largely intact. Although a relatively open area that had once been a city park, the helicopter faced simple tin and wood structures on three sides and a tin fence ran along behind the crash site. The aircraft hadn't caught alight and to those watching in the JOC, there was a good chance of survivors.

Colonel Matthews ordered the surviving sniper Black Hawk, Super 62, to make a low pass over the crash site, looking for signs of life. They saw Durant struggling to free himself from the cockpit. They also saw movement from Chief Warrant Officer Ray Frank, Durant's co-pilot, and some indication that perhaps one or both of the crew chiefs in the rear of the Black Hawk had survived the impact. Captain Jim Yacone, Goffena's co-pilot in Super 62, reported the sightings to Matthews in the C2 helicopter.

Upon learning of the survivors, the three-man Delta sniper team on board Super 62 immediately volunteered to be dropped near the crash site to establish security until a ground force could fight their way to the location. Their request was denied as Matthews and Harrell examined their options. CSAR had already been deployed and with the extra Ranger platoon removed from the force package, there was no immediate reaction force that could be ferried into the site to secure it.

Matthews instructed Super 62 to provide covering fire from the air whilst he vectored in AH-6 support. Super 62's snipers and doorgunners began

# "WE ARE THEIR ONLY HOPE"

engaging targets to stem the flow of Somali militiamen and armed civilians moving toward the crash site. Goffena, who would tragically pass away in 1998 in an aircraft accident shortly after retiring from the Army, would bring the Black Hawk in low to disperse the mobs with his rotorwash, exposing the ever-present RPG gunners to the Delta snipers and doorgunners. The pilots even dropped flashbang grenades into the crowds in an attempt to dissuade them from nearing the crash site.

Tom DiTomasso commented:

> Originally we had two Black Hawks circling the objective providing overwatch, Super 61 and Super 62, with Army snipers on board. So when Super 64 went down they moved Super 62 over to the 64 crash site to give General Garrison some security of the second crash site. General Garrison and the guys in the JOC could see what was happening there and they could see guys crawling out of the helicopter so they knew that there were crew members still alive. They could also see crowds starting to form around the second crash site.

Colonel Matthews dispatched two of the Barber callsigns to join Super 62 in protecting the crash site until a recovery mission could be mounted. The first to arrive was Barber 51, the flight lead piloted by Randy Jones and Hal Ward. They were met by three RPGs launched at their Little Bird. Despite the RPG fire, Barber 51 managed to get close enough to the crash site to see Ray Franks still alive in the wreckage and to throw down an infrared strobe to mark the location of the helicopter.

Barber 51 attempted to keep back the mobs with repeated minigun gunruns whilst the command team in the C2 Black Hawk weighed their few options. Garrison, Boykin, Matthews, and Harrell had a difficult decision to make. Karl Maier commented: "Task Force Ranger had only 450 people in it, including all of the support guys, so when we're out on the assault, we've got everybody with us. We didn't have a dedicated QRF or anything like that."

Tom DiTomasso explained:

> We'd already employed our CSAR asset. The vehicles – the Humvees and the five-ton trucks – that came forward to the first objective area ... some of the Humvees went back with Blackburn, the rest had loaded up the prisoners and

they were already heading north to try to get to the first crash site but they were getting ambushed so bad and they were so shot up they were losing men, prisoners and vehicles ... General Garrison had nothing else to respond with, except the snipers on Super 62.

Major Ron Cugno, commander of the MH-6 flight in Star 44, even made a request to Matthews for his Little Birds to insert their co-pilots to defend the crash site until friendly ground elements could fight their way through. That would give at least another four guns on the ground, all armed with SAWs. As courageous as the request was, Matthews, understandably concerned that another helicopter might be downed during the insertion, denied repeated requests from Cugno to put his pilots in.

Whilst awaiting a decision from their commanders, Super 62 continued to provide vital fire around the Super 64 crash site, holding the swarming Somalis at bay. The Delta snipers engaged armed militiamen whilst the miniguns kept back the crowds. All the while, the helicopter continued to attract substantial small-arms and RPG fire. Both pilots could hear the rounds striking the aircraft and could only hope that a vital component wasn't hit.

**1655 HOURS: UNABLE TO LEAVE CRASH SITE #1 – CANNOT RECOVER 1 X KIA IN AIRCRAFT.**

There were no easy answers. The Ranger chalks and Delta assaulters from the objective were still fighting their way up to the first crash site and had sustained significant casualties, including the death of Fillmore and the gravely wounded Smith along with a large number of lesser wounded. CSAR and Chalk 2 had their hands full simply securing the first crash site.

DiTomasso recounted:

> I was under the first Black Hawk trying to defend it when I heard on the radio that another Black Hawk had been shot down. Initially we thought, "Okay we're going to go secure it," but we still had [the body of] Cliff Wolcott trapped in the helicopter. We didn't have enough men to secure the crash site and then pick up our casualties and move. We had three men on litters that would take six men to carry in combat any distance at all. All but two guys from Chalk 2 were wounded – you had guys shot in the arm, shot in the leg, but still fighting.

> I watched one Sergeant Major from the SMU [special mission unit] that was on a litter on his back, still shooting his pistol at enemy that would try to climb in through the window where we had the casualties at.

Meanwhile, McKnight's ground convoy had run into ambush after ambush and was struggling to reach the first crash site. Struecker's three-Humvee convoy had made it back to the airfield and was now heading back out in a reinforced convoy of Humvees in an attempt to reach the second crash site. It too was running into continual ambushes and its progress was slowed by roadblocks. From the air, Super 62's pilots could see they would never make it in time.

The snipers in Super 62 were again asking to be inserted near the Super 64 crash site. They could see the growing crowds and knew that the helicopter would be overrun within minutes. Yacone, receiving updates on the situation on the ground and at the first crash site, conveyed the likelihood that it would be some time before the Delta snipers would be relieved by a ground convoy. He discussed options for them to withdraw to an identified landing zone with any wounded they could recover where they could be picked up by Super 62. There simply wasn't room for the helicopter to land directly at the Durant crash site and they had already jettisoned their fast ropes during the initial insertion at the target building.

Boykin recalled: "I said, 'stay above them, use your sniper rifles and just take out anyone you can, fire on anybody who tries to get near that crash.'" One of the snipers, Master Sergeant Gary Gordon, called back and explained that there were simply too many enemy converging on Super 64 and that the crash site would soon be overrun by hostiles: "Sir, put us in." Again Boykin and Garrison refused. Boykin explained that he told them to "use the doorguns on the helicopter if you have to, knock 'em down but don't let 'em get near that crash."[8]

Tom DiTomasso takes up the story:

> The other sniper Black Hawk, Super 62, calls up on the radio and requests permission to put their three Delta snipers into the crash site to defend it because they can see the crowds starting to build there. General Garrison told me this years later; three times they called, three times permission was denied to put Super 62 in. The last time they call, Master Sergeant Gary Gordon, the

Delta team leader, got on the radio and called General Garrison and said "Sir, you've got to put us in."

General Garrison said "Gary, do you know what you're asking for?" And Gary Gordon said "Yes sir, we are their only hope." I submit that this example by Master Sergeant Gordon and Sergeant First Class Shughart is the ultimate leadership lesson. They lived the creed ... "I will never leave a fallen comrade." So Super 62 flies over to Mike Durant's area. They can't use their fast ropes because they've already used them on the target. So they had to find a place where they could hover where the snipers could jump off and run over to the crash site.

As they're making their way over to the crash site, they [Super 62] get hit by machine-gun fire and one of the crew chiefs in the back of the Black Hawk gets shot in the hand, so the youngest sniper Brad H steps up to man the machine gun, that's why only Shughart and Gordon jumped off the bird.

Crew chief Sergeant Paul Shannon had been struck in the hand by a burst of ground fire. At the same time, his minigun suffered a stoppage. The second crew chief, Sergeant Mason Hall, moved across and took over the minigun, clearing the stoppage and getting the weapon back into action. Brad H, the third Delta sniper, took over Hall's minigun on the right hand side of the Black Hawk.

If anyone could pull off such a rescue against all odds, it was the two Delta snipers. Master Sergeant Gary Ivan Gordon, nicknamed "Lobo," was the Sniper Team Leader. A former member of the 10th Special Forces Group before passing Selection and the Operator Training Course, he had joined Delta in 1986. Gordon was a combat veteran of Panama including the Acid Gambit rescue and had deployed to Saudi Arabia on standby to conduct special operations should Saddam Hussein break the ceasefire agreement negotiated to end Operation *Desert Storm*.

Despite his profession, one that he undoubtedly excelled at, Gordon was a study in contrasts. He wrote poetry to his wife whilst on deployments, built furniture, and was a budding author of fiction for children. Alongside Gordon was Sergeant First Class Randall D. Shughart, a former Ranger from the 2nd Battalion. Shughart was raised on a dairy farm but from a young age knew the military was his calling. He joined the Rangers straight from high school. He passed OTC and had also joined Delta in 1986 as an

# "WE ARE THEIR ONLY HOPE"

Assistant Team Sergeant. Both were very experienced and respected operators in C-Squadron's 3 or Sniper Troop.

The pilots of Super 62 spotted the only clear landing zone amid a sea of decrepit buildings and debris and flared over it to blow away some of the rubbish littering the ground. They hovered briefly to allow the two snipers to jump the five feet from the aircraft. Shughart became entangled in his safety harness as he exited the Black Hawk and had to be cut free by a crew chief. Gordon leapt out but fell hard as he landed. They both righted themselves and looked to the Black Hawk pilot for an indication of the direction they should head.

DiTomasso explained:

> Jim Yacone was one of the pilots on Super 62 and he says that when Shughart and Gordon got off, the only thing Jim could do was point in the direction of the crash site and say, "It's that way." Remember back then we didn't have GPS, guys didn't have GPS on their wrists, we didn't have airborne ISR [Intelligence, Surveillance and Reconnaissance] helping these guys navigate.

One of the crew chiefs then threw a smoke grenade to mark the direction of the crash site. Boykin recalled, "They kicked down a small wall and fought their way in to the crash."

Whilst they hovered, Yacone undid his seatbelt and grabbed his MP5 submachine gun to accompany the two Delta snipers "as he had a better idea of where they were. The pilot in command [Goffena] reached over and grabbed him by the arm and said, 'No, I need you up here to help me fly the aircraft, you don't need to be jumping into this hornet's nest – you're not an infantryman. You're not going to be as much help as you think you will,'" recalled Gerry Izzo. Yacone stayed in the aircraft. "They find this area 300 meters away from Durant's helicopter and Shughart and Gordon jump off that bird with an M4 [CAR15], a modified M14, and two .45-caliber pistols," continued DiTomasso.

**1701 HOURS:** SUPER 62 TAKING REGULAR/CLOSE RPG FIRE; MOST FROM WEST SIDE OF 2ND CRASH SITE.

Super 62 lifted out and moved into an orbit overhead of the crash site, attracting numerous RPGs which trailed through the air around the helicopter. Delta sniper Brad H and one of Super 62's crew chiefs continued to engage the gunmen from the air with the miniguns, trying to buy Shughart and Gordon some vital time whilst the two operators moved toward the crash site, engaging approaching Somalis with single shots or fast double-taps.

The AH-6s were making gunruns to slow down the crowds racing toward Super 64 whilst Goffena dropped flashbang grenades from his cockpit to try and disperse the mobs. The co-pilots in the Little Birds were even using their personal M16s to try and pick off militiamen. Shughart and Gordon continued to "… make their way 300 meters through the village, through the neighborhood, and find the helicopter. They navigated through that shanty village and found the Black Hawk. They pull everyone out of the Black Hawk, they put them under cover to include Durant and they defend that helicopter," said DiTomasso.

"That's one of those that makes you ask, 'Where do we find men like that?'" Colonel Gary Harrell later remarked. "It wasn't like they just decided they'd hop off the helicopter and thought that somebody would come to their rescue. We had two helicopters down. We had the capacity to get one. We didn't have the capacity to get two. They knew what was going on."[9]

Ten minutes after Super 64 crashed, the Delta operators had arrived at the site. Shughart carried a 7.62mm M14 battle rifle, Gordon a camouflage-painted and sound-suppressed CAR15 carbine. In common with all of the snipers deployed on Super 61 and 62, neither man wore a helmet. The snipers went to the aid of Durant first. Durant told the author that he had no warning that the Delta snipers had arrived: "I did not hear Super 62. They literally appeared at my side." They quickly ascertained the extent of Durant's injuries. He told them, "I thought my leg was broken and I thought there was something seriously wrong with my back, but I had no idea what," and they carefully extracted him from the aircraft.

The snipers then placed Durant on the ground in some concealment, ensured his MP5K submachine gun was loaded and ready to fire, gave him a spare 30-round magazine and then returned to Super 64 to extract the other casualties. First they brought out the grievously injured crew chief Bill Cleveland and then went back for Ray Frank and the other crew chief Tommy Field, attempting to establish some form of casualty collection point. Durant believes today that his crew chiefs were alive when Super 64 crashed but may well have died soon after. He saw his co-pilot Ray Frank get himself up and out of his seat in the cockpit and sit in the open door of the Black Hawk just before the snipers arrived.

Barber 52 was now overhead and caught a glimpse of the scene below: Ray Frank had been extricated from the wreckage and was sitting behind the aircraft near a tree, Bill Cleveland was being examined by one of the snipers, the other operator was covering the left hand side where another crew member lay on the ground.

With enemy fire increasing minute by minute, Shughart and Gordon tried to locate a closer landing zone as they would have both been acutely aware that they would face extreme difficulty moving two seriously wounded and two critical casualties any distance back to the landing zone previously agreed with Yacone. Durant remembered: "I could tell they were trying to figure out how to get out of there. Because they basically had four litter patients."[10]

The pilots of Star 41 who had earlier extracted Delta snipers Busch and Smith from the Super 61 crash site had heard the call and they were going to attempt another rescue. After dropping off their casualties, Star 41 flew back to the Task Force Ranger hangar to refuel and link up with the rest of the Star flight. As they were refueling, Maier heard "that Mike got shot down on the radio. So I took off and I called Matthews and said, 'Hey I'm heading over there'. We landed at the same spot the Black Hawk dropped off the two operators. The Black Hawk [Super 62] had already taken off." Maier continued:

> It was really the only area [to land]. It looked like there used to be a pretty good-sized building but this was like what was left of the foundations. Everything else around there was a bunch of shanties. So I decided to stay on the ground there rather than risk flying around because at this point any aircraft that was circling around was a) getting shot at and b) was a beacon for everybody to move toward. So that's why we decided to stay on the ground and hopefully hear from Shughart and Gordon.
>
> I never did see the crash site but I thought they would know I was there as it was the only spot you could land near that area. I waited there to hear from somebody. I'm listening to all the radio nets – we had four radios, I had the Air to Air up, the Ground Force Commander net and the team I had been carrying, the assault force, their frequency. I could pretty much hear everything that's going on.

> I'm going to guess we were on the ground for 10 or 12 minutes and then we got another call [from Matthews]: "Get out of there – the crowds are converging." Well, this time we did because we could see them, they were coming. So we waited a little longer until they got a little bit closer and then we pulled pitch. When I took off I tried to find Mike's crash site but I never could get it in sight. Once I got in the air, the boss told me to head back to our base.

Maier related that, even after he returned to the airfield, he wanted to go back in and attempt another extraction:

> I wanted to go back in there with two of our guns [AH-6s] as escort and get vectored in, because the guys up in the C2 could see the crash site, and land on the damned crashed helicopter and get those guys out of there. I wanted to try something. I was jumping up and down in the TOC and finally the Colonel told me to get the hell out of the TOC!

It is difficult even after interviewing multiple participants who were overhead at the time, and with access to the operations log's contemporary timeline, to be entirely accurate regarding how long the snipers fought. Gerry Izzo in Super 65 thought that "20 minutes is about right," but conceded "we're all shaky on time," certainly understandable after the intervening 25 years. Maier agreed with Izzo's estimate but added that it could've been a little longer.

Shughart and Gordon had placed Durant in a tactically advantageous position. From his location next to a tree on the right side of the helicopter, with the tin wall behind him, he could cover that entire side of the Black Hawk. Any Somalis hoping to approach had to maneuver around the wall that Durant had covered some 15 feet away from him. The snipers gently extracted the grievously wounded Bill Cleveland from the wreckage and laid him down behind Durant.

Hearing voices through the thin tin wall, Durant fired off some rapid shots from his MP5, surprising both Delta snipers who hadn't realized the pilot still had fight left in him. Durant experienced multiple stoppages with his MP5, believing he hadn't been strict enough on his weapons maintenance regime. Frustratingly he was forced to eject a number of live rounds to clear the weapon.

The Delta snipers had moved back around the front of the aircraft on the left hand side and were engaged in a vicious firefight as the militia closed in. Durant could hear the AK47s being met with single, aimed shots as the operators engaged them. As he registered the sounds of Somalis moving behind the tin wall, he would fire single shots through it in an effort to discourage them.

He engaged another Somali who attempted to climb over the wall. The pilot killed a Somali who had been attempting to sneak up on the snipers but he was low on ammunition, already down to his last magazine. Finally, he fired his last round and the MP5 clicked empty. Durant explained that for whatever reason he didn't even remember his 9mm Beretta M9 pistol in its drop holster. Despite this, he incredibly still managed to bat away a hand grenade that was thrown over the wall with his empty MP5.

The operators were firing both their rifles and their .45 pistols, transitioning to the sidearms as they changed rifle magazines. Both were beginning to run low on ammunition. The AK47 fire was now constant with rounds aimed from all directions at the helicopter. One of the snipers was finally hit by a Somali bullet. Whether it was Gordon or Shughart is still open to question. Durant initially recalled it as being Shughart who was hit first, remembering him crying out, "I'm hit." The pilot didn't see the operator get shot as both snipers were around at the front of the downed Black Hawk, out of Durant's field of vision. He later said in a CNN interview that: "It's like being shot down initially, because now one of the guys you thought was indestructible has just been taken down."[11]

As Super 62 made another pass overhead, Goffena saw one of the operators get hit. Moments later, Goffena's aircraft was struck by an RPG. "Super 62 had no doors fitted because it was summer time and an RPG came through that door, hit Brad H in the leg, [causing a] traumatic amputation of the leg. It knocked the two pilots out cold," recounted DiTomasso. The wounded Delta operator used his own belt to apply a tourniquet to his leg to manage the bleeding. He later became the first man to be fitted with a bionic prosthesis and became so adept with the device that he rejoined Delta before finally retiring from the Army as a Sergeant Major and becoming a certified prosthetist in 2002.

Super 62 was in a bad way. Goffena had been momentarily stunned by the impact. His co-pilot, Jim Yacone, was unconscious. "One of the pilots woke up, the cockpit was full of smoke but the helicopter was still flying," DiTomasso explained. Goffena was quoted as saying: "I thought we had already hit the ground, but when I came to my senses, I realized we were still in the air. All the warning lights came on. My co-pilot was completely out and leaning on the controls."[12] The left side minigun was unmanned but the blast had damaged its firing controls and it continued to fire until it ran through its ammunition belt.

Smoke trailed from the aircraft. Goffena knew he was losing power and height. Up ahead was a set of power lines. The pilot struggled to keep altitude to pass over the wires. Moments later he crash landed at the New Port, bringing the aircraft in hard but in one piece. Had it not been for the incredible skills of Mike Goffena, Task Force Ranger would have been forced to deal with a third downed aircraft in the city.

At the Super 64 crash site, the situation was desperate. Whilst the Little Birds did what they could from the air, the lone surviving sniper was in a single-handed struggle against hundreds of Somalis. The Medal of Honor citations for both men state that Shughart was killed first. Mark Bowden interviewed Delta operator Paul H who said that he believed it was in fact Gordon who was killed first. All of the operators interviewed for this book concur. Durant to this day is unsure, having never met either man personally.

One of the operators, most likely Shughart, returned to the pilot's location after Gordon was hit and asked him whether there were any small arms on board the helicopter as he was running low on ammunition. Durant recalled:

> Then Randy [Shughart] came back up around the nose of the aircraft and he was almost out of ammunition and I was already out of ammunition and he asked about weapons in the aircraft. The crew chiefs had M-16s, so I told him where those were and he came back out and he gave me what I believe to this day was Gary's weapon [a suppressed CAR15]. He made a quick call on the survival radio and we were told that a reaction force was en-route, but what we didn't know was that it was going to take seven hours to get there.[13]

Tragically the 7.62mm M134 miniguns mounted on both sides of the aircraft were useless as they relied upon electrical power generated by the helicopter to operate. Surprisingly there was no backup power source carried for such emergencies. A similar scenario was encountered almost a decade later when a 160th SOAR MH-47 Chinook was shot down by al-Qaeda-affiliated Uzbek insurgents on a remote mountain called Takur Ghar in eastern Afghanistan. Again, the miniguns would have been a distinct advantage in the resulting firefight, but power was lost to the weapons when the Chinook was struck by an RPG.

Shughart had asked the pilot for the radio frequency for the Fire Support Net. Ecklund and McNerney in their Naval Postgraduate School report on the battle confirmed this directly with General Garrison himself:

> the only AN/PRC-112 survival radio ever activated belonged to Durant. Shughart used it to contact 1LT James O. Lechner on Channel B, the Fire Support Net. Lechner forwarded the call to LTC Matthews and LTC Harrell in the C2 MH-60, who in turn ordered him to inform Shughart that "a reaction force is en-route." The Somalis were in control of that radio shortly after that transmission.[14]

Lieutenant Lechner himself recalls:

> one of them took Durant's survival radio, tuned to the fires support net, and sent out the call for help which I received. I passed on the call to the Command and Control ship. I was ordered to inform them that a relief column from the 10th Mountain Division had been requested and was on the way and to hold on. As I was in the middle of a fire mission, I had to abruptly end the conversation. I had no way of knowing it would be the last thing heard from them alive.[15]

It was unusual for the operators to not be to being carrying their own PRC-112 radios but as Kurt Smith recalled, both the Rangers and Delta were guilty of leaving behind mission-critical pieces of equipment based upon their requirements developed over the previous six missions. Indeed Smith specifically mentions leaving behind the survival radio: "I compromised and left behind some non-lethal munitions, my PRC-112 survival radio, and, most significantly, my NODs [night observation device]."[16]

The operators all carried their own Motorola Saber intra-team radios and Shughart also used this at least once to contact Norm Hooten, who carried two such radios, one set on the command frequency, the other on the intra-team frequency. He explained that using preset channels was difficult under fire but even carrying the two dedicated radios became confusing in the heat of battle.

> I remember when I was going toward the first crash site, I got this phantom call from Randy Shughart and he was like, "Where you guys at?" and I said, "We're on our way to the crash site." [Shughart said] "How long you going to be before you get here?" I said, "Hopefully five minutes." I didn't know about the other crash site, we didn't know that another bird had gone down.

Hooten is unsure but thinks fellow operator John M from 3 Troop, Shughart's fellow snipers, may have also received a radio call from him.

After Shughart left Durant with Gordon's CAR15, the surviving sniper returned to the far side of the helicopter. In the CNN interview, Durant said that "the volume of gunfire was unbelievable. I kind of knew there was no way he could hold them all off."[17] Durant described the amount of fire by likening it to the sound of a thunderstorm: "It was like being at the range when there's a company or battalion of people shooting. There was a huge volume of fire and it lasted for a couple of minutes and then it went quiet except for that crazed mob that started to overrun the site."[18] At least 25 Somali corpses surrounded the crashed Black Hawk, a testament to the shooting skills of the two brave Delta defenders.

Garrison, Boykin, and the staff at the JOC watched the horrifying live feed from one of the OH-58Ds as the Somalis overran the crash site: "Garrison turned away from the monitor while shaking his head in disgust; with his ground forces immobilized, he was virtually powerless to affect the battle."[19]

Durant fired off the last of the magazine in the CAR15 and, realizing that both snipers were gone, laid the carbine across his chest and crossed his hands over it.

He commented:

> I mean, I've got no rounds left. I still had my 9mm pistol still in its holster and to be honest with you, I've never been able to explain why I never thought of it. I never even acknowledged that it was there. Don't know why.

C-Team after the successful capture of Osman Atto on September 21, 1993, with Star 42 in the background. Paul Leonard is carrying the M249 second from the left. Note the pilot to his left carrying the compact MP5K submachine gun. (Courtesy Paul Leonard)

B-Team in front of their assigned Little Bird, Star 41, piloted by Karl Maier and Keith Jones. Michael Moser, the team's breacher, is second from the right. Note the operators wear AWS chest rigs over their Faust body armor. (Courtesy Michael Moser)

C-Team from 1 Troop and a wild hog from one of Delta's informal "aerial safaris." Gary Keeney can be seen at the left, next to him is Paul Leonard, and next to Paul is Matt Rierson, C-Team's Team Leader. (Courtesy Paul Leonard)

F-Team pictured with their assigned Little Bird, Star 44. Norm Hooten is to the far right of the image. (Courtesy Paul Leonard)

Bravo Company, 3rd Battalion Rangers posing for a group shot just prior to October 3. Note the mix of desert- and woodland-finish Humvees and the black Progressive Technologies vests worn by the Rangers in the background (including John Belman's CSAR element in the center). Most of the Rangers in the foreground wear the brand new Ranger Body Armour (RBA) vests with woodland pattern covers. (Courtesy 75th Ranger Regiment)

Elements of Bravo Company, 3rd Battalion of the Rangers at the hangar. The building behind them housed the JOC and J-2 team. Note the collapsed rotors on the Little Birds. (Courtesy 75th Ranger Regiment)

The Combat Search and Rescue (CSAR) element pose in front of Super 68, "Razor's Edge." The difference between the Delta Faust vests and the Progressive Technologies vests is obvious. Note the operators using ProTec helmets with goggles. (Courtesy John Belman)

John Belman of the CSAR SST (SAR Security Team) in front of Super 68. Note the RBA vest. (Courtesy John Belman)

Delta operators returning to the hangar after a previous mission. The two MH-6 Little Birds feature "people pods" (officially the External Personnel System) and Fast Rope Insertion/ Extraction System (FRIES) mounts are visible. (Courtesy Private Collection)

A Cargo Humvee (or "Cutvee" as the SEALs christened them) at the New Port in Mogadishu. This particular vehicle belongs to the 5th Special Forces Group but is very similar to those employed as part of the Ground Reaction Force by Task Force Ranger. (HOCINE ZAOURAR/AFP/Getty Images)

US troops in Mogadishu aboard an M923A2 five-ton cargo truck. The same type, with the same field expedient sandbag protection, was used by Task Force Ranger to transport the prisoners from the objective. (HOCINE ZAOURAR/AFP/Getty Images)

The Star MH-6 (unarmed Little Bird with external passenger pods carrying Delta operators) flight launching from the airfield on October 3. (Courtesy US Army)

The Barber AH-6 (armed AH-6 Little Bird) flight launching from the airfield on October 3. Each helicopter carried a pair of 2.75-inch unguided rocket pods and a pair of 7.62mm miniguns. (Courtesy US Army)

A modern image of the MH-6 Little Bird showing the "people pods" and the Fast Rope Insertion Extraction System to good effect. (Luke Sharrett/Bloomberg via Getty Images)

General Mohamed Farah Aideed pictured just before the June 15 raid on the Abdi House. Note that prior to the arrival of Task Force Ranger, Aideed often appeared in public to bolster his supporters. (ALEXANDER JOE/AFP/Getty Images)

The remains of Super 61 after it was destroyed by demolition charges placed by the C-Squadron EOD technician. Note the tumbled-down wall to the left rear, part of the damage caused when the helicopter crash-landed into the alleyway. (STR/AFP/Getty Images)

Another view of the Super 61 crash site looking west toward the intersection with Marehan Road. Karl Maier and Keith Jones landed their Little Bird just to the left of the intersection. Just visible is the building strongpointed by Captain Miller and his operators. (STR/AFP/Getty Images)

The only known image from the ground during the battle, taken from Chalk 1's position at the southeast blocking position looking back along the wall that surrounded the objective building. Tim Watson's Chalk 3 can be seen in the background at the intersection with Hawlwadig Road. The courtyard gate that Delta breached through can also be seen (the blue-colored wall section). A section of the target building is just visible above it. (Courtesy US Army)

Master Sergeant Gary Gordon, who gave his life defending the Super 64 crash site and was posthumously awarded the Congressional Medal of Honor: "Master Sergeant Gordon's extraordinary heroism and devotion to duty were in keeping with the highest standards of military service and reflect great credit upon him, his unit and the United States Army." (Courtesy US Army)

Sergeant First Class Randy Shughart, who gave his life defending the Super 64 crash site and was posthumously awarded the Congressional Medal of Honor. The citation notes that Shughart and his fellow sniper Gary Gordon "unhesitatingly volunteered to be inserted to protect the four critically wounded personnel, despite being well aware of the growing number of enemy personnel closing in on the site." (Courtesy US Army)

An aerial view of the Super 64 crash site taken on October 20, 1993. The tree under which Durant was placed is visible along with the tin wall. The image underlines the close ranges faced by Shughart and Gordon with ample cover and concealment for attackers to approach within meters of the downed Black Hawk. (Courtesy US Special Operations Command)

I was totally focused on the MP5 and we believe it was a CAR15 that Randy gave me, and when I was out of ammunition in my mind I was out of ammunition. Quite honestly, in looking back, and trying to speculate, I probably would have just gotten myself killed as they came around the corner if I had been pointing a pistol at them. So maybe it was a good thing. Still regardless, I still had the 9mm [pistol] and never pulled it out of the holster.[20]

With the two Delta snipers dead, the Somalis raced forward in a bloodlust toward Super 64, howling like injured animals. Durant awaited the inevitable as the mob surged into and around the helicopter, a screaming, teething mass of violence hammering their fists against the metal skin of the crippled Black Hawk.

# CHAPTER 6

# "RANGER, RANGER. YOU DIE SOMALIA"

*"Every time we stopped, bad shit was happening."*

**Sergeant Matt Eversmann, Chalk 4**

## "RANGER, RANGER. YOU DIE SOMALIA""

At the Super 64 crash site, it didn't take long for Durant to be spotted by the Somali mob. They swarmed over him, mercilessly punching and kicking him, and tearing off his equipment. A militiaman hauntingly declared, "Ranger, Ranger. You die Somalia!" as the mob attacked him. At one horrific point he was clubbed over the head with a dismembered arm, torn from one of his crew mates or from one of the fallen Delta snipers. His nose, cheekbone, and eye socket were all broken in the onslaught. Durant recounted:

> It was minute to minute. I think initially, I thought it was over. I mean, we'd been briefed on what they would probably do. When I do talk about this with people, I compare it to what happened to the Blackwater guys at the bridge in Fallujah [in 2004].* I mean, that's what they did. It's the same thing. So, I'm thinking that's what's gonna happen and I can't stop them.[1]

At least two of his compatriots suffered such a grisly fate, torn limb from limb in a macabre display of brutality. All of Task Force Ranger knew that this was the grim likelihood if they fell into Somali hands. Earlier that year, Nigerian peacekeepers had been mutilated and Somali civilians had been reported as playing football with their decapitated heads. Capture was a pilot's greatest fear.

The mob tried to tear Durant's uniform off but when they discovered he was not wearing any underwear they inexplicably left his trousers on. He was still being beaten senseless by the mob when gunshots rang out and SNA militiamen stepped forward to stop the crowds. The SNA claimed Durant as the property of Aideed and carried him roughly away to a waiting truck, surrounded by the mobs that still continued to strike him despite the presence of the militia. The women were particularly vicious, Durant noted that they were grabbing his genitals and attempting to castrate him.

"At the crash site, I could only see men, but as I was carried through the streets there were women who attacked me. I couldn't see much, but caught glimpses of them," Durant explained. He was later told by his captors that the Somali women were indeed the cruelest when exacting revenge. One wonders if women were involved in the desecration of the flight crew and snipers'

---

\* Four private military contractors from Blackwater USA were killed in Fallujah, Iraq on March 31, 2004, after their soft-skinned SUVs were ambushed. Their burnt bodies were mutilated and hung from a bridge.

bodies. Nothing, not even the vaunted SERE [Survival, Evasion, Resistence, and Escape] School, had prepared Durant for the experience of being surrounded by a violent, baying crowd intent upon his death. "Even if they [SERE] tried, I don't see how it could come anywhere close to the real experience," he added.

"They [the Somalis] grab Durant, he's the last one they find, they strip off all of his equipment, and an elder steps forward and says 'Let's keep this one alive for negotiations,'" commented Tom DiTomasso. James Lechner noted an alternative motivation for the capture of Durant: "[Durant] was only saved by the timely intervention of the son of Osman Atto, who happened to be at the scene, and wanted a live prisoner in the hopes of trading for his father."[2] This alternate scenario has never been confirmed.

Mike Durant was roughly carried to a flatbed truck, covered by a blanket or tarp and then sat upon by militiamen, further injuring his broken leg and the crushed vertebrae in his back. The femur had now broken through the skin and was bleeding profusely. As he later learned, the covering they threw over him was to disguise his presence from other Somali clans and bandits as much as from the American helicopters overhead. Durant was told after his release that the Navy P-3 had recorded the overrun of the crash site and the Somalis carrying him away but they had lost the trail once he disappeared into the teeming mobs. "And they're reporting this over the radio, we're all hearing it but there's nothing we can do about it," DiTomasso remembered, the frustration still evident in his voice decades later.

Back at the objective, McKnight's Ground Reaction Force had been ordered to move to the first crash site minutes after Super 61 was shot down. The prisoners had been restrained and placed in one of the five-ton trucks and the convoy left the target building intending to conduct a straightforward movement north and then east to arrive at the crash. What looked to be a relatively simple movement on paper, or from on high up in the C2 Black Hawk, proved to be anything but down on the ground.

The convoy consisted of three Humvees in the lead, including the SEAL Cutvee, followed by the two remaining five-ton trucks, and with three more Humvees in trail behind the trucks. One of the five-tons carried C-Team, the pair of Delta snipers, and the detainees along with the wounded Ranger Staff Sergeant who was now on a collapsible litter. The prisoners were probably in the safest place in the truck, down on the floor surrounded by sandbags. The other five-ton was empty save for its driver, Ranger Private Richard "Alphabet" Kowalewski.

Matt Eversmann was one of the last to climb aboard as the convoy headed off. He recalled:

> We're stuffing everyone onto vehicles wherever we can. I was the last on because I was doing the last sweep to make sure we haven't left anybody and the vehicles start to move. Thankfully they stop. I remember climbing up one of these pick-up truck style ones with the wooden sides [cargo Humvee] and turning around and leaning backwards because I wanted to be able to face out and I toppled over with my legs hanging over the side. I couldn't sit up and that was without a doubt one of the scariest moments for me. I remember sitting there thinking "We're going into harm's way and I can't even sit up to shoot back," I was thinking "I hope it doesn't hurt!" It wasn't until we made a turn someplace and stopped that I was able to position myself upright.

The Somalis were now split between those heading to the undefended southern crash site of Super 64, the northern crash site of Super 61 where CSAR and Chalk 2 were defending the perimeter, and the original target building. Reinforcements were still channelling from the northern end of Hawlwadig Road and the GRF ran into an incredible amount of fire as they attempted to head east from the objective.

Paul Leonard, in the first of the five-ton trucks, guarding the prisoners, recalled: "They were blocking the road, they were lighting fires. It was crazy trying to get out of there. We were losing guys left and right." Eversmann added: "There was a ton of them. Someone smarter than me said there were estimates of 10,000 Somalis fighting for Aideed on October 3rd and 4th."

Leonard noted:

> Every time we went through an intersection it was like there was more and more Somalis at each intersection. Every time we went a block there'd be more people shooting at us. The Rangers would stop – I told the driver, "Don't stop at the intersections," because we were sitting ducks. Each intersection was like an ambush. It was their inexperience unfortunately. You know the Rangers are best at what they do. The Rangers then were the best small unit fighting force – but they just weren't used to working with the level

of soldier that we were. In fact lots of Delta operators were Ranger prior to coming to the Unit.

As the convoy worked its way north, McKnight was informed that Super 64 had been downed, south of the Olympic Hotel. The new orders were still to head to the Super 61 crash site, load all personnel back onto the convoy's Humvees and trucks and then head down to the second crash site. McKnight was also told the 10th Mountain QRF had been scrambled and were heading to the airfield prior to launching a second ground convoy to secure the Super 64 crash site.

The GRF's vehicles were already fully loaded meaning that, even if they made it to the second crash site, they would be unable to drive everyone out on the vehicles. In the absence of another CSAR asset or the standby platoon of Rangers that had been trimmed from the force package, it was, however, the best, and only, plan they had. Unknown to McKnight and the GRF, Struecker's battered three-Humvee convoy, reinforced by a scratch force drawn from the cooks, armorers, and security detail at the hangar, would also soon enter the fray attempting to reach the second crash. As we shall see, this heroic effort was frustrated by both continual Somali ambushes and the quality and timeliness of the directions given to Struecker from the air.

The GRF continued its lethal traverse of the city. A number of times the convoy abruptly halted, either due to confusion on the directions supplied by the C2 helicopter or because they had run into another roadblock. The fire was intense but no more so than at the intersections, which saw Somalis on either side wildly firing at the convoy.

"[When the vehicles are stopped] clearly it's a lot better to get out of the vehicles and fight. It also seemed that at each stop someone was wounded and was lying in the street. You'd get up to administer aid and get them to safety," said Matt Eversmann. "[At the intersections] it was the most unbelievable thing. You could see these people – their battle drill was just to line up on both sides of the street, face center and then shoot while the Americans are passing through. There's no telling how many casualties the Somalis inflicted on their own. Unbelievable to watch this happening."

Gary Keeney noted:

> That convoy stopped three or four times during the entire lost convoy fiasco. One of those times, the worst of it happened. Every time that convoy stopped

we were a target and people were dying and people were getting shot, people were getting injured. As long as the convoy was moving, we were safer. We were harder for them to hit us with RPGs.

Keeney remained on the truck carrying the prisoners. He explained:

> The six operators posted three to each side of the five-ton truck: front left Mike F, front right Matt Rierson, middle right was Paul Leonard, and I was in the back right corner. Alex and Joe were on the left side. Because I was in the back I had visibility of [Ranger Private Richard "Alphabet"] Kowalewski [who was driving the truck behind Keeney and the operators] and he kept stopping at the intersections so he's receiving fire up and down, left and right. We were trying to tell him that – "Don't stop at the intersection. Stop short or come up with us and stop forward." The one stop that cost him his life was that he stopped again at a spot that wasn't good. The RPG that hit his vehicle came from an alley directly to his left side.

Kowalewski had already been shot once in the shoulder and was struggling to control his vehicle under the constant hail of gunfire. Keeney continued:

> It was like slow motion, I didn't see the RPG flying through the air but I saw the RPG's explosion hitting the front left of the truck around the driver's door, between the driver's door and the engine compartment. When it exploded I saw a head, and it wasn't a head it was a helmet, but I thought it was a head, flew out the passenger window. He was alone in the vehicle, the only guy in the front cab.
>
> Kowalewski went unconscious or was immediately killed, his foot came off the brake and his truck rolled forward and collided with our truck. His truck then stalled. Our driver separated us from his truck and that's when I got down off the truck. Matt Rierson said "Greedy, go help with that casualty" or something to that effect. I ran around to the truck and a [Ranger] E5 was already there and looking at me and hollering for my assistance. "Sergeant, Sergeant, I can't get him out, I can't get him out, he's stuck." So I climbed into the five-ton through the passenger door and I looked at Kowalewski and I knew he was gone.
>
> So I crawled up on top of him to work out why he was stuck and basically all it was, was a piece a webbing from his LBE [load bearing equipment] that

was stuck around some jagged metal. Once I unhooked it off the jagged metal, he came right out. So I pulled him out and then me, and that E5 threw him in the back of the nearest Humvee that ended up having [Delta Direct Support Special Forces Medic] Glenn I in it. When I went back into the [immobilized] five-ton to recover any equipment, I grabbed his pistol … and I looked down at the floorboard and part of his arm and hand were there. I remember picking it up and I gave it to the E5 who was standing there and I said, "Throw this in the vehicle with him."

Kowalewski had actually been struck by a second RPG that hadn't detonated or was struck by a part of the first as it exploded. In either case, there was what appeared to be a live RPG warhead embedded in his body. "I didn't know there was an RPG in his chest," said Keeney. "I didn't see it, I didn't observe it. What came out later when we pulled him off [the Humvee] was that there was a live ordnance RPG round inside his body. I don't even know if it was a full round, it might've actually just been the tailfins, I don't know. That second five-ton never went back with us. When we pulled Kowalewski out of there we left the vehicle." The Explosive Ordnance Disposal detachment at the airfield were notified of the RPG as the convoy finally headed back and Kowalewski's body was later placed in a sandbagged bunker before the warhead could be made safe.

Again, the convoy began to slowly move off under intense fire from all directions. Somalis were firing down from rooftops, alleyways, and doorways, spraying a manic burst or launching an RPG before ducking back into cover. As they braved the gauntlet of fire, another Ranger was shot and killed, this time Ranger Specialist James Cavaco who had been manning an Mk19 on one of the Humvees.

Paul Leonard recalled the incident vividly:

I was in the back of this five-ton and Cavaco, I saw him get shot right in the face. The Rangers weren't getting up on the Mk19 because they'd get shot at. The Rangers seemed to be getting a little freaked out. I look at Matt [Rierson] and say "Hey Matt, want me to get on that gun?" and he says "Get on it" so I run back there. This is where my inexperience in combat comes in – I take my CAR15 and lay it in the back of the Humvee and Matt's yelling at me – he goes "Hey put that gun around your neck!" so I put my CAR15 back over my neck and get up on top.

Matt Eversmann, who had been out in the street assisting with the casualties ran to get on board one of the departing Humvees only to make a grim discovery: "I jumped into the back of a Humvee and I jumped on top of a young Ranger who'd been killed and I think it was Cavaco." Keeney remembered the effect Cavaco's death had on his fellow Rangers: "When Cavaco got shot, I remember a couple of Rangers in that vehicle, they allowed the situation and the death of their team leader to overcome their emotions and their actions," He recalled. "They just went to tears because that was the first time they'd seen someone die. It kinda messed them up there for a little bit until they got back in the fight at some point."

Paul Leonard was now on Cavaco's Mk19. He recounted:

We're sitting there and I've only got several rounds left before I needed to reload. I asked "Do we have another can of Mk19 rounds?" The Rangers told me we had another can. So not to waste the few rounds I had left before I needed to reload, I saw a few bad guys moving up the road towards us. Bounding from parked vehicles on the side about 800 yards away.

I was inside the Humvee while we were waiting to move to avoid being shot at. I tap the 18-year-old Ranger who was driving on the shoulder. Watch this, I pointed [out] one of the guys bounding toward us, I fired a single round at the guy, and I almost couldn't believe it myself, the round landed right in front of him and exploded. I repeated that several times, I was having a lucky day. I reloaded the Mk19 before we started to move again.

The convoy had by now turned north, heading on a road parallel to Hawlwadig and were directly east of the target building when the third Humvee in the column was hit by an RPG. Paul Leonard recalled:

Just soon after that, we went around a corner, took a left, then right, and I remember a huge concussion [wave] as an RPG hit Grizwold's [Tim Martin's] vehicle. It literally turned it sideways. It turned our vehicle sideways. I was shooting at a bunch of people in front of us and I yelled at a Ranger to help Grizwold. Grizwold was on the ground. It looked like his legs were split and were up by his ears, he was so messed up. And his chest, where most of us keep our magazines for the CAR15, all the springs were popping out of his [magazines]. It was crazy looking.

Tim Martin was grievously wounded, although not to the same extent as shown in the film where he is depicted being blown in half. Matt Eversmann said:

> There were a couple of guys lying in the street and I jumped out of the Humvee. Tim Martin was lying there, he's still alive and I remember running right up to him. He'd been hit right through his hip, his leg was at a terrible angle and disfigured. The first thought is to get him behind some cover.
>
> I reached down to grab him and drag him to cover but he had on Nomex gloves and they slipped right off. So I grabbed his shirt or his vest or something. By that time somebody else was there. I know there were more people there quickly with more medical skills than I do. [Ranger Private] Adalberto Rodriguez got hit and was lying there too. He got hit through the thigh. We moved him, at this point it was get back on the vehicles and let's get out.

The two operators who took over from Eversmann were Gary Keeney and "Doc" Don H, a Delta Direct Support Special Forces Medic who both "grabbed Griz off the street and we put him in the five-ton with us, the other operators. He was still conscious."

Leonard was still firing the Mk19 to suppress the enemy fire:

> I remember a woman pointing at us. I took my eye off what I was doing for a brief moment, then I told someone to take care of Grizwold and then I shot this lady in front of me that was pointing at me. I could see a gun around the corner of a wall so I took off the side of the wall with the Mk19 – I only had like three rounds left. I took my focus off what I was doing because I was obviously focusing on shooting somebody before they shot me and I got shot.
>
> All of a sudden, it was like a hot hammer hit me in the leg, it was like a hot poker. The Rangers are trying to get me off the vehicle and I was still shooting. I told myself, "I don't have time for this nonsense. I'm too busy." My peripheral vision was diminishing because of the blood loss – from that point also my vision was black and white, I didn't see color anymore – and I'm asking the Rangers to get a tourniquet around my knee, "Who's got a tourniquet?" and nobody had because they were using them on everyone else so I took a first aid bandage, put it behind my knee and cranked on it

## "RANGER, RANGER. YOU DIE SOMALIA'"

to put some pressure on it. I felt like I was going to black out. There was a case of litre bottles of water and I drank two of them and I felt better. My vision seemed to improve some but the colour did not return for several days.

The Rangers are trying to bandage my leg while I'm still shooting the Mk19. They wouldn't move until they got my leg bandaged up, I said "Okay, bandage my leg up and let's go!" It was an AK round that took off the front of my shin, it was pretty messed up, I'm very fortunate to have my leg.

Matt Eversmann was likely in the back of that same Humvee and helped trying to treat Leonard's wound. He recalled: "I do remember somebody got shot in the leg, I kinda remember trying to wrap a bandage on and it could have been him [Paul Leonard]."

"I remember looking over and seeing Paul had been hit. He wasn't all the way up on the gun and there was a look between me and him and there might have been some words that weren't heard but were spoken that he was letting me know that he was fucked up, he was hurting in a bad way," recalled Gary Keeney. Still the convoy rolled on.

Delta operator Tim "Griz" Martin in the five-ton was still conscious. Gary Keeney was with him:

> I will never forget this. We were coming back in that five-ton after we'd gotten moving again after that last terrible and tragic stop and Griz reached up to grab my hand. He wanted to hold a fellow comrade's hand. The fact that he wanted to hold my hand … he knew he was in a bad way and he needed to reach out to somebody and I was the guy there. He's holding my hand and I'm trying to reassure him it's going to be okay and we're heading back.
>
> It didn't last long, maybe 30 seconds or 20 seconds and then once I said, "Griz, I kinda need that hand back because it's got my trigger finger on it." As soon as I said that, he let my hand go. He was a professional to the end. All this time Doc H is there, packing his wounds full of Kerlix. He's just working on him. Looking back on it, Griz was in shock.

More tragedy unfolded. Ranger Sergeant Lorenzo Ruiz who had replaced the wounded Private Othic on the .50 cal on the rear Humvee was shot, the round penetrating under his right arm into his chest and causing what is known as a sucking chest wound. Ruiz would later be evacuated from the airfield to the US trauma hospital in Germany but sadly died during the flight.

At the third stop, Eversmann lost one of his Chalk 4 Rangers, Sergeant Casey Joyce. He recounted:

> We stop, we all get out, I'm on one side of the street with Dave Diemer and Telscher and Joyce are on the other side of the street. This is where they decide we're going to turn around, turn the whole convoy around, and move back ostensibly in a different direction. I don't see it happen but Sergeant Joyce goes to shoot around a corner and he gets shot right under his left armpit. Jim Telscher and someone bring him over to my location and we start working on him the best we can while the vehicles are getting turned around. "Let's get him on board, we're going to head back to the airfield." I think one of the vehicle commanders said "He's dead."

"They tried to drive north and then east and then get to the crash site but they got ambushed so bad … that's when Casey Joyce who was on Chalk 4 got shot," remembered DiTomasso. Keeney agreed: "We were dealing a lot of death but the longer we stayed, the more we were getting fucked up and the more casualties we took."

Eversmann had climbed into another Humvee after Joyce was shot:

> At some point I got into the back of another Humvee, I'm scrunched in the back of this Humvee and the bad guys are shooting. I remember opening the door so I could start engaging to the front right of the vehicle [through the gap between the body of the vehicle and the inner edge of the door] and that was a great plan until I realized we're screaming toward a parked car, we might hit this car and it's going to snap my weapon in half!

The nightmare battle continued as Eversmann recalled: "At some point, Jim Telscher wound up getting blown out of a Humvee that got hit by an RPG and was dragged by the vehicle for however long attached to the cargo strap … There were so many bad guys. Three dimensional battlefield. Rooftops, corners, on the street, behind vehicles."

The GRF had initially headed north behind the target building, parallel to Hawlwadig before turning west for several blocks. They then headed back down Hawlwadig past the objective before making a U-turn and traveling east toward the first crash site. They then drove north, driving past and missing the crash site by a block before finally heading for Armed Forces Way, a route that would take them back to the airfield.

Paul Leonard recounted:

> We turned around again and now we were the furthest distance away from town and this is when Matt [Rierson] got out of the truck and ran up to me and said, "Hey what's going on?" And I'm like, "I know as much as you do." He runs up to McKnight. The road we were on had a little hill and in front of McKnight this [Somali] car fishtailed and did a 90 degree turn – a sedan, it had a bunch of people in it. I was trying to tell McKnight to get out of the way because he was about 100 feet in front of me and the back of his head was right where I was going to shoot into this vehicle with the Mk19. The Rangers again are not shooting at it, their .50 cal. could have just lit it up. Anyway McKnight jumps in his vehicle and I pop several rounds over the top of his head. The 40mm rounds went right through the rear window and it just explodes.

Apart from Schilling, McKnight, and the occupants of the lead Humvee, there seems to have been confusion about the route being taken and why, and even the objective of the mission at this stage. The other vehicles in the convoy weren't aware that they were headed for the Super 61 crash. Keeney noted:

> I never knew that we were given the command to go to crash site one. The antenna was broken from my radio. All this time I'm thinking that we're supposed to be going back to the airfield. I never knew there was an order given for the lost convoy to go to crash site one. That would have countered the GFC's [Ground Force Commander] order from Scott Miller.

Tom DiTomasso graphically explained the situation:

> That convoy is under fire, they are traveling down a single lane road and they are being shot at from both sides of the road. They're also trying to drive as fast as they can to get out of the line of fire. The instructions to turn left or right are coming from a helicopter but that helicopter had to go and refuel.

So the P-3 is now giving directions to the JOC and the JOC is trying to relay them to the convoy but by the time that transmission occurs, the convoy has already gone past the turn. It was just so chaotic.

By now, the second convoy had been launched from the airfield led by Struecker and Lieutenant Larry Moores and it too was receiving directions from above. To add insult to injury, at times the seemingly conflicting directions were being received and acted upon by the wrong convoy. Dan Schilling had taken over navigation for the convoy from McKnight who had been wounded by fragments; he "seemed dazed and was slow to respond to issues. I think also that the situation was overwhelming to him, as it put him a bit out of his element. Ranger commanders aren't used to working vehicle convoys or so I've been told," noted Schilling in his book.[3]

Danny McKnight in his own memoir notes that in his view:[*]

> there was no "lost" convoy … I believe this misperception may have been presented by many in the convoy because it seemed so to them, and that is understandable. That is probably because the planned route of movement changed after Super Six One was shot down in the city. The new route was created on the move with no time to stop and brief everyone on the new movement plan.[4]

After realizing the contradictory state of the directions he was receiving, Schilling took the initiative to contact one of the reconnaissance helicopters overhead, likely an OH-58D, and asked them to direct him to the crash site. Unfortunately he didn't specify which crash site and the helicopter directed them back down Hawlwadig past the objective toward Super 64. Schilling realized the error and the helicopter began to finally direct them toward Super 61. Gary Keeney recalled:

> We were missing turns and ending up on roads that were blocked. At some point making all of these turns, we passed by the ground force element

---

[*] Although in sporadic contact for more than a year, the author failed to interview McKnight despite numerous attempts.

moving to the crash site. We'd already stopped one or two times and received some casualties and were kinda in a bad way and I distinctly remember seeing [fellow operator] Phil P and we exchanged one of those looks like, "What the fuck, man? I don't know what's going on with this convoy but we're not supposed to be seeing you." They probably didn't even know we were heading to the crash site. We didn't know it. I guess McKnight knew it.

Leonard agreed: "We went up and down the same road two or three times and I'm thinking 'What is going on?'" The route was further complicated by some of the narrow streets the convoy was directed to use by the C2 aircraft: "These aren't all two- or three-lane streets – there's not room for a big Humvee to get down a particular alley," said Eversmann. Keeney shared their frustration: "We were on Armed Forces Way, we were out of the mess. Then Colonel McKnight or whoever was leading this convoy did a U-turn on Armed Forces Way, went back traveling east and then made a right and went back south into the badlands! When that happened I was like, 'Holy shit, what the fuck is going on here?'"

Jeff Struecker, the Ranger Sergeant with the best understanding of the maze-like road network, had returned to the Task Force Ranger base with the three Humvees carrying Blackburn, leaving McKnight's GRF without any experienced navigators. Instead the GRF had to rely upon directions provided from the C2 helicopter. When it had to return to the base to refuel, the task became even more problematic. Coupled with the fragmentary and often late directions from overhead, the Rangers weren't used to conducting vehicle movements, particularly in a city, and basic drills like advising each vehicle as to its destination were missed.

Struecker recalled that as a key lesson learned:

One of the things we didn't do well was we didn't allow anyone else to navigate – I was the only guy who did navigation for the vehicles so when I pulled out [to take Blackburn back to the hangar], no one had any clue about how to get around the city. They are totally dependent on the helicopter. That's part of the reason that McKnight's convoy goes back and forth down the same street more than once because they don't know how to navigate through the city. We really didn't do that well. We should have spread that navigation responsibility around but we didn't.

The longer they were on the ground, the greater the number of roadblocks that appeared. Whether by design or accident, the Somalis were trying to isolate the crash sites from the convoy. Leonard recalled:

> They had tires, they had barbed wire, they had wood, rocks, over four foot high – these things were pretty formidable roadblocks – they were big enough that you couldn't get the Humvees over unless you were experienced and the Rangers just weren't. These roadblocks had people behind them shooting at us. I described it one time as being like the movie *Saving Private Ryan* – when they come up on the beach and the gate drops and you've got all of these rounds flying at you – that was it.

Keeney, in the truck with Leonard, agreed: "We were in the fatal funnel over and over again. We were just sitting ducks to anyone firing from a rooftop or doorway …" Leonard added:

> One time we hit a barrier and he [the driver] couldn't get over it. I'm sitting up there [on the Mk19] and seeing people running down the road shooting at me so I get down in the vehicle and the driver says "I'm stuck." So I kicked the gear and said, "Now push on the brake a little bit" – none of these guys knew how to engage the four wheel locking out. On Humvees you have to apply pressure to the brake, give it gas and watch out! So he went right up over this three-foot berm and he couldn't believe it.

**1654 HOURS: GRF #1 REPORTS NUMEROUS CASUALTIES (NUMBERS/TYPE UNKNOWN).**

Gary Keeney reported:

> The driver of our five-ton was injured and he wasn't driving very well as the result of his injuries. Ultimately [C-Team operator] Mike F had to get into that vehicle and drive it for him. I remember Mike telling me he had to push the guy out of the way and as he's driving the five-ton, he's shooting out his window with his .45 [pistol].

Ranger Specialist Eric Spalding in the passenger seat had been shot twice through the legs whilst Ranger Private John Maddox who had been driving had been hit in the helmet by an AK47 round, the force temporarily blinding him.

Twice the convoy passed frustratingly close to the Super 61 crash site. "I could hear the gunfire. Literally I could hear the .50-caliber machine guns and the 40mm grenades going off. I could hear them in the distance and then they would stop and then they'd get further away. And then they'd get closer. The ground convoy was trying to break through," said Tom DiTomasso with Chalk 2 at the crash site.

Kurt Smith, on foot with F-Team, remembered seeing the convoy go past whilst they were on their foot movement to the crash site:

> We traveled east for two blocks and arrived at an intersection. The Ground Reaction Force drove by from north to south. There was a distinct difference in operating procedure when I saw it. Instead of Rangers and operators boldly pulling security from their positions on the vehicles, they were maintaining very low silhouettes as if they had driven through several ambushes [as they already had]. The convoy passed, and we continued east one more block before turning north.[5]

As the convoy again headed onto Armed Forces Way, Schilling made a final attempt to head to the Super 61 crash site. They turned east in this last attempt but were again engaged by an ambush, narrowly avoiding an RPG fired at their Humvee. With the .50 cal. firing to cover their withdrawal, Schilling's and McKnight's Humvee turned around and pulled back around the corner to discover the rest of the GRF still waiting on the main road. Due to yet another communications breakdown, the convoy had not followed them east and instead stopped.

Finally, after consultation with Harrell and Boykin, Colonel McKnight was forced to make the painful decision to abandon efforts to reach either of the crash sites and instead try to nurse his shot-up convoy back to the airfield. McKnight himself had been hit in the neck by a fragment from an RPG next to his carotid artery and was wounded in the right arm. Matt Eversmann agreed with McKnight's decision to head for the base: "The sheer number of wounded ... I think the reality was we couldn't even stuff any more people on these vehicles anyway. It was a smart call."

With the number of dead and wounded on the GRF, and taking into consideration the state of their vehicles, there is little doubt that even had they been able to break through to the Super 61 crash site, they may have done as much harm as good. Although they would have been able to reinforce and likely expand the defensive perimeter around the alleyway, they would have added significantly to the already stretched medical resources at the site.

Delta Ground Force Commander Scott Miller later remarked: "The convoy going back, as we listened to the debriefs afterwards, was in a terrible firefight, convoys were riddled with RPGs and automatic weapons fire, they are losing individuals, KIAs, individuals wounded in action, and they are fighting their way back trying to get back to the airfield."[6]

Most importantly, with two five-ton trucks now out of action and several of the Humvees shot to pieces, they simply wouldn't have had the cargo capacity to actually load up the CSAR team, the Ranger chalks and the Delta assault force. The Humvees were jam-packed with casualties already. If the GRF had made it through, a longer and more hazardous version of the later "Mogadishu Mile" would have occurred with the able-bodied Rangers and operators forced to run back to the airfield alongside the GRF vehicles. They undoubtedly would have incurred significant casualties, as the relatively short Ranger and Delta foot movement to the Super 61 crash site had already demonstrated.

"Two more intersections and now we do another U-turn and we're heading back to the airbase because we've lost too many guys. We went up and down that road three or four times and we had a lot of casualties," recalled Leonard, still manning the Mk19 on Cavaco's Humvee despite his leg wound. Even on Armed Forces Way, they were still receiving significant fire: "We passed this intersection [when] I see up ahead of me the same kind of truck we had, a military five-ton, but unloading a bunch of Somalis, and again the Rangers don't shoot."

Even at this stage of the battle some of the young Rangers were hesitant to fire, either due to inexperience, combat shock, questions about the rules of engagement, or a combination of all three. "The .50 cal. goes by and didn't even light them up and I'm like, 'What is going on?' So now it is so close, maybe 15 feet, maybe 25 at the greatest, it was really danger close [a military term denoting weapons being employed in dangerously close proximity to friendly troops] using the Mk19. I'm bouncing rounds into the ground and into the vehicle and it blew up the vehicle and the gas tank." After Leonard's Mk19 was finally empty, he resorted to his CAR15 and eventually his pistol. He recounted:

I was sitting on Cavaco. The Rangers freaked out about that but I was using him to support my leg. The [Ranger] First Sergeant was there too and he was really confused – I felt sorry for him: "Who do I shoot at? Who don't I shoot at?" I was pointing out people to shoot out. I actually gave my gun [CAR15] to a Ranger. I said, "Why aren't you shooting?" and he goes, "Because my gun's broken," so I handed him my CAR15 and I pulled out my pistol. I didn't shoot anyone with it because we were almost back to the airfield. It was just crazy, the confusion.

The militias were brazenly attempting to take advantage of the American rules of engagement, counting on the likelihood that the Rangers and operators would not fire on unarmed civilians. Struecker recounted:

I watched it with my own eyes where a 25-year-old guy runs across the street, picks up an AK47 and shoots at the Humvees, we drop him and don't even think about it. A guy who's 17 years old runs across the street, picks up the AK, shoots at the Humvees [and we] drop him without thinking about it. Seven-year-old kid runs across the street, picks up the same AK47, shoots at the vehicles and everyone on the vehicles hesitates because inside they're thinking "Well that's just a kid, I can't kill a kid" and it's not until I start to shoot that they decide, "Well I better shoot because otherwise he's going to kill me."

I don't think they were asking, "Is it lawful for me to kill them?," they were more saying, "Isn't it wrong if I kill this woman?" I came to the opinion that the people in Mogadishu have lived under war and famine for so long that human life just doesn't mean anything. Human life just doesn't have value there.

Just as it appeared that Leonard's fellow Delta operator Gary Keeney would escape unscathed, his luck ran out as they headed for home. He recalled:

When we got back out on Armed Forces Way and turned left again, for the second time and the last time, that's when I got shot. I was still engaging people but the fire had reduced significantly and that's when all of a sudden, "Bam," I got struck in the leg. It just scared me because I wasn't expecting it like all the other times. [Delta Medic] Don H who was still working on Griz at the time looked up at me and goes, "Greedy, you okay?" and I just kinda looked down and said, "Yeah, I'm fine, man."

**1703 HOURS:** SECOND RANGER GROUND (GRF #2) ELE [ELEMENT] RECONSTITUTED AS RECOVERY FORCE FOR 2ND CRASH SITE.

While the GRF convoy was fighting its way through ambush after ambush, at the Task Force Ranger base, the second ground convoy was being assembled. Chief amongst it would be Sergeant Jeff Struecker who had earlier led the Blackburn MEDEVAC convoy out of the city. He explained, "I had a couple of guys wounded but still able to fight, [Dominick] Pilla's dead, Blackburn – at this point it doesn't look like he's going to make it – a couple of guys just light gunshot wounds, nothing that would prevent us from going back out, but the vehicles are in real bad shape." Struecker continued:

> We had the search-and-rescue force that was already going in at the first crashed Black Hawk, Cliff Wolcott, I didn't know this as I'm on the way back with Blackburn. By the time I get back, Durant's Black Hawk has crashed and we don't have anybody else to go out to a second crash site. When I got back [Lieutenant Larry] Moores is waiting for me, saying, "Hey, you need to get your guys back on the Humvees, we're going back out to the crash site." And I'm like, "What crash site? We've got a search-and-rescue bird." "No, the second crash site," answered Moores. When 64 went down, I didn't even know 61 had gone down.
>
> Lieutenant Moores was preparing the cooks and the ammunition guys and the intel guys to get on to the five-tons and ride in the middle of the convoy. It was basically, "Anybody who has a gun, get on the big trucks." This was the point that [Major] Craig Nixon [the Ranger battalion executive officer who had been acting as the Task Force Ranger liaison to the 10th Mountain] joined us at the back on Larry Moores' vehicle. He gave me a specific amount of time to get more fuel, get more ammunition, get the vehicles ready to go back out and just like you see in the movie, one of the special operators [Sergeant John M] who came back on my Humvee said, "Jeff, go clean your Humvee up" ... so we cleaned the blood out of the back of that Humvee.

Struecker was thinking the same as every other man who had run the gauntlet already that day: "Everything inside of me was saying don't do this. Don't do this because you're going to get every one of your men killed if you go back out there. Personally, I was thinking it was a suicide mission. If I drive back through what I just went through, I'm going to die in the next few moments, no question about it."[7]

He later credited Nixon with inspiring him to lead his men out once more:

> He [Nixon] said, "Any idiot can go in on a hot landing zone the first time. But, it's asking guys to go back into the exact same LZ after they've already been there and after they know how dangerous it is, that takes real courage and takes real leadership skills. You need to get your men ready for what we're about to ask them to do."

The incident shown in the film where a young Ranger is hesitant to go back out actually occurred. Struecker spoke to him: "'I'm not going to make you do this, but I need you on those Humvees. The rest of the guys who are on the city streets fighting for their lives – they need you," and as the vehicle convoy mounted up, he spotted the young man climb aboard a departing Humvee with his SAW.[8]

Moores and Nixon had recruited virtually every support Ranger at the airfield: mechanics, cooks, armorers, clerks, analysts, and those providing perimeter security. "They loaded up all the headquarters personnel because they needed more Rangers. They washed out all the trucks and loaded up all those headquarters personnel and those guys kept on trying to come back out to us," added DiTomasso.

Christened GRF #2, the convoy consisted of four Humvees and three five-ton trucks carrying a 27-man mixed force of Rangers and a scattering of operators. Struecker was in the lead vehicle, with Moores and Nixon in the Humvee directly behind him. Both lead Humvees mounted .50 cal. machine guns.

The Ranger GRF #2 would soon be plagued by the same communications mishaps as McKnight's convoy. Struecker explained:

> We don't know exactly where Durant's Black Hawk crashed so he [Moores] gives me the instruction to turn my radio to the air frequency to talk to the

helicopters and get directions from the helicopters. What he [Moores] didn't know was that Danny McKnight was on the same frequency getting directions from the same aircraft. So the same [C2] aircraft is giving directions to two convoys. McKnight doesn't know that, I don't know that, so McKnight is turning when I'm supposed to be turning.

The newly established convoy was first engaged by enemy fire barely after they had left the airfield gates. It was as if the whole city was looking for an opportunity to shoot at the Americans. GRF #2 then proceeded to the K-4 Traffic Circle and, already under now heavy fire, drove north on Via Lenin and then turned east onto National. They had also incurred their first casualties. Ranger Specialist David Eastabrooks, driving one of the Humvees, had been shot in the hand. Struecker himself suffered another close call. An RPG had impacted next to his Humvee, lifting one side of the vehicle off the ground.

**1720 HOURS:** GRF #2 APPROACHING 2ND CRASH SITE; ROAD HAS BEEN BLOCKED WITH TIRE FIRES; GRF #2 RECEIVING HEAVY FIRE.

Struecker recounted:

> At this point the clans are pretty adept at directing us, so now the battle is in their backyard and they're going to force us to go where they want us to go. One of the routes that the helicopter gave me was, "Jeff, take this right turn and go down the road for two blocks and take a left," and I can't go two blocks because they've set up all of this garbage, concertina wire, tires ... the kind of stuff you can move by hand. And its four foot high and you can't get over it. So the helicopter doesn't know that they are doing that so they can direct us into an ambush.

Along with the temporary roadblocks, the Somalis had seemingly used earth-moving equipment to establish an earthen berm on one road that forced GRF #2 to yet again turn around to attempt to find another passage through. Struecker continued:

> These guys [Somalis] know what they're doing and they're doing it pretty well given their capabilities and their technology. To this day I'm pretty impressed

by their resolve. There was significantly less enemy fire but it was well coordinated. There was [one] well-coordinated vehicle ambush that could have been really, really devastating if they had pulled it off well.

They initiate on my Humvee, the first Humvee, with an RPG and then I get hit from probably 10 automatic weapons from the side of the road which is about 10 feet away but it's all directed on the first two Humvees. The rest of the convoy backs up and we're stuck in the middle of this ambush. The two of us return fire and back out of there. During that whole ambush, nobody on either of those two vehicles gets hit ... [The Somalis] must have been shooting with their eyes closed to miss us! It was a well-coordinated, well-executed vehicle ambush, if they'd hit the big trucks in the middle it would've been textbook. They were just stupid enough to open up on the first Humvee which gave everyone else the chance to run away.

Struecker was forced to reverse and ram the second Humvee to escape the ambush:

I told [Private First Class] Jeremy Kerr, who was driving my Humvee, to put it into reverse, stomp on it, and run into Moores, he'll figure out what we're doing, he'll back out of here. We're returning fire as we're getting out. I called back up to the helicopter and said, "I can't take the road that's blocked, can't go down this road because it'll kill a bunch more guys in the Humvees, find us another route."

At one point, GRF #2 could even see the Super 64 crash site in the distance as they crested a rise, but the path to the south was blocked by roadblocks and burning tires. Many of the Somalis who had been moving toward the objective building and Durant's helicopter now took the opportunity to fire on the convoy. GRF #2 drove through the murderous fire, all the while being forced to reverse and turn around multiple times in the narrow streets as one route after another was blocked.

**1740 HOURS:** GRF #2 LINK-UP W/GRF #1 AT K-4 CIRCLE. GRF #2 ATTEMPTING DIFFERENT ROUTES; RECEIVING HEAVY FIRE WHEREVER HE GOES; CHANCE LINK-UP ... RETURNING TO COMPOUND TRANSLOAD PC AND WIA FROM DISABLED VEHICLES – ENTIRE FORCE RTB.

In another miscommunication, the Rangers on GRF #2 were unaware that McKnight's convoy was headed back to the airfield until they literally ran into each other north of the K-4 Traffic Circle. Paul Leonard was surprised to see other American vehicles: "I didn't know about it, another convoy coming out. They obviously knew we were coming back. I saw several Humvees drive past us."

McKnight's convoy had been heading west whilst GRF #2 was heading east. It took some time to turn the GRF #2 vehicles around and transload the wounded from McKnight's Humvees and the surviving five-ton. Struecker was stunned by the damage incurred by McKnight's vehicles. He recalled:

> We were in bad shape but those guys were really, really in bad shape. I was kind of shocked when I saw their vehicles: "What the heck happened?" What we just went through was bad but what those guys went through was a lot worse.
>
> Most of them were limping out of the city, so shot up that they couldn't keep going. One Humvee was totally destroyed and a five-ton was pushing it down the road. We link up with them [McKnight's GRF] on Via Lenin Road. They were so shot up that we just stopped what we were doing and put most of the dead and the wounded on the five-tons and on our Humvees. Moores made the decision to take them back to the base. One of the Humvees – they had fired all of their ammunition, the only thing they had left was the guy on the top who had his pistol out and he had about five rounds left.

At this time, another Humvee was hit by an RPG and disabled, wounding the three Rangers inside. On fire, it was abandoned in the street. The SEAL "Cutvee" was running on its rims and was so badly damaged it had been pushed down the road by the five-ton driven by the Delta operator. The decision was made to disable it and leave the bullet-ridden wreck at the K-4. "We set thermite grenades on the [immobilized] Humvee, stripped it of everything, and then took the rest of the vehicles back," remembered Struecker.

With the wounded and dead loaded onto the GRF #2 vehicles, Moores conferred with McKnight and the C2 helicopter and it was decided to withdraw back to the airfield with GRF #2 providing force protection for McKnight's battered convoy. Although enemy fire was lessening as they neared the edge of the Habr Gidr territory, a GRF #2 Humvee was struck by an RPG and the Humvee carrying Matt Eversmann was hit by gunfire as they crested a rise and got their first glimpse of the ocean and the Task Force base, wounding the vehicle's driver, Ranger Sergeant Mark Luhman.

Suddenly all firing stopped and an eerie quiet descended as the combined convoys headed toward the airfield. They were now in another clan's territory, one friendlier to the United Nations forces. "It was like an imaginary DMZ [de-militarized zone]. I remember all of a sudden it stopped. Wow, like there's nobody shooting," said Eversmann.

**1735 HOURS:** QRF DEPART FOR CRASH SITE #2.

Along with the scratch rescue force drawn from the Task Force support personnel, Struecker was aware that the 10th Mountain QRF also had the capability to come to their aid: "We knew we had a company from 10th Mountain that was available should we really get in a jam. They had launched. I didn't know that they got within a couple of blocks of the target building and just got shot to pieces."

In fact, the 10th Mountain Quick Reaction Company or QRC had launched a platoon-sized rescue element soon after the second ad hoc Ranger convoy had departed from the airfield. The combined Ranger convoys of GRF #1 and #2 actually ran into the QRF convoy as they headed back to the airfield after their link-up, speeding through Lieutenant Colonel Bill David's force who had dismounted to clear an ambush.

It had been previously agreed between Nixon and the 10th Mountain that the QRC would be placed on a 30-minute warning standby whenever Task Force Ranger launched on a mission. If and when they launched, the QRC would be placed under the temporary operational command of Garrison and Task Force Ranger. Barely six minutes after the downing of Super 61, the QRC received the request to assist from Garrison in the JOC. On the rotational QRC duty on October 3 was callsign Tiger, C-Company of the 2nd Battalion, 14th Infantry Regiment of the 10th Mountain. This same QRC company had been involved in the battle to reach the downed Courage 53 a week earlier.

After negotiating a circuitous route known as MSR Tiger that would keep them out of Habr Gidr territory, the QRC arrived some 45 minutes later.

C-Company would be reinforced by a small number of Ranger and Delta personnel on four Humvees and three five-tons, including Delta Colonel Lee Van Arsdale who had been leading the JSOC headquarters element for Task Force Ranger. The QRC and Ranger element departed the airfield for the Super 64 crash site 20 minutes after the QRC arrived. The 10th Mountain soldiers were in a total of six five-ton trucks reinforced with sandbags carrying a pair of infantry platoons and some ten Humvees, two with the 2-14th battalion commander (Lieutenant Colonel Bill David) and C-Company commander on board. Several of the five-tons were empty in anticipation of carrying out the Task Force Ranger personnel from one of the crash sites.

Their route was similar to the one taken by Struecker, Moores, and Nixon: straight up to the K-4 Traffic Circle, north up Via Lenin and then turning to the right and heading east along National until they reached Hawlwadig. From there they would turn right again, heading south until they reached the Super 64 crash site past the Olympic Hotel and the original objective. If they were prevented from reaching National, the plan called for them to head further north and turn at a disused milk factory before working their way south, bypassing National.

The QRC soon began to run into ambushes and several Humvees were struck by RPGs just past the K-4. Lieutenant Colonel David's men had spotted the two destroyed Task Force Ranger Humvees near the K-4 and the 10th Mountain soldiers bravely cleared the area under fire, searching for any wounded or dead Rangers in or near the vehicles. They remounted their own vehicles and pushed on, just managing to reach National but coming under a withering amount of small-arms and RPG fire from the east which halted their progress.

Instead of trying to drive head first into the enemy fire, the QRC followed the alternate plan and swung north before running into a massive ambush near the milk factory where they came under fire from numerous RPGs and heavy machine guns including Soviet 12.7mm "Dushkas." The QRC infantry platoons again dismounted and conducted an assault against the enemy positions; one Ranger and one 10th Mountain soldier were wounded during this action which succeeded in suppressing the enemy machine-gun positions.

The C-Company commander, then-Captain Michael Whetstone, later noted: "The SNA militia had effectively sealed off the area around the Rangers against any penetration by thin-skinned vehicles." As they attempted to push through, the QRC were thwarted at every turn. Finally, the QRC was ordered to return to the airfield as Garrison attempted to organize United Nations armor to accompany another rescue effort.[9]

AH-6s were overhead but experienced difficulties differentiating between friend and foe on the ground and were subsequently not "cleared in hot" to conduct gunruns. This proved to be another important lesson learned as communication difficulties between the Tiger callsigns and the AH-6s, along with the airspace initially being restricted to only Task Force Ranger aircraft, meant that the 10th Mountain QRC could not call upon its own integral attack helicopter component either. The four AH-6 Barber callsigns were also overstretched trying to protect both crash sites and provide some air cover for GRF #1 and GRF #2 as they returned to base.

**1830 HOURS: QRF RECONSTITUTES FORCE AFTER BREAKS IN CONTACT CAUSED BY AMBUSH; RTB TF RANGER COMPOUND.**

Garrison informed the 10th Mountain command that a request had been placed with the United Nations for access to Pakistani M48 main battle tanks and Malaysian Condor armored personnel carriers to form an armored reaction force that would fight their way into the city. The QRC infantry company would form an integral element of that effort, which became known as Task Force David after its commander, and thus they were reluctantly directed to return to the airfield after more than 90 minutes trying to fight their way through to the Super 64 crash site.

Even as they attempted to withdraw, the Tiger Company soldiers were forced to fight another dismounted action to break contact with the enemy, allowing the convoy's vehicles to turn around. Two 10th Mountain soldiers, Private First Class Eugene Pamer and First Sergeant Gary Doody, were awarded the Silver Star for their bravery during the battle. As the vehicles began to move, the soldiers ran alongside to suppress enemy fire until they could board their vehicles. Almost an hour after their first contact, their own organic Cobra gunships were finally overhead to provide air cover as they returned to the airfield to rearm, regroup, and receive medical treatment for their three seriously wounded soldiers.

DiTomasso, hunkered down at the Super 61 crash site, remembered:

All afternoon and into the evening we kept hearing them making contact with the enemy. They made several attempts plus they were trying to get to Durant's crash site but they just couldn't get to it because they didn't have armored vehicles. I knew Lieutenant Larry Moores was trying to get his platoon on Humvees to the crash site. I knew he would make it through eventually.

Whetstone has remarked in his excellent account of his battalion's service in Somalia, *Madness in Mogadishu*, that he felt that, had his QRC been launched earlier, they might have been able to make it through to one of the crash sites. His men were on their vehicles and ready to move minutes after Super 61 was shot down. He believed that any delay surrendered the initiative to the militia, allowing them to erect roadblocks and channel any rescue attempt. Nonetheless he also understood that, in the fog of war when hard decisions had to be taken immediately, holding the QRC back until the status of the McKnight and Struecker convoys could be ascertained made tactical sense.[10]

At the Task Force Ranger base, the bloodied Ranger GRF #1 and #2 convoys finally staggered through the gate. Struecker's and McKnight's respective convoys had suffered an astonishing 36 casualties between them, including a number of fatalities. Little Bird pilot Karl Maier recalled: "The convoy was coming back and they were unloading people and parts [of people]. They were hosing them out to get ready to go back out. Most of them, their tires were flat but they were still using them. It was a mess."

Gary Keeney in the last surviving five-ton from GRF #1 remembered the grim task that awaited them:

When we got back to the airfield the first thing we do is unload all of our injured guys first. We didn't have any dead on our truck. Then we started unloading the prisoners and in the course of that I realized that four of those guys were dead. I don't know how many were injured. At least two of them were shot in the head.

Paul Leonard was still up on the now empty Mk19 when they swung into the compound. He recalled:

So we pulled in to the airport which was being blocked by another convoy. I got the [Ranger] 1st Sergeant out of the vehicle to get our vehicles in. The five-ton [was] just full of wounded people. I wouldn't let them put me on the gurney until all the [wounded] Rangers had gone first. So I eventually went into the tent to get evaluated and there was a nurse who was trying to get an IV into me. She was very nervous, so I told her, "Hey, just calm down, you do this all the time."

I then asked another nurse, "Am I going to lose my leg?" and she said, "Can you move your toes?" and I wriggled my toes and she said, "No, you're not going to lose your leg," and from that point on, I didn't care what anyone said, you're not taking my leg. More than you know, they wanted to take my leg below my knee and I wouldn't let them do it.

As the wounded were treated and the most serious stabilized for flights to Landstuhl in Germany, the walking wounded and the able-bodied men of Task Force Ranger and the 10th Mountain resupplied themselves with water, ammunition, and grenades. Most importantly they all retrieved their night-vision goggles and weapon sights in anticipation of a further rescue attempt later that night alongside the Pakistani and Malay armored units.

Jeff Struecker and his men prepared to go back out into the city. He explained:

McKnight wisely goes back to the Operations Center and puts [Major] Craig Nixon in charge of all the vehicles on the ground and Nixon kind of comes up to me and says, "Jeff, I think we're going to go back out there but we've got to wait to see what happens with 10th Mountain" and then he comes back to me, and we're getting our vehicles ready, and says "Hey, 10th Mountain got shot to pieces, we're going back out there but we're waiting for the United Nations to help us out." That took a while.

# CHAPTER 7

## THE LONG NIGHT

*"What came next was hours of fighting between ninety-nine Americans and tens of thousands of the Somali militia, all armed with rifles, grenades, and rocket-propelled grenades and determined to kill as many Americans as possible."*

Colonel Jerry Boykin, Commanding Officer, 1st SFOD-D (A)

# THE LONG NIGHT

As the numerous relief convoys fought their way back to the airfield, the mixed Ranger and Delta element strongpointed in the buildings along either side of Marehan Road, just south of the Super 61 crash site, were in the fight of their lives. Norm Hooten explained that the Somalis "had a lot of ammunition. They had an abundance of RPGs. They were not professional soldiers by any stretch of the imagination and it's probably a good thing for us that they were not. These guys mortared the airfield every day for three months and only managed to hit one time, but they weren't afraid to fight." The Americans were also vastly outnumbered. One militia commander later claimed that the Super 61 crash site was surrounded by some 360 SNA militiamen supported by several hundred additional armed civilians.

Tom DiTomasso noted the location of the various units as night fell on the crash site: "Captain Steele and the Rangers all occupied the buildings on the right side of the road, the east side, and the Delta troop got on the left side and cleared from building to building all the way up and came abreast of the crash site. Now we had all those guys [Captain Scott Miller and G-Team] at the crash site as well."

Ranger Corporal Jamie Smith's condition continued to worsen. "He was shot in the leg, but he was shot way up close to the hip, so you couldn't get a tourniquet on him, you know. And we kept pushing IVs into him for hours and he would say, 'Am I gonna die?' And we would say, 'No, you're not gonna die,'" remembered Hooten. Delta Medic Kurt S tried everything to stem the bleeding and save the young man's life. At one point he was forced to tear the wound further open to be able to access the artery and try to clamp it with his own hands. Kurt S had run out of the blood and IV solution that Smith desperately needed.

Water had also become an issue. "It was hot. People were dehydrated and without water. I don't believe there were any true heat casualties. We all had cramps, but there were more important things to think about at the time," recalled another Delta operator who preferred to remain anonymous. A faucet was discovered near the eastern end of the crash site and several Rangers refilled their canteens, preferring to drink and take their chances with dysentery.

**1820 HOURS: ASSAULT FORCE AMMO GETTING CRITICAL.**

Ammunition was also a problem. The operators recovered Dan Busch's M249 and delinked the ammunition to reload their CAR15 magazines, but many men were down to their last magazines (a pair of night-vision goggles had also been found in the downed aircraft and were given to a Ranger machine-gunner guarding the perimeter). At that point, if the Somalis had made a concerted and coordinated effort to overrun the crash site, there was a good chance that the Rangers would have run out of ammunition.

Mike Moser explained:

> As the evening settled in, and it became apparent I would remain static in this CCP for the time being, I naturally began to run through a number of themes. The possibility of being overrun was certainly there. I realized that the force would have considerable difficulty walking out on our own given the number of non-ambulatory folks. I tried to put myself in the Somali position – it would have been a tremendous coup not just to defeat us but to completely annihilate [or] capture our force.
>
> That was a very remote possibility, but if they had acted quickly – massing and coordinating early enough to make us extinguish all of our ammunition before any rescue force was capable of assisting – they may have succeeded. Anyway, I became a little concerned that they may send some very committed guys at us through the walls of the housing units rather than in the main alleys. I knew that they most likely had no explosives breaching capability, but an RPG or two might provide access. At any rate we had guys watching every doorway and window that led to us.

**1836 HOURS:** NUMEROUS RPG LAUNCHES IN VIC [VICINITY] N [NORTH] CRASH SITE; STILL HAVE ONE BODY TRAPPED IN ACFT [AIRCRAFT] – UNABLE TO GET DUE TO NUMEROUS SMALL-ARMS.

Tom DiTomasso was also low on ammunition and reliant upon the AH-6s to engage any large groupings of Somalis they spotted:

> My Forward Observer was talking to the aerial fires assets which were the AH-6s at that time and continually calling fire missions to keep the Somali gunmen off of us. They just kept attacking – if they had better command and control, if they were better organized, they might have been able to overwhelm us at that point as we were running out of ammo. They just kept attacking in threes and fours and running at the building and climbing in through the

windows. We were able to fight them in small groups. The Rangers would fight to the death for each other, and it showed. I owe my life to them forever.

There were several times during the battle that we should've been overrun – there were only seven of us there initially and then there was 15 from Chalk 2. If the enemy had mounted a very quick and large counterattack they could have overrun us very, very quickly. We may have been outnumbered, but the Rangers fought as a team, and were fighting for a bigger prize: each other and our fallen comrades in the aircraft.

**1908 HOURS:** SUPER 66 WILL DROP RESUPPLY ITEMS AT CRASH SITE #1; DZ [DROP ZONE] MARKED BY IR [INFRARED] STROBE; AH-6 SUPPORTING WITH GUNS. ASSUME FRIENDLIES AT THE STROBES. TAKING FIRES FROM 9 O'CLOCK; RESUPPLY SUCCESSFUL. AT LEAST 20 ENEMY WITH AKS IN VIC.

The shortage of ammunition and water led to a very courageous resupply mission conducted by Super 66 as DiTomasso recalled:

We'd already run out of water, we'd already run out of medical supplies. We'd almost run out of ammunition. General Garrison made the decision to send in the resupply bird, Super 66. After dark, they decide to load up the resupply bird with water, ammunition, and medical supplies and they fly it into the target area. A Little Bird used a laser pointer to show Chief Warrant Officer Stan Wood flying Super 66 which building to go to.

The MH-6s were told to "stay on the ground and stand by for a mission." Their flight lead, Karl Maier, had volunteered for the resupply mission, figuring that the MH-6s would be more agile and face less of a risk than the lumbering Black Hawk, but was turned down and the mission went to Super 66. The other surviving Black Hawk, Super 65, also remained on standby in case another resupply or an emergency MEDEVAC was cleared in. "We stayed on the ground and we kept running all night long. We stayed running until about 7:30 in the morning," confirmed Gerry Izzo.

Hooten still remembers the resupply. He recounted:

We ran dry until we had the Black Hawk come over and kick out a bundle. We were short on ammo and a lot of guys were out of water – that was a big issue. They [Super 66] were there for maybe 10 seconds and they were taking a lot of ground fire. RPGs are going everywhere but they were not very effective. They were shooting but they don't have any night sights plus they weren't very good with them during the day and they were even worse at night.

Mike Moser recalled the tremendous amount of fire directed at Super 66 and the supporting AH-6s as they attempted to suppress the enemy firing points:

I definitely heard that [resupply mission], [it] sounded like it was directly above us when she finally came in. We could hear brass [expended cartridges] raining down on our tin roof, mostly from gunship strafing runs as they prepped and delivered fire missions for our guys before and afterward. I was still monitoring our assault net and knew of the intent to risk the delivery. The aircraft's approach and hover, to me anyway, seemed painfully slow as the enemy fire climaxed all around. I did at some point become concerned that she [Super 66] might come crashing down through the roof on top of us if she didn't conclude her business soon.

Another operator commented that he couldn't hear Super 66's miniguns because of all the Somali fire being directed at the helicopter. The ammunition and bottles of water were packed in Mk19 ammunition boxes and dropped out the side of the aircraft by two members of Delta's sniper troop who had volunteered for the mission – Alex S and Joe V. Both had survived the earlier gauntlet of the McKnight convoy, traveling in the five-ton with C-Team and the prisoners.

DiTomasso recounted:

As soon as he came into the area he started to take machine-gun fire. He came in and pushed out the supplies but he received so much fire that he started to lose hydraulics, but they managed to make it back to the airfield and crash landed it there. [Unfortunately] all the water shattered on the ground, a lot of the ammunition shattered when it hit the ground. We were picking up bullets out of the sand, bringing them back and loading them in our weapons. Our machine guns were overheating so we actually took our bayonets and punctured the oil can underneath a car that was parked in the garage of the building that we were defending and used that to lube up our machine guns, both the M60s and the SAWs.

**2025 HOURS:** ASLT [ASSAULT FORCE COMMANDER] ADVISES THAT "IF QRF DOES NOT GET THERE (NORTH CRASH) SOON, THERE WILL BE MORE KIAS FROM PREVIOUSLY RECEIVED WIA; GET THE ONE STAR [GENERAL] TO GET HIS PEOPLE MOVING!"

Tragically the resupply hadn't included any blood which Delta medic Kurt S desperately needed, but it had provided bags of IV solution that Schmid immediately administered to the wounded Corporal Jamie Smith. Perino and other Rangers were taking turns at keeping pressure on Smith's wound in an attempt to stem the bleeding. After refusing for many hours, as it might dangerously lower his respiration rate, Kurt S finally agreed to provide morphine which took the pain away for the young Ranger.

Super 65 pilot Gerry Izzo:

> At one point in the battle, after the resupply, the senior Delta operator on the ground [Miller] called Colonel Harrell who was in the C2 bird and he said "We need an immediate MEDEVAC, I've got two guys who are going to die if I don't get them out of here." We got the aircraft ready, I figured I would land on the roof of the building, but this was the same building they had done the resupply mission to that had got shot to ribbons, so I'm thinking I've got about 30 seconds to get in there and get these guys and get out. I remember I took my pistol out and jacked a round into the chamber, I grabbed my M16 and I thought, "Well, at best I'm going to get shot down or I'm going to get killed."
>
> I'm thinking all of this and on the radio Colonel Harrell and Captain Miller are talking and Harrell said [to Miller] "Scottie, just hang on, I can't send any more Black Hawks in, [and] I'm running out of helicopters. We're going to get some tanks and armored vehicles and we'll punch through to them with those." I was frustrated but at the same time I was relieved.

Lieutenant Perino later wrote:

> Smith was deteriorating; he was losing blood at an alarming rate. We were running critically short of IVs, and I realized that Corporal Smith would die

if he was not evacuated immediately. I requested MEDEVAC on three separate occasions, but each time I was denied – enemy fire was just too great, and we had already lost three helicopters to enemy fire. All we could do was post security and wait. Despite all attempts to keep my soldier alive, Corporal Smith died at 2027 hours.[1]

Norm Hooten remembered the horror of that night: "You try to tell him 'No, son, you're not gonna die, you're gonna live.' And he died and that … that's one of the things that … you know, keeps me up at night sometimes – that, that horrible lie that you tell someone trying to keep his spirits up."[2] "There were calls for a MEDEVAC that were refused by the command bird and the reason was because they felt they couldn't get the bird in there safely, they would've lost the MEDEVAC bird and I agreed with them on that," added Hooten sadly.

**2027 HOURS: ASLT FORCE ADVISES 1 X CRITICAL WIA AT CRASH SITE #1 IS NOW KIA.**

Delta Medic Bart B continued to treat the other wounded Rangers and operators at the second CCP with Captain Steele. He recalled:

> The casualties I treated were all very cooperative. I was the primary care provider for some, and others came to "my courtyard CCP" already self/buddy treated. The ones who were seriously wounded and needed it were given morphine. They couldn't walk or fight anyway. Others who were still able to fire their rifles were given injectable Toradol [an anti-inflammatory pain reliever] if needed. I explained to them all that we may very well be in for a long stay, and everyone needed to be able to fight and move without being "under the influence." I never saw any excessive screaming or psych cases.[3]

When Captain Miller wanted Captain Steele to move his force to link up with Miller's element to shrink the perimeter and make it easier to both defend and to allow the Little Birds a clearer "kill box," Steele refused after initially agreeing to the request as relayed by Colonel Harrell. His senior NCO, Sergeant Watson, argued that with the number of wounded they had suffered, such a move was suicidal. Harrell apparently refused to directly order Steele to move, leaving the management of the ground force and all its elements to Miller.

# THE LONG NIGHT

Norm Hooten recalled:

We got a call from Captain Miller, who said "Come on over to my location. Move everybody up here and we'll try to establish a proper perimeter around the aircraft." So [B-Team leader] John B, [A-Team leader] Jon Hale and I are getting ready to move forward. We had our teams together and we had fragments of the Ranger blocking positions and Captain Steele was there as well.

We went to him and said, "How long until you can get moving? We've got to move up to put a perimeter around the aircraft. How long do you need before you're ready to move?" He said "Five minutes." So what happened was we went back after the five minutes and said, "Okay, are your guys ready to move?" and he [Steele] says, "I want to readdress this, I don't think it's a good idea," and I said, "It doesn't matter what you think, this is what's happening. The Ground Force Commander has made the call and we are moving." Still Steele resisted.

So [B-Team leader] John B and I are talking through a hole in the wall and he says, "What in hell is taking you guys so long?" and I said, "I've got an issue. I think I've got a personality conflict with Captain Steele. Why don't you come over here and see if you can convince him to move?" So John B goes over to "Mr Personality" [Steele] and says, "Hey, what's your problem?" and he goes, "I don't think this is a good idea," and John B took his headset off and goes, "Get on the radio to Scott Miller, the Ground Force Commander, and tell him you don't think it's a good idea." Captain Steele wouldn't take the headset.

With Steele refusing to move, Miller instead ordered John B, Hooten, and the three other Delta operators at Steele's position to link up with him and his command element opposite the alleyway leading into the crash site. Hooten said:

We moved out and got lit up. The plan was to move up to Scottie Miller's position. I was concerned that, along with the Somalis, every man in that assault force might light us up as well. I was making sure on the radio that [everyone knows] we have friendlies moving across the streets. We managed to get one house up and that put us directly on that corner where Earl [Fillmore] had been hit.

Hooten's element then prepared to bound across to a house directly opposite to close the gap between them and the crash site perimeter. Hooten reported:

> We were getting ready to cross the street into the corner house and we were going to light it up before we moved. We got all of our 203 gunners lined up to unload on the house and just before we did we saw a flash of a light. So we called over [the radio], "Are we sure that we have no friendlies in that house?" and everybody confirmed, "Nope, you have no friendlies in that house." And just before we did we saw a light come on and it was [Ranger Sergeant] John Belman and that was our first link-up with anyone from the crash site.

Belman also remembered the moment vividly. The operators believed they had seen a tactical light affixed to Belman's CAR15 when in fact it was a flashlight owned by a Somali civilian woman in the house which incredibly still had batteries. She had switched the light on at an opportune moment, likely saving Belman's life. Hooten then "went over to link up with Scott Miller so I took my team over to Scott Miller's location directly across the street from the house Belman had moved back to."

An operator who requested anonymity said that the Somalis continued to probe their positions all night long, mainly in twos and threes but sometimes in larger groups: "The skinnies [Somalis] kept trying to sneak up on us but most were killed." The operator believed that the AH-6s were instrumental in holding back the Somalis: "early on I thought this [being overrun] was a possibility, but after a prayer and the AH-6s all seemed well!"

The AH-6s flew all night. The five-man airfield services detachment "loaded more than one hundred rockets and fifty thousand rounds of minigun ammunition while pumping 12,500 gallons of fuel to 'hot-fuel' the helicopters."[4] Combat Controller Jeff Bray called in danger close Little Bird gunruns all night long. "Danger close" is the US military term signifying that friendly troops are dangerously close to the intended enemy target and pilots should take particular care to ensure against fratricide. Bray had placed infrared strobes around their location to mark the location of friendlies and guided the AH-6 pilots onto his targets using the AIM-1 infrared laser mounted on his GAU-5 carbine (the Air Force personnel carried a slightly different version of the CAR15 called the GAU-5).

Many of the Rangers and CSAR team remembered the expended brass from the miniguns of the AH-6s raining down on their heads as the Little Birds zipped by overhead. PJ Tim Wilkinson recalled with some understatement: "When Jeff was calling in danger close missions on the wall right next to us – that I'm almost leaning up against – and hot brass is raining down on my head, and the whomp of the rockets they are shooting is shaking the house, you have a sense that things are indeed grave."[5]

AH-6 pilot Chief Warrant Officer Paul White recalled Bray talking him onto targets: "I will always remember the calm demeanor and professionalism [Bray] showed over the radio even as I heard bullets hitting very near his position each time he keyed his radio microphone."[6] He was awarded the Silver Star for his efforts to defend the crash site.

His citation reads in part:

> While serving with a US Army Ranger element trapped and surrounded inside a building in the city, Staff Sergeant Bray coordinated helicopter gunship fire on targets all around his position throughout the night. He developed tactics and techniques on the spot that allowed him to mark friendly forces' locations so that helicopter gunships could destroy close enemy concentrations. By his gallantry and devotion to duty, Staff Sergeant Bray has reflected great credit upon himself and the United States Air Force.[7]

Gerry Izzo explained the process of calling in the air support: "The Little Birds [would] make several dry dummy runs to make sure the target the guys on the ground were talking about was the same target before they would fire. They were engaging targets with the miniguns within 10 meters of friendly troops and they were engaging targets with the rockets within 30 meters." It was the first time in the combat history of the 160th that Little Birds "Winchestered" or ran out of ammunition before they ran out of fuel. Jeff Struecker recounted:

> The tide of the battle changed when the Little Birds started firing rockets. We could tell the Somalis became defensive and they said, "Okay, now we are officially outgunned." There had been a lot of concern about casualties to civilians. The flight lead for the Little Bird gunships said, "Give us credit for using the proper weapon at the proper time." They used HE rockets, not the fletchette rockets.

> First time I heard a rocket from one of our aircraft was 2 or 3 o'clock that morning and I thought "I thought we weren't supposed to be using rockets": then it dawned on me that we had now thrown the rules of engagement out the window and said, "We're going to do whatever it takes to keep each other alive."

At any one time there would be a pair of AH-6s refueling and rearming, whilst another pair were flying over the battlespace. At the Super 61 crash site, one AH-6 would be flying gun runs whilst its partner provided overwatch, keeping an eye out for Somali RPGs or heavy weapons that could threaten the Little Birds. As they ran low on fuel or ammunition, they would be replaced in a constant cycle as the others refueled and rearmed.

Karl Maier did what he could to help the Barber crews, as did the other 160th SOAR air and ground crews. Maier explained:

> I would meet them at the FARP [forward armament and refueling point] and either hold the flight controls so they could go and pee or I brought them coffee and food – whatever I could do to help them because they flew for about 18 hours straight. They went through thousands of rounds of ammunition and hundreds of rockets.
>
> Randy Jones, the flight lead for the guns [AH-6s], came in and he said, "Hey, could you get something to wipe the windshield off?" I'm wiping it and looking at it and its dark so I don't really know what I'm messing with and then I saw blood and hair and half of a jaw, someone's jaw on the windshield. Probably from a rocket.

Thankfully the Somalis had no night-vision equipment and whilst they could hear the AH-6s approaching, the first they would see of them was as the miniguns or rocket pods opened fire. The crews flew almost completely blacked out with night-vision goggles. Night-vision devices would have been beneficial for the Task Force Ranger personnel on the ground too, particularly for the Ranger M60 and SAW gunners who were providing the bulk of the suppressive fire.

Kurt Smith recalled that "many TF members began leaving gear behind because the precedent set for six missions dictated that certain pieces of equipment would not be required. It was a gradual process, but, by the time the seventh mission started, some of the gear being left behind included ballistic 'chicken' plates, survival radios, 'excess' water, and night observation devices."[8] Tom DiTomasso added: "I left my night-vision goggles on my bunk. Every mission in the Army I did after that, I always brought my night-vision goggles with me!" Hooten and his operators also left them behind: "No, I did not [take them on the mission], none of my team did. We recovered some later from the pilots."

John Belman believes, however, that whilst they would have been an advantage, the Rangers were surviving without the technological aids. He explained:

> The impact of that from a Ranger perspective is somewhat overstated. For the crew-served weapons [M60s] and the SAWs they had night-vision scopes [available] – I'm not sure who brought their night-vision scopes or not – but those would have been important to have. Delta had dual reticle [goggles] but we have PVS-7s which were monocles with no depth perception – in terms of using it with an IR [infrared] laser to shoot, they were next to useless. They just weren't very effective. The NVGs the Delta guys had [however] were great.

RPGs continued to strike the building housing the northern CCP closest to the crash, slowly demolishing the flimsy structure. At one point, the Somalis deployed a crew-served heavy machine gun, possibly a 12.7mm "Dushka," the Soviet equivalent of the vaunted US .50cal Browning. Tracer rounds from this machine gun tore through the northern CCP until the gun was silenced by a well-aimed 2.75-inch rocket fired from an AH-6 vectored in by Bray.

The 12.7mm was likely mounted on a tripod rather than on the back of a technical, as Belman explained:

> I know we took some heavy-weapons fire but I don't recall seeing technicals, not like in the movie where they're waiting around the corner with a .50 cal.! Technicals, at least around the crash site, would have had a pretty difficult time. They would have had to drive right up on us. It's a bad place to be [with AH-6s in the air] to be a technical.

The CSAR team eventually used a C4 breaching charge in an attempt to blow a hole through into an adjacent building. They planned to move the casualties further into the building to protect them from the murderous fire on the street. Their first charge instead opened a man-sized hole out onto an exposed external courtyard. A second charge was more successful and the wounded were moved through, giving them a brief respite from the continual RPG fire. DiTomasso recounted:

> We pulled all the casualties in, put them in the center of the building, and defended that building. We split the defense with a Delta Captain [Bill C] – he took the northern side, I took the southern side. He had all of the CSAR guys with the special equipment so he continued to work on Cliff [Wolcott] at the helicopter. My job was to run the casualty collection point and secure the perimeter.

Belman added:

> Once it got dark I was inside with our casualties pulling security. It seemed like there was less fire but that might've been because I was inside. Direct fire effectiveness was less, simply because the Somalis didn't know where we were at that point. At that point you've got people who weren't necessarily in the initial fight, grabbing the RPG off the mantelpiece and running to go and have some fun!
>
> It was early on October 4th. I remember thinking prior to that, "Okay, how long are we going to sit here before we have to run out? We need to be preparing to carry guys because we need to get out before it gets light." If we're going to run out without vehicles we won't be able to do that in daylight. Doing the mental math, how many wounded, our ammunition, what if the ground convoy couldn't get to us … I accepted the possibility, if not the likelihood, that we were not going to get out.

**1900 HOURS: PLAN APPROVED FOR QRF TO MOVE TO CRASH SITE W/2 X MALAYSIAN MECH COMPANIES & 1 X PAKISTANI ARMOR [PLATOON].**

Some three kilometers away in the JOC, a rescue plan was being hatched. Garrison, working with Boykin, Montgomery, and the 10th Mountain leadership, had sketched out a rough plan – the QRF would form the backbone of the rescue package. They would be supported by the Malaysian APCs and

Pakistani tanks who would break through roadblocks and lead in the rescue force. The Italians had also offered the use of their armor but their base was at least two hours away in the northeast of the city and speed was of the essence.

The Italians would, however, move their forces into the city early that morning, pre-positioning themselves for another rescue attempt should the QRF become pinned down and unable to complete the link-up and extraction of Task Force Ranger. The Indian United Nations contingent also agreed to help and stood up their forces, including a number of Soviet-manufactured T72 main battle tanks. Montgomery told them, "I will only use your force if I have Americans in extremis."

"There were only eight tanks in Mogadishu ... they were old American tanks that had been given to the Pakistanis, and of those only four were operational, and they were at the airport, which is where the Ranger headquarters was. And so I called the Pakistani Commander and told him that I might need those tanks, and he said okay," recalled Major General Montgomery.[9]

The M48s were outdated Cold War-era US models but still packed a significant punch with their 105mm main guns. They were also heavily armored and could shrug off all but the most unlucky RPG strike. The real threat to the M48s was understandably landmines, a point made clear by the Pakistani tank commanders who later forced the Americans to manually search roadblocks for mines before they drove through them.

Colonel Lawrence Casper commanding the 10th Mountain QRF had immediately dispatched both the remaining A and B Companies from 2-14th of the 10th Mountain to the airfield in anticipation of another movement into the city to relieve the embattled Rangers. Both companies now formed up with their C-Company comrades at the airfield and awaited the order to move. At 20:52, the combined 2-14th and Task Force Ranger convoy, along with four attached Pakistani M48A5 tanks and a Pakistani mechanized infantry platoon in M113 armored personnel carriers, drove out of the airfield gates and headed toward the United Nations facility at the New Port to link up with the Malaysians who had volunteered their vehicles to assist in the rescue mission.

They arrived at the New Port at 21:30 to organize and integrate some 32 Malaysian Condor armored personnel carriers into the convoy and head for the Super 61 crash site as soon as possible. The Condors, painted in glaring United Nations peacekeeper white, were a German-made four-wheel light

APC mounting a turret equipped with twin MAG58 general-purpose machine guns. A number were alternately equipped with 20mm cannon. Although lightly armored, and thus vulnerable to RPGs, the vehicle could carry up to a dozen soldiers, making it ideal to ferry out Task Force Ranger. The Pakistani M113s were tracked and thus better at clearing obstacles than the wheeled Condors but also suffered from relatively light armor.

**2228 HOURS:** MG MONTGOMERY REQUESTS QRF CONVOY ROUTE FOR POSSIBLE "IMPROVEMENT" PLANNING PRIOR TO DEPARTING. NO ESTIMATE ON WHEN CONVOY WILL PROCEED TO CRASH SITES FOR TF RANGER RELIEF.

Organizing the Pakistani and Malaysian forces was problematic for both sides. Most of the Pakistani and Malay officers spoke at least some English and agreement was reached to dismount the Malaysian infantry in their APCs to make room for the Task Force Ranger personnel they would eventually be transporting back out of the city. The crews of the Condors spoke virtually no English and had to stay with the vehicles as they were the only ones trained to operate the APCs.

Originally the plan called for a movement back through Habr Gidr territory and onto the main paved road, National, but this was changed when the Pakistanis offered a safer route up a road called Via Jen Daaud that skirted the Habr Gidr zone. The Pakistani route would allow the convoy to access National from the southeast, turning west onto National and heading for Hawlwadig. One company would dismount around the Olympic Hotel and link up with the defenders of the Super 61 crash site. A second company, accompanied by a number of Delta operators, would head to the Super 64 crash to ascertain the situation and extract any survivors who might be in hiding nearby.

Jeff Struecker, returning into the city for the third and final time in his bullet-ridden Humvee, recalled:

> We went to the Port to link up with this multinational task force. It was little more direct from there. The Pakistanis showed up with tanks, the Malaysians had 30 or 40 armored personnel carriers, 10th Mountain in the middle and us, a handful of Rangers on Humvees, in the middle of the 10th Mountain. All of us rolled out together, heavy armor first, light armor second, and then

light-skinned Humvees third. When we get there I think the plan was to send the armored personnel carriers to the crash site but they didn't know exactly where they were going … so we ended up sending Humvees from 10th Mountain or guys on foot to the crash sites.

Colonel David ensured that each of his elements was as well briefed as possible on the intended route and ensured that all of his men carried as much ammunition as possible, with most taking double the typical combat issue. Struecker and his men also took what they thought was abundant ammunition. He recalled: "We all went out there with NVGs [night-vision goggles], we had enough water, I had what I thought was enough ammunition but it became pretty clear that [we] had to conserve ammo. Fire single shot and only when you see a target because we'll run out of ammo."

Navy SEAL Captain Eric Olson, in command of the SEAL sniper element attached to Task Force Ranger, and two of his SEALs went out with the seven Task Force Ranger Humvees attached to the convoy. Olson took the trail vehicle to ensure none of the convoy got separated or left behind in the confusion of the rolling enemy contacts. Delta Colonel Lee Van Arsdale, in charge of the Task Force Ranger component, was in one of the lead vehicles. "He was the JSOC Operations Officer over in the TOC. When he heard everything that was going on, he cobbled together this reaction force – elements of 10th Mountain, Malays, and Pakistani tanks. So he left his position with JSOC and took charge of that extraction force," explained Hooten.

The final force included most of the 2-14th spread out between their own trucks and Humvees and the Malaysian Condors, their antitank platoon and their scout platoon, a Military Police element, an additional antitank platoon from C-Company of 1-87th Infantry, all in Humvees and some 40 mixed Ranger, Delta, and SEAL personnel from Task Force Ranger including Matt Rierson from C-Team. The Task Force Ranger elements were temporarily placed under the operational control of Colonel David and the QRF. B-Company of 2-14th was assigned as the standby reaction force with a plan developed to insert them by helicopter at an off-set landing zone should they be required.

Liaison officers were attached to the command vehicles of the Pakistani and Malaysian contingents with an American officer riding in the lead M48. Air support would be provided by the AH-1 Cobras and OH-58Ds of the 2-25th Aviation Regiment until the convoy reached National where the role would be passed to the AH-6 Barber callsigns of Task Force Ranger. The OH-58Ds would also be able to "sparkle" the route for the convoy using infrared lasers only visible through night-vision devices.

## 2323 HOURS: QRF DEPARTING NEW PORT.

Struecker recounted: "Malaysians, Pakistanis, some elements from the 10th Mountain and me and my men in those same two Humvees. We all ride out there about 11 o'clock at night and spend until 9 o'clock the next morning out there." The 93-vehicle convoy made it to the vicinity of National largely unscathed and in good time, a scant 30 minutes after rolling out from the airfield.

Until that point, they had only received intermittent small-arms fire. As they approached the turn onto National, however, the multinational structure of the rescue force broke down. The Pakistani tank commanders decided that they would no longer lead the convoy. They were fearful of using their white-light headlights to drive as they had no night-vision devices and were concerned the headlights would likely draw Somali RPG fire.

After fruitless negotiation with the American liaison officer, the Pakistani armor pulled off the road and the Condors took the lead. The tanks would, however, stay and secure the far western end of National, and the planned egress route, once the convoy linked up with the crash sites. Now in the lead was A-Company in the Condors. Captain Charles Ferry, the company's executive officer, wrote that: "1st Platoon had the mortar and fire support squad, a medic, and three APCs; 2nd Platoon had the engineer squad, a medic and three APCs; 3rd Platoon had a medic and two APCs."

As they turned onto National, they were taken under heavy enemy fire. The two lead Condors made a wrong turn to the south, inadvertently heading toward the Super 64 crash site. The American infantry they carried from 2nd Platoon of A-Company under Lieutenant Mark Hollis, a recent Ranger School graduate, and an attached Engineer squad, could see nothing but knew the vehicles were accelerating away. Hollis later recounted in an article for *Infantry* magazine:

> We started going over curbs and obstacles in the road … Unknown to me, at the same time the first vehicle, which held the 1st Squad leader, and my vehicle, the second, began pulling away from the rest of the column. This effectively

separated me and my two lead squads from the rest of the company ... At this time, I was totally disoriented and had not realized we were on our own.

The two APCs continued west on National Street, then turned south toward Crash Site 2 and continued past it. I believe they were trying to return to the New Port facility. The vehicles were about one kilometer beyond Crash Site 2 when they entered a Somali ambush. RPG fire struck the lead vehicle head-on, mortally wounding the Malaysian driver. My vehicle was struck a moment later in the engine compartment ... the blast felt like someone had lifted the vehicle up ...[10]

Both Condors were immobilized by the RPGs with the Malaysian driver, Private Mat Aznan, later dying of his wounds after being rescued from the wreck by a 10th Mountain soldier. The vehicles would later be "denied to the enemy" by attached Cobra attack helicopters.

Both American squads dismounted and engaged their attackers whilst the Malays stayed in the vehicles. Hollis's men resourcefully used a demolitions charge to enter a nearby compound which they then strongpointed. Hollis remarked that the charge was perhaps a little too large for the task: "It not only made a hole in the wall but knocked down the wall and a small building on the other side. The squad leader reported that part of the wall on his side had come down on his soldiers as well."[11] Hollis himself was hit in the face by a piece of flying concrete that dented his night-vision device.

On National Street, the battle was now in full swing. The M48s were engaged, with an estimated 7 to 10 RPGs fired at the lead tank. It responded with main-gun fire. The Mk19s on the 10th Mountain Humvees hammered targets on the south side of National as they approached the Olympic Hotel. "We were now by the main intersection of National Street and the street the Olympic Hotel was on [Hawlwadig]. The company was stretched out about three city blocks on both sides, with the APCs in the middle," recalled Ferry.[12]

Norm Hooten remembered hearing the firing from the convoy and being immediately concerned about fratricide: "The first sign of that convoy coming in was the main gun on a tank going off. I remember calling on the radio and saying 'Be careful with those things' – I was afraid they were going to shoot us – that was my concern." Belman at the crash site CCP also recalled the tremendous amount of fire as the convoy snaked its way toward them: "The volume of fire when the UN convoy started coming our way – it was just enormous both from the convoy itself and people shooting at it."

Mike Moser at the southern CCP agreed: "The approach of the convoy through the city toward us was easy to monitor, partly through radio but also via the sounds of meandering firefight – incoming and suppressive outgoing – that bounced around the room, growing louder and louder."

Ferry and his men managed to get the APCs moving again and made the turn right onto Hawlwadig, heading north, only to be stopped again by a tremendous amount of fire from the vicinity of the Olympic Hotel. The 10th Mountain soldiers could see the still burning wreck of the Task Force Ranger five-ton truck that had been destroyed outside the objective hours earlier.

Ferry recounted: "Both 1st and 2nd Platoons were taking and returning a large amount of small-arms fire from the Olympic Hotel and nearby buildings and alleys. One APC was up next to the lead platoon."[13] Private First Class James Martin, an assistant M60 gunner, and the M60 gunner himself, Specialist Boynton, were deployed to suppress fire from the Olympic as others cleared a roadblock to allow the APCs to move up.

A Somali gunman popped up behind them and sprayed them with AK47 fire. Both were wounded, Martin fatally, with a round hitting him under his helmet at the base of his skull. "The battalion surgeon, the First Sergeant and two soldiers from 1st Platoon moved into the intersection under fire to give them aid. Nearby, soldiers laid down heavy suppressive fire until the casualties could be pulled into the relative safety of a depression next to a building."[14]

At this point, the Malay APCs were stationary and refusing to move forward due to the weight of enemy fire and concern for their missing comrades. The infantry they carried had dismounted and were fighting block by block up National and Hawlwadig. An Mk19-equipped Humvee from the Military Police was brought forward and used to silence the key enemy firing points outside the Olympic in a hail of 40mm grenades. This effort got the convoy moving again and the force headed up Hawlwadig whilst the dismounted 1st Platoon headed east toward the Super 61 crash site.

**0155 HOURS: LINK UP BETWEEN TFR AND LEAD QRF ELEMENT; ENSURE GOOD ACCOUNTABILITY PERSONNEL PRIOR TO MOVEMENT & CUT KIA OUT OF ACFT.**

One of the lead squads from 1st Platoon spotted the infrared strobes that the Delta operators had placed around the perimeter of the crash site through their night-vision goggles and knew they were close. With the 1st Platoon soldiers shouting "10th Mountain, don't shoot!" to avoid fratricide, the defenders responded with "Rangers!" Moments later, the lead element met up with the Rangers protecting the intersection to the west of Super 61.

Captain Drew Meyerowich of the 10th Mountain met with Captain Steele, who was apparently reluctant to give up command to the rescue force and tried to tell Meyerowich where to place the APCs. Meyerowich was clear to Steele that 10th Mountain was in command of the rescue effort, particularly in light of their recent experience conducting a similar operation at the Courage 53 crash site. Delta Lieutenant Colonel Lee Van Arsdale intervened before the situation became even more heated and told Steele simply: "Mike, let them handle it. They are in charge."[15]

Several APCs were brought forward and stopped near the intersection to allow the Task Force Ranger wounded to be loaded on board. Although the firing had decreased, mainly due to the arrival of the convoy which had now attracted many of the enemy combatants, the occasional RPG was still being fired at the stationary APCs. Captain Meyerowich's A-Company of 2-14th deployed around the perimeter of the crash site to reinforce the Task Force Ranger personnel.

One of the A-Company soldiers was wounded by an RPG fired from a nearby building and an AH-6 swung into action. "An attack helicopter hit the building with [miniguns] and 2.75-inch rocket fire. I thought the helicopter was firing on our position until I saw the tracers hitting the building only 50 meters north of our position," related Ferry. "The expended shell casings dropped into the perimeter. I had never been so close to an air strike, and all of us were plenty scared. For the next several hours, aircraft continued to fire all around our position 35 to 60 meters from us."[16]

The 10th Mountain and Task Force Ranger perimeter continued to receive intermittent volleys of RPGs and largely inaccurate small-arms fire all through the early hours of the morning. The RPGs would be met by return fire and a hastily vectored AH-6. At Super 61, the men worked frantically to free Wolcott's body whilst still under enemy fire.

**0249 HOURS: NO BODIES FOUND AT CRASH SITE #2 (SUPER 64) & NO ONE ANSWERS TO AIRCREW'S NAMES IN VIC (4 X AIRCREW PLUS 2 X DELTA SNIPERS SHOULD HAVE BEEN THERE).**

As 10th Mountain linked up with the Rangers and operators at the first crash site, 1st Platoon soldiers from Whetstone's C-Company, accompanied by three Delta operators and guided by an OH-58D overhead, had made their way into the shantytown surrounding the crash site of Super 64. They were immediately contacted by the enemy as they began making their way through the maze of structures but fought their way through, using their night vision to engage the enemy. Finally, Super 64 was in sight.

Whetstone recalled:

> Super 64 lay diagonally across a small courtyard, pocked with holes from the earlier gunfight as the Super 64 crew and the Delta sniper team tried to hold off the Somalis. John M had a list of the guys that should have been at this site. Under sporadic fire, we began calling out those names that will haunt me forever: Frank … Cleveland … Field … Durant … Shughart … Gordon … Using NVGs, we followed blood trails over 100 meters into the dangerous darkness. The feeling was horrible; there was nothing, no sign of life, no remains in or around the aircraft.[17]

The 10th Mountain soldiers helped John M and his two Delta RTOs recover sensitive materials from the Black Hawk and finally set thermite grenades in the wreckage. The men collapsed their perimeter and fell back to the waiting 3rd Platoon who were guarding their exfiltration route back onto National Street. Struecker, at this point commanding one of the Ranger Humvees on National, sadly recounted: "Some operators went on foot to the Durant crash site to confirm no one was left or no one was alive and they came back and said, 'Everybody's gone, everybody's missing.'"

For Lieutenant Hollis's squad from 2nd Platoon, A-Company, trapped for several hours near the immobilized Condors, salvation finally arrived in the form of Whetstone's C-Company. AH-6s had been vectored to rocket surrounding buildings but Hollis's situation remained dire, surrounded by Somali militiamen. Whetstone requested a visible signal to direct his men. Hollis fired a red parachute flare into the sky and they established they were perhaps a kilometer apart. Whetstone needed the Condors on National to fight through to Hollis's position.

Again communication difficulties between the Americans and Malays delayed any action for another hour as the Malaysians discussed and debated the situation because their battalion commander was concerned about further casualties due to the large numbers of RPGs present. Eventually Whetstone ordered his men to advance on foot and C-Company began a slow and deadly house-to-house fight to reach Hollis's trapped platoon element. Hollis and his men were already moving toward C-Company and had fought some 300 meters toward them when Sergeant Cornell Houston, an attached Engineer, was shot in the chest and two other soldiers wounded.

Hollis himself was attempting to shoot the gunman:

> Just as I ran out of ammunition and was changing magazines, the gunman moved around the corner and began shooting at my location. His actions gave the squad leader enough time to draw a bead on him and kill him. I was so eager to ensure he was dead that I grabbed grenades from the medic and hurled them into the building. We had no more shots from that gunman.[18]

Another Somali opened fire from the north, suppressing one of the squads. One of the squad leaders fired an M203 flare round to mark the gunman's location for close air support, but it hit the wrong building. An AH-6 that had arrived on-station engaged the marked building, destroying it. Hollis told his RTO to tell the AH-6 to follow his tracer and he stood up and emptied a magazine at the correct building. He recalled: "Little Bird came in perpendicular to our location, fired his 7.62mm [mini] gun, then his rockets, and the building disappeared."[19]

C-Company were now only 100 meters distant from Hollis and preparing to charge across the gap when suddenly two to three of the Malaysian Condors appeared behind them. The Malaysian vehicles pulled up near Hollis's men, hosing the upper stories of the surrounding buildings with their twin machine guns and cannon. Hollis's RTO had apparently been directing the Condors toward their location after their commander bravely disobeyed a direct order from his leadership and decided they must attempt to rescue his trapped countrymen and the embattled American infantry.

Whetstone ordered C-Company to follow the Condors and they soon had Hollis's men, including a number of critically injured soldiers, inside the APCs. Once everyone was on board, the Condors pulled out onto National Street and sped away, heading for the Pakistani-controlled soccer stadium to the north. Despite all efforts to halt their wild movement, the Condors kept going until they reached the stadium. They, and the 10th Mountain soldiers on board, were now out of the fight. Sergeant Houston would tragically die from his wounds in Landstuhl, Germany several days later.

At the Super 61 crash site the CSAR team, now reinforced by further Delta operators, were still working to free Cliff Wolcott's body. Delta operator John M and the two other operators who had searched the Super 64 site had brought a diamond-bladed mechanical cutting saw with them to hopefully speed up the process of cutting Wolcott clear of the wreckage, but the saw was only making slow progress.

**0453 HOURS:** ASSAULT [FORCE COMMANDER CAPTAIN MILLER] REPORTS HE HAS 200 DISMOUNTED, (QRF/ASSAULT FORCE/RANGER BLOCKING FORCE) WILL LINK W/ TRANS[PORT] ON NATIONAL ONCE BODY RECOVERED.

Norm Hooten's F-Team who had earlier arrived at Captain Miller's location were dispatched to assist with freeing Wolcott's body from the wreckage:

> [Super 61 co-pilot] Donovan Briley had already been taken out of the aircraft by John Belman I believe and Cliff was still in the aircraft. When the bird crashed, the whole upper part of the Black Hawk had collapsed on him. Somalis are still shooting and throwing hand grenades over the wall at the aircraft. So basically we had to disassemble that aircraft and still couldn't get him out. It was at that point that I linked up with [Delta CSAR medic] Bob M and [Delta sniper troop Sergeant Major] Rick W. At this point the vehicles had also arrived.

Hooten recounted how they tried every means possible to free Wolcott:

> We started using manual breaching tools to rip that aircraft apart and that took a while, then we used the Humvees with fast ropes to try and pull the aircraft apart. There were [cargo] straps aboard the Humvees too so straps and fast ropes. Doing it in the middle of a gunfight is even harder. They were still out there harassing us but they couldn't see what they were shooting at.

Hooten knew that it was imperative that they complete their task before sunrise; the first hints of dawn were already visible on the horizon. Eventually

Hooten and the operators were successful. "We got what we could of the body out and at that point the sun was coming up. I remember being in the aircraft and seeing the sky starting to turn – it added to the sense of urgency."

Kurt Smith reported:

> Dawn was falling over Mogadishu, and we didn't want to be here when it got light. Lieutenant Colonel Lee Van Arsdale finally commanded, "Alright, enough of this. Get him out of there." I reached down into the wreckage and managed to wrap the tow strap over his neck and under one of his arms. It was the best I could do. The Humvee pulled slowly as the tow strap began riding up under Cliff's arm. I pushed his arm down fearing his arm was going to snap and spray blood all over me, but we were able to pull Cliff's body from the wreckage after some difficulty. We then bagged Cliff's remains and loaded him in the Humvee.[20]

C-Squadron EOD technician Luke V, who was assigned to Delta in 1986 and stayed for over a decade, was assigned to place demolition charges on the remains of Super 61 whilst the complicated process of loading up all of the remaining Task Force Ranger and 10th Mountain personnel began. "It just takes a long time. I remember loading bodies and wounded onto the vehicles, you've got to coordinate the link-up … there's a lot of stuff you've got to do to get moving. It's a lot of coordination," explained Belman.

The wounded were loaded into the APCs that had been brought forward to the Super 61 crash site. The dead were strapped on top. Once Wolcott was freed, the plan called for the APCs to drive out with the wounded first. The 10th Mountain and Task Force Ranger would fall back to the intersection of National and Hawlwadig where the Task Force Ranger Humvees waited, positioned with the Pakistani tanks. They would then mount up in the Humvees and Condors for the ride out, destined for the soccer stadium.

Mike Moser was loaded into a Condor. He recalled:

> Exfil vehicle for me was a Malaysian APC. Following the actual link-up with our element, my team had rejoined us by that point, and after some coordination we [the wounded] were ushered out into the street bit by bit for loading. The APC I entered already had a couple guys from our Sniper Troop.

After I was loaded, we loitered there or perhaps a short distance away some considerable time for the extrication of 61's pilots. I recall seeing the sky grow lighter and lighter through the Malay gunner's hatch above me and thinking I'd much rather be making the run home in the dark. It was relatively quiet; I recall little firing during this time aside from maybe an incoming RPG or two, but one or two guys expressed somewhat heated frustration with the time it was taking to cut Cliff and Bull out. I later learned more about why this was so problematic.

**0530 HOURS:** BODY RECOVERED. DESTRUCTIVE CHARGES SET ON HELO. AH-6S PROVIDING COVER FIRE FOR WITHDRAWAL FROM CRASH SITE #1.

Now the race was on to get out of the city before the sun rose. Jeff Struecker and the Rangers were only too aware of what daylight would bring: "As the sun starts to come up it is noticeable, every minute enemy fire is picking up, more volume, more accurate … Everyone in the city knows where we're at. Everyone who wants to kill Americans knows exactly where to go." Tom DiTomasso added: "We defended that crash site all night long until the commander made the decision to leave at 5 o'clock the next morning. The Somalis started coming out again."

As the sky lightened, the Pakistani tanks abruptly started their engines and, without a word, drove off to the east, likely headed for the New Port facility. With the light came renewed Somali small-arms and RPG fire. One of the Task Force Ranger Humvees was immobilized at the intersection as they waited for their comrades to move from the Super 61 crash, down Hawlwadig, and to their location.

Ranger Captain Lee Rysewyk later wrote:

> One RPG landed next to the GRF2 cargo Humvee with the Ranger weapons platoon leader, the cooks, and other headquarters personnel in it, disabling the vehicle and wounding four Rangers. One Ranger, Sergeant First Class Rick Lamb, complained of a massive headache. He had a small amount of blood coming from a scratch on the forehead, but he continued to fight. Later, the Ranger found out that he had a piece of shrapnel from an RPG lodge two inches into his forehead between the lobes of his brain.[21]

Lamb recounted the incident:

> There was an RPG flash off to the right side. You could hear the guys in the back yelling RPG and everything slowed to where you could almost follow it with your eyes. It hit in the alleyway to my left. I can remember my head going back and watching a spurt of blood hit the running lights on the dashboard and I remember swearing under my breath and saying, "Damn it, I just got killed," and everything went to a white pristine point of light, everything got quiet. I was almost feeling pretty good; you're wet, you're sweaty, it's noisy, it's stinky, and everything was feeling "nirvana-ish," then I remember focusing on that white spot of light then thinking about my kid, what about my wife? Then the guys in the back hit me in the back of my head and yelled, "Don't stop here, don't stop here!"[22]

Rick Lamb survived and later had surgery to remove the fragment. The veteran Ranger had previously served during Operation *Eagle Claw* in Iran and in Panama where he was involved in the hunt for Noriega. Most famously, he was also instrumental in the November 1984 defection of a Soviet citizen across the DMZ in Korea which resulted in a 40-minute firefight with North Korean troops who were attempting to kill the defector. He has since gone on to an illustrious career with US Army Special Forces.

Also on Rick Lamb's Humvee was Navy SEAL Homer N. This was the second Humvee that he had been traveling on to be destroyed. The SEAL luckily escaped without a scratch and was later awarded the Silver Star along with the other four SEALs for "conspicuous gallantry and intrepidity in action while serving as a member of a US Navy SEAL Team, US Naval Special Warfare, assigned to Task Force Ranger."[23]

**0350 HOURS: REEF POINT VERY BRIEFLY PICKED UP 2 X PLS [PERSONAL LOCATOR SYSTEM] IN VIC CRASH SITE #2.**

During the night, the PLS (Personal Locator System) built into the PRC-112 survival radios carried by the aviators on Super 64 transmitted at irregular intervals after their crash site was overrun. At one point, at 23:57 according to the logs, this led the JOC to suspect that Shughart and Gordon and perhaps some surviving aircrew may have managed to withdraw to the vicinity of the former Saudi Arabian Embassy compound south of the crash. Another log notes at 01:22 on the morning of October 4 that "friendlies believed to be in abandoned building approx. 100M south of old Saudi embassy." Sadly, this was the movements of the Somalis who had stripped the bodies of their clothing and equipment, including the survival radios.

One of the features of the PRC-112 is that it will continue to transmit a unit's location if an aircraft within line of sight is equipped with the necessary equipment; the AN/ARS-6 Pilot Locating System. The AN/ARS-6 will "ping" the PRC-112, which responds with data on its location. As the Somalis moved around the city with the stolen survival radios, this process was continuing, giving "false reads," and false hope, to the JOC.

Later that morning, as Task Force Ranger were finally extracting out of the city, the log notes another possible PLS transmission at 08:15. At 08:45, they related: "Voice came in over beacon saying, 'my arm is broken.' Attempting to DF [direction find] source." This may have been Durant, but it seems unlikely and was probably a ghost transmission. One final, heart-wrenching, log entry was made at 09:15: "Continued attempts to establish comms with Beacon station unsuccessful. Beacon being turned on or off." This was the last recorded transmission from the PLS.

Super 68 pilots Dan Jollota and Herb Rodriguez had transferred to the spare Black Hawk at the airfield and with a new composite CSAR team on board took off to look for any survivors from Super 64. "The soldier in me is always very optimistic that everyone is OK on the ground," Jollota said. "So, when I analyzed Mike Durant's site, I believed that those guys had successfully landed their aircraft and gotten out of the aircraft. I believed they were moving from their crash site ... I spent the rest of the night ... flying over that city, getting rocked by RPGs, looking for those guys only to find out later that the Somalis had found their radios and turned them on to give us false indications."[24]

# CHAPTER 8

# THE MOGADISHU MILE

*"I can remember how tired everyone looked and how I felt. As we came to major intersections, I watched Rangers summon all their energy to sprint across the intersection. Bullets strafed the streets, kicking dirt up around their feet."*

Lieutenant Tom DiTomasso, Chalk 2 and 2nd Platoon Commander

**0542 HOURS:** ASSAULT MOVING ALL ELEMENTS OUT OF TARGET SITE. AH-6 ELE CONTINUES FIRE SUPPORT.

After Wolcott's body was finally released, the first APCs set off from the Super 61 crash site carrying the wounded as the surviving Rangers, operators and 10th Mountain soldiers began to collapse their perimeter. Tom DiTomasso recalled the bittersweet feeling:

> As we moved across the street to link up with the rest of the company, I could hear the explosions [of the charges placed on Super 61] and see the black smoke rising above the helicopter where friends had died.
>
> Captain Steele briefed us that we would have to move by foot to National Street, approximately two miles away. From there we would link up with Malaysian and Pakistani armored vehicles, Humvees from the 10th Mountain Division and 3rd Platoon. Everyone was exhausted. Lieutenant Perino's platoon, Chalks 1 and 3, would lead the run out; my Chalk 2 would pull rear security. Chalk 4, the other element of my platoon, had exfiltrated back to the airfield on Humvees, after numerous attempts to link up with me at the crash site.

"It was communicated by Scott Miller and Van Arsdale – we loaded up the KIAs first and then we put the wounded on and did a combined foot and vehicle movement. The APCs were moving and we were moving alongside of them like a mechanized infantry unit," remembered Norm Hooten. Unfortunately, once the first Condors reached Hawlwadig and began taking small-arms fire, several sped away, leaving many of the Rangers and operators dangerously exposed.

**0605 HOURS:** NOT ENOUGH TRANSPORT, 50 PAX [PEOPLE] STILL DISMOUNTED. ASSAULT REQUESTING MORE APCS.

Kurt Smith recalled:

> There was no room inside the APCs for the 40–50 TF members who were able to move on their own. Norm [Hooten] instructed the team that we would run alongside the APCs and use them for cover on the way out. The APCs began moving down the street past the target building and turned

south on Hawlwadig Road. At this point, they accelerated to about 30 miles per hour and left us behind.[1]

A number of the Rangers were hit as they attempted to run along with the departing APCs. One of the Ranger medics Richard "Doc" Strous, who had been wounded earlier by an RPG fragment, was struck by a round that ignited a flashbang on his webbing. It detonated and the medic disappeared in the explosion, only to reemerge unharmed moments later. Sergeant Randy Ramaglia was hit by gunfire as he crossed one of the intersections:

> I remember just running across the road, just blindly shooting and hoping sounds of the shots is enough to get somebody's head down. We get to the intersection where we set up our initial blocking position … They're still shooting; I'm beside this wall … and this is when it felt like somebody had walked up behind me and just hit me with a ball bat in the shoulder. It slung me forward … I just remember, you know, kinda recovering for a moment and "what happened?"
>
> I'm figuring somebody shot a piece off the building or threw … a rock. And that's when [Specialist John] Collett said he'd been shot … and then his eyes just got huge. And, he's like, "Sergeant, you've been shot" … I did all my vital signs. [Shoulder] just felt tight, it just felt like somebody had wrapped it up in a bandage. But it didn't hurt … And I'm thinking I got shot in the back, in the torso. And if it came through it more likely is gonna penetrate a lung or at least bust a rib. And that was like the biggest thing I was concerned about.[2]

With some of the Condors gone, around 25 Rangers and operators were left with none of their rolling cover. The men on foot fought their way out on the infamous "Mogadishu Mile." They paused at each intersection and placed suppressive fire down each thoroughfare to enable their teams to cross. Smith recalled:

> The situation was desperate. If we had taken a single casualty on the run out of the area, the TF could have been rendered immobile again. We had also had enough of allowing the Somalis to exploit the ROE [rules of engagement] to their advantage. On this run down Hawlwadig Road, if we saw a single

Somali trying to interfere with our movement, he was put down immediately: man, woman, or child. We moved down Hawlwadig Road for eight blocks before turning east on National Street. There, a number of Humvees were lined up on the side of the road. We were still taking fire from Somali militia. F-Team consolidated behind a Humvee.[3]

**0620 HOURS: ALL PAX LOADED, CONVOY MOVING OUT.**

In one of the Condors, wounded Delta operator Mike Moser was considering his chances of survival in the lightly armored vehicle:

> When we were at last under way, I recall no rounds striking our APC during the drive to the Pakistani stadium. There was certainly a great deal of shooting going on outside – I attributed this to the revised ROE – we were quite ready to suppress [or] destroy anything at all in order to move safely. I remember being consumed with the question of what my final milliseconds might feel like if an RPG were to pierce the skin of our APC. I really preferred to take my chances moving on foot rather than ride inside this massive target. My legs were still working fine and I always regret not voicing my wish to run alongside my team.

Ranger Lieutenant Perino was moving with his men from the crash site: "AH-1 Cobras and our AH-6 Little Birds began to strafe the streets parallel to us. The whole force moved from building to building, using doorways and the APCs for cover. Each time a Ranger would reach an alleyway, he would fire down it while another Ranger would leapfrog around him."[4] Awaiting the Ranger chalks, operators and CSAR team were "approximately five Humvees and three APCs." Perino and his men clambered aboard a Pakistani M113.

John Belman from the CSAR team said: "I do recall Malay vehicles with their guns elevated just shooting, not actually shooting at anybody but guns elevated at a 45-degree angle and firing. When I saw that I was like, 'Are they really doing that?' but they were. Those rounds have to come down somewhere." Jeff Struecker agreed. "They are just tearing everything up – twin MAG58s, I get it, you want fire superiority but you're going to run out of ammunition."

Struecker was waiting with the Task Force vehicles. He explained:

The plan was for [Lieutenant] Larry Moores and I to be the last two vehicles to leave and we didn't have any hatches, we didn't have any doors [on the Humvees]. Everybody else drives away. The guys on foot were told to go down National Street, the vehicles are waiting there. The plan was never "You run all the way out of the city." Somehow the word came down that we got everybody, everybody is on the Malaysian APCs so we make the decision to leave. Tanks leave, APCs leave, 10th Mountain leaves, and we are the last vehicles.

I told Paulson who was on the .50 cal., who at this point had been shot twice, to face the gun to the rear because we were the last vehicle. Paulson said, "Hey Sergeant, there's like 50 guys running down the road chasing after us." I said "Paulson, light them up, man, because we've got everyone on the vehicles" and he says, "No, those are our dudes."

Larry Moores and I backed up, back to the target building and as many guys as physically could jumped into our Humvees, and I mean jumped into the back, jumped into the doors, literally hanging off the bumper with their feet dangling on the ground and probably 15 to 17 guys on each Humvee but we couldn't take everyone – they had to run out the rest of the way on foot. Jeremy Kerr had the pedal to the floor and the vehicle was going 30 kilometers an hour.

He remembers it was as if the population of Mogadishu had woken up and all decided to shoot at them again: "It was crazy – getting shot from both directions as you crossed the intersection. The intersections were bad, real bad and the fire was overwhelming. We kind of split the convoy up so no one would be in the intersections."

Combat Controller Jeff Bray was one of the last running along on foot, often running backwards to direct AH-6 strikes as the Little Birds flew top-cover for the embattled column, trying to suppress enemy fire. "There was a lot [of fire] on the way out, RPGs and all sorts of stuff," confirmed Belman. "I didn't have any ammunition, I got a little bit from the 10th Mountain guys but I was on my last magazine. There was a Delta guy called John B and he threw one to me as we were running toward where the vehicle pick-ups were."

Up ahead, Norm Hooten and his team were trying to keep pace with the APCs. Hooten explained:

> When the armor stopped at intersections, we'd shoot under the wheels. We were much more aggressive going out than going in. Going in we'd only shoot identified targets, going out we'd shoot suppressively down intersections. Instead of waiting to find a target, suppress whilst your team is crossing. Suppress the road then move to the next road and suppress that one. I remember [earlier] talking to my team, one of my team mates fired a 203 and I said, "Hey, careful where you shoot that, make sure you have a target," and on the way out I really didn't care where he shot it!

A number of 10th Mountain Humvees were waiting at the eastern end of National Street, some 1200 meters from the intersection where the Olympic Hotel was located, to carry out those who couldn't fit into the APCs. "We moved out maybe a half mile and we linked up with 10th Mountain. They had a lot of vehicles in and around a parking garage and when we got there some of us loaded into vehicles, some of us went on foot and we moved back to the Pakistani stadium," Hooten added.

John Belman recounted:

> [Sergeant First Class] Al Lamb and I jumped on the same 10th Mountain Humvee on the way out but other than that everybody else [from the CSAR team] came out on a collection of three Humvees. We ended up getting separated from the main convoy going to the Pakistani stadium and went off on our own lost patrol back to the airfield. I don't know how we got separated but we drove into the far end of the airfield. Then we had to go back out because one of their vehicles [from 10th Mountain] was missing and we had to go find them. And just as we're about to go back out, with no ammo, we heard the [missing vehicle] had made it to the Old Port.

"Captain Steele put Chalk 2 at the rear of the foot movement and we were the most wounded. When Chalk 2 got to the link-up point, all the vehicles were gone. The crowd kept coming so we just kept running," recounted Tom DiTomasso. He was down to his last magazine and most of his Rangers were out of ammunition for the last 45 minutes of the exfiltration. Delta Sniper

Troop Sergeant Major Rick W even used his custom .45 pistol to shoot a number of gunmen after his CAR15 ran dry. "I heard the story of Rick W, the Delta Sergeant Major on our bird, pulling his .45 and taking a couple of people out," confirmed Belman.

After the QRC commander learned of the dismounted Rangers and operators, he called an immediate halt for all vehicles not yet at the stadium to ensure that those running the "Mogadishu Mile" were retrieved. DiTomasso and his men, however, were finally picked up by other Rangers. He explained:

> Larry Moores, the platoon leader for 3rd Platoon, was at the Pakistani stadium looking for me. When the guys rolled in with the Malaysians and Pakistanis, Larry's saying "Where's Chalk 2?" So he took his guys, loaded them back up in their Humvees and drove back into the city. Basically he saw us running down the road, he stopped, did a U-turn, we jumped on his Humvees and they took us to the Pakistani stadium.

"It took us probably until 8 o'clock the next morning. We went to the soccer stadium. It would have been too much of a fight to go back to the base so we took everyone to the nearest UN [location] which was the Pakistani soccer stadium," remembered Struecker. He recalled the peculiar sensation of the enemy fire ceasing as they left Habr Gidr territory:

> Seven warlords had split the city up and said, "This city block is mine [and] that city block is yours," and when we crossed the line we were no longer in that warlord's territory and it was like somebody flipped the switch. We had rough ideas where those lines were but we didn't know exactly where they were.
>
> The imagery that I'll never forget was driving away with all of these [Rangers] hanging off Larry Moore's vehicle, the sun is coming up and the road has so many bullet casings on it that the road looks like it's glittering from gold. It dawned on me that those were bullet casings – that's how many bullets we fired tonight – and then you cross the line and the firing stops completely.

Norm Hooten was similarly taken aback:

> I can distinctly remember being in a gunfight and then being in a friendly neighborhood where everyone was cheering for us. It was like crossing a line – from running down the street shooting at every intersection and then linking up with 10th Mountain and into an area where all the Somalis are on the side of the road cheering – it was just surreal. It sums up Mogadishu, it's split up by tribe and clan. So we'd rolled out of the control of the Habr Gidr clan …

Finally, after 18 hours of pitched battle, Task Force Ranger returned to the Pakistani-controlled soccer stadium. "As much as the UN weren't exactly our friend up until that point, I will say on the day the Malaysians and Pakistanis they put themselves in the line of fire and were able, along with 10th Mountain and the residual forces from Task Force Ranger, to put something together that was pretty remarkable," recalled John Belman.

**0630 HOURS: CONVOY PULLING INTO PAKISTANI STADIUM.**

At the stadium they were greeted by a scene of devastation. Colonel Boykin said years later he recalled: "A five-ton truck, and we had it stacked with bodies, dead and wounded. My soldiers. And we dropped the tail on that truck and the blood poured out the back of it, like water." The CIA Station Chief was horrified at the thought that his intelligence and his recently recruited Somali source in Team Three may have led Task Force Ranger into an ambush. He asked SEAL Captain Eric Olsen, "Did I take these guys into an ambush?" "No, it wasn't an ambush," Olsen replied, "It was just a shootout."[5]

Belman remembered:

> I walked over to where they had a bunch of ammunition stacked and grabbed a bunch of magazines so that I had all the ammo and everything else that I needed and then I walked back and started talking to [Ranger Sergeant] Alan Barton who was another guy who'd been on the CSAR team. He started telling me all the people who'd been killed and that's when it first hit me.

Tom DiTomasso summed up the feelings of his men, saying: "It was an immense feeling of sorrow, that's the best way I can describe it. It was not celebration."

Wounded Delta operator Mike Moser recalled the moment they arrived:

At the Pakistani stadium, upon exiting the APC I was greeted with the sight of a much larger CCP than our little neighborhood courtyard [back near at the Super 61 crash site]. I saw quite a few guys covered up, and many more on litters being tended to. [Delta surgeon] Doc Marsh may have been right there but I have no memory of him. I needed no real treatment since my little scratch was certainly not getting worse.

Steve D, a sniper from Super 61 – who also happened to be an 18D Special Forces medic – and who was relatively unscathed, [I] think his back was damaged though, was treating several guys, including our Squadron Sergeant Major, Tommy C, who was shot following his exit from the CSAR Black Hawk onto Super 61. I walked over to Tommy to check on him and give him a thumbs up and a smile. I made a half-assed attempt to be useful to Steve, but he and the other medical folks had things under control.

I began to review the corpses, curious who we had lost, Ranger or ours, but for some reason felt it was bad taste to peek under the tarps. Through a few conversations here and there I tried to gain an understanding of who was hurt [or] killed. Maybe here I learned about Super 64. As this triage process was still unfolding, there was an evacuation shuttle which began to transport guys back to the Task Force HQ area at the airport.

Within an hour or so I was loaded onto an old Huey MEDEVAC bird outfitted with litter racks and lifted out. At the airfield, I was met by our CI [Counter-Intelligence] guy, who took custody of most of my kit. At some point I was triaged. My wound was relatively minor, so I was sent to the Swedish combat hospital for surgical exploration/cleaning – our JSOC medical team concentrated on the urgent folks.

Great narcs [drugs] – I remember a very slow, hallucinatory return to consciousness watching a ceiling fan spin above me. No real repairs done, [the surgeons] just opened me up to accommodate the swelling to come. Despite the small geography of the elbow, that round did not blast the joint apart as I had thought – just a tiny bone chip. Radial nerve trauma, however, made the arm useless and it would remain so for months to come.

Struecker also recalled the Hueys:

> We coordinated with some Huey UH-1Hs to fly the guys who were really, really bad back to our surgeon [Doctor Rob Marsh, Delta's surgeon, was located at the airfield with his JMAU]. Those helicopters just kept on flying turn after turn, fully loaded with wounded and that's when it kind of overwhelmed me – "Holy crap, a lot of people just got killed or wounded" – and I walked away without a scratch.

**0810 HOURS:** BEGIN SHUTTLE OF RANGERS, FROM STADIUM RTB. NET MONITORING WEAK INTERMITTENT TRANSMISSIONS FROM VIC OF CRASH SITE #2.

The surviving lift Black Hawks ferried the survivors back from the Pakistani stadium to the Task Force Ranger hangar. "We were cycling back and forth from the stadium to bring guys back. I think I did three round trips and [Super] 67 did four," recalled Izzo. The Star flight MH-6s also flew the Delta operators back to the hangar.

The most serious casualties were flown to the US military medical facility in Germany. Moser explained:

> At some point I was returned to a bay full of Task Force wounded and saw some other familiar faces including Rick Lamb, who amazingly caught the sliver of RPG steel between the halves of his brain and lived, though at the time I think he was still unaware of his wound's severity and told me it was a scratch. Don't recall how many days it took, but we all were lifted out to Landstuhl on a C-141 STRATEVAC [Strategic Evacuation].
>
> I briefly got to shake some hands at the Task Force on the way out as we were loaded. At the Landstuhl hospital, I underwent another surgery – actually the first one was never closed – to examine the extent of damage and more cleaning/debridement. Within a day or two I was transported to Walter Reed Army Hospital in Washington DC, where I stayed on the ward for several days until I was finally released.

Others were inevitably second-guessing themselves amid their grief. Super 65 pilot Gerry Izzo admitted that he struggled for years with questions over whether he should have flown into the Super 64 crash site or followed orders:

I did what I was told and stayed in holding. It's not just my life, I've got my crew and I'm responsible for them. And of course you think you're the only one with doubt, with survivor guilt but you find out that everyone from General Garrison down to a private Ranger was going through the "coulda, shoulda, woulda" thing. You can't help it. It's natural.

Task Force Ranger casualties for the October 3 mission were 16 killed; five from Delta, five from the 160th SOAR, and six from the Rangers; and an incredible 83 wounded. A later analysis showed that 55 percent of the Task Force Ranger casualties were from bullets or direct hits by RPGs, 31 percent were fragmentation injuries primarily from RPGs and hand grenades, 12 percent were blunt force trauma including the casualties sustained by the aircrews, and 2 percent were burns. The International Committee of the Red Cross estimated the number of Somali dead at somewhere between 200 and 300 with approximately 700 wounded. Radio Mogadishu reported slightly higher figures; 364 killed and 754 wounded. Other Somalis claim as many as 500 were killed and twice that number wounded. We will never know for sure.

The 10th Mountain suffered 22 wounded and two killed in action during the eight-hour operation to extract Task Force Ranger. Matt Eversmann noted that "When I think about (2-14th Infantry's) virtually 'no notice' mission to head out to support us, I am thankful that those warriors were there to answer the call."[6] Their role was covered briefly in the Bowden book but almost completely excised from the film, leading to understandable discontent amongst 10th Mountain veterans.

Without the 10th Mountain intervention, the number of additional casualties incurred by Task Force Ranger would have been much higher. Some personnel would have undoubtedly made it out of the city on foot with the AH-6s flying above, but exactly how many is open to question. 10th Mountain played a significant and sometimes underreported role in the events of October 4, as did the Malaysians and Pakistanis. The Malays suffered two men killed and seven wounded whilst the Pakistanis had two of their own tank crewmen wounded. A later report noted, "By operation's end, 'Task Force David' had successfully achieved what many believed to be impossible. The fact that so few casualties were sustained by this ad hoc organization, in the execution of a near insurmountable task, was nothing short of miraculous."[7]

## DAY OF THE RANGERS

**0916 HOURS: GROUND COMMANDERS REPORT ALL PERSONNEL ACCOUNTED FOR EXCEPT FOR THE 4 CREWMEMBERS AND 2 SNIPERS INSERTED INTO CRASH SITE #2.**

On the morning of October 4, many of the members of Task Force Ranger were just learning of the missing aircrew and Delta snipers at the Super 64 crash site. "We didn't know the true fate of any of them. I didn't really know what was going on at Crash Site 2 for a long time," explained Karl Maier. "We knew the crowd overran them because the C2 bird could see that. When I heard they had Mike Durant, I was like, 'Okay, what about the rest of them? Where's everybody else?' We were kinda in the dark."

Delta's Operational Support Troop prepared a small team to venture out into downtown Mogadishu in the hope of recovering those missing in action. The Operational Support Troop was known as F-Troop, one of the most clandestine sub-units within Delta, and one that conducts close target reconnaissance and advanced force operations often prior to a Delta squadron's arrival in a conflict zone.

Uniquely, F-Troop included women, and at least one deployed to Somalia. In the film, it was incorrectly shown as Eric Bana's Hooten that was tasked with such a mission whilst in the book, another operator, John M, was mentioned as having conducted it. A number of operators confirmed instead that in reality it was the Operational Support Troop: "They were the guys that went back out. They negotiated the return of the remains of Shughart and Gordon."

The true horror of what happened to the Super 64 aircrew and the snipers would soon become all too evident as stomach-churning images appeared on CNN of their bodies being dragged through the streets of Mogadishu. A shocked America began asking questions about a country few had even heard of.

One naked body, likely from the Super 64 aircrew, was paraded through the streets on a wheelbarrow. A Pakistani UN contingent near the K-4 Traffic Circle saw the body and realized that it was one of the missing Americans. After trying to intercede, they were threatened by the mob and left the area.

Another nude body was dragged through the streets by ropes in a horrific display of savagery. In one small mercy, all of the aviators and both of the operators had been shot dead before their bodies were desecrated.

The bodies of Gordon and Shughart were likewise treated with savage indifference. The Somalis tore them to pieces. As noted previously, one of their severed arms was used to club Durant into near unconsciousness. Still images exist of the atrocious treatment of the bodies, but these are not reproduced in this book as a mark of respect to the families of the fallen.

A Habr Gidr militia member interviewed by American broadcaster PBS tried weakly to explain the savagery:

> A person who's [sic] father was killed, don't you expect him to drag a dead body? If a person gets very angry he wants to vent his anger, he wants something to have all his anger accrued on. We as militia did our part of the fighting through the bullets, those people who were dragging the bodies were only small children and women, and that was their way of expressing their anger.[8]

Gerry Izzo remarked: "When we saw the video of them dragging those bodies, our attitude changed. It hardened very much and it's probably good that we never engaged them again because we probably would have shown much less restraint, much less control." Similar feelings were voiced by a number of Delta personnel who even after the brutal battle of October 3 were champing at the bit to return to the city to rescue Durant. The feeling on the ground was not surprisingly one of barely suppressed rage: "We were pissed off, we knew they had guys missing, had guys killed. We were ready to go kill somebody," said Delta Sergeant First Class Kelly Venden, a member of A-Squadron who flew in to reinforce the Task Force.

Contained within a plastic garbage bag, one set of remains was unceremoniously dumped outside the US Embassy. Another was delivered by CIA informants. Tommy Faust mentioned: "HUMINT sources reported a body left at a tire roadblock in the city, and then managed to recover the body. It was one of us."[9] Another body was returned by the ICRC:

> The Red Cross brought in the remains of one of our casualties to the Swedish hospital at the airport. The Red Cross delivered several pieces of what appeared to be a black corpse, a total of less than 60 pounds. All of our casualties were white. However, the remains were evacuated to Dover AFB [Air Force Base] and DNA testing confirmed it was one of our SF soldiers. Evidently, the body had been temporarily covered in lime and buried which accounted for the discoloration. The other two MIAs, less CW3 Durant, were accounted for [and] were changed to KIA.[10]

A-Squadron would arrive in Somalia on October 5, 1993 to relieve their battered and bruised colleagues in C-Squadron. Venden explained:

> Charlie was already there and after October 3rd, A-Squadron was ready to replace C-Squadron in the normal rotation. We were due to rotate in soon after October 3rd. October 3rd happened, we were already palletized to go over and once things went down we were called in and immediately flew out. We showed up on the 4th if not early morning of 5th October and took over the lead finding Aideed and finding our guys who were missing.

Ultimately, the deployment of A-Squadron and A-Company of the Rangers was an incredibly frustrating time which only made the Task Force Ranger losses even harder to comprehend as Venden recalled:

> We spent about six weeks there and after the first couple of weeks it became more of a "We're just here to let people see us here, we're not really looking for anybody," there's political talks, there's been communications with Aideed so we're really just there as a show of force. The next thing is that we're flying Aideed around in our [US] helicopters – it was pretty pathetic from our point of view. Extremely frustrating. Once the politics took over, we just sorta hung out, did a lot of PT, ran on the beach …

Venden confirmed that although Delta and the newly arrived Rangers were ready to strike, either against Aideed or in a hostage rescue mission to recover Durant, they never "spun up" on another mission: "When we first got down there, we were planning on hitting heavy. We were looking for Aideed, looking for Durant, our goal was to go and find these guys. We did not ever do a dry hole, we never had a location, and we never had any solid intel that I recall on either Durant or Aideed."

Still out in the city was Mike Durant, his status unknown. The overrun of the Super 64 crash site had been seen by the C2 helicopter and filmed by the Reef Point, so the JOC were aware Durant had been hauled away by the mobs, but they had no idea if he was still alive or had been executed – he was listed only as missing in action (MIA). The lack of remains at the crash site also gave rise to speculation that his crew and the Delta snipers might have also been captured, but they too were initially classified as MIAs.

Durant had in fact suffered yet another terrifying incident as he was being transported away from the vicinity of the crash by the SNA militia. Whilst on the truck, Durant's captors were, in the words of the official history of the 160th SOAR, "intercepted by local bandits who took Durant intending to use him for ransom. He was taken back to a house where he was held, interrogated, and videotaped. Later, when Aideed paid his ransom, Durant was moved to the apartment of Aideed's propaganda minister." He was held by the bandits for the first 24 hours of his captivity.[11]

During those first hours, Durant could still hear the firefight continuing in the city as the eventual United Nations and 10th Mountain relief convoy fought its way into and out of the city. Durant heard helicopters overhead and mentally prepared for a Delta Force assault to rescue him, a rescue that sadly never eventuated. At some point before the transfer, the pilot was shot in the shoulder by a cowardly AK47-wielding bandit, inflicting a further wound upon the battered aviator. Once transferred to Aideed's custody, the conditions of his imprisonment improved somewhat with ICRC packages and a Somali doctor visiting.

The video Durant had been forced to participate in was transmitted by the world's media, a still from which infamously made it onto the cover of both TIME and Newsweek Magazine along with newspapers worldwide. The videotaped interview makes uncomfortable viewing even today, as he is clearly in severe pain and being forced to answer questions. Gerry Izzo remembered watching the footage with other members of Task Force Ranger:

> As soon as I saw his leg turned 90 degrees and his beat-up face and everything, I thought he might have been mutilated. I could see the way he was trying to take the pressure off his back with his hands because he had fractured his L4, L5 vertebrae. I was watching that video and you're sick in the stomach for him. I was hoping as I was watching it that the camera was then going to pan to the right and his co-pilot would be there, his crew chiefs would be there, but that wasn't the case.

The 160th SOAR aircrews rigged up a speaker system on a Black Hawk and flew nightly flights over the city, calling out to Durant to reassure him that they would not leave Somalia without him. "You could hear other US soldiers calling his name from above [through megaphones]; they didn't know where he was but they were circling around above saying, 'Mike, we won't let you down. We won't leave without you. We'll get you home,' said International Red Cross Committee representative Suzanne Hofstetter, who spent a total of 18 months in Somalia and who later visited Durant in captivity.[12] The aircraft also played music including Durant's favorite, "Hell's Bells" by rockers AC/DC, in an effort to keep his spirits up.

Hofstetter was taken to a house somewhere in southern Mogadishu to conduct a welfare check on Durant. She gave him a care package that included a Bible. Durant used the Bible as a means of recording what had happened to him in enigmatic marks and notations that would make little sense to his captors. When Hofstetter returned from her visit, she was asked questions by the Task Force Ranger J-2 staff but she could not provide any information due to the ICRC's strict neutrality. If the Somalis discovered that she had assisted the Americans, Durant's life, and the lives of future prisoners in war zones, would be placed at risk.

Nonetheless Durant managed to sneak a covert message into one of the letters he was allowed to write to his family and to his unit. At the bottom of the page, he wrote "NSDQ," a cryptic reference that only fellow Nightstalkers would recognize as the unit's motto "Night Stalkers Don't Quit." In fact, the ICRC were suspicious of the "NSDQ" reference and scratched it out before handing over the letters. The initials were thankfully still legible when it arrived at Task Force Ranger. The J-2 teams pored over the letters looking for clues, in one instance focusing on Durant's mention of looking forward to eating pizza upon his release as a possible indication that he was being held in or near a pizza shop.

He was also provided with a radio that allowed him to listen to the BBC World Service and the local Armed Forces Network. On the latter, he heard his wife's voice one morning. She had been interviewed by CNN and was replying to Durant's letter the ICRC had delivered to her. In her statement she made a telling reference to the Nightstalker motto that Durant knew that his unit had asked her to include. Asked by the author what kept him going through his captivity, the aerial messages, the ICRC visit, or the interview with his wife, he replied, "All of the above, (and) my one-year old son, and being part of a unit culture that considers quitting to be an unacceptable alternative."

After the intercession of Admiral Howe, who passed a stark warning to Aideed that if Durant was not unconditionally released, the US would launch an all-out assault on Mogadishu in an effort to recover him, and by implication kill Aideed, the warlord ordered Durant to be freed the next day. Durant was delivered to the United Nations compound and immediately wheeled in for treatment at the American medical facility there. Word soon got back to Task Force Ranger and three Delta operators arrived to quiz him on the location and details of his captivity, with the hope that other members of Super 64's aircrew or their team mates may have still been held at the same location.

Durant later wrote a best-selling account of the mission and his captivity, *In the Company of Heroes*, which is highly recommended to all readers who wish to understand in greater detail the horrific 11 days he endured as a prisoner of war of Aideed. The pilot courageously managed to return to flight status and again piloted Black Hawks with the 160th SOAR until his retirement from the Army in 2001.

In an October 6, 1993 National Security Council meeting, President Bill Clinton decided the hunt for Aideed was over and that the much-mooted dual-track political settlement would now be sought with the warlord. Launch authority was removed from Garrison and his staff. If Task Force Ranger wanted to launch any sort of operation, they would now require express Pentagon approval. Many felt understandably betrayed by the decision.

On the same day, thousands of miles away in Mogadishu, a final tragedy was to befall Task Force Ranger. General Downing and Colonel McKnight were talking outside the hangar, leaning against a Humvee. A number of other Rangers and Delta personnel including Doc Marsh were also present in the vicinity. Tommy Faust also passed by on his way from the showers, pausing to briefly talk with Downing and McKnight before continuing on into the airport building his intelligence cell operated from.

Moments after, an SNA mortar round landed where Faust had stood. It detonated, severely wounding 16 Task Force Ranger personnel including Downing, Marsh, and McKnight, and killing Sergeant First Class Matt Rierson, the seasoned assault team leader who had been so instrumental during the battle and on McKnight's convoy.

"They'd been trying to hit that airfield every day for three months," said Norm Hooten. "Especially for someone like Matt who had gone through so much on that convoy and he had two small sons, a great family and was going to be a future leader in the Unit … he was really respected, one of the heart and soul members of C-Squadron. It was a blow to all of us." Today, Rierson, a formidable pistol shot, is remembered within Delta by the Matt Rierson Trophy awarded during the Operator Training Course to the best pistol marksman during the training program.

For Task Force Ranger, Operation *Gothic Serpent* was over. Delta's C-Squadron and Bravo Company of the Rangers along with their attached Air Force and Navy personnel were soon rotated back to the United States. Their replacements, A-Squadron from Delta and A-Company from the Rangers, would soon follow.

The last United Nations representatives left Somalia in March of 1995, effectively admitting defeat and ceding control to the clans. Aideed declared himself the President of Somalia, a position that not surprisingly failed to be recognized by the international community. He was eventually killed the following year after suffering wounds inflicted leading his forces against his former ally and Task Force Ranger target, Osman Atto.

# CHAPTER 9

# MAALINTII RANGERS

*"I talked to Aideed at great length about the day of the battle in Mogadishu and the tactics involved. And he made the determination that the helicopters were the vulnerability, or the center of gravity."*

**General Anthony Zinni, United States Marine Corps, Commander of the Combined Task Force, Operation *United Shield***

In the wake of any battle come the inevitable questions. What were the failings? What could be learned that might prove useful in future conflicts? The battle of Mogadishu or, as the Somalis now call it, "Maalintii Rangers" or the Day of the Rangers, was no different. A number of important lessons were learnt from the October 3 battle which have since changed the way such operations are conducted and have saved many lives during the post September 11, 2001 Global War on Terror.

There were also the equally inevitable controversies. Would the provision of light armor to Task Force Ranger have made a difference? What was the truth about alleged al-Qaeda involvement? Did the battle of Mogadishu make the White House and Pentagon gun-shy of deploying special operations forces throughout the rest of the 1990s?

# AC-130 SPECTRES

"I remember thinking at the time 'It'd be cool to have Spectre' but I didn't give it a second thought. Maybe ignorance is bliss."

SERGEANT MATT EVERSMANN

Perhaps no single issue has generated as much controversy as the lack of AC-130 Spectre gunship support for Task Force Ranger. Trimmed from the force packages, there is little doubt that the AC-130 would have been a game-changer if it had been available on October 3. It is also an issue that understandably still raises the ire of Task Force veterans. Tom DiTomasso gave his thoughts:

> In my opinion, anybody that says that AC-130s and armored vehicles would not have mattered in Mogadishu is either lying or they have no idea of what they're talking about. We could've dragged that helicopter out of the city with armored vehicles, and the AC-130s would have put a ring of fire around the second crash site. I think that was one of the strategic failures.

Another survivor of the battle at the Super 61 crash site, John Belman, agreed:

Spectre would have been extremely helpful once the first crash occurred and this thing became a massive firefight. Once it went from being a quick surgical hit in a semi-permissive environment to "We're going into heavily defended very hostile territory in daylight." It seems to me if you could have subbed in a Spectre instead of using the Black Hawks as sniper platforms, you would have had a higher firepower, safer resource.

Particularly during the night when Spectre has the ability to see and paint targets and hit targets with a high degree of accuracy, I think that would have been very, very helpful. It could've helped the ground convoy out too – it could've passed directions more effectively and [with] the ability to basically hammer anything that might threaten the ground convoy.

Gerry Izzo was equally adamant:

The AC-130 absolutely would've helped. If we had had the AC-130, because the Delta operators and the Rangers all knew how to call for fire, they could've kept that AC-130 over the objective area and we could've then taken the [AH-6] gunships and sent them over to Mike's crash site with the rest of the Black Hawks and maybe the [MH-6] Little Birds to get them out.

Remembering the effect of Spectre during the UNOSOM II strikes on Aideed's infrastructure targets back in June 1993, Izzo explained, "The AC-130 gunship was sorely missed. The Somalis were terrified of that thing because they had no defense against it. They could have blown those roadblocks, they could have hit them with 105[mm] shells ... As that gunfire came raining down on them, the Somalis would've pulled back. They respected it, they were terrified of it." Bill Garrison himself agreed in his Senate testimony: "The Somalis were petrified of the AC-130."

Karl Maier also thinks that the AC-130s could have proven hugely beneficial: "Number one: they can see a lot of things, they have great sensors. Number two: they could have used their 40mm or their 20mm cannon to isolate the siege area. Yes, it would have been very helpful. Both as a sensor and as a defensive weapon to keep people away from the area."

Danny McKnight wrote in his memoir of the battle: "I truly believe my five brothers-in-arms would be alive today had the AC-130 been available ... I think Gary Gordon and Randy Shughart would have been able to render medical aid and provide the needed close-in security while the AC-130 kept the enemy from massing and overrunning the Six Four crash site."[1]

Amid such widespread support from the operators on the ground, why then was the AC-130 not deployed? During the pre-deployment exercises at Fort Bragg, Task Force Ranger personnel had trained with Air Force AC-130H Spectre gunships as a constant orbiting presence, providing an aerial safety net with their impressive firepower and sensors.

Officially at least, it is important to note that of the three force packages discussed for the *Gothic Serpent* mission only "Cadillac," the largest option, had integrally attached AC-130H gunships. The author has been unable to verify whether there were discussions regarding adding the Spectres to the other packages. Air Mission Commander Tom Matthews noted: "We planned to do it as we train. We got direction to make it [the force package] smaller. We resisted – we wanted to do it as we train."[2]

General Joseph Hoar, then head of Central Command, who had overall responsibility for operations in Somalia, did not support the AC-130 request, believing instead that the Task Force's AH-6 Little Birds and the AH-1 Cobras of the QRF were sufficient. The justification was to limit the size of the American footprint at a time when the United States was attempting to disengage from Somalia and hand over responsibilities to the United Nations. Hoar confirmed:

> The AC-130s were dropped in view of the number of capabilities available to the Task Force. That was my recommendation up the line. My position was to give them what they needed and no more. If we weren't careful, we would have had 1,000 troops over there. There was a three-way discussion among Downing, Powell, and me about the deployment of Little Birds, troop carriers [presumably the MH-60 Black Hawks], etc. I felt, and Downing agreed (he certainly told me he did), that we didn't need AC-130s.[3]

In fact General Downing, the then-commander of Special Operations Command and the parent command of the Joint Special Operations Command, seems to have preferred to have retained the Spectres, but conceded that the Task Force Ranger mission could be accomplished without them. He said: "The AC-130s were part of every package we looked at … We talked about the force package. I advised that I would like to have the AC-130s. General Powell advised that we needed to keep the numbers down … I said that I thought the

AC-130s should be included and I so recommended since they were an integral part of the package.

"But I also advised that the force could do the mission without them. I had the option to say don't send the force without the AC-130s, but it was then and is now my professional judgment that they would have been useful but we could do the job without the AC-130 gunships as long as the helo gunships went with the force. I decided not to fall on my bayonet. I believe my voice was the most influential with respect to the force package."[4]

It is interesting to note that Downing seems to have believed that the AC-130s were part of all of the force package options presented, as did the Senate Armed Services Committee who conducted their own enquiry into the battle in 1994. With many documents still classified, as noted it has proven impossible to definitively state that the Spectres were or were not included in each of the three packages. "Cadillac" certainly included them.

Undersecretary of Defense Frank Wisner who represented the Secretary of Defense, Les Aspin, explained:

> I was aware of and supported the Joint Staff's recommendation that AC-130s not be included in the force package because they were unnecessary and inappropriate for the mission especially considering the extensive collateral damage they could be expected to cause in an urban environment. I still believe that they were inappropriate for the mission due to the risk of collateral damage.[5]

General Colin Powell as then-head of the Joint Chiefs of Staff does appear to have agreed with Wisner, noting that the earlier deployment of AC-130s in support of the UNOSOM II force in Somalia, "wrecked a few buildings and it wasn't the greatest imagery on CNN."[6] Powell also does not specifically recall AC-130s being a part of any of the force packages, but concedes they must have been. Aspin took a similar line and also argued that he "was never aware that AC-130 gunships were ever in a Ranger Task Force package. They must have been pulled out before the request came to me."[7]

The fact that the AC-130s would have likely been based in nearby Kenya and thus would not have increased the actual US footprint in Somalia would appear to call into question at least some of the arguments set forth by Hoar, Powell, and Wisner. Downing felt that the key sticking point was with the Joint

Chiefs and the political leadership who were almost fanatically attempting to minimize the numbers but, for whatever ultimate reason, and a mixture of political will and fears of collateral damage seem the most likely, the AC-130s were not deployed.

Until darkness fell on October 3, the AC-130s may have been of little assistance as the aircraft are typically forbidden from flying during daylight hours. During the 1991 Operation *Desert Storm*, Spirit 03, an AC-130H operating in support of Marine ground callsigns in Khafji, Saudi Arabia, was downed by an Iraqi SA-7 surface-to-air missile. Gerry Izzo believes that the threat level in Mogadishu for the Spectre was not as high, saying: "I don't think they had heat-seekers [surface-to-air missiles] and the AC-130s could have stayed off-set and provided absolutely deadly fire support."

Ironically, after *Gothic Serpent* was aborted, the newly arrived US reinforcements to Somalia included a complement of Spectres. "We had four AC-130 aircraft in the theater; they were stationed in Mombasa [Kenya]. We could have kept AC-130s overhead 24 hours a day, 7 days a week if we wanted to. Sometimes we'd just keep them overhead and refuel them from KC-135s," noted General Carl Ernst, who took over command of US forces in Somalia days after the October 3 battle.[8]

The Senate Armed Services Committee report would later conclude: "It is difficult to understand the decision to omit the AC-130 gunships from the Joint Task Force Ranger force package. The AC-130s were part of all the force package options and were included in all of the training exercises. This decision is inconsistent with the principle that you fight as you train."[9]

## ARMORED VEHICLES

*"We had guys driving in Somalia in Humvees and getting shot to shit. That's ridiculous. If you're going to be driving in an urban environment, you need armor."*

### SERGEANT FIRST CLASS NORMAN HOOTEN

The use of largely unarmored Humvees, let alone Humvees without doors and the completely open cargo variant, was certainly a factor in the number

An image taken on October 14, 1993 of children playing on a rotor blade amongst the remains of Super 64 after it had been destroyed by thermite grenades placed by Delta operators on the morning of October 4. Note the shanty town surroundings. (Scott Peterson/Liaison)

Another image of the final resting place of Super 64 and the site of the last stand of Shughart and Gordon. Note the tree in the background – this was likely the spot Durant was placed with the tin wall immediately to his right, through which he fired his MP5. (Scott Peterson/Liaison)

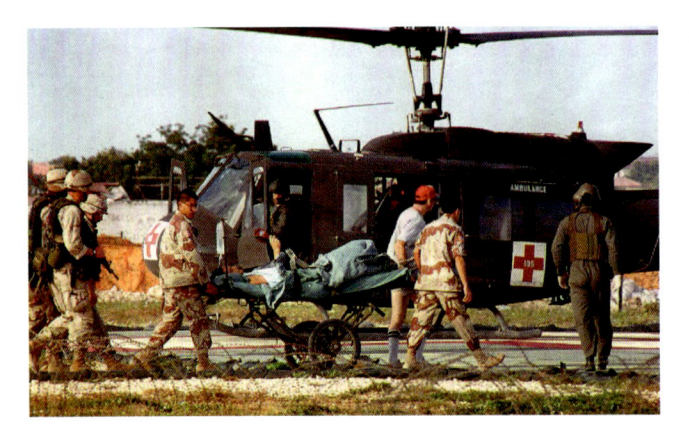

Super 64 pilot Mike Durant pictured beginning his journey back to the United States from the 46th Combat Support Hospital on October 15, 1993. Note the Ranger security element trailing the gurney. (HOCINE ZAOURAR/AFP/Getty Images)

Mike Durant gives the thumbs-up as his litter is carried to a waiting aircraft by fellow aircrew from the 160th SOAR. Each soldier present was given a thimble of watered-down whiskey from a bottle kept stashed by Durant for his return to the United States.
(Courtesy US Special Operations Command)

An AK47-armed militiaman next to a burnt-out Malaysian Condor armored personnel carrier, likely one of the two that became separated from the main effort as the UN rescue convoy arrived on Hawlwadig on the night of October 3/4. (ALEXANDER JOE/AFP/Getty Images)

The wreckage of a Task Force Ranger Cargo Humvee after it was abandoned near the K-4 Traffic Circle and set alight with thermite grenades by Delta operators. (STR/AFP/Getty Images)

Malaysian Condor armored personnel carriers painted in United Nations white seen in Mogadishu on October 13, 1993. Note that both feature the twin 20mm cannon mount rather than the more usual twin FN MAG machine guns. (Scott Peterson/Liaison)

A grainy view of the Pakistani-controlled soccer stadium where Task Force Ranger and Task Force David eventually exfiltrated after the battle. (Courtesy Gerry Izzo)

General Garrison leading the remembrance service for the fallen following the October 3 battle. (Courtesy 75th Ranger Regiment)

A close-up view of the traditional upturned rifles and helmets in remembrance of the six Rangers and five Delta operators (a sixth, Matt Rierson, would be killed within days of the ceremony) lost in the battle. The five Little Birds (one is out of shot) each represent one of the fallen members of the 160th. (Courtesy US Army)

President Bill Clinton awarding the Congressional Medal of Honor to the wives of Randy Shughart and Gary Gordon. (Courtesy United States Department of Defense)

Jim Yacone standing next to the damage inflicted upon Super 62. The RPG struck just behind his seat, knocking him and pilot Mike Goffena briefly unconscious. Thankfully Goffena awoke and managed to land the crippled Black Hawk at the New Port facility. The third Delta sniper on board, Brad H, lost a leg to the RPG in the incident.
(Courtesy Gerry Izzo)

Pilot of Super 65 Gerry Izzo pictured with his Black Hawk in October 1993 and 23 years later in the same helicopter, which was purchased by a private company who intended to return the Black Hawk to its original fit-out from 1993. (Courtesy Gerry Izzo)

Super 68, the CSAR helicopter, on display at the Army Aviation Museum in Alabama. Super 68 continued to serve with the 160th and flew in Iraq and Afghanistan as a Direct Action Penetrator (DAP), the armed MH-60 variant. It is shown here with a full DAP weapons load.
(Courtesy US Army Aviation Museum)

**INSET** Restoration work on Super 68 at the US Army Aviation Museum included recreating the famous "Razor's Edge" paintwork. (Courtesy US Army Aviation Museum)

Tom DiTomasso, Anton Berendsen, Danny McKnight, John Waddell, and medic Richard Strous pictured at Fort Benning in 1994. (William F. Campbell/The LIFE Images Collection/Getty Images)

Veterans of Task Force Ranger visit the grave of Corporal Jamie Smith in February 1994. (William F. Campbell/The LIFE Images Collection/Getty Images)

Reproduction of a US Army Ranger. Note the Nomex flight gloves, "chocolate chip" pattern helmet cover (not enough of the new three-color DCU pattern covers had been delivered) and the blood type written on the boots. The figure carries a standard 5.56mm M16A2 assault rifle. (Courtesy US Army Airborne and Special Operations Museum, Fayetteville, North Carolina)

Artifacts from Tom DiTomasso. These include his ALICE "fanny pack" at the top, Somali currency, his "chocolate chip" boonie hat featuring first lieutenant rank, his boots (marked with his blood type, A + POS), his map (behind the boots), and a Bible given to him by the chaplain of the 160th SOAR. (Courtesy US Army Airborne and Special Operations Museum, Fayetteville, North Carolina)

Reproduction of US Army Rangers showing an M249 SAW gunner lying next to a rifleman. Both figures wear the RBA vest, but the kneeling soldier has the later version which featured a back trauma plate. The gunner's fast-rope gloves are to his side and a length of fast rope is visible to the right. (Courtesy US Army Airborne and Special Operations Museum, Fayetteville, North Carolina)

of casualties suffered by Task Force Ranger. To their credit, the Humvees performed as advertised and survived being riddled with gunfire and RPGs, managing to limp home even after all tires were shot out thanks to their run-flat design. The use of the M923A2 five-ton trucks was understandable in the limited role of extracting prisoners but, once contacted by the enemy, these completely unarmored vehicles proved to be far less than optimal.

Special operations forces working with armor was largely an unknown in 1993. Darby's Rangers during World War II had famously operated with 75mm-equipped M3 half-tracks although their primary mission was to engage German armor, not to provide protection for the infantry. A decade following the Mogadishu operation, Delta itself formed "Team Tank" in the western Iraqi desert with an embedded platoon of M1A1 Abrams main battle tanks, again to deal with enemy armor. John Belman explained:

> We had not worked with armor in those days. The only vehicles we had in the Ranger Regiment were the RSOV [Ranger Special Operations Vehicle] Land Rovers which were completely unsuitable [for Mogadishu] and Delta had some desert mobility vehicles [Pinzgauer Special Operations Vehicles], they didn't even have Humvees so they had to commandeer vehicles from the SF [Special Forces] Groups. None of us had ever worked with tanks. a) it's a mindset shift and b) trying to coordinate that and make that effective takes some doing. Having said that, anything's better than an unarmored Humvee.

Along with the AC-130 controversy, the lack of armored vehicles is a constant theme when discussion turns to the battle of Mogadishu. Armored vehicles, whether wheeled or tracked, would have provided three powerful capabilities to US forces. One, the ability to punch through roadblocks that would defeat Humvees and other soft-skins; two, the capacity to extract wounded under armored protection; and three, the overwhelming firepower of even the 25mm Bushmaster cannons mounted in a Bradley turret, let alone the 120mm main gun of the Abrams, would ensure that any such force could fight their way into and out of the city.

General Hoar had received a faxed request from General Montgomery in August for an armored battalion of tanks and Bradley infantry fighting vehicles. This had nothing to do with Task Force Ranger and was driven by Montgomery's assessment of the increasing risk to his forces. Under Secretary

Wisner, working for Aspin and who had been involved in the decision to cut AC-130s from the Task Force Ranger deployment, was hesitant about acceding to such a request in the face of increasing calls from the civilian leadership to decrease, not increase, the US presence.

After receiving a lukewarm political reception to the idea of an armored battalion, Hoar discussed with Montgomery the idea of reducing the request to a company-sized group of four Abrams and 14 Bradleys. Montgomery agreed and the amended request was sent on September 14, including the rationale that the armor would be used to "deter or defeat militia/bandit attacks on US forces" and "provide a critical roadblock-clearing capability for our vulnerable thin-skinned vehicles." He added that "I believe that US forces are at risk without it."[10] On September 23, the request was denied by Secretary of Defense Les Aspin.

The US Army's Somalia history notes:

> General Montgomery had discussed additional mechanized and armored units with CINCCENT [Commander in Chief, US Central Command] in August and had formally requested a mechanized infantry team with a platoon of tanks and an artillery battery in early September. However, CINCCENT deleted the artillery before forwarding the request to the Chairman of the Joint Chiefs and, despite the chairman's recommendation for approval, Secretary of Defense Aspin disapproved the request in late September.[11]

Defending his refusal to grant the request, Aspin later claimed that he was unaware that the request was based on force protection of US troops: "[it was] never put in terms of protecting troops; it was put in terms of the mission of delivering humanitarian aid," he claimed in an interview with the American ABC television network.[12]

Garrison admitted in testimony to the Senate Armed Services Committee in 1994 that, even if armor had been available to him, he most likely would not have included it in the force committed on October 3. The entire plan was for the assault and blocking forces to complete their mission in under 30 minutes and be on their way back to the airfield before the Somalis could muster a concerted resistance. He did acknowledge, however, that armor would have improved the survivability and increased the speed of the eventual relief column.

The question of equipping units like the Rangers and Delta with their own integral armored vehicles would be one that was thoroughly debated during the years since the battle. Even amongst veterans of the October 3 battle, opinions were mixed. Jeff Struecker, who drove out into Mogadishu three times on October 3, argued:

> I went to Afghanistan nine times and to Iraq five times, most of those with the Ranger Regiment and I was involved for almost ten years in the whole armor/Humvee debate. My job is to get on the ground with a gun and kill bad guys and armored Humvees or light armored vehicles are just a taxi-cab. What armor does is [it] sometimes gives a false sense of security – when things start to get crazy guys start to hunker down behind the armor because they don't want to get shot. It can be a dangerous false sense of security.

He does concede, however, there is a place for vehicles in special operations:

> Make them fast and light and carry lots of guns and get the heck off the vehicle when the bullets start to fly. I'm not a big proponent of light armored vehicle carrying light infantry but I'm heavily in the minority. Everybody else was like, "If we can save a life why don't we?" and I said that there was a psychological component to all of this. Rangers can employ GMVs [Ground Mobility Vehicles – a heavily armed SOF version of the Humvee] with great effectiveness in Afghanistan and Iraq – I'm a big fan of the GMV ... but my experience in Somalia is that the vehicles are bullet magnets.

Delta veteran Kelly Venden added another perspective to the debate:

> We are by nature a short-lived, no logistics train, operational group that goes in, takes care of business and leaves. The more robust [in terms of equipping with armor] we are, the more we lose our flexibility, our ability to react because now you need heavier duty aircraft [to transport the armor], you need ground support and mechanics [to maintain the vehicles], you need all these different things that take away from our ability to be that quick reaction, "we're in, we're out," "we were never there" type thing. You know, "it was the local guys who did all the work." Now there's a signature that we have to try to break.

Obviously the guys who were getting shot at would love to have armored vehicles but conversely that was never our mission. What happens is that you get comfortable having that capability – you get used to the protection and the lack of mobility and you start planning based on the capabilities of your infil vehicle rather than the capabilities of the Unit, you start limiting what you can offer to the Command [JSOC].

Delta's Norm Hooten takes another view:

That was probably the single biggest thing out of Somalia. It was a lesson learnt that went on to save a lot of lives [but] that was not a done deal in the Unit, we had to fight to get Pandurs [six-wheeled APCs], even amongst guys who had been to Somalia. It basically tore the Unit apart. We fought [over the issue internally] for two or three years!

Mike Moser agreed: "We immediately saw the requirement for a rapid, armored troop ground delivery platform. Eventually we (the Unit) obtained a solution, but lining the vehicle walls with sandbags and cannibalizing the extra helo Kevlar plates was what we had at the time."

Hooten continued:

We went in and started looking back and said, "We crashed birds in Iran, we crashed a bird in Grenada, we crashed a bird in Panama, we crashed birds in the Gulf War and we crashed birds in Somalia. Every time we do this we have to call someone else to get armor." In Grenada, we had to call someone and get light-skinned vehicles to drive in and recover survivors. In Panama, we had to get Task Force Gator, which was a conventional mechanized infantry unit with M113s, to recover Delta Force operators on the ground. We didn't have vehicles because we were just too cool for vehicles. In Somalia we called on the Malaysians and the Pakistanis. Every SWAT team in America has an armored vehicle and we're the only guys who don't!

We still believed that we could fly around in a helicopter in a skateboard helmet and a black Faust vest and everybody's going to lay down and give up because they know Delta Force is in town and that's just not true. But there were guys in the Unit who really fought against it – "it's too much trouble, we're going to have to maintain these things, and they'll take up a lot of training time."

There was another half of us that fought very strongly to get it [the capability]. Sanity won out and we got the Pandurs. General Shinseki, who was Chief of the Army, came to see us one day for a capabilities demonstration and he saw the vehicles and he was skeptical at first – "If you need armor, why don't you have a Bradley?" He started to listen to why we had wheeled vehicles – they're easier to transport by helicopter, you can put 'em on transport planes, you can maintain them easier, you can train in them anywhere because they have rubber wheels that don't do any damage to the roads and all the different reasons why we picked them. He put together this task force to basically develop an Army version of it and that version became the Stryker, the Stryker really originated out of Mogadishu.

Delta did eventually decide it needed an integral light-armor capability, and a requirement for what later became known as the Armored Ground Mobility System or AGMS was issued in 1998. This resulted in the purchase two years later of a number of General Dynamics/Steyr Pandur six-wheeled armored personnel carriers. A SOCOM spokesperson was quoted at the time as saying: "Particularly, these vehicles will provide our small teams with a degree of force protection while they are operating independently from other friendly forces,"[13] naturally without mentioning Delta as the receiving unit. The vehicle would be fitted with General Dynamics SURMAX flexible composite armor to protect against armor-piercing rounds.

A number of years later, as the Iraqi insurgency was heating up, the British SAS also attempted to buy a number of Pandurs after noting Delta's positive experience, but allegedly the manufacturer could not supply within the Regiment's timelines, and instead a number of Australian Bushmasters were purchased and customized for their mission. Delta's Pandur remains in service to this day and has been seen in action in Syria, even including one variant mounting a TOW II antitank guided-missile system for use against Islamic State suicide car bombs. "Simply by having that vehicle reduces the number of people who can kill you by a whole lot. Now they [Delta] don't go anywhere without them," concluded Hooten.

After experimenting with a number of platforms including the German-made Wiesel, the Rangers too adopted an armored vehicle, although it was the bitter counterinsurgency fight in the streets of Iraq that finally prompted the move. Instead of the Pandur, the Ranger Regiment received 16 Stryker variants in 2005. The Stryker is an eight-wheeled infantry carrier vehicle capable of transporting an infantry squad and equipped with a remote weapons station mounting either the .50 cal. or the 40mm Mk47 automatic grenade launcher, the replacement for the venerable Mk19 that had served so well in Mogadishu. The Rangers also still use the Stryker and a number have been seen in Syria, all modified for their specialist role.

## HELICOPTER VULNERABILITY

*"They routinely flew in low circles above the ground force at about 500 feet – well below the burnout elevation of an RPG … It was almost as if they thought they could not be hit."*

GENERAL THOMAS MONTGOMERY

Much has also been made of the use of helicopters in a sprawling urban environment like Mogadishu, and in particular the employment of two low-flying Black Hawks as aerial sniping and surveillance platforms. Today, many of the veterans concede that the tactic perhaps displayed an overconfidence in their abilities. Many also argue that it showed a lack of appreciation for their enemy, particularly after the September 25 downing of the QRF helicopter, Courage 53.

John Belman from the CSAR team recalled on the day: "I remember thinking the Black Hawks were flying low and slow. In retrospect that probably was a bad idea. Two of the three that went down were performing that role [sniping and aerial observation]." Norm Hooten was also wary of the tactic, commenting:

> To slow down to the speed that is necessary for a guy to take a single shot with a sniper rifle is really not the best use of a Black Hawk. If I'm going to be shooting from a helicopter I want to use something really effective like a rocket or a minigun, I don't want to slow down and take a single shot. Not a good use of a helicopter, I could do the same thing putting me down on a roof and coming back and getting me later.

The technique had found its genesis in Delta's Aztec or counterterrorism mission where helicopter-borne snipers provided aerial overwatch for the assaulters as they broke into a hijacked aircraft, train, or bus. Indeed, Hooten noted that to use the tactic: "It would have to be in a very permissive environment where I had no risk to the aircraft." Mike Moser also noted his uneasiness with the tactic: "From the very beginning, I, and I'm sure others, were concerned that our aerial platforms were quite vulnerable. Infil needed to be quick and accurate; keeping the sniping birds hovering made me nervous."

Karl Maier agreed: "Sooner or later, when you have a 22,000-pound aircraft flying around at 100 feet off the ground doing circles, you're going to get nailed. And it's daylight. It was definitely something the bad guys took advantage of." Indeed, Marine General Anthony Zinni later all but confirmed this after speaking with Aideed himself:

> And so when they held a meeting, he put people on the roofs of the houses around the meeting place with the machine guns and rocket launchers, and they were to concentrate all their fire on the helicopters. He really believed if he shot a helicopter down, that would cause them to gather around the helicopters. They could fix them and pin them in one area.[15]

MH-60s are still used today in the aerial sniper support role, although lessons have been learnt from the Somalia experience. Close-range, intimate sniper support in dense urban environments has become increasingly a capability delivered by the smaller, more agile MH-6. The raid on the al Qadisiyah research center, codenamed Objective Beaver, in western Iraq in March 2003 is a very useful comparison between the helicopter tactics used in Mogadishu 1993 and in Operation *Iraqi Freedom* a decade on and is worth examining in detail.

At al Qadisiyah, in the same manner as the October 3 infiltration, two AH-6s led the armada and were tasked to overfly the target and ensure there was no imminent threat to the assault force. If air defenses, RPGs, or heavy machine guns were seen, the AH-6s would engage them and neutralize the threat before the lift package arrived. Just behind the AH-6s were a pair of MH-6s with SEAL Team 6 snipers perched on the people pods, one on each side of the aircraft.

Next came the blocking force in four MH-60Ks carrying chalks from the 2nd Battalion of the Ranger Regiment. As in Mogadishu, the Rangers would establish four blocking positions around the objective, the Black Hawks landing to deposit their cargo rather than fast roping the troops in. Immediately behind the lift helos were a pair of DAPs or Direct Action Penetrators, the armed version of the MH-60 equipped with a 30mm cannon, rockets, and miniguns. As we have seen earlier, DAP kits were taken to Mogadishu and the flight crews trained with them, but they were not employed on October 3.

The DAPs were there to provide dedicated close air support along with the AH-6s and the snipers aboard the MH-6s. Two MH-47E Chinooks trailed behind the DAPs, each carrying a contingent of SEAL assaulters. Finally two further MH-47Es brought up the rear, one carrying the CSAR team and one carrying a Ranger Immediate Reaction Force (IRF).

The Black Hawks of the lift package were the first to come under fire as they landed to insert their Rangers. The last Black Hawk received significant small-arms fire, critically wounding a Ranger; the bullet entered his back, missing the rear trauma plate of his body armor, passed through his chest and embedded itself in the front trauma plate. Once the MH-60Ks lifted out of the target location, they flew to a nearby desert runway previously secured by the Rangers and Air Force Special Tactics where a surgical team was standing by to treat casualties.

Notably, unlike Mogadishu, here the MH-60Ks landed, engines running and rotors spinning, awaiting the call to return to the target location. As the MH-47Es landed at the target and the SEALs ran down the ramps, the second aircraft was peppered with small-arms fire and a Nightstalker crew chief was shot through the jaw. The Chinook flew the wounded man directly to the forward surgical team whilst his fellow aviators and a SEAL provided emergency first aid.

Importantly for our discussion, at the target location the DAPs moved out of the immediate area and flew at altitude, engaging technicals that appeared to be intent on reinforcing the enemy on Objective Beaver. Only the Little Birds stayed aloft over the target, the AH-6s suppressing fire from buildings with their rockets and the SEAL snipers delivering precision fire from the bench seats of the MH-6s. Their agility, size, and relative speed improved their survivability over the much larger MH-60Ks.

After the site was secured and the SEALs conducted their Sensitive Site Exploitation (SSE) looking for evidence of chemical or biological weapons, the assaulters were picked up by the CSAR and IRF Chinooks as the transport Chinooks that had initially inserted the operators had sustained too much battle damage to safely fly. The MH-60Ks returned to pick up the Rangers from the blocking positions, all under the watchful eyes of the Little Birds and DAPs. The mission lasted a scant 45 minutes from touchdown to extraction. Both the wounded Ranger and Nightstalker recovered.

What can be gleaned from Objective Beaver and what lessons from Mogadishu have been applied to heliborne SOF assaults? Firstly, the presence of what are effectively two CSAR elements, a doubling of capability since Mogadishu – the Immediate Reaction Force could land to secure a crash site, recover wounded or dead personnel, cut off fleeing enemy, or reinforce ground forces. It has since become a staple of heliborne SOF missions.

Secondly, the MH-60Ks were moved out of the danger zone as quickly as practicable and held at a secure location nearby until extraction was requested. They were not flying over the objective acting as tempting targets for RPGs. Thirdly, the job of close air support on the target location was given to the Little Birds. Even the larger DAPs orbited further out, and at a higher altitude, to reduce their exposure. The DAPs were available if required, but concentrated on securing the outer perimeter from enemy reinforcement. Aerial snipers were employed from the people pods of the MH-6s, not from the larger and slower Black Hawks.

In their history of CSAR, authors George Galdorisi and Thomas Phillips argue that "survival at low altitude depended on staying very low and on immediate suppression of hostile ground fire by aggressive gunners. The MH-60s were low but not low enough, and not maneuverable enough, because of their size amongst the obstacles of city housing. Black Hawks are sixty-four feet in length, with a fifty-five foot rotor diameter ... big birds."[16]

"Challenged to mask effectively because of their size, [the MH-60s] could not hang around in such an environment for too long, or they would eventually be hit by even unsophisticated enemy fire." The authors proceed to emphasize that none of the Little Birds were shot down during the October 3 battle, arguing that the size and agility of the Little Bird platform was far better suited for urban special operations.[17]

It is something that Karl Maier commented upon:

> I think in that city there were very few places for a Black Hawk to land so all of the infils we had to fast rope. I might be a little biased because I'm a Little Bird guy but there were way more places for us to land and it might've been a better idea to have all of us in Little Birds. We even talked about not using blocking positions, just going in with the assault force so we could get them out real

quick and didn't have a whole bunch of people on the ground. The Little Bird has a really small slice of the pie but that slice we have is the urban environment.

The amount of RPGs available to the Habr Gidr was severely underestimated by Task Force Ranger in Mogadishu. Had the RPG threat been understood, changes to the plan to use two of the Black Hawks as sniper platforms would have been made. One report argued:

> TFR failed to develop a plan and execute an operation that protected its tactical decisive point – its helicopters. MH-60, the most vulnerable helicopter, was kept in orbit within Somali RPG range for forty minutes (1540–1620) after the initial assault … While the ground force was coming under sporadic fire, no crisis existed on the ground that required MH-60s to be used in the ground support role. AH-6s with miniguns or MH-6s with snipers could have been used instead if necessary. MH-6s and AH-6s are much smaller, faster, [and] more maneuverable, and would have been much more difficult for the Somalis to hit with RPGs.[18]

To a man, veterans interviewed felt that the AH-6s had literally held the tide against the enemy during the October 3 mission, particularly around the first crash site. Tom DiTomasso summed up the feelings of many when he said: "The Little Birds saved our ass. They don't have a lot of ammo on them, they just kept on flying and coming back. If they had not done that I don't think we would have survived because we were running out of ammo."

## COMBAT LEADERSHIP

*"In this dire circumstance that every infantryman wonders about, the men reacted in textbook fashion."*

SERGEANT MATT EVERSMANN

At Ranger squad and platoon level, small-unit leadership during the battle was exemplary. Many cite Lieutenant Tom DiTomasso as a perfect example of combat leadership. He made tough calls in a situation that had escalated beyond his control, particularly as a relatively inexperienced junior officer. Sergeant Matt Eversmann too, on his first day on the job as chalk leader, and his team leaders held their blocking position against murderous enemy onslaughts. Lieutenants Larry Moores and Larry Perino and Sergeant Jeff Struecker have also been noted in their adherence to the Ranger creed, repeatedly leading their often battle-weary and bloodied men back out into the city to rescue their comrades. There was no lack of bravery on display during the battle.

Sergeant Eversmann commented on the quality of the individual Rangers under his command:

> Young Rangers were able to shoot, move and communicate under fire with little or no direction from me. I remember at one point of the battle doing a quick assessment of the perimeter and smiling as I watched the men aggressively engage the enemy from three directions. We had a debate with my platoon leader about SLA Marshall's claim concerning how many men would actually pull the trigger under fire. We had 12 of 13 and I have to believe that if he could have, Ranger Blackburn would have done the same thing.

Where some Rangers may have hesitated to engage targets, particularly in the vicinity of unarmed civilians, most of whom were certainly combatants, this is understandable considering their relative inexperience and the ambiguities in facing such an asymmetric enemy, let alone the shock of being involved in such a high-intensity urban battle. The vast majority of the Rangers had never heard a shot fired in anger. When Rangers hesitated, their team leaders and the Delta operators gave them guidance which to their credit they followed unfailingly.

Jeff Struecker agreed:

> The greatest compliment I can make to the young Rangers was that despite how terrified they were – and they were terrified – they loyally did whatever I as their leader asked them to do. When the bullets were hitting all around them, their eyes were on me: "What do you want me to do now, boss? I'm going to do exactly what you tell me to do next, otherwise we're going to die." They didn't react to the enemy without first hearing from their leaders.

Matt Eversmann explained:

> A big concern was the ROE, again a very real first [for the young Rangers]. It was very detailed and the situation was complicated by the fact that there were, for instance, some Somalis who were allowed to carry weapons (e.g. those working for the UN) and others that couldn't. It took briefings from the staff Judge Advocate General and the commander to spell out everything so that every 19-year-old [Ranger] understood the ROE. "What can I do when the bullets are flying and x happens? Do I shoot or not?"[19]

Much praise was reserved for Lieutenant DiTomasso. Karl Maier's comments were representative of the high esteem in which he was held by the other members of the Task Force:

> He had to fight his way from the original objective to the crash site and had already gone through a little bit of hell to get there. At the time he was a pretty young lieutenant and I was pretty proud of him. I'll tell you a story [about DiTomasso]: fast forward to Iraq, Baghdad in maybe 2006 or 2007 and I've walked into the TOC [Tactical Operations Center] and he's there, and now he's a Lieutenant Colonel, and he points at me, didn't miss a beat and said "Oh look, there's the guy who tried to kill me!" He's a funny guy!

The much-maligned Captain Steele, commander of the Rangers' Bravo Company and a man who so divided opinion within the Task Force, took his own lessons from October 3. He appears to have believed that his Rangers were unprepared for the kill-or-be-kill environment they found themselves in on the streets of Mogadishu. According to a profile in *The New Yorker*, Jerry Boykin said: "Somalia left Mike Steele with a determination that he would never go into combat with soldiers that he was responsible for without making sure that they were fully prepared. I think he thought that it was problematic that some of the young soldiers were not expecting the impact of trauma, not prepared emotionally for the impact of seeing dead bodies."[20]

Steele was instrumental in a program known as Psychological Inoculation of Combat that was taught at Fort Campbell to his unit after he left the Ranger Regiment. Based in part on the writings of retired Colonel Dave Grossman and his contentious book *On Killing*, the program was an effort to desensitize his soldiers to killing. Once deployed to Iraq, his command guidance to his troops was brutally direct. A "kill board" was established to rank the number of insurgents killed, with the best-performing troops rewarded with a challenge coin known as a "kill coin."

His interpretation and indeed understanding of the rules of engagement in place at that time were questionable. On one mission – Operation *Iron Triangle* – he appears to have ordered all positively identified military-age males to be killed, whether armed or unarmed. This command culture had its inevitable and tragic consequences. The Army found that, "Although clearly unintentional, confusion regarding the ROE was the proximate cause of the death of at least four unarmed individuals, none of whom committed a hostile act or displayed hostile intent."[21]

Four soldiers from Steele's unit were also later charged with murder when unarmed detainees were executed. Two pleaded guilty to murder whilst another pleaded guilty to negligent homicide. The fourth was convicted of a lesser assault charge. Another inquiry found that Steele had not "encouraged illegal, wanton, or superfluous killing"[22] and Steele wasn't charged with any offence, but his reputation was indelibly tarnished and his Army career over.

Military historian Thomas Ricks quotes Steele's brigade's former commander, Colonel James Hallums: "The supermacho image that Steele projected permeated his unit, and in my opinion, led directly to atrocities."[23] This "supermacho" posturing was commented upon by a number of Task Force Ranger veterans interviewed for this book. Some noted "a big man complex" in Steele, who viewed serving as a Ranger as "a purely physical thing."[24] Another's candid assessment was that Steele "was overbearing, stubborn, and a bully."[25] An operator mentioned that "The Rangers on the ground did what they were told, it was just that one of their leaders was a bully."[26]

Mike Steele could not be reached for interview for this book.

## TEMPLATES

### "If you use a tactic twice, you should not use it a third time."

#### COLONEL ALI ADEN, SOMALI NATIONAL ALLIANCE

Task Force Ranger based all of their operations on variants of two basic templates – one for targets that were in a building, the second for targets that were mobile in vehicles. This approach has received criticism in some quarters for telegraphing American tactics to Aideed and his militia. In response, it must be remembered that there are only so many ways to "skin a cat," as one operator explained.

Tom DiTomasso agreed, arguing:

> A lot of people say, "Well, you set a pattern," but there's only five ways to get from point A to point B – you can fly, drive, walk, swim, or parachute. You're not going to parachute and you're not going to swim so we infiltrated by foot, by vehicle, and by helicopter and tried to mix it up as much as we could. I felt that every time we went and did a mission, the enemy found out more about us – that's true with any military action. Same thing occurred in Bosnia, same thing occurred in Iraq and Afghanistan. The more we do missions the more the enemy learns about us so every time you go out it gets a little more dangerous.

Mike Moser explained: "When we embarked on this operation, I was very confident in the 'mousetrap' mechanism – the flight package, if triggered by timely and accurate intelligence, was capable of successfully capturing any HVT [high value target]. However, as we settled in, each time we performed another 'Signature Flight' or an unsuccessful hit, the enemy learned more and more about how to counter us."

Another Delta operator, Kelly Venden, added: "When you start doing daylight rather than nighttime hits … we have never in all my years done a daylight hit because we own the night. Over time, complacency kills," although he conceded that "One thing I've learnt is that Murphy is always there. You just never know when things will go wrong. It's a dangerous business, so sometimes things just go bad."

On the decision to launch on a daylight raid, more than two decades later, DiTomasso is still adamant:

> The decision to launch that day was made by General Garrison and I absolutely support it. There are lots of factors you have to weigh to make that decision – what is the mission, what is the value of the target, is it fleeting in nature, is it a time-sensitive target, do we think we're going to be able to find him again? You also have to understand how well your guys are trained and what risk are they taking. As a commander, this is a constant evaluation. Your

job as a commander is to mitigate the risk to your guys as much as possible, and accomplish your mission. Major General Garrison is one of the best commanders I have ever worked with. If he called me today, I would show up.

Counterinsurgency specialist David Kilcullen wrote in his later study of urban asymmetric warfare:

> In the case of Mogadishu, the Rangers had poked a hornet's nest in the Black Sea district: they had attacked the city itself, only to be chewed up and spat out, stunned and bloodied ... even today local civilians know [the battle] as "Maalintii Rangers", "the Day of the Rangers", marking it as an unusually intense episode – even for a city that had already become habituated to enormous bloodshed during the civil war ...[27]

Kilcullen believes that:

> previous raids (in particular, an attack on a Mogadishu house [the Abdi House on July 12] by helicopters that fired ... missiles, killing fifty-four people, including many noncombatants) had generated intense hatred of the Rangers and even greater hostility toward their helicopters. This contributed to the ferocity with which local fighters – Aideed's militia and armed civilians alike – responded after the two aircraft went down on October 3. By assaulting straight into the area [of the Bakara Market], in broad daylight, TF Ranger was directly challenging Aideed's powerbase and courting a strong counterpunch.[28]

# FOREIGN FIGHTERS

*"[It] was a starting point for the long war between the mujahideen of al-Qaeda Organization and America. Sheikh Osama himself pointed this out in his speeches and he mentioned that they got to witness the weakness of the American soldier and his fragility through this war."*

AHMED ABDI GODANE, AL-SHABAAB

In 2011, the leader of Somali insurgent group al-Shabaab claimed that three al-Qaeda representatives had been present in Mogadishu: "Actually, they had a prominent role that includes many fields. For example, the field of training, supplying help in actual participation in the fighting, etc." The al-Shabaab leader who made the claim, Ahmed Abdi Godane, was later killed in a 2014 drone strike. In a final irony, the Reaper unmanned aerial vehicles responsible were from JSOC.[29]

A later study also claimed:

> The Habr Gidr received external advice from Islamic fundamentalists from Sudan who had experience combating Russian helicopters in Afghanistan. From the Sudanese the Habr Gidr learned some clever techniques on the use of RPGs in an anti-helicopter role for which the weapon had never been intended ... New tactics included methods of concealing the shooter from the helicopter gunners, waiting for the helicopter to pass overhead before rising to shoot, aiming at the tail rotor – the helicopter's most vulnerable spot, and shooting from pits that enabled a skyward shot. Heartened by the success of downing the QRF Black Hawk, the Habr Gidr deliberately planned to concentrate their RPGs on helicopters in future engagements with the Rangers.[30]

Jim Yacone, formerly of the 160th SOAR and one of the pilots of Super 62, left the Army to join the Federal Bureau of Investigation where he became the commander of the Bureau's elite Hostage Rescue Team. In a 2001 trial of terrorists accused of bombing US embassies in Tanzania and Kenya, Yacone said, "I am not really sure who was training Aidid's [sic] group." He did contend that "you probably have to get some training" to be able to engage helicopters with RPGs. He also testified that the signals intelligence intercepts of the mortar strikes against the Task Force hangar were in Arabic: "It led intelligence people to tell us there may be other people here training Aidid's clan."[31]

Ahmed Abdi Godane's self-serving proclamations aside, it has never been conclusively proven that foreign jihadists were involved in either the training of the SNA or actively assisted them on the ground on October 3. Usama bin Laden later made statements that October 3 had encouraged al-Qaeda as it had shown the Americans could be beaten, but he never actually claimed any fighters allied to his organization had taken part. On the balance of probabilities, it seems probable that the SNA success against Task Force helicopters had more basis in the incredible number of RPGs fired than any external training.

# THE POLITICAL DIMENSION

"Mogadishu ... spooked the Clinton administration as well as the brass, and confirmed the Joint Chiefs in the view that SOF should never be entrusted with independent operations."[32]

PROFESSOR RICHARD SCHULTZ

Clausewitz famously declared that "War is the continuation of politics by other means." Mogadishu and the *Gothic Serpent* mission was no different. By September 1993, the White House was actively looking for a political solution that would allow the United States to disengage from the Somalia mission. Elements within the Department of Defense had expressed doubts as to the ability of Task Force Ranger to find its target and supported Department of State efforts to increase their efforts at finding a political agreement with Aideed and, by extension, with the United Nations.

The White House seems to have decided to allow the *Gothic Serpent* missions to continue, despite the chance of friendly casualties, to provide leverage against Aideed to join the negotiating table – a carrot and stick approach that was apparently never communicated to Garrison and Task Force Ranger.

In a cable to Powell and Wisner in early September, General Hoar admitted the overall humanitarian operation in Somalia was lost: "After four months of operations with extraordinary help from the U.S., the U.N.'s successes have been modest. A coherent plan which encompasses the political, humanitarian and security needs for the country has yet to emerge. Control of Mogadishu has been lost."[33]

Admiral Howe explained:

> We weren't going to negotiate with him directly, but either through the ... Ethiopians and Eritreans who were trying to help, or through our direct contacts. We could meet with some of his people, and we even got to a point

later on in which we were discussing who could be there at the table and so forth. Of course, it was in our interest to guarantee the safety of anybody that would come to these kinds of discussion. We got to the point [later] where we said we may have to call off these arrest operations that were being run by the Rangers and Delta because we had gotten to a point where there was genuine reciprocation in terms of interest in working this thing out peacefully. We never got quite to that point. But certainly it was in our minds.

... As a general proposition in these sort of complex situations, in which you hope you'd never have to use force, I think you always have to have a peace track that is available, and hopefully you can persuade the right people that are causing the problem, or at least their followers, to follow that track and to get on that track. I certainly think that the force that was sent in in August, the Ranger [and] Delta Force, provided [that] pressure because I think there was a real concern perhaps on Aidid's [sic] part that he would be captured. These were serious forces, they were very capable and therefore this alternative of finding this peaceful resolution became more attractive.[34]

Whether such dual-track strategies seem duplicitous or not, they are a constant in warfare and an intelligent commander like Garrison would have known that such overtures were likely. As Howe noted, Task Force Ranger was operating as the impetus that was forcing Aideed to rejoin the political settlement process. In the aftermath of October 3, his SNA was critically wounded, undermining his power. Soon after, however, the United States decided to leave Somalia to its fate and Aideed to live another day.

One claim that often appears in certain sectors of the media, and particularly on the internet, is that the operation was somehow doomed as it was under United Nations command. This is patently untrue, both in terms of Task Force Ranger and the wider Joint Task Force-Somalia. Both were under direct US command and operated under their own rules of engagement. The only real effect of the UN presence on the October 3 mission was the provision of armored vehicles that proved pivotal to the relief of Task Force Ranger. In fact, the Senate hearings on the matter went out of their way to note "the willingness of allied forces to respond ... foremost in this regard were Malaysian and Pakistani forces."[35]

*Gothic Serpent* did cause significant political repercussions for the American special operations community. In some quarters of the military it rekindled old arguments and biases dating from Vietnam that SOF should be restricted to supporting roles rather than as the main effort. There was still an institutional distrust of SOF, best exemplified by General Norman Schwarzkopf during Operation *Desert Storm*, who had resisted nearly all attempts at integrating SOF apart from embedding Special Forces as liaisons with Coalition partner forces and a limited role for Delta hunting the infamous SCUDs.

In Vietnam, Schwarzkopf had experienced SOF getting into trouble only to require bailing out by conventional forces under his command. The debacles in Grenada and to some degree in Panama had only reinforced his thinking. The efforts of Delta in Iraq's western deserts went some way to alter his thinking, but the specter of Mogadishu undid much of their good work. Indeed *Gothic Serpent* may well have contributed to the reluctance of President Clinton to deploy JSOC against Usama bin Laden in 1998 when a valid opportunity existed to launch a Delta-led assault on one of his training camps in Afghanistan.

The mission also reinforced Vietnam-era fears of mission creep and increasing American casualties in an unwinnable conflict that many felt the United States should not have been involved with in the first place, particularly after the first American soldiers and Marines began returning in body bags. Ironically, the events of September 11 cured the public's fear of casualties as the long and bloody war in Iraq and the continuing "forever war" in Afghanistan have demonstrated.

*Gothic Serpent* also effectively ended the US military's involvement for many years in humanitarian and peacekeeping efforts. The so-called "Mogadishu Effect" has been blamed for inaction during the genocide in Rwanda to the later commitment of US troops to the Balkans. During the 1990s, October 3 hung over American foreign policy as a constant reminder of what might go wrong on such operations.

The mission also understandably angered the families of the fallen, often directed at then-President Bill Clinton. Herbert Shughart, Randall Shughart's father, attended the Medal of Honor presentation ceremony at the White House, where he refused to shake hands with President Bill Clinton. He then proceeded to criticize the president, reportedly saying, "You are not fit to be President of the United States. The blame for my son's death rests with the White House and with you. You are not fit to command."[36]

# TACTICS, TECHNIQUES, AND PROCEDURES

"The future [of war] may well not be 'Son of Desert Storm,' but rather 'Stepchild of Somalia and Chechnya.'"

GENERAL CHARLES C. KRULAK, FORMER UNITED STATES MARINE CORPS COMMANDANT

Mogadishu produced many lessons learned which were adopted across the special operations community. Many of these led directly to reduced casualties and greater success in the thousands of missions conducted during the Global War on Terror. Delta operator Norm Hooten commented: "We learnt lessons that day that helped us in future conflicts in Iraq and Afghanistan."

In terms of personal equipment, the lack of night-vision devices available during the night of October 3 was a grave miscalculation. Mike Moser recalled: "We received some criticism regarding the decision to cut our NVGs before this raid, anticipating an early return. I really believed that reduction of weight would translate to better performance (more agility, faster response, etc.), and I was always looking to cut more. I wouldn't do that again."

"Oh, and always having extra batteries for any [and] everything electronic on your person," he added. "This was really already a standard, but on the Radio Mogadishu hit my NVGs died and apparently I neglected to restock my spares – very disconcerting." Today, every operator and Ranger carries at least one night-vision device into combat without exception.

Indeed, within several years of the battle of Mogadishu, the Ranger Regiment adopted a new basic load-out for each Ranger rifleman that each soldier carried into combat, which included a pair of AN/PVS7 night-vision goggles. Other newly issued items included a squad communication system allowing individual Rangers to communicate similar to those used by Delta on October 3, improved Ranger Body Armor with front and back trauma plates, and a number of items of personal protective equipment including gloves, ballistic goggles, and knee, elbow, and shin pads.

Following Delta's use of chest rigs over their body armor, the Rangers issued a system known as RACK or Ranger Assault Carry Kit that carried their water, ammunition, grenades, and medical and breaching kit in a vest over their RBA. The Rangers also followed Delta's lead and began to issue infrared laser pointers called the AN/PEQ-2 laser illuminator mounted on their then-new M4 carbines. Their M4s also mimicked Delta with Aimpoint red dot sights as issue.

Such advances were also experienced within Delta, although the Unit had its own integral research and development team that was constantly innovating: "As far as gear we now have helmets that we can shoot with that will stop frag, we have better ammunition, [although] weapons are similar [but with] better sights, better body armor, better water containers ... Medical gear and tourniquets are the biggest and most important improvement."

Hemorrhage-control tourniquets were indeed perhaps the key lesson from Task Force Ranger. The development of effective one-handed tourniquets, including a version produced by Delta medics, has led to a marked increase in survivability on the battlefields of Afghanistan and Iraq. Tourniquets are even more important in these environments where IEDs routinely traumatically amputate soldiers' limbs.

A history of the development of the modern combat tourniquet noted:

> After the 1993 Somalia conflict (Operation *Gothic Serpent*), the United States Special Operations Command (USSOCOM) held many after-action reviews in which tourniquets were a major lesson learned. These lessons anticipated many things seen later in Iraq and Afghanistan – the need for more tourniquets, forward transfusion, field antibiotics, and better pain control, as well as definition of associations between better armor and survival rates with junctional injuries.
>
> Soon, an SOF medical working group started developing tourniquet designs that were refined incrementally over the years; these three veteran SOF experts later made the first prototypes of the Combat Application Tourniquet. In 1997, US Navy SEALs and the 75th Ranger Regiment, an SOF unit, adopted Tactical Combat Casualty Care (TCCC) techniques including the use of tourniquets.[37]

In the case of the Rangers, this was the Ranger Ratchet Tourniquet.

Another innovation was the Combat-Ready Clamp, which might have saved Corporal Jamie Smith. The device works like a junctional tourniquet by applying direct pressure on the groin to manage femoral artery bleeds and is now standard issue in the trauma kits of field medics after being adopted in 2010. By 2012, an estimated 2000 service members' lives had been saved by tourniquet and clamp use in Iraq and Afghanistan – an incredible achievement that can be directly related to the courageous Delta, Ranger, and Air Force medics who worked tirelessly to find better ways of saving lives after their experiences in the streets of Mogadishu.

Aerial resupply was another area Moser explained was improved upon in light of the battering Super 66 took as it conducted its dangerous low-level resupply:

> We also saw a void with respect to airdropped resupply – shortly after our return some of the guys developed a friction device, similar to a Petzl D11, which was scaled for a fast rope. It could be used to limit the station time of a Black Hawk and safely deliver loads. We also developed a remote-control parachute delivery system using a ram-air canopy similar to our free-fall rigs.

Intelligence, Surveillance, and Reconnaissance (ISR) technology was another innovation that saw its genesis in Mogadishu. During October 3, there were at least the Navy P-3 Orion and the OH-58 Kiowas providing full-motion video that was beamed back to the JOC. This gave Garrison and the headquarters team a unique and unparalleled view of the battlefield in real time, the first time in history that technology enabled such an event. From these humble beginnings, ISR technology has now advanced to a stage where armed unmanned aerial vehicles can loiter over a battlespace for hours, transmitting video feeds that can be viewed by squad leaders in real time by carrying a tablet-like receiver.

Training for combat was revolutionized almost overnight by the experiences of October 3. An operator who was part of the assault force summed it up: "It had everything to do with training, and still does today. From shooting, mission planning, medical training … " Norm Hooten added: "Train like you fight," he said. "Don't train like you think you're going to fight. Don't train like you want to fight. Do a real good analysis of the enemy, because he's 50 percent of that equation, and then train like you will fight. Get used to being creative and adapting to the enemy's actions."

The Rangers soon took this on board. The Rangers' Regimental Training Guidance spelled out the change from a European-focused "wooden environment" to "our most probable combat situation [is] physically grueling, lethal operations encountered in a night, MOUT [military operations in urban terrain] environment."[38]

The Ranger Regiment also identified four principles that needed to be mastered by all Rangers: physical fitness, battle drills, medical training, and marksmanship. Physical fitness now focuses on foot marches with full equipment to improve endurance, combat-related physical training, and an extensive combatives (hand-to-hand combat) program based on Brazilian jujitsu. Every Ranger is now a combat lifesaver with an EMT (Emergency Medical Technician) trained soldier in every squad and a medic in every platoon.

The Regiment realized after Mogadishu that standard Army qualification shoots did not prepare soldiers in any way for shooting in combat – a vastly different animal. Prior to this only the special mission units like Delta conducted any kind of advanced "stress-shoots" and close-quarter battle shooting. The Ranger Marksmanship program soon focused on four key areas: day qualification, night qualification, close quarters marksmanship (CQM), and combat or stress firing.

The Ranger CQM sums up their objective succinctly: "Who shoots the fastest and most accurately lives." The "stress-fire" component focuses on firing accurately whilst on the move in an urban environment, from all shooting positions including using the off-hand and firing around obstacles. Shooting techniques were also influenced by the lessons learned. One Ranger instructor explained to veteran SEAL and historian Dick Couch: "Shoot until the enemy goes down. The double tap (firing two shots) is not a guarantee. We train using controlled pairs in as many multiples as needed."[39]

Simunitions, plastic training ammunition that can be fired through modified versions of all standard small arms, was another innovation that progressed from Delta to the Rangers. It allowed so-called force-on-force training where soldiers assaulting an objective could engage live role-players acting as the enemy who were themselves equipped with Simunitions. Unlike live ammunition, it also allows training in a wider variety of locations due to the reduced risk of injury.

Breaching also became a more widely disseminated skill within the Ranger Regiment. Each Ranger squad was issued a set of mechanical breaching tools, including the Halligan Tool (a pry-bar-style entry tool first developed by New York firefighters and now standard amongst infantry and SOF units) and an eight-pound sledgehammer.

Each squad was additionally now issued a shortened 12-gauge Remington 870 shotgun with specialist Hatton ammunition designed to destroy door locks and hinges. The Regiment's Master Breachers also developed a standard breaching charge known as a close-proximity charge that was designed to explosively breach most types of doors safely with a charge small enough to fit within a cargo pocket.

The Rangers also identified a need for an "enclosed space, shoulder-fired AT/breaching weapon," specifically from their experiences in Somalia. A lightweight rocket that could be employed from within a building to explosively breach into another or suppress an enemy firing point located in an adjacent building would have enabled Task Force Ranger far greater freedom of movement, particularly at the first crash site. This need was eventually realized in the CS (Confined Space) variant of the AT4 (M136) 84mm single-shot launcher. Delta were experimenting with a thermobaric variant a few years later. The key to the AT4 CS was its employment of a unique saltwater counter-mass that absorbed much of the backblast of launch, meaning Rangers could fire the AT4 CS from within structures relatively safely.

Pistols began being issued to every Ranger: "I am a believer that every soldier should have a sidearm ... being in the back of a Humvee with enemy surrounding you and having to pass a 9mm [M9 Beretta pistol] around to whoever has a shot because the unit is short on [9mm] ammunition is a bad, bad situation to be in," noted Matt Eversmann. "You can only plan so deep, and you can only carry a finite amount of ammo. I shot 13 [M16] magazines, as did most. In a situation where you must shoot or die, it is a terrible feeling to know that you are out of ammo."[40]

Field first-aid training was also revolutionized. The effect of this training and the introduction of widespread use of the tourniquet has meant that not a single Ranger with treatable wounds has died from those wounds in Afghanistan. Then-Colonel Stanley McChrystal had ensured in 1998 that the Tactical Combat Casualty Care (TCCC) program became one of the four pillars of Ranger training.

The Air Force also took away their own lessons from the battle. According to Gene Adcock's history of Air Force Special Tactics including the Pararescueman Jumpers, after Mogadishu:

> Special Tactics recognized the need for a more effective system for extracting personnel from downed aircraft. The rapid extraction deployment system (REDS) kit is now standard issue and the search and rescue (SAR) Security

Team reflects the tactics, techniques and procedures (TTPs) learned from the Somali operation. Day and night urban close air support (CAS) tactics were reevaluated and modified to assure compatibility with current tactics. The most significant outcome was the shift in attitude among sister-service commanders. Special Tactics proved to be essential to the joint team effort.[41]

# SOMALIA

"The African Union troops have been very effective, helped and trained by US Special Forces and others. They have attacked and thrown al-Shabaab out of most of their strongholds. They are on the run, but they are not out yet."

GENERAL JAMES MATTIS ON AL-SHABAAB

In the wake of the United States' and later United Nations' departure from Somalia in 1994, the country descended even further into open warfare between the clans. Aideed pronounced himself the country's de facto president in opposition to Ali Mahdi Muhammad, who had been recognized by the United Nations as the country's leader. Aideed struggled against rival clans until his violent death in 1996, shot three times by gunmen loyal to his former colleague Osman Atto.

In a bizarre twist, Aideed's son, Hussein Mohamed Farrah Aideed, a naturalized US citizen, had served with the US Marine Corps in both Operation *Desert Storm* and with *Restore Hope* in Somalia. After leaving the service he returned to Somalia and was declared president by the SNA days after his father's death. They also declared him the new leader of the Habr Gidr clan. He later became part of the United Nations-brokered Transitional Federal Government and still resides in Mogadishu.

The nascent presence of jihadist elements hinted at in some of the Task Force Ranger intelligence reports eventually spawned a Salafist (an extreme form of Sunni jihadism) insurgency by an al-Qaeda-linked terrorist organization called the al-Itihad al-Islami (AIAI), who had begun in Ethiopia but soon spread to Kenya and Somalia. The AIAI provided support for the al-Qaeda bombings of the US embassies in Kenya and Tanzania in 1998 but, in the aftermath of September 11, many of the jihadists fled to Yemen. Those remaining in Somalia faced an incursion by the Ethiopian military, intent on destroying the organization. Some survived and established the Eritrean-backed Islamic Courts Union (ICU) and its militant wing, al-Shabaab.

By the turn of the millennium, a fledgling federal government had been formed in Somalia and the Somali military was beginning to be re-formed to battle the ICU, which had grown into a major power and controlled much of the southern part of the country. It was also receiving operational funds from al-Qaeda associates. United States military SOF and CIA Special Activities Division personnel began covert operations in Somalia under Operation *Black Hawk*, seemingly chosen in memory of Task Force Ranger, often recruiting local clan members to conduct missions against al-Qaeda, who had infiltrated into the country.

JSOC's Task Force Orange, another name for the Intelligence Support Activity, monitored cellular traffic to assist in the targeting of al-Qaeda members by these locally recruited gunmen. Importantly, their targets were members of al-Qaeda's East Africa cell, not the ICU and al-Shabaab. After prolonged fighting, the ICU actually managed to briefly seize power in June 2006, capturing Mogadishu. Ethiopia, alarmed at the prospect of a jihadist-controlled neighboring state, invaded Somalia at the end of the year. JSOC operators, including a number from Delta, were secretly embedded within Ethiopian ground forces and called upon two AC-130s based in Ethiopia to strike concentrations of al-Shabaab fighters.

The Ethiopians managed to wrestle control of Mogadishu from the jihadists and, in late 2007, the United Nations-supported African Union Mission in Somalia (AMISOM) began peacekeeping operations. Al-Shabaab was forced to retreat from the capital into both central and southern Somalia, where they still operate to this day. The US has continued to conduct operations into Somalia, carrying out both air strikes and kill/capture raids targeting al-Shabaab and al-Qaeda leaders.

In 2017, the US military suffered its first casualty in Somalia since the events of October 3, 1993. Elements drawn from SEAL Team 6 were operating in a low-profile role within the country, conducting what is known as "Train, Advise and Assist" alongside Somali Army SOF. Whilst accompanying a local force on a raid against al-Shabaab in their base area of Bariire, a SEAL was killed and two of his colleagues severely wounded in a firefight. In August of 2017, Bariire fell to combined Somali and AMISOM forces, assisted by United States special operations forces on the ground. In Somalia, the war continues.

# FINAL THOUGHTS

### "The way I see it, we went into the tiger's cage. We took his bone. And we came out."

#### THE LATE STAFF SERGEANT JEFF BRAY, 24TH SPECIAL TACTICS SQUADRON

"The mission was a success in that we captured the two SNA lieutenants we were after that day. It came at great losses. The enemy got lucky that day," said Tom DiTomasso. "They rallied the civilians to basically fight where they were at, and there was some command and control but it wasn't organized enough that they could defeat us – think about what we had, maybe 30 guys at the [Super 61] crash site and they couldn't overrun the crash site. We stayed until we decided to leave. I see many articles saying 'the Rangers were pinned down in Mogadishu' – that's absolute bullshit – we left when we wanted to leave. We stayed there to get Cliff Wolcott out of the helicopter. As hard as it is to say, this was a tactical success. We were never overrun, we stayed there as along as we had to remove Cliff out of the helicopter and then we left and that's that." Matt Eversmann agreed: "I believe in my heart that it will always go down as a complete tactical victory and a dismal strategic failure."

DiTomasso continued:

> We released all the prisoners we had captured, we released them all. On October 2nd the mission was important enough to the United States to have Task Force Ranger there. On October 3rd, after 73 casualties and 18 men killed, all of a sudden it wasn't that important any more and they pulled us all out. I disagree with this course of action.

Colonel, now General, Boykin, the Delta Force commander noted in a statement to the House of Representatives: "These men battled against incredible odds to defend fallen comrades and did so without hesitation or reservation. Honor was preserved but at a price. Given the same dilemma again, it is a sure bet that every man would do the same thing."[42]

The fallen are remembered every day at their respective units, but never more so than on the anniversary of the battle when veterans gather for a day of remembrance. The 20th anniversary in 2013 included a visit to the Delta compound at Fort Bragg where operators made a presentation to the veterans highlighting all of the lifesaving tactical and technical advancements that were the result of the battle of Mogadishu.

Task Force Ranger was the subject of a stunning exhibition at the Airborne & Special Operations Museum, which ran from 2014 to 2016 and which won the Society for History in the Federal Government's John Wesley Powell Prize for "an outstanding contribution to furthering history." Exhibits were donated by Task Force Ranger members and included Mike Durant's Bible in which he made secret annotations detailing his capture and confinement by the Somalis, and the recovered main rotor assembly from Super 61.

In 2013, two civilian companies working in Somalia managed to recover a number of significant items from the crashed Black Hawks. The US Army's Special Operations Aviation Command assisted in the repatriation of the remains of the main rotor assembly and foot pedals from Super 61 and an M134 minigun from Super 64. A former Army intelligence officer, David Snelson, and his wife, former war correspondent Alisha Ryu, were instrumental in recovering what could be salvaged from the Super 61 crash site. The couple run the Aran Guest House in Mogadishu along with a security service for visiting business people and journalists.

Individuals have also been memorialized. There is for instance now an "SFC Earl Fillmore Army Health Clinic" and US Navy training ships named after Randy Shughart and Gary Gordon, along with a number of training facilities. Rick Lamb, Jeff Struecker, Craig Nixon, and Larry Moores would all be inducted into the Ranger Hall of Fame.

Keni Thomas and Jeff Struecker returned to Mogadishu to film a short film, *Return to Mogadishu: Remembering Black Hawk Down*, in 2013, revisiting the K-4 Traffic Circle, Hawlwadig Road, the Olympic Hotel, and the target building. Struecker mentioned that even today he remembered those streets and could note battle damage caused on October 3.

Tragically, the battle is still being fought for some veterans of Mogadishu. At least four of their number have taken their own lives and some still struggle with deep psychological wounds. Others carry the marks of the battle on their bodies. Many have hearing problems, whilst others have continuing serious health issues directly related to wounds suffered on October 3 and 4.

Matt Eversmann explained:

> We realized that the reality of combat is that, no matter what, the best-trained soldiers are going to die at the hands of an inferior, poorly trained, poorly equipped enemy. That's just a fact. Nothing replicates that in training, but you train people to a high standard, hold them accountable, and make sure they know what they're supposed to do – that goes a long way.

Delta operator Norm Hooten summed up the thoughts of many:

> I look back and I've had a very full and rewarding life with my family and I've [gone on] to do other things and I think of guys like Matt Rierson whose children were the same age as my kids, guys who never got to live their life, and I still feel a little guilty you know?
>
> I've had a great life and it would've been wonderful for those guys to have that as well, so I regret that they didn't get to experience the full life that I have lived. I think of them a lot. Their loss also makes me much more thankful for the things I've been given in life because I know they would've loved to have had even one more day of it.

# APPENDIX 1

## BLACK HAWK DOWN, THE MOVIE

*"It's a movie, not a documentary, and as such it was very good – it's weird hearing your friends' names and callsigns used and some of the tactics we used shown."*

**Gerry Izzo, Super 65**

Whenever a film is produced of a historic battle, there will be the inevitable mistakes, omissions, and "dramatic license" of the film makers to muddy the waters. Participants will understandably view any such endeavor with a keen critical eye – for veterans, "getting it right" is more than historical accuracy, it is ensuring their friends and colleagues are accurately represented on the big screen. *Black Hawk Down* was no exception.

Although based on Mark Bowden's excellent book, the film makers chose to include a number of incidents either wholly manufactured or by a process

# APPENDIX 1

of amalgamating several incidents into one. The aim of this appendix is not to detail every single diversion from the historical record during the transformation of Bowden's work to celluloid, but to give the reader a glimpse into what veterans of October 3 think about the film. Nor is it to denigrate the film, which in the end is one of the better Hollywood depictions of combat.

Ranger Lieutenant Tom DiTomasso pointed out perhaps the key difficulty veterans have with the movie: "The uniforms in the movie were good and accurate. The helicopters were accurate. Pieces of the storyline were accurate, but he had the characters rolled up into one – to make the movie more sensational they rolled several guys into one character. For the people that were there, that rubs them a little bit."

This was a common refrain amongst veterans interviewed by the author for this book. The act of creating composite characters is a standard Hollywood device to present a complex story through the eyes of just one character, making it easier for the audience to follow the story. Inadvertently, it also leads to confusion for those who are well versed in the source material or indeed for those who rely on the film for their understanding of a particular event. Many viewers will consider the film version to be a true retelling of events as they have no wider frame of reference.

In *Black Hawk Down*, the key characters of Matt Eversmann and Norm "Hoot" Gibson were composites of several real-life individuals. In Eversmann's case, the character played by Josh Hartnett was shown conducting actions that were in real life carried out by a number of Rangers, principally Tom DiTomasso but also Larry Perino and James Lechner. One of the most glaring examples of this is when Josh Hartnett's Eversmann leads a foot movement of his Ranger chalk to the Super 61 crash site. Not only did the real Eversmann and Chalk 4 join McKnight's vehicle convoy rather than join the foot movement, but it was DiTomasso and half of Chalk 2 that secured the crash site moments before the CSAR aircraft arrived.

The real Matt Eversmann explained:

It was such a surreal, absurd experience for me and for anyone else whose name was used, but … the elephant in the room [was] that they made this kid, Josh Hartnett, the star of this show and he happens to be Sergeant Eversmann! Understanding their film formula, you can only have five or six characters, so everyone's going to be a composite of other people.

Jerry Bruckheimer wants to tell the story as accurately as he can but 18 hours into two and a half hours, there's gotta be some leeway. All the movie people were pretty straightforward about how they were going to do it, what they were trying to accomplish, to the point where I'm like, "Okay, I can buy into that," but I gotta be ready to make some explaining when somebody says, "Hey, Matt, you didn't do that," and I'm like, "Yeah I know, this is why it's in there."

Gerry Izzo agreed: "I do know one thing with Sergeant Eversmann in the movie – they took what Sergeant Eversmann did, what Lieutenant DiTomasso did, what Lieutenant Moores did, what Lieutenant Lechner did … they took the actions of all four of those guys and they put them all into Eversmann. That's fine because otherwise you've got too many main characters."

Izzo himself didn't feature in the movie, as he laughingly recalled:

Nobody played me. The closest that they came was when the Black Hawks did the assault and they're coming out and you hear a voice on the radio say, "This is Super 65, my chalk is in, I'm going to holding" – what I actually said was "Super 65's coming out straight up" because I was coming out of the dust and I wanted to let the two guys who were orbiting [know] that I was coming out straight up.

Eric Bana's character, Norm "Hoot" Gibson, was clearly based primarily on Norm Hooten but also included actions and dialogue attributed to other Delta Force personnel. We have already touched on the infamous "This is my safety, sir" scene earlier in the book, but "Hoot" Gibson is also shown carrying out an undercover reconnaissance mission in what appears to be the Bakara Market.

Such operations were actually carried out by the Advanced Force Operations element of C-Squadron from the Operational Support Troop and by the Intelligence Support Activity/Office for Military Support.

The same thing happens in the closing scenes when Gibson is shown getting prepared to go back out into the city to track down the missing in action members of Task Force Ranger.

This mission was again the responsibility of the Operational Support Troop. Gibson's opposite number, Jeff Sanderson, played by William

# APPENDIX 1

Fichtner, was a composite of the Ground Force Commander Scott Miller, Matt Rierson, and likely another Delta operator, John M. All of the names of the operators were fictionalized for the film for personal security reasons.

Along with the composites, there are a number of factual inaccuracies that crept into the script. Some of these are particularly jarring for veterans, as Gerry Izzo pointed out: "At one point in the movie they said 'DiTomasso's wounded and he's out of action,' and he [DiTomasso] said afterwards, 'Like hell I was!' Tom was wounded, but he continued to fight and to lead his men throughout the battle. He was never out of action."

The aerial vehicle intercept of Osman Atto was inaccurate – Gary Keeney was particularly adamant: "How that was depicted in the movie was bullshit, it was not factually correct. The only thing that was a little bit close was that they depicted him [Atto] as being extremely defiant and arrogant." As we have seen earlier in Chapter 2, Keeney was a member of the Delta element that identified the captured Atto.

In reality, the aerial intercept was against a single vehicle, a green Fiat, not a three-vehicle convoy of 4WDs as shown in the film. As depicted in the movie, Atto's vehicle was initially engaged by Jim Smith firing his CAR15 into the engine block – not shown was the doorgunner on the Black Hawk adding the firepower of his minigun to the fusillade to immobilize the car. Atto later claimed the vehicle was hit more than 50 times.

In the film, he is shown being captured cleanly with an AH-6 hovering in front of Atto's vehicle after the sniper shoots into the engine block. As again detailed in Chapter 2, Atto's bodyguard, Ahmed Ali, in fact raised his AK47 and was deliberately shot in the legs to disable him. Atto managed to escape the scene and take refuge in a nearby garage where Delta located him. He was then exfiltrated by Little Bird from the rooftop.

During the assault on the target building, the landing locations of the Little Birds depicted were incorrect. In particular, at least one MH-6 is depicted landing on the roof of the target building, but, as we have noted, all landed on the streets surrounding the objective. The situation Eversmann's chalk faced, at least two blocks north of their intended insertion point, is not shown. Similarly, when the operators were moving into the objective, the film depicts them shooting several Somalis. In fact all of the enemy personnel at the objective immediately surrendered once the operators burst in.

Ranger Scott Galentine is shown as a member of Eversmann's chalk as they move to the first crash site. As mentioned, this chalk was actually Chalk 2 under Tom DiTomasso and Galentine was actually wounded back at Eversmann's blocking position. Their destination, Super 61, is depicted as having crash landed at what appears to be a major intersection rather than the far tighter alleyway to the north east of Marehan Road.

The nature and extent of the wounds suffered by Tim "Griz" Martin were greatly exaggerated in the movie. He was not blown in half. Colonel McKnight was also nowhere near him when he was wounded, but he is shown, portrayed by Tom Sizemore, as being amongst the first to react. Eversmann, Keeney, and the Delta medics recovered and treated Griz. The circumstances of Dominick Pilla's death are also incorrectly shown. As we have noted in Chapter 3, he was in the back of Jeff Struecker's Humvee when he was hit, firing his M60, not manning the .50 cal. It appears as if Pilla's death may have been confused with Cavaco, who was manning a heavy weapon when he was killed.

Many of the scenes depicting Task Force Ranger members being wounded or killed are out of sequence with reality or are shown in a fictionalized light – Tom Sizemore playing McKnight again appears when Kowalewski was hit by an RPG whilst driving the second 5-ton truck. Sizemore's McKnight is shown opening the door to the cab to discover the mortally wounded Ranger. In reality, as detailed in Chapter 6, this was Gary Keeney assisting an unknown Ranger Sergeant. On McKnight's convoy, the movie also shows the Somali detainees in the back of Humvees, which did not occur – they were in the 5-ton protected by C-Team and their attached snipers.

The arrival of the rescue convoy is another sequence that is factually incorrect. Tom Sizemore's Danny McKnight is depicted being greeted by Mike Steele when it was in fact the QRC Company Commander. McKnight, wounded twice, had handed command of his Task Force Ranger element to Nixon and Van Arsdale. As mentioned in Chapter 8, Steele became involved in a verbal altercation with Captain Drew Meyerowich of the 10th Mountain before Lee Van Arsdale overrode him.

Finally, the sequence depicting the Mogadishu Mile, whilst visually stirring, jars with reality. The movie shows a number of Rangers and operators running all of the way to the Pakistani-controlled soccer stadium. In fact, as noted in Chapter 8, the Rangers and operators ended up being extracted by

# APPENDIX 1

ground vehicles after the commander of the 10th Mountain QRF realized there were still men left behind on foot. They did have to run down most of Hawlwadig and National, exposed to tremendous amounts of enemy fire, to meet the vehicles, and it was this movement that was christened the Mogadishu Mile. They did not run, however, all of the way out of the city to the stadium as depicted in the film.

The film tries, in its closing credits, to make a connection between Aideed's death and the retirement of General Garrison occurring within days of each other, perhaps hinting that Garrison waited until his adversary was dead before he felt comfortable hanging up his spurs. The idea makes for a suitably dramatic ending for the Hollywood version of October 3 but not surprisingly has no basis in reality. The prosaic but inevitable mountain of paperwork involved in retiring from the military can take months, if not longer, to wind its way through the bureaucracy, particularly for officers of Garrison's rank.

A number of scenes in the film were also added despite having never occurred in reality. The entire sequence involving two of DiTomasso's men, M60 gunner Specialist Shawn Nelson and SAW gunner Specialist Lance Twombly, was fabricated in its entirety. Nelson and Twombly moved with their respective half-squads to the Super 61 crash site, Nelson with DiTomasso and Twombly with Yurek. The scene involving the deafness suffered by Nelson was correct, the result of Twombly firing his SAW near Nelson's head.

The scene showing Gibson and his team killing the crew of a technical mounting a recoilless rifle commanded by a fictional version of the leader of the local Habr Gidr militia, Yousuf Dahir Mo'alim, is also made from whole cloth. No such action occurred. As noted by numerous participants, technicals were not deployed during the battle, particularly during the evening when the skies were owned by the AH-6s. It is also questionable that the operators would have used choke holds rather than their carbines or grenades to disable the crew of the vehicle!

There were several deleted sequences which added some historical scenes back into the movie, although these ended up being cut from the final production version. One shows a Delta element, most likely Norm Hooten's F-Team, initially storming another building before they entered the objective. Another shows a Ranger SAW engaging E-Team in the objective building which, whilst still not completely accurate as E-Team were on the roof when this occurred, at least gives a nod to the dangers of fratricide.

The film looks superb from a technical standpoint, helped in large part by the contributions of the Ranger Regiment and the 160th SOAR. The Black Hawks and Little Birds shown in the movie were flown by members of the 160th SOAR including a number of Mogadishu veterans. For the fast-roping sequences, the US Army loaned a number of Rangers to the production. The Pentagon also assisted by facilitating "boot camps" for the actors to immerse themselves in the worlds of the men they portrayed.

A number of uniform inaccuracies in the movie were largely down to the film makers' attempts to identify the different units and individuals for the audience. In particular, the addition of the names of the Rangers on their helmets was done for exactly this reason. The operators were also shown with longer than standard length hair and unshaven when in fact, to blend in with the Ranger component, they had Ranger-style "high and tights" and were clean shaven.

There were also a number of weapon inaccuracies, although many less than a typical Hollywood war film. "One of the big things about the movie – when they would show those RPG rockets coming at everybody, those damned things were going at the speed of a model airplane. Somebody in a wheelchair or a walker could've gotten out of the way of those! Those things come at you [in reality] like a bullet. There's no watching it coming in," remembered Gerry Izzo, laughing. Likewise when Super 61 is shown being hit by an RPG team lead by Yousuf Dahir Mo'alim, the backblast would have killed or severely injured him and a second RPG gunner standing nearby if they had fired as depicted.

Another, albeit minor, inaccuracy is that Dan Busch is shown using a CAR15 when in fact he carried and employed a SAW at the Super 61 crash site. In the same sequence, his fellow snipers Jim M and Steve D are nowhere to be seen, although Jim Smith is briefly depicted helping to carry Busch to the Little Bird. Additionally, Star 41 is shown landing within meters of Super 61 when in reality they had to land around the corner due to the tight confines of the alleyway in which the Black Hawk lay.

Despite the laudable use of real Black Hawks and Little Birds, the production was understandably unable to source actual Condor APCs, so what appear to be Spanish BMRs were used in the film. Additionally no tanks were shown in the movie; again these would have been difficult to source, particularly accurate M48A4s as used by the Pakistanis. Pakistani M113s are depicted, complete with blue-helmeted crew in a rare nod to the United Nations forces involved in the rescue convoy.

# APPENDIX 1

One inaccuracy in the film was seemingly forced upon the film makers by the Pentagon. Ranger company clerk John "Stebby" Stebbins, who featured extensively in the Ridley Scott film, and was played by Scottish actor Ewan McGregor, was found guilty of child molestation and the rape of his own six-year-old daughter in June 2000 by a military courts martial. He was sentenced to a minimum 30-year prison term. During the making of the film, the US Army requested Stebbins' character be renamed and Scott complied, allegedly to maintain Army material support such as the provision of the Black Hawk helicopters, and called the character John Grimes instead.

A number of veterans helped out with the film. Matt Eversmann noted:

Jerry Bruckheimer and Ridley Scott were very smart and they hired Tom Matthews and Lee Van Arsdale. They had just retired. So Lee and Tom were there and they made sure shit was wired tight and I think the major reason it turned out as well as it did was because those two warriors were there. They knew the story and they lived the story and they made sure it was as accurate as you could probably get.

Additionally the scene showing Star 41 landing at the Super 61 crash site was recreated by an MH-6 piloted by none other than Keith Jones, Karl Maier's co-pilot on October 3.

Izzo and Maier both thought that the depiction of the operators was very well done, including their disdain for structures of rank. Izzo: "William Fichtner and Eric Bana really captured how those guys are. They're kinda these low key, confident, very informal … For years I would plan missions and I wouldn't know if I was talking to a Sergeant, a Captain, or a Major!"

In the final wash, the film for the most part manages a creditable job of explaining the battle in its medium as a Hollywood blockbuster. It also paid tribute to the fallen, particularly Randy Shughart and Gary Gordon. John Belman from the CSAR team summed it up well: "If you take it from the perspective that it's Hollywood and they have to do certain things to dramatize the event, I think it was a decent portrayal of what happened." Gerry Izzo agreed: "Mike Durant said one time that he'd give it an A+ for patriotism and a B+ for accuracy and I'd say that's about right."

# APPENDIX 2

## THE WEAPONS AND EQUIPMENT OF TASK FORCE RANGER

Task Force Ranger were equipped with a range of standard US-issue and specialist small arms and equipment to accomplish their mission. The Rangers had some limited leeway in selecting equipment, adding scopes and sound suppressors for instance, but Delta could and did have almost unlimited freedom in choosing the right weapon for the job. In the close-range infantry fight of October 3, it is worth examining the small arms used by both Task Force Ranger and the Somali militia.

Mogadishu was awash in small arms, mainly of Russian, Chinese, and former Warsaw Pact origin. The Somalis principally used the ubiquitous AK47-pattern assault rifle in 7.62x39mm from a range of manufacturers. The AK47 is simple to use and is extremely reliable, particularly well suited for militiamen for whom weapon maintenance was probably a low priority.

Several interviewees noted that the Somalis tended to empty a magazine in the general direction of US forces, rather than using the sights. They also mainly fired from the hip or without looking, over or around obstacles. Karl

# APPENDIX 2

Maier recalled a Somali emptying an AK47 magazine at him from close range and not registering a single hit. The Somalis managed to inflict casualties not through accuracy but purely through an overwhelming weight of fire.

A number of 7.62x51mm Heckler and Koch G3 battle rifles were also seen in the hands of militiamen. The older semiautomatic Russian SKS 7.62x39mm carbine, and the Chinese Type 56 copy, were also used, but the AK47, with its capability for fully-automatic fire and larger 30-round magazine, was much preferred.

7.62x39mm RPK light machine guns and 7.62x54mm PKM medium machine guns were employed, as was a limited number of 12.7mm DShK heavy machine guns, at least one of which was used to engage the casualty collection point near the Super 61 crash site. There appears to have been at least some form of organization to the SNA militia but it is unknown at what rate these heavier support weapons were issued.

Along with the AK47, the most prolific weapons system in Somali hands was the RPG-7. Although the acronym is often mistakenly referred to as "rocket-propelled grenade," it in fact translates from the Russian as "handheld antitank grenade launcher." RPGs in Somalia included the RPG-7 and 7V along with the Chinese Type 69-I, distinctive for its folding bipod. As we have discussed in Chapter 4, it seems very unlikely that Somalia RPG rounds were modified to airburst in an attempt to engage Task Force Ranger helicopters and most likely were in fact operating as advertised, detonating at 920 meters.

There appears to be no first-hand evidence of recoilless rifles used on October 3, although these were a common weapon platform on Somali technicals. Despite their depiction in the film *Black Hawk Down*, there were no technicals engaged in the October 3 battle. Some were seen, particularly early on as Delta operator Norm Hooten confirmed, but none played any role in the battle itself. As we have noted, technicals were jealously guarded by the warlords and Aideed knew that they would be prime targets for the AH-6 Little Birds.

Along with copious numbers of AK47s and RPGs, the militia also seemed to have access to large numbers of hand grenades, although their provenance and reliability were open to question. Several veterans interviewed mentioned enemy hand grenades failing to explode. No grenade launchers were encountered, nor were any mortars, although the SNA certainly had both 60mm and 82mm Chinese and Soviet models, evidenced by the mortar strike with tragic consequences on October 6 against the Task Force Ranger hangar. There is no evidence that mortars were employed on October 3 despite dubious Somali claims that they intended to bracket the Super 61 crash site but decided against risking civilian casualties.

The Rangers were equipped for the most part with the then-standard-issue Ranger small arms and equipment, with some notable exceptions. In terms of personal weapons, Ranger riflemen carried the US Army 5.56x45mm M16A2 assault rifle, an M16 variant that offered both semiautomatic and three-round burst settings. The three-round burst setting was largely shunned, with Rangers trained to fire aimed single shots. Whilst not ideal for urban close combat because of its length, its 20-inch barrel did offer greater accuracy and range than the shorter CAR15 carbine.

The CAR15 was carried by a small minority of Rangers, most notably platoon commanders, radio operators and the security element assigned to the CSAR aircraft. These CAR15s were actually mainly Colt Model 727 carbines but were referred to by both Delta and the Rangers by the Vietnam-era name, the CAR15, although, strictly speaking, the CAR15 was a specific Vietnam-era variant, the XM177E2. Mini-Maglite flashlights were affixed under the barrel of some of the M16A2s and CAR15s by Rangers in emulation of Delta practices and were modified with removable red filters for night operations (red light does not destroy night vision like white light).

Rangers assigned to the CSAR team modified their CAR15s with Aimpoint 2000 or 3000 model red dot sights. The Aimpoints displayed a red dot within the optic that was zeroed to the bore of the weapon and could be employed with both eyes open, improving both speed and accuracy. A later model, the M68, became standard issue with the Rangers during the late 1990s and later across the whole US Army.

Their carbines were also fitted with AIM-1D infrared lasers that could be employed at night to mark targets (the infrared beam only visible through night-vision devices) and sound suppressors to reduce the report of their weapons. Although many commentators have assumed that these came from Delta, they were actually from the Ranger Regiment, which held limited stocks at that time: "We had our own Aimpoints, they came from the Regiment. Delta had their own version. They may have had the 5000 model. We also had the IR lasers, the AIM-1s, they were Regiment stock too," recalled John Belman.

## APPENDIX 2

"The rationale [on the suppressors] was that we might be coming into a situation that we would want to be stealthy in our approach in terms of shooting and so hence the suppressors – they also look cool!" explained Belman, laughing. "What we found though, and this is why I took mine off, was that with those kinds of suppressors the carbon build-up in the action of the weapon was just so bad that it would render it pretty much unfireable. The guys who kept them on, found that out, and ended up swapping out weapons with people who had been wounded. So suppressors [were] not a win there!"

Two to three Rangers in each chalk carried M16A2s mounting the 40mm single-shot M203 grenade launcher. The M203, looking like a stubby shotgun under the M16's barrel, could deliver high-explosive grenades out to 400 meters. Each chalk also had two 5.56x45mm M249 squad automatic weapons or SAWs, light machine guns equipped with a folding bipod that fed from a 200-round plastic box. The SAWs, although bulky, provided a tremendous firepower advantage and were designed to suppress enemy targets at ranges out to 600 meters with a cyclic rate of fire of 850 rounds per minute.

Each chalk also had an M60 medium machine-gun team. The M60 was being replaced at the time by the M240, based on the Fabrique Nationale MAG58, and a number were shipped to Somalia, but the M60 was deployed on October 3. A Delta source noted that the MAG58 had been employed by the Rangers on at least one earlier mission. Delta had in fact purchased the MAG58 several years earlier to replace their HK21 medium machine guns and had deployed with it on Operation *Desert Storm*.

The M60 was belt fed and fired the heavy 7.62x51mm NATO round at a cyclic rate of around 550 rounds per minute. This rate of fire cannot be maintained without burning out the barrel and thus the weapon is fired in short controlled bursts. A spare barrel is typically carried by the assistant gunner to allow an over-heated barrel to be swapped out using a special asbestos glove. The M60 served as the primary suppressive fire weapon for the Ranger chalks.

Ranger sniper teams brought along the big semiautomatic .50 Barret M82A1 antimaterial rifle but none were deployed during the events of October 3. Some of the snipers carried scoped M16A2 carbines fitted with folding Harris bipods and at least one Ranger carried a Colt 727 carbine mounting the M3A ten-power telescopic scope from the Army's M24 sniper-rifle system. Again none of these sniper rifles were used on October 3.

For the ballistic breaching of doors, the Rangers had available shortened 12-gauge Remington 870 pump-action shotguns fitted with top folding stocks or pistol grips. Ranger Sergeant Keni Thomas of Chalk 3 carried one such shotgun, attached by Velcro to his belt. The shotguns were issued at a rate of one per chalk and were only used for breaching purposes. At least two Rangers in each chalk also carried the M72 LAW or Light Antitank Weapon. A 66mm disposable single-use rocket, it was useful against fortified positions or technicals and was used a number of times during the foot movement to the first crash site.

In terms of ammunition, each Ranger initially carried the standard load of seven 30-round 5.56x45mm magazines and two fragmentation grenades. The M60 gunners carried 600 rounds in linked belts; additional belts of ammunition were distributed amongst the other members of the chalk and dropped off to the gun team once positioned. The SAW gunners had 800 rounds in their green plastic drums. Only officers and NCOs carried the issue sidearm, the 9x19mm M9 Beretta: "Back then it wasn't the standard, some of the SAW and M60 gunners had sidearms, but it wasn't a standard issue deal to have a sidearm in the Ranger Regiment," noted Belman.

Others such as Combat Controller Staff Sergeant Dan Schilling carried only two spare GAU-5 magazines along with the magazine in his weapon on the infiltration on October 3, along with a .45ACP M1911A1 pistol with four seven-round magazines. The Combat Controller's main role was not combat but to use magazines loaded with tracers to assist in marking targets for the AH-6s. Upon his return on the United Nations/10th Mountain convoy, however, he carried more than a dozen magazines for his GAU-5, an Air Force variant of the CAR15.

Along with their weapons, each Ranger carried whatever else he needed for his specific role. Medics carried their trauma kits, the RTOs carried multiple radios. Most carried a range of less-than-lethal munitions and demolition charges designed to blow holes in walls. John Belman recalled: "I had flashbangs, maybe a concussion grenade, some smoke, some demo [explosive breaching charges] with me and medical gear." Ranger Sergeant Jeff Struecker said: "I had concussion grenades and flashbangs and in the open, concussion grenades work a lot better. Flashbangs do pretty well in a room, concussion grenades are way overkill inside a room so I carried a number of concussion grenades with me to throw in the open."

# APPENDIX 2

The Rangers had also received a quantity of a new body armor type that was lighter and more flexible than the PASGT system worn by most US infantry at the time. The RBA or Ranger Body Armor was a brand new design in 1993 and the Rangers of 3rd Battalion deployed to Somalia were the first to use it in combat. Unlike later variants, the original model only featured a single trauma plate held in a pouch on the chest, protecting the heart and lungs. This trauma plate was rated to stop the Soviet 7.62x39mm round fired by the AK47 family of assault rifles. The remainder of the RBA was constructed of Kevlar that provided protection against fragmentation.

Along with the RBA, some Rangers wore Progressive Technologies (PT) body armor. The Progressive Technologies vests had been sourced by Delta from Army Special Forces Groups as it became evident during build-up training that there were simply not enough RBA vests to fully equip the Ranger contingent. Priority for the superior RBA went to those Rangers assigned to the blocking-position chalks. Most of the Rangers on the CSAR element by contrast wore the black PT vest, which had the advantage that it held trauma plates in both front and back. Belman explained:

> When we first deployed to Fort Bragg to stage for the Somalia deployment, Rangers still had the old flak jackets. They were just making the RBA. From what I can recall, Delta secured additional body armor for us as well as a few armored HMMVs, which neither we nor the Unit had at the time. Now from pictures, the body armor appears to be the same as the Delta body armor but the Delta body armor was very different – the plates were a lot smaller and lighter. The ones [plates] we had were just so large and heavy … I took my plates out, both front and back. Some people on the CSAR bird took them out, some people didn't. What people on the ground did I don't know.

The reasoning for taking out the trauma plates was a question of speed for the CSAR team. They knew that if they were required to attend the crash of a helicopter, they would likely be under fire immediately and needed to get clear of their own helicopter as quickly as possible. Thus whatever they could do to reduce weight and improve speed was considered a reasonable compromise. Other Rangers have noted that it was almost impossible to go prone wearing the PT vests as the front plate would strike the user under the chin.

Belman continued:

It ended up proving to be the right call, given that our helicopter did get hit while we were roping in. The bottom line was that I felt like I would not be able to get off the helicopter fast enough with that stuff on and as we weren't anticipating a massive firefight, the feeling was that speed was more valuable than personal protection. Those vests were very, very heavy and those plates were gigantic – all the way down from your chin down to your belt buckle. It was like wearing a suit of armor! The RBA for example had a much smaller plate – these things were gigantic.

Delta operator Kurt Smith agreed:

One can achieve a high level of protection by wearing ballistic helmets, body armor, ballistic "chicken" plates, groin flaps, collars, etc. But, once a soldier is wearing all this, in addition to all the other kit an assaulter may be required to carry, his mobility drops significantly. The decrease in mobility by wearing all this kit is more dangerous. You are more likely to be hit by enemy fire for not moving fast enough.

The Rangers' uniform itself was standard for US infantry operating in arid environments. Most of them wore the newer Desert Camouflage Utility (DCU) pattern fatigues then being issued, although a few still had the older Desert Battle Dress Uniform (DBDU) or "chocolate chip" pattern uniforms. As stocks of helmet covers in the DCU pattern had yet to arrive, most Rangers used the "chocolate chip" PASGT helmet cover. Their webbing at the time was the standard ALICE (All-Purpose Lightweight Individual Carrying Equipment) LBE (Load Bearing Equipment), a webbing set that included magazine pouches, canteens, and a small pack affixed to the belt.

Delta in contrast had a long tradition of carrying non-standard or heavily modified weapons and equipment. Delta tested everything that was available on the commercial market and used whatever worked for them, as they enjoyed their own discretionary budget to purchase what they required. Individual operators also had a wide degree of latitude in choosing their own loads based on the mission at hand, a fact that impacted on October 3 with many choosing to leave behind their night-vision devices.

# APPENDIX 2

The primary weapon carried by the operators was the Colt Model 723 carbine, known within the Unit as the CAR15. Their Colt 723s had a notched barrel allowing underslung attachments such as the M203 grenade launcher or 12-gauge Master Key breaching shotgun to be fitted. Unlike the later M4 that allowed the mounting of sights directly above the receiver via the Picatinny rail system, optics on the Somalia-era Delta carbines were mounted directly onto the top of the carrying handles.

Delta carbines featured a number of other unusual features. Most were fitted with the Aimpoint 2000, although the Aimpoint 5000 was also used. According to Norm Hooten, the 3000 model was felt to be less reliable and was largely shunned by Delta, although some were employed by the Rangers. The Unit had been experimenting with a range of such optics for many years, inspired by the Son Tay raiders who had mounted Single Point optics to their CAR15s for their prisoner-of-war rescue mission in North Vietnam in 1970.

A range of tactical lights including the first iteration of what would later become the Surefire 6P weapon light were affixed under the barrel of operators' CAR15s. In Panama, operators used diving flashlights fitted to their weapons by clamps. Some carried two 30-round magazines taped together but separated by a device known as a Redi-mag, which allowed either magazine to be quickly fitted without the need to turn the magazine over – this also protected the lips of the magazine from damage when in the prone position. Some also affixed flashbang or smoke grenades to the magazines of their CAR15s for easy access when breaching as they could manipulate the grenade with their left hand whilst still pointing the carbine with their right.

Delta snipers used Ops Inc. suppressors affixed to their CAR15s. Some were also fitted with the Israeli-manufactured Elbit Systems AIM-1D infrared laser light. Delta's SAWs also mounted the AIM-1D, as did some individual CAR15s used by the assaulters. One operator on an assault team noted: "I didn't have one on my rifle at that time, I had another IR aiming device that went inside the charging handle, which is why our Aimpoints were attached differently than most. The AIM-1 was used on heavy weapons and some of the helo weapons, later on we all had those before we went to the PEQ." The PEQ was a later design of infrared illuminators that have since found wide acceptance amongst both infantry and special operations forces.

Within each Delta team, one operator typically mounted a 40mm M203 grenade launcher on his CAR15. Gary Keeney explained:

My role on the team was M203 gunner and mechanical breacher. I didn't carry any of those specific [breaching] tools or a shotgun on this mission. So on that day I was solely the 203 gunner. I think I had 8 to 12 HEDP [High-Explosive Dual-Purpose] rounds in a pouch on my left hand side. I can tell you when the lost convoy got back to the airfield, I didn't have any left!

One operator on each chalk, the assigned breacher, would also carry a breaching shotgun. For ballistically breaching doors and locks, shortened pistol-grip Remington 870 shotguns were carried. Knight's Armament Company's Master Key shotguns were also used by some operators. The Master Key was a shortened 12-gauge Remington 870 that was mounted under the barrel of the CAR15 in a similar fashion to the M203 grenade launcher. It was designed to allow an operator serving as a breacher the use of the shotgun for breaching and a rapid transition to the CAR15 to engage any hostiles as he entered the room. At least one operator who carried the Master Key on October 3 used it during the Mogadishu Mile to engage targets as he ran low on 5.56mm ammunition.

Some former operators have since remarked that they found the Master Key to be overly heavy and awkward to use, and Delta appears to have shelved the Master Key soon after Mogadishu. Kelly Venden from A-Squadron, which replaced C-Squadron in Mogadishu, explained: "They were more cumbersome. I used to carry a really shorty 870 [sawn-off pistol-grip shotgun] for breaching doors and stuff. It all comes down to preference but when you have a tool that you use perhaps 1 percent of the time, I'd rather have it out of the way and not interfering with my main armament."

Exactly what weapons a particular operator carried was largely down to the individual and his team. Another operator recounted: "I carried a Remington 870 sawed-off shotgun for breaching and a CAR15 with Aimpoint. I did not carry a 1911 since I had the shotgun, many guys did though. I did not carry any less-lethal munitions, but some did for their shotguns." Kelly Venden agreed: "That was the one thing I always valued, everybody can do whatever they want as long as they're efficient and able to accomplish the mission."

Others, including operator Kurt Smith on F-Team and Paul Leonard on C-Team, carried the SAW before transitioning to the CAR15 during the initial infiltration: "After the Lig Legato hit, I now carried a CAR15 slung across my chest, and I kept my SAW in my hands. It was tethered to the aircraft. I would use it on infil and exfil only and assault with my CAR15." The idea was to enable the operators to fire from the Little Bird to suppress anyone threatening their landing zone before leaving the bulky SAW with the aircraft. Leonard noted that the version employed by Delta had been customized by Unit armorers with a shortened barrel and collapsible stock; some were also fitted with vertical forward grips.

Mike Moser, a tactical breacher on B-Team, explained that decisions on weapons were largely governed by whichever mission template would be employed:

> Throughout the deployment I had essentially two configurations of kit and primary weapon, depending on which mission "template" we were to execute. These two templates were: a) Vehicular Convoy Intercept and b) Building Assault. The intelligence apparatus that would trigger a stand up of the TF [task force] would include some information as to whether our HVTs [High-Value Targets] were likely to be in transit (vehicle intercept) or static (building assault). After the team leaders were assembled in the TOC [tactical operations centre] and collectively worked out the particulars of the hit, I would reach for one or the other sets of equipment kept at the foot of my cot.
>
> My primary weapon in the "Convoy Intercept" template was to carry an M249 SAW with the purpose of stopping the lead vehicle by engaging its engine compartment and trying not to damage the people inside. The SAW was a clumsy tool to accomplish this, and horrible for room clearing – I threw out my back badly during an earlier hit – but its high volume of fire made it the choice for persuading a car driver to stop.
>
> My primary weapon in the "Building Assault" template was my CAR15. Regardless of which primary weapon and harness I carried, I would also have my M1911 .45 pistol. Typically there were carried by most guys in "drop holsters" on the primary leg; however, my thighs' real estate was dedicated to breaching charges and firing systems. I therefore kept my pistol in a Velcro holster affixed to my chest/body armor.

In terms of specialist breaching kit, Moser carried:

> a modified Claymore mine bag slung on my right thigh filled with a variety of breaching charges and firing systems. I had a small axe as well, but no larger

mechanical forced-entry tools. My team leader chose to carry a shorty 12-gauge shotgun slung under a shoulder as a backup breaching device. He preferred to have it [although] generally the breachers will carry them. In the event of an explosive misfire, I would be occupied with retrieving and safeing the charge and he could instantly employ the shotgun to gain entry.

Delta's pistols were customized .45ACP Caspian M1911A1s. In fact the Unit issued two .45s to each operator – one a 5-inch-barreled Government Model and the other featuring a compensator more commonly seen on high-end competition pistols. The compensated model, which reduced barrel rise and recoil, was used principally for counter-terrorist missions, whilst the Government Model was carried on general combat operations. The Unit had traditionally chosen the .45ACP pistol in favor of the issue 9mm Beretta as in the early days of Delta's formation few reliable hollowpoint designs were available in the 9mm caliber. It was felt that the .45ACP was a safer option as with its lower velocity it carried less of a risk of overpenetration that could wound or kill hostages.

The snipers of 3 Troop employed both suppressed CAR15s and a range of customized 7.62x51mm M14s and M21s with competition-grade triggers. Other rifles including the M24 bolt-action sniper rifle were also available but were not employed on October 3. The Delta M14s used a Brookfield Precision Tool scope mount to attach an Aimpoint 5000 red dot optic. At least one, Randy Shughart's weapon, was also fitted with the AIM-1D infrared laser. Sniper Jim Smith confirmed that there were no AR-10s or SR-25s used, only the M14s/M21s.

As noted earlier, some of the Delta snipers carried both the M14/M21 and CAR15s in the helicopters. This gave them the choice of platform in case they were dropped off to provide sniper support from a nearby building. In that case, the operator could take the M14/M21 to provide extended range, while the CAR15 was used for sniping from the aircraft as it could be rapidly fired in volleys against ground targets.

In contrast, most of the SEAL snipers carried modified CAR15s fitted with early ACOGs and longer 16-inch barrels. The ACOG or Advanced Combat Optical Gunsight was a fixed four-power magnification optic ideal for short- to medium-range precision shooting. One SEAL carried a modified M14. The SEALs also brought with them .300 Winchester

# APPENDIX 2

Magnum bolt-action Remington 700s in McMillan aftermarket stocks and these were used whilst providing overwatch for at least one of the earlier missions. In terms of sidearms, each SEAL was issued the 9mm SIG-Sauer P226, the same pistol then in use with the British SAS and known for its accuracy.

All operators carried hand grenades. Flashbangs were carried by some operators on the assault teams but they were mainly "kept on the aircraft for crowd dispersion," according to Hooten. Instead he carried fragmentation grenades. Many of the operators and some of the Rangers used the Dutch V40 mini-grenade, a "mini-frag" that had been in use since the Vietnam War. The advantage of these grenades was their small size, enabling a considerable number to be carried, and their relatively small detonation radius, making them ideal for using within buildings.

Stingball riot grenades were also used. When these detonated, they sprayed rubber pellets which, whilst non-lethal, were nonetheless painful. These were also carried on some of the helicopters for crowd control. Some of the breachers used AN-M14 thermite grenades for demolitions work or for denying immobilized vehicles or aircraft to the enemy, as they could burn through metal and armor. These were employed on the immobilized 5-ton truck at the objective and on the two Humvees abandoned at the K-4 Traffic Circle. They were also used by John M and his team at Super 64.

Delta wore their own non-standard protective equipment. Instead of the Kevlar PASGT worn by the Rangers, nearly all of the operators chose the lightweight plastic ProTec hockey or skateboard helmet. Although offering zero ballistic protection, many operators felt that the principal risk facing them was hitting their heads when climbing through windows or otherwise operating in tight spaces.

The ProTec helmets had debuted during Panama four years earlier. Some ProTec helmets were wrapped in tape to reduce their infrared signature, others were hand painted in desert colors. Most had an infrared strobe attached. The snipers chose to wear no helmets at all as it impeded their cheek-weld with their weapons. One operator did continue to wear the standard-issue PASGT helmet, nicknamed the "K-Pot," a more ungainly and heavier helmet but one that afforded some degree of ballistic protection. At least one operator noted after the battle that he had made a very smart choice. Delta quickly adopted ballistic helmets soon after Mogadishu.

The operators wore modified Desert Camouflage Uniforms with extra pockets sewn onto the upper sleeves. Glint tape was affixed to their upper sleeves and on their helmets. This allowed them to be seen and identified as friendly forces through night-vision devices. Most also wore lightweight knee pads. Their communications were via TASC-1 microphones running through Motorola radios. This allowed them to communicate within their teams, a luxury the Rangers did not have. As Hooten mentioned, Delta team leaders often carried two Motorolas – one set to the team frequency, the other to the Assault Force Commander's frequency.

There has been much confusion over the years about the black body armor worn by Delta. In Mogadishu they wore the NATO Special Forces model manufactured by TG Faust with custom-configured AWS chest rigs to carry magazines and grenades worn over the top of the vest. The operators had large colored US flag patches affixed on a Velcro strip on the chest portion of their body armor. "I'm pretty sure our body armor at the time was Faust. I know we used Faust for a long time. Paraclete were used later on," confirmed Hooten.

Although small arms were a weapon of absolute last resort for the aircrews of the 160th SOAR, they carried a range of personal defense weapons. Their primary weapon was the 9x19mm Heckler and Koch MP5K and MP5A3 submachine gun. The A3 model featured a collapsible stock whilst the ultra-compact K model had no stock but instead featured a vertical forward grip. Firing from a 30-round magazine, the MP5 was an accurate and dependable weapon, effective to perhaps 100 meters. The pilots also wore standard Army issue 9x19mm Beretta M9 pistols in thigh holsters.

Pilot Mike Durant confirmed that he used an MP5K to help defend the Super 64 crash site. He also only carried one spare magazine with him. He noted a number of stoppages with the weapon, unusual for the normally reliable MP5, but admitted his weapon maintenance may not have been all it could have been. MH-6 pilot Karl Maier used his own MP5A3 to good effect, holding back the mobs at the Super 61 crash for a considerable period.

The pilots liked the MP5 as they were easy to access in the cramped confines of a cockpit but recognized a longer-range weapon would be preferable should the unthinkable occur and they were forced to defend a crash site. The 9x19mm caliber was also considered ineffectual in comparison to the rifle-caliber carbines used by Delta and the SEALs. Indeed the

# APPENDIX 2

5.56x45mm Heckler and Koch HK53, a rifle-caliber version of the MP5, was tested as a possible replacement but was considered too heavy and unwieldy.

Assault rifles were available; crew chiefs stored a pair of 5.56x45mm M16A2 rifles in the rear of the aircraft. As mentioned previously, the aircrews also had access to less-than-lethal grenades and dropped these into crowds as they tried to buy time for the ground convoy to reach the Super 64 crash site. After Mogadishu, the MP5 was replaced with the Colt carbine in 5.56mm which offered ammunition compatibility with their "customers."

As we have noted, the Little Birds carried SAWs in the rear cargo compartment for use by operators during the infiltration phase of the mission. Additionally, some Little Bird crews carried M16A2s and at least one AH-6 pilot was recorded using his M16A2 over the Super 64 crash site to engage targets on the ground, perhaps after running out of minigun ammunition.

The 160th SOAR aircrews tended to wear tan flight suits or DCUs along with black American Body Armor A1-TAC-DSPO vests that featured both front and rear trauma plates and SPH-4 aviator helmets. Most wore modified SRU-21 survival vests with a belt rig. Some wore spare MP5 magazines in a thigh-mounted pouch, and indeed a drop holster for the MP5 was trialed but not deployed to Mogadishu.

In closing, it was the individual marksmanship skills of the Rangers and Delta operators that kept them alive during the Day of the Rangers. Somali small-arms fire was heavy but inaccurate. Indeed, several veterans are astounded that they were not hit by the tremendous weight of fire directed toward them. October 3 once again proved that it was the training and ability of the shooter to quickly place accurate fire upon an adversary that won the day.

# APPENDIX 3

## FULL JOINT OPERATIONS CENTRE OPERATIONS LOG

## MOGADISHU, OCTOBER 3-4, 1993

| TIME | EVENT |
|---|---|
| 1350 | BLANK [likely CIA] reports possible Salad/Qeydid mtg [meeting] at house near VIC [vicinity] Olympic Hotel (GRG sheet 24, 12.8/M.8; UTM NH36122665). |
| 1403 | Recce launch (2 x H-530 & 1 x OH-58D): [P3] Reef Point previously on station. |
| 1410 | Coords [coordinates] passed to Capt. Donahue (UNOSOM LNO). Confirmed no NGO [non-government organization] in vicinity of target. MG Montgomery notified. |
| 1415 | BLANK [likely CIA] reports source/signal may have occurred prior to arrival of Recce. |

## APPENDIX 3

| | |
|---|---|
| 1424 | Recce reports white Toyota land cruiser parked in front of hotel – fits description given by source. |
| 1427 | Source vehicle (silver with red stripes on the doors) stopped in front of target house and raised hood IAW [in accordance with] prearranged instructions to let us know he was at target. |
| 1434 | BLANK [likely Recce helicopters] will remain on meeting house location; BLANK [likely P3 Reef Point] will track white Toyota vehicle. |
| 1447 | Source may not have given prearranged signal in front of target house (gave signal only to let us know he was in the vicinity); Recce possibly on wrong target; J2 attempting to reconfirm/pinpoint actual target location. |
| 1450 | Source will drive around block again and give signal to reconfirm target location (approx. location 1 block northeast Olympic Hotel; GR sheet 24, 12.9/M.5). |
| 1459 | Source confirmed on target. Recce maneuvering to provide video of both sides of building. Recce advises this area has reported numerous small-arms fire in recent past. Aircrews/ground forces brief mission. |
| 1505 | Confirmed airspace deconfliction with QRF [quick reaction force] helos. |
| 1509 | Recce provides obstacle/hazard info on planned helos. |
| 1519 | BLANK [likely P3 Reef Point] reports 1+00 fuel on-station remaining BLANK = 1+10. |
| 1523 | (AH-6) Flight repos to FARP [forward armament and refueling point]. |
| 1527 | Assault force route passed to Recce; BLANK [Barber AH-6] flight will have rockets – no pre-planned fires at this time. Convoy route (K4 – National – Olympic) 9 x HMMWV & 3 x 5 tons: will depart when helo force departs airfield. |
| 1529 | Assault force pax [personnel] loaded and ready for launch. |
| 1530 | Recce reports 2 x roadblocks (burning tires) VIC of 21 Oct Rd and National. Route checked against possible land mine locations. |

| | |
|---|---|
| 1532 | Helo assault force launches. |
| 1535 | Ground reaction force convoy departs TF Ranger compound. |
| 1537 | Initiate assault codeword [Lucy] passed to all elements. |
| 1540 | Recce passes convoy route is clear of all obstructions. |
| 1542 | Helo assault commences on target/exact target building unknown/city block will be cleared. |
| 1543 | Super 61 reports ground force hitting the ground; Recce is providing flight following instructions to ground force. |
| 1545 | Ground reaction force at pre-planned hold point. |
| 1546 | AK-47s sighted/reported in compound; BLANK [Barber AH-6] reports forces too close to hotel to fire rockets. |
| 1547 | Large crowd coming up National toward target. Ground forces report sporadic ground fire contact – no KIA/WIA [friendly killed in action/wounded in action]. |
| 1550 | Super 61 reports friendlies on roof of target building. |
| 1551 | Recce reports 8–9 enemy (militia) approx. one block over and en route to target. |
| 1553 | RPG/small-arms fires reported 1 block east next to green water tank; ground reaction force moves to effect link-up with assault force. |
| 1555 | Super 62 will engage green water tank; man with RPG ran down street and is in small shack – Barber [AH-6] will engage. Women/children in area; Star [MH-6] ELE [element] to RTB [return to base] for FARP. |
| 1558 | RPG reported hit 5-ton – one WIA (gunshot to leg) and vehicle disabled. |
| 1600 | Recce reports troops with AK-47s moving toward target. |
| 1602 | LTC [lieutenant colonel] McKnight reports 9 x PC [precious cargo – prisoners] with possible principal captured. |
| 1604 | All forces to begin collapsing to building #1 for link up and ground exfil of all forces and PC. Will use bldg. #1 roof PZ [pickup zone] if required. |
| 1610 | Super 61 reports RPG burst over target; location of fires passed to Barber [AH-6]. |

# APPENDIX 3

| | |
|---|---|
| 1613 | McKnight reports one critical WIA will evacuate by ground ASAP [as soon as possible]; helos will provide guns as required. GRF #1 at building #1 for exfil. |
| 1620 | Super 61 shot down by RPG – Somalis approaching crash site. GRG sheet 24, 16.2/0.7, UTM NH 36142685. Ground reaction force 1 moving to secure crash site. Survivors climbing out of wreckage – ACFT [aircraft] is not on fire. Assault force personnel (approx. 7) securing the position. Report: area secure for MH-6 ELE to effect exfil of casualties (2 x KIA, 2 x WIA). |
| 1622 | Report: Large crowd of Somalis approaching crash site. |
| 1624 | MH-6 has landed at crash site – Super 62 providing cover – RPG gunner reported in target area – Barber inbound. |
| 1626 | GRF #1 will move to crash site with ASLT [assault] force and PC; move to crash site #1 approximately 1635. PC en-route back to TF Ranger compound via 5 ton with HMMWV security. QRF assistance requested; QRF to report to TF Ranger compound to link-up. |
| 1628 | Super 68 (SAR) [search and rescue] infils SST [SAR security team] at crash – Super 68 hit by RPG – require RTB ASAP. |
| 1630 | Super 68 lands TF Ranger compound. Crew trans-loads to spare aircraft. |
| 1631 | MH-6 exfil 2 x WIA from crash. |
| 1634 | Report: RPG fire 200 meters east of crash site. |
| 1641 | Super 64 is down – RPG; Grid 36402625, Super 62 fast-ropes 2 x snipers on site. BLANK [likely C2 helicopter] directs assault force assist ASAP. Reports: large crowd moving toward second crash site. |
| 1644 | RPGs being launched from numerous locations. |
| 1654 | GRF #1 reports numerous casualties (numbers/type unknown). |
| 1655 | Unable to leave crash site #1 – cannot recover 1 x KIA in aircraft. |
| 1656 | GRF #1 reports heavy sniper fires. |

| | |
|---|---|
| 1701 | Super 62 taking regular/close RPG fire; most from west side of 2nd crash site. |
| 1703 | Second Ranger ground (GRF #2) ELE reconstituted as recovery force for 2nd crash site (27 pax on 7 HMMWVs). |
| 1710 | QRF arrives compound. |
| 1713 | PC w/security and WIAs en-route to TF Ranger compound. GRF #1 continuing to crash site #1 under heavy fire. |
| 1715 | BLANK [likely Barber AH-6] ELE RTB to FARP. |
| 1720 | GRF #2 approaching 2nd crash site; road has been blocked with tire fires; GRF #2 receiving heavy fire. |
| 1723 | BLANK [likely C2 helicopter] RTB to FARP; BLANK [likely Garrison] requests GRF #1 return to crash site #1 to reconstitute. U64 [Uniform 64 – McKnight] has numerous casualties – cannot return to crash site. |
| 1726 | ASLT Force elements move overland to crash site #1 and secured. |
| 1727 | Super 62 hit – going down at new port- require MEDEVAC [medical evacuation] ASAP – numerous casualties. |
| 1730 | Super 68 (spare) en-route to new port to evacuate casualties. |
| 1734 | BLANK [likely CSAR] 2 x urgent casualties at northern crash site – need GRF assist ASAP; also live casualties at southern site still in ACFT – need GRF to secure that site also. |
| 1735 | QRF depart for crash site #2. |
| 1740 | GRF #2 link-up w/GRF #1 at K-4 circle. GRF #2 attempting different routes; receiving heavy fire wherever he goes; chance link-up … returning to compound transload PC and WIA from disabled vehicles – entire force RTB. |
| 1743 | Super 68 will pick up remaining pax at Super 62 (New Port). |
| 1744 | AH-6 continues taking RPG fires (approx. 50M north of |

## APPENDIX 3

|      |   |
|---|---|
|      | 2nd crash site); BLANK [likely Barber AH-6] reports aircraft has taken numerous rounds – can still fly. |
| 1745 | QRF in firefight VIC K-4 circle; will proceed to crash sites ASAP. |
| 1746 | Somali road block being built at 2nd crash site – Barber [AH-6] will engage to dissipate crowds. |
| 1751 | Require EOD [explosive ordnance disposal] to disarm possible active grenade at TF Ranger compound on remains- 10th Mountain notified (TF Ranger EOD w/ assault force). |
| 1755 | ASLT force reports running short of ammo and med supplies. |
| 1758 | AH-6 right gun jammed – will RTB and get it replaced. |
| 1801 | AH-6 rockets only capable – at crash site #1. |
| 1808 | AH-6 taking fires – no damage. |
| 1810 | QRF ([Lee] van Arsdale w/BN C2 [battalion command and control]) pinned down at K-4 circle. |
| 1820 | ASLT Force ammo getting critical. |
| 1830 | Super 68 will RTB & P/U [pickup] ammo and IV [intravenous] bags/QRF reconstitutes force after breaks in contact caused by ambush; RTB TF Ranger compound. |
| 1836 | Numerous RPG launches in VIC N [north] crash site; still have one body trapped in ACFT – unable to get due to numerous small arms. |
| 1854 | AH-6 break from K-4 and RTB north crash site. |
| 1855 | AH-6 taking RPG fires. |
| 1856 | North crash site still working recovery of body from ACFT – will not leave the body. |
| 1900 | Plan approved for QRF to move to crash site w/2 x Malaysian mech [mechanized] companies & 1 x Pakistani armor. |
| 1908 | Super 66 will drop resupply items at crash site #1; PZ marked by IR [infrared] strobe; BLANK [likely AH-6] supporting with guns. Assume friendlies at the strobes. Taking fires from 9-o'clock; resupply successful. At least 20 enemy with AKs in VIC. |

| | |
|---|---|
| 1926 | ASLT requests QRF get to crash site #1 ASAP!! Need to look at driving to Paki stadium then get air exfil to AFLD [airfield]. BLANK [likely P3 Reef Point] reports 21 Oct hwy [highway] is clear/quiet. |
| 1947 | Report from ASLT. Pilot still pinned in crash, will need jaws to retrieve him, requests evac (again) for 2 x critically wounded pax ASAP. |
| 2025 | ASLT advises that "If QRF does not get there (North crash) soon, there will be more KIAs from previously received WIA; Get the one star [general] to get his people moving!" |
| 2027 | ASLT force advises 1 x critical WIA at crash site #1 is now KIA. |
| 2032 | BLANK [likely OH-58D] will sparkle RPG site which just fired on AH-6 ELE, AH-6 will service. |
| 2035 | There is a lot of frustration over QRF/QRC [quick reaction company] not moving to assist. MG Garrison, BLANK [likely Boykin], and LTC McKnight discussing QRF plan of attack with BG Gile and QRF staff. |
| 2100 | SITREP [situation report] crash sites. Crash site #1: 99 total pax (13 x WIA/3 x KIA). Crash site #2: No report, situation unknown. |
| 2108 | BG Gile reports to CG [commanding general – Garrison] QRF will probably not be able to move until approx. 2200. |
| 2130 | QRF en-route to link-up with Malaysians at New Port. |
| 2200 | QRF arrive New Port/link-up w/Pakis [Pakistanis] & Malaysians/finalizes plan: establish holding area between crash sites; move 1 company to each crash site, reconstituted Ranger Force (& 8 x HMMWV, 56 pax) to secure area/act as reserve. |
| 2224 | BLANK [likely Hoar] called. Covered OPREP [operation report] 3 report with him. |
| 2228 | MG Montgomery requests QRF convoy route for possible "improvement" planning prior to departing. No estimate on when convoy will proceed to crash sites for TF Ranger relief. |

# APPENDIX 3

| | |
|---|---|
| 2230 | Final PC status: 24 detainees; 1 x WIA, 3 x KIA = 24 total; enemy KIA are currently in 507th Mortuary Support ELE (at AFLD). |
| 2300 | Telecom between BLANK [likely CIA] requests stop jamming – BLANK [likely J2] said no – not until all TF Ranger forces recovered; BLANK [likely J2] request BLANK [likely CIA] put up cash reward for anyone who aids Americans or helps recover remains; Also, try to get "sources" in VIC of crash sites to inform on what's going on. |
| 2305 | BLANK called BLANK and requests plus-up LONG BLANK [unknown but likely relating to CIA activities, possibly launching CIA aircraft]. |
| 2323 | QRF departing New Port. |
| 2345 | QRF receiving fire en-route to holding area. |
| 2350 | QRF arrive holding area/A Company dispatched to crash site #1. |
| 2353 | AH-6 will break for fuel. |
| 2357 | QRF convoy and crash sites taking heavy small-arms fire. Friendlies believed south of southern crash site based on PLS [personal locator system] codes being picked up in that VIC (old Saudi embassy). |
| 0002 | QRF believes location approx. 200M from TFR [Task Force Ranger] crash site #1 under heavy contact. Lead ELE of QRF (TF Ranger LNO [liaison officer] ELE) has Quickie Saw to cut remaining body from aircraft. |
| 0026 | Pakistani tanks refuse to move on/APCs very reluctant to move, but eventually do. Roadblock removed by hand, by dismounted QRF troops. |
| 0036 | BLANK [likely P3 Reef Point] relays QRF troops dismounted way too soon. Approximately 3–4 blocks from TFR forces. |
| 0120 | BLANK [likely P3 Reef Point] reports QFR approx. 300M from TFR location. |
| 0122 | Friendlies believed in abandoned building approx. 100M south of old Saudi embassy (crash site #2). |
| 0148 | Enemy forces approx. 150M east of crash site #1. |

## DAY OF THE RANGERS

| | |
|---|---|
| 0155 | Link-up between TFR and lead QRF element; ensure good accountability personnel prior to movement & cut KIA out of ACFT. |
| 0210 | QRF en-route to crash site (#2). |
| 0227 | Crash site #2 secure – no sign of aircrew. |
| 0230 | CG receives approval to bring replacement aircraft into theatre. C5 will bring 5 x MH-60 and 2 x AH-6 with supplemental crews. |
| 0239 | BLANK [likely P3 Reef Point] reports 4 x barrel gun firing (possibly Paki) have them check fire. Enemy illumination at site #2. |
| 0248 | QRF (TF Ranger LNO) advises several hours required to cut free/recover KIA in ACFT at site #1. |
| 0249 | No bodies found at crash site #2 (Super 64) & no one answers to aircrew's names in VIC (4 x aircrew plus 2 x BLANK [Delta] snipers should have been there). |
| 0300 | Thermite grenades set on crash site #2 (south) – no confirmation they have been lit. |
| 0336 | AH-6 returns to airfield with inoperative fuel gauge and "Fuel low" light. |
| 0348 | Pakis request to fire mortars into Villa Somalia (mortar position). |
| 0350 | Reef Point very briefly picked up 2 x PLS in VIC crash site #2. |
| 0400 | AH-6 service RPG launch location VIC crash site #1. |
| 0409 | Pakistanis cleared road from Paki stadium to CP207, no mines reported. |
| 0415 | AH-6 RTB for main rotor blade replacement, estimated 30 min downtime. |
| 0420 | Phone con from BLANK [likely Van Arsdale] report 2 x Malaysian APCs reported hit by RPGs vicinity grid NH363265. Requesting assistance from TF Ranger gun helos. Passed to TF Green [Delta]. |
| 0424 | Pakistanis report they have not cleared road from stadium to CP207. Pakis have a guide to RDVZ [rendezvous] W/ BLANK [unknown] at CP [check point] on National. |

## APPENDIX 3

| | |
|---|---|
| 0438 | BLANK [likely Miller or Van Arsdale] querying avail of additional transport to pick up dismounted troops. |
| 0453 | ASLT reports he has 200 dismounted, (QRF/assault force/Ranger blocking force) will link w/transport on National once body recovered. |
| 0500 | ASLT query about possible resupply of 5.56/40MM/and water to BLANK [likely Miller] advises redistribute rom vehicles, high helo threat. Still at least 20 minutes to cut body from wreckage. |
| 0515 | ASLT reports attempting to cut out majority of body from wreckage. |
| 0523 | LNO reports no control over Malaysian vehicles, APCs abandoned Dragon 6 position, Malays appear returning to Paki stadium. |
| 0530 | Body recovered. Destructive charges set on helo. BLANK [likely Barber AH-6] providing cover fire for withdrawal from crash site #1. |
| 0542 | ASLT moving all elements out of target site. AH-6 ELE continues fire support. |
| 0550 | Terminator & Kilo elements linking up with Dragon ELE. |
| 0605 | Not enough transport, 50 pax still dismounted. ASLT requesting more APCs. |
| 0610 | 30 pax mounting APCs. |
| 0620 | All pax loaded, convoy moving out. |
| 0627 | Cobras making TOW [anti-tank guided missile] shot on abandoned APCs. |
| 0630 | Convoy pulling into Paki stadium. |
| 0715 | Confirming names of 20 pax RTB to New Port so BLANK [likely Van Arsdale] can check his headcount. |
| 0720 | BLANK [likely Reef Point] RTB. |
| 0734 | AH-6 ELE all on standby at FARP. |
| 0745 | AH-6 or ASLT feels that 2 snipers inserted to crash site #2 are possibly responsible for taking bodies and equipment from site. Might be in hiding near site. |

# DAY OF THE RANGERS

| | |
|---|---|
| 0810 | Begin shuttle of Rangers, from stadium RTB. Net monitoring weak intermittent transmissions from VIC of crash site #2. |
| 0815 | BLANK [likely SIGINT] possible beacon transmission, frequency being investigated. |
| 0827 | BLANK [likely Reef Point] being launched. AH-6 being stood down. |
| 0845 | Voice came in over beacon saying "my arm is broken." Attempting to DF [direction find] source. |
| 0915 | Continued attempts to establish comms with Beacon station unsuccessful. Beacon being turned on or off. |
| 0916 | Ground commanders report all personnel accounted for except for the 4 crew members and 2 snipers inserted into crash site #2. |

# GLOSSARY

| | |
|---|---|
| **AC-130** | Armed version of the C-130 Hercules transport aircraft, also known as Spectre |
| **AGMS** | Armored Ground Mobility System |
| **AH-1** | Cobra attack helicopter |
| **AH-6** | Little Bird helicopter variant armed with rockets and miniguns |
| **AIAI** | al-Itihad al-Islami, a Somali insurgent group |
| **AMISOM** | African Union Mission in Somalia |
| **ASLT** | Assault Force Commander |
| **AWSS** | Authorized Weapons Storage Sites, UN cantonment areas for illegal heavy weapons and technicals |
| **BP** | Blocking Position |
| **C2** | Command and Control |
| **CAP** | Combat Air Patrol |
| **CAR15** | Colt 5.56mm carbine carried by Delta and some Rangers – predecessor to the M4 |
| **CAS** | Close Air Support |
| **CCP** | Casualty Collection Point |
| **CCT** | Combat Controller, US Air Force special operations personnel trained to guide in close air support |
| **CENTCOM** | Central Command, US military headquarters responsible for |

| | |
|---|---|
| | operations in the Middle East, Central Asia, and northern Africa |
| CI | Counter Intelligence |
| CP | Command Posts |
| CQB | Close Quarter Battle, techniques for breaching and clearing rooms and shooting at close range |
| CQM | Close Quarters Marksmanship |
| CS | Confined Space |
| CSAR | Combat-Search-and-Rescue: on October 3 the Black Hawk known as Super 68 was assigned the mission |
| DAP | Direct Action Penetrator, a kit allowing the MH-60 to be transformed into an attack helicopter variant armed with 30mm cannon, miniguns, and rockets. Taken to Mogadishu by 160th SOAR but not deployed. |
| DMZ | Demilitarized Zone |
| DO | Directorate of Operations, CIA command responsible for field operations |
| EDRE | Emergency Deployment Readiness Exercise |
| ELE | Element |
| EMT | Emergency Medical Technician |
| EOD | Explosives Ordnance Disposal |
| FARP | Forward Armament and Refueling Point |
| FLIR | Forward-Looking-Infrared Laser |
| FO | Forward Observer |
| FSO | Fire Support Officer |
| GMV | Ground Mobility Vehicle |
| GRF | Ground Reaction Force, Ranger units mounted in Humvees and trucks |
| HMMWV | High Mobility Multipurpose Wheeled Vehicle, designation for Humvee |
| HUMINT | Human Intelligence, using agents on the ground to gather intelligence |
| HVT | High-Value Target |
| ICRC | International Committee of the Red Cross, a humanitarian organization |
| ICU | Islamic Courts Union, a Somali insurgent group that preceeded |

# GLOSSARY

|  | al-Shabaab |
|---|---|
| **IED** | Improvized Explosive Device |
| **IR** | Infrared |
| **IRF** | Immediate Reaction Force |
| **ISA** | Intelligence Support Activity, US Army covert unit (also known as Centra Spike and Office of Military Support) |
| **ISR** | Intelligence, Surveillance, and Reconnaissance |
| **J-2** | Intelligence Cell |
| **JCS** | Joint Chiefs of Staff |
| **JOC** | Joint Operations Center, the Task Force Ranger headquarters |
| **JSOC** | Joint Special Operations Command, the parent organization responsible for the special mission units such as Delta and SEAL Team 6 |
| **KIA** | Killed In Action |
| **LBE** | Load-Bearing Equipment |
| **LZ** | Landing Zone for helicopters |
| **M14** | 7.62mm nettle rifle used by some Delta and SEAL snipers |
| **M16A2** | Colt 5.56mm assault rifle carried by most Rangers |
| **MEDEVAC** | Medical Evacuation, usually by air |
| **MH-6** | Unarmed troop-carrying variant of the Little Bird helicopter |
| **MH-60** | Special operations modified version of the UH-60 Black Hawk helicopter |
| **NCO** | Non-Commissioned Officer, a sergeant or corporal |
| **OH-58** | Kiowa reconnaissance helicopter |
| **OMS** | Office of Military Support, another cover name for the Intelligence Support Activity |
| **OPSEC** | Operational security |
| **PC** | Precious Cargo, codeword for prisoners |
| **PJ** | Pararescueman Jumper, US Air Force special operations personnel trained to rescue trapped aircrew |
| **PKM** | Heavy weapons system, the Russian 7.62 x 54mm medium machine gun |
| **PLS** | Personal Locator System |
| **PZ** | Pick-up Zone, normally for helicopters and often within an urban environment such as from a rooftop |
| **QRC** | The QRF's standby Quick Reaction Company |

| | |
|---|---|
| **QRF** | Quick Reaction Force drawn from the 10th Mountain Division |
| **RBA** | Ranger Body Armor |
| **REDS** | Rapid extraction deployment system |
| **Reef Point** | Modified surveillance version of Navy P-3 Orion |
| **RG-8** | Schweizer glider surveillance aircraft operated by CIA |
| **ROE** | Rules of engagement, the conditions under which an enemy combatant can be engaged |
| **RPG** | Ruchnoi Protivotankoviy Granatomyot or antitank grenade launcher. Incorrectly but widely mistranslated as Rocket-Propelled Grenade. |
| **RTO** | Radio Telephone Operator, the radioman |
| **SAD** | Special Activities Division, CIA paramilitary unit |
| **SAR** | Search and Rescue, also known as CSAR |
| **SAS** | Special Air Service, UK Special Forces |
| **SAW** | Squad Automatic Weapons, the Belgian-designed M249 or Minimi light machinegun |
| **SEAL** | Sea, Air, and Land, US Navy commandoes |
| **SERE** | Survival, Evasion, Resistance, and Escape |
| **SFOD** | 1st Special Forces Operational Detachment-Delta (Airborne), official title of Delta Force |
| **SIGINT** | Signals Intelligence |
| **SMU** | Special Mission Unit, term used to describe Delta, SEAL Team 6 and the Intelligence Support Activity |
| **SNA** | Somali National Alliance, a clan militia of the Habr Gidr clan |
| **SNM** | Somali National Movement, an insurgent group in the Somali civil war |
| **SOAR** | 160th Special Operations Aviation Regiment, the Nightstalkers |
| **SOCOM** | US Special Operations Command, the parent organization responsible for all US military SOF units |
| **SOF** | Special Operations Forces |
| **SOP** | Standard Operating Procedure |
| **SSE** | Sensitive Site Exploration |
| **TCCC** | Tactical Combat Casualty Care |
| **Technical** | Militia armed pick-up truck |
| **TF** | Task Force |
| **TFR** | Task Force Ranger |

# GLOSSARY

| | |
|---|---|
| **TOC** | Tactical Operations Center |
| **TOW** | Tube-launched, Optically tracked, Wire-guided; an American anti-tank missile fired from AH-1 Cobra attack helicopters |
| **TTP** | Tactics, Techniques, and Processes |
| **UNOSOM** | United Nations Operations in Somalia, the UN humanitarian mission in Somalia |
| **USC** | United Somali Congress, a clan militia of the Hawiye Clan |
| **USSOCOM** | United States Special Operations Command |
| **VIC** | Vicinity |
| **WIA** | Wounded In Action |

# NOTES

### Chapter 1

1. https://www.csmonitor.com/1993/0614/14011.html
2. UN Mission Statement: http://www.un.org/Depts/DPKO/Missions/unosomi.htm
3. http://www.nytimes.com/1991/12/08/world/factional-fighting-in-somalia-terrorizes-and-ruins-capital.html?pagewanted=all
4. Baumann, Robert F. and Yates, Lawrence A. with Washington, Versalle F., *My Clan Against the World: US and Coalition Forces in Somalia 1992–1994* (Leavenworth: Washington Combat Studies Institute Press, 2003), p. 108
5. https://www.pbs.org/wgbh/pages/frontline/shows/ambush/interviews
6. Wasdin, Howard E. and Templin, Stephen, *SEAL Team Six* (New York: St Martin's, 2011), p. 177
7. https://www.pbs.org/wgbh/pages/frontline/shows/ambush/interviews/howe.html
8. Ibid.
9. https://www.csmonitor.com/1993/0614/14011.html

# NOTES

10. https://www.washingtonpost.com/archive/politics/1993/06/16/somali-warlords-tactics-confound-un/2c574b6f-8741-44b2-ad84-1aa9dacee2e0/?utm_term=.3fcc29a15cd7
11. Baumann and Yates with Washington, *My Clan Against the World*, p. 139
12. Ernst Presentation, MOUT 2000 Conference
13. https://www.pbs.org/wgbh/pages/frontline/shows/ambush/interviews/howe.html
14. Senate Review of Circumstances Surrounding the Ranger Raid on October 3–4, 1993 in Mogadishu, Somalia (hereafter "Senate Review")
15. https://www.pbs.org/wgbh/pages/frontline/shows/ambush/interviews/howe.html
16. Ibid
17. Senate Review
18. Ibid
19. http://www.independent.co.uk/voices/profile-how-to-turn-a-warmonger-into-a-hero-general-aideed-top-bad-guy-on-americas-hit-list-1485338.html
20. Senate Review
21. Baumann and Yates with Washington, *My Clan Against the World*, p.139
22. Senate Review
23. McKnight, Lieutenant Colonel Danny, *Streets of Mogadishu* (Chester: Leading for Freedom, 2011), p. 84
24. DiTomasso, Captain Thomas, *The Battle of the Black Sea: Bravo Company, 3rd Ranger Battalion, 75th Ranger Regiment, 3–4 October 1993* (Fort Benning: Infantry Officer's Advanced Course, 1994); www.benning.army.mil/library/content/Virtual/.../DiTomassoThomas%20CPT.pdf
25. Smith, Captain Kurt, *Task Force Ranger in Somalia: 1st Special Forces Operational Detachment-Delta, 3–4 October 1993* (Fort Benning: Infantry Officer's Advanced Course, 1994); www.benning.army.mil/library/content/Virtual/.../other/.../SmithKurt%20CPT.pdf
26. Ibid
27. Senate Review

28. Ibid
29. Department of Defense, *Subject: After Action Report for TASK FORCE RANGER Operations in Support of UNOSOM II; 22 August–25 October 1993* (USSOCOM, 1994); http://www.socom.smil.mil/socs-ho/aarll/somalia
30. Ibid
31. Smith, *Task Force Ranger in Somalia*
32. DiTomasso, *The Battle of the Black Sea*

## Chapter 2

1. Smith, *Task Force Ranger in Somalia*
2. Faust, Colonel James T., *Task Force Ranger in Somalia: Isaiah 6:8* (US Army War College, 1999); http://www.lc-vans.lintcenter.org/wp.../08/TF-Ranger-Part-1-Paper-with-Prologue-pp-0-29.pdf
3. Smith, *Task Force Ranger in Somalia*
4. Senate Review
5. https://www.pbs.org/wgbh/pages/frontline/shows/ambush/interviews/haad.html
6. Faust, *Task Force Ranger in Somalia: Isaiah 6:8*
7. Senate Review
8. http://articles.chicagotribune.com/1993-08-27/news/9308270330_1_delta-force-mohamed-farrah-aidid-somalia
9. Ibid
10. http://articles.latimes.com/1993-10-22/news/mn-48499_1_american-policy
11. Rysewyk, Captain Lee, *Experiences of Executive Officer from Bravo Company, 3d Battalion, 75th Ranger Regiment and Task Force Ranger during the Battle of the Black Sea on 3–4 October 1993, in Mogadishu, Somalia* (Fort Benning: Infantry Officer's Advanced Course, 1994); www.benning.army.mil/library/content/Virtual/.../RysewykLee%20A.%20CPT.pdf
12. Lechner, Captain James O., *A Monograph of Combat Operations in Mogadishu, Somalia Conducted by Task Force Ranger* (Fort Benning: Infantry Officer's Advanced Course, 1994); www.benning.army.mil/library/content/Virtual/.../LechnerJamesO%20%20CPT.pdf

# NOTES

13. Ibid
14. Ibid
15. Carney, Colonel John T. and Schemmer, Benjamin F., *No Room for Error: The Covert Operations of America's Special Tactics Units from Iran to Afghanistan* (New York: Ballantine Books, 2002), p. 250
16. McKnight, *Streets of Mogadishu*, p. 166
17. Bowden, Mark, *Black Hawk Down* (London: Bantam Press, 1999), p. 34
18. Thomas, Keni, *Get It On! What it Means to Lead the Way* (Brentwood: B&H Publishing Group, 2011), p. 137
19. Ibid
20. *United States Forces, Somalia: after action report and historical overview: the United States Army in Somalia, 1992-1994*
21. Karcher, Major Timothy M., *Understanding the Victory Disease, from the Little Bighorn, to Mogadishu, to the Future*; www.dtic.mil/get-tr-doc/pdf?AD=ADA416034
22. Kassinger, Jack, *Holding Hands with Heroes* (Pittsburgh: Dorrance Publishing, 2010), p. 154
23. Ernst Presentation, MOUT 2000 Conference
24. http://smallwarsjournal.com/jrnl/art/intelligence-challenges-in-urban-operations
25. https://www.washingtonpost.com/archive/lifestyle/magazine/2000/02/27/after-action-report/3c474a43-ea21-4bf5-afc5-02820b8579e5/?utm_term=.fbffa8f6d588
26. Wasdin and Templin, *SEAL Team Six*, p. 197
27. Ibid, p. 209
28. Smith, Michael, *Killer Elite: The Inside Story of America's Most Secret Special Operations Team* (London: Orion, 2006), p. 187
29. Faust, *Task Force Ranger in Somalia: Isaiah 6:8*
30. Ibid
31. http://www.pacom.mil/Media/Speeches-Testimony/Article/795839/special-operations-command-pacific-change-of-command/
32. Ernst Presentation, MOUT 2000 Conference
33. Naylor, Sean, *Relentless Strike: The Secret History of Joint Special Operations Command* (New York: St Martins, 2015), p. 59

34. Allard, Kenneth, *Somalia Operations: Lessons Learned* (Washington DC: National Defense University Press, 1995), p. 51
35. http://www.pbs.org/wgbh/pages/frontline/shows/ambush/interviews/haad.html
36. Rysewyk, *Experiences of Executive Officer from Bravo Company*
37. Smith, *Task Force Ranger in Somalia*
38. Department of Defense, *Subject: After Action Report for TASK FORCE RANGER Operations in Support of UNOSOM II*
39. Ibid
40. Faust, *Task Force Ranger in Somalia: Isaiah 6:8*
41. Smith, *Task Force Ranger in Somalia*
42. Rysewyk, *Experiences of Executive Officer from Bravo Company*
43. Senate Review
44. Ibid
45. Smith, *Task Force Ranger in Somalia*
46. Faust, *Task Force Ranger in Somalia: Isaiah 6:8*
47. Ibid
48. Smith, *Task Force Ranger in Somalia*
49. Ibid
50. Ibid
51. Faust, *Task Force Ranger in Somalia: Isaiah 6:8*
52. https://www.cbsnews.com/news/the-holy-warrior/
53. Sangvic, Major Roger N., *Battle of Mogadishu: Anatomy of a Failure* (Fort Leavenworth: School of Advanced Military Studies United States Army Command and General Staff College, 1999); www.dtic.mil/get-tr-doc/pdf?AD=ADA366316
54. https://www.pbs.org/wgbh/pages/frontline/shows/ambush/interviews/montgomery.html
55. Sangvic, *Battle of Mogadishu: Anatomy of a Failure*
56. Lechner, *A Monograph of Combat Operations in Mogadishu*
57. Faust, *Task Force Ranger in Somalia: Isaiah 6:8*
58. Department of Defense, *Subject: After Action Report for TASK FORCE RANGER Operations in Support of UNOSOM II*
59. Levin, C. and Warner, J., *Subject: Review of Circumstances Surrounding the Ranger Raid on October 3-4 1993 in Mogadishu, Somalia* (Washington: Senate Committee on Armed Services, 1995)

# NOTES

## Chapter 3

1. Faust, *Task Force Ranger in Somalia: Isaiah 6:8*
2. Smith, *Killer Elite*, p. 188
3. Faust, *Task Force Ranger in Somalia: Isaiah 6:8*
4. Senate Review
5. DiTomasso, *The Battle of the Black Sea*
6. https://www.dvidshub.net/news/165185/career-sof-senior-nco-receives-2015-bull-simons-award
7. https://www.cbsnews.com/news/black-hawk-down-site-revisited-20-years-later/
8. http://www.defensemedianetwork.com/stories/interview-michael-j-durant-2/
9. Ibid
10. Smith, *Task Force Ranger in Somalia*
11. https://www.army.mil/article/135695/Soldiers_reflect_on_Battle_of_Mogadishu/
12. Smith, *Task Force Ranger in Somalia*
13. Ibid
14. http://www.pbs.org/wgbh/pages/frontline/shows/ambush/interviews/haad.html
15. Thomas, *Get It On!*, p. 53
16. http://edition.cnn.com/2001/LAW/04/23/embassy.bombings.trial.01/index.html
17. Bowden, *Black Hawk Down*, p. 53
18. Butler Jr., Captain Frank, Hagmann, Lieutenant Colonel John H. and Richards, David T., "Tactical Management of Urban Warfare Casualties in Special Operations" (*Military Medicine*, 165, Supplement 1, 2000)
19. https://www.brooksidepress.org/Products/.../DATA/.../SOMALIA7May1999.doc
20. Ibid
21. Ibid
22. McKnight, *Streets of Mogadishu*, p. 127
23. http://articles.orlandosentinel.com/2002-01-19/news/0201190359_1_blackburn-commandos-rangers

24. https://www.pbs.org/wgbh/pages/frontline/shows/ambush/rangers/berendsen.html
25. Durant, Chief Warrant Officer 4 Michael J. and Hartov, Steven, *In the Company of Heroes* (New York: GP Putnam's Sons, 2003), p. 39
26. https://www.youtube.com/watch?v=97hbJzK7SU8
27. http://www.pbs.org/wgbh/pages/frontline/shows/ambush/interviews/haad.html
28. http://www.pbs.org/wgbh/pages/frontline/shows/ambush/rangers/berendsen.html
29. http://www.defensemedianetwork.com/stories/interview-michael-j-durant-2/
30. Perino, Captain Larry D., *The Battle of the Black Sea: Mogadishu Somalia* (Fort Benning: Infantry Officer's Advanced Course, 1994); www.benning.army.mil/library/content/Virtual/.../PerinoLarryD%20%20CPT.pdf
31. http://www.pbs.org/wgbh/pages/frontline/shows/ambush/interviews/haad.html
32. Eversmann, Matt and Schilling, Dan, *The Battle of Mogadishu: Firsthand Accounts from the Men of Task Force Ranger* (New York: Presidio Press, 2004), p. 185
33. Ibid, p. 69

## Chapter 4

1. Lechner, *A Monograph of Combat Operations in Mogadishu*
2. DiTomasso, *The Battle of the Black Sea*
3. https://www.cbsnews.com/news/black-hawk-down-site-revisited-20-years-later/
4. Boykin, Lieutenant General William G., *Never Surrender* (New York: Hachette, 2008), p. 265
5. This is a direct quote from a Delta operator who wished to remain anonymous
6. http://www.pbs.org/wgbh/pages/frontline/shows/ambush/etc/script.html
7. https://www.cbsnews.com/news/black-hawk-down-site-revisited-20-years-later/

# NOTES

8. Butler, Hagmann and Richards, "Tactical Management of Urban Warfare Casualties in Special Operations"
9. Boykin, *Never Surrender*, p. 266
10. Butler, Hagmann and Richards, "Tactical Management of Urban Warfare Casualties in Special Operations"
11. https://www.army.mil/article/108840
12. http://www.24sow.af.mil/News/Article-Display/Article/162683/pj-scott-fales-receives-2012-bull-simons-award/
13. https://www.army.mil/article/156778/Veterans_reflect_on_Battle_of_Mogadishu/
14. Smith, *Task Force Ranger in Somalia*
15. https://www.cbsnews.com/news/black-hawk-down-site-revisited-20-years-later/
16. http://www.24sow.af.mil/News/Article-Display/Article/162683/pj-scott-fales-receives-2012-bull-simons-award/
17. Ibid
18. Ibid
19. http://www.24sow.af.mil/News/Article-Display/Article/162683/pj-scott-fales-receives-2012-bull-simons-award/
20. http://content.time.com/time/magazine/article/0,9171,163897,00.html
21. http://arits.org/biographies/279-sfc-earl-fillmore
22. Smith, *Task Force Ranger in Somalia*
23. Ibid
24. Thomas, *Get It On!*, p. 106
25. Perino, *The Battle of the Black Sea: Mogadishu Somalia*
26. Ibid
27. Ibid
28. Ibid
29. Ibid
30. http://www.24sow.af.mil/News/Article-Display/Article/162683/pj-scott-fales-receives-2012-bull-simons-award/

## Chapter 5

1. http://www.defensemedianetwork.com/stories/interview-michael-j-durant-2/
2. Ibid
3. Bowden, *Black Hawk Down*, p. 167
4. Grau, Lester W., "A Weapon For All Seasons: The Old But Effective RPG-7 Promises to Haunt the Battlefields of Tomorrow" (*Infantry Magazine*, May–August 1998); http://fmso.leavenworth.army.mil/documents/weapon.htm
5. Rottman, Gordon L., *The Rocket Propelled Grenade* (Oxford: Osprey, 2010), p. 46
6. DeKever, Andrew J. and Durant, Chief Warrant Officer 4 Michael J., *Here Rests in Honored Glory: Life Stories of Our Country's Medal Of Honor Recipients* (Merriam Press Military, 2012), p. 322
7. https://www.defensemedianetwork.com/stories/socom-year-in-review-2008-2009/
8. https://www.youtube.com/watch?v=Ioo3HnN8rKI
9. http://www.socnet.com/showthread.php?t=75147
10. http://www.defensemedianetwork.com/stories/interview-michael-j-durant-2/
11. http://edition.cnn.com/2016/03/14/us/mike-durant-rewind/index.html
12. DeLong, Kent and Tuckey, Steven, *Mogadishu! Heroism and Tragedy* (Westport: Praeger Publishers, 1994), p. 43
13. http://www.defensemedianetwork.com/stories/interview-michael-j-durant-2/
14. Ecklund, Marshall V. and McNerney, Michael A., *Personnel Recovery Operations for Special Operations Forces in Urban Environments: Modeling Successful Overt and Clandestine Methods of Recovery* (California: Naval Postgraduate School Monterey, 2004); https://calhoun.nps.edu/handle/10945/1159
15. Lechner, *A Monograph of Combat Operations in Mogadishu, Somalia Conducted by Task Force Ranger*
16. Smith, *Task Force Ranger in Somalia*

# NOTES

17. http://edition.cnn.com/2016/03/14/us/mike-durant-rewind/index.html
18. https://www.defensemedianetwork.com/stories/interview-michael-j-durant-2/
19. Ecklund and McNerney, *Personnel Recovery Operations for Special Operations Forces In Urban Environments*
20. https://www.defensemedianetwork.com/stories/interview-michael-j-durant-2/

## Chapter 6

1. https://www.defensemedianetwork.com/stories/interview-michael-j-durant-2/
2. Lechner, *A Monograph of Combat Operations in Mogadishu, Somalia Conducted by Task Force Ranger*
3. Eversmann and Schilling, *The Battle of Mogadishu: Firsthand Accounts from the Men of Task Force Ranger*, p. 185
4. McKnight, *Streets of Mogadishu*, p. 164
5. Smith, *Task Force Ranger in Somalia*
6. https://www.dvidshub.net/news/printable/165185
7. https://www.army.mil/article/135695/soldiers_reflect_on_battle_of_mogadishu
8. Ibid
9. Whetstone, Lieutenant Colonel Michael, *Madness in Mogadishu: Commanding the 10th Mountain Division's Quick Reaction Company during Black Hawk Down* (Mechanicsburg: Stackpole Books, 2015), p. 215
10. Ibid

## Chapter 7

1. Perino, *The Battle of the Black Sea: Mogadishu Somalia*
2. https://www.cbsnews.com/news/black-hawk-down-site-revisited-20-years-later/
3. https://www.brooksidepress.org/Products/.../DATA/.../SOMALIA7May1999.doc

4. Carney and Schemmer, *No Room for Error*, p. 254
5. http://www.airforcemag.com/MagazineArchive/Pages/1994/June%201994/0694heroes.aspx
6. Carney and Schemmer, *No Room for Error*, p. 255
7. http://www.courier-tribune.com/news/20161105/bray-lived-dream-he-wanted-to-be-soldier
8. Smith, *Task Force Ranger in Somalia*
9. https://www.pbs.org/wgbh/pages/frontline/shows/ambush/interviews/montgomery.html
10. Ibid
11. Ibid
12. Ferry, Captain Charles P., "Mogadishu, October 1993: A Company XO's Notes on Lessons Learned" (*Infantry* Magazine, November-December 1994); https://www.benning.army.mil/magazine/1994/1994_6/fa02.pdf
13. Ibid
14. Ibid
15. Casper, Colonel Lawrence E., *Falcon Brigade: Combat and Command in Somalia and Haiti* (Boulder: Lynne Rienner Publishers, 2001), p. 79
16. Ferry, "Mogadishu, October 1993: A Company XO's Notes on Lessons Learned"
17. Whetstone, *Madness in Mogadishu*, p. 168
18. http://www.battleofmogadishu.com/Cms_Data/Contents/mog/Media/.../JAN_APR_98.pdf
19. Ibid
20. Smith, *Task Force Ranger in Somalia*
21. Rysewyk, *Experiences of Executive Officer from Bravo Company*
22. https://www.dvidshub.net/news/165185/career-sof-senior-nco-receives-2015-bull-simons-award
23. http://www.homeofheroes.com/valor/02_awards/silverstar/6_PostRVN/10_somalia.html
24. https://www.army.mil/article/135695/soldiers_reflect_on_battle_of_mogadishu

# NOTES

## Chapter 8

1. Smith, *Task Force Ranger in Somalia*
2. https://www.pbs.org/wgbh/pages/frontline/shows/ambush/rangers/ramaglia.html
3. Smith, *Task Force Ranger in Somalia*
4. Perino, *The Battle of the Black Sea: Mogadishu Somalia*
5. https://www.washingtonpost.com/archive/lifestyle/magazine/2000/02/27/after-action-report/3c474a43-ea21-4bf5-afc5-02820b8579e5/?utm_term=.517e38c186d4
6. www.drum.army.mil/mountaineer/Article.aspx?ID=7891
7. Ecklund and McNerney, *Personnel Recovery Operations for Special Operations Forces In Urban Environments*
8. http://www.pbs.org/wgbh/pages/frontline/shows/ambush/interviews/haad.html
9. Faust, *Task Force Ranger in Somalia: Isaiah 6:8*
10. Ibid
11. http://www.governmentattic.org/2docs/Army_160thSOAR_Histories_1991-2001.pdf
12. http://www.dailylife.com.au/news-and-views/dl-culture/black-hawk-down-us-prisoner-of-war-mike-durant-reunites-with-the-aid-worker-who-saved-him-20150518-gh41z5.html

## Chapter 9

1. McKnight, *Streets of Mogadishu*, p. 169
2. Senate Review
3. Ibid
4. Ibid
5. Ibid
6. Ibid
7. Ibid
8. Ernst Presentation, MOUT 2000 Conference
9. Senate Review
10. Ibid

11. Baumann and Yates with Washington, *My Clan Against the World*, p. 22
12. https://www.washingtonpost.com/archive/politics/1993/10/31/the-words-behind-a-deadly-decision/061d5a21-d93a-4c7d-8ad5-4a0c10688595/?utm_term=.65ae1a4b6a57
13. http://www.worldaffairsboard.com/showthread.php?t=41259
14. Faust, *Task Force Ranger in Somalia: Isaiah 6:8*
15. http://www.pbs.org/wgbh/pages/frontline/shows/ambush/etc/script.html
16. Galdorisi, George and Phillips, Thomas, *Leave No Man Behind: The Saga of Combat Search and Rescue* (St Paul: Zenith Press, 2009), p. 505
17. Ibid, p. 505
18. Sangvic, *Battle of Mogadishu: Anatomy of a Failure*
19. Eversmann, MOUT 2000 Conference
20. http://www.newyorker.com/magazine/2009/07/06/the-kill-company
21. http://www.nytimes.com/2007/01/21/world/middleeast/21abuse.html
22. http://www.newyorker.com/magazine/2009/07/06/the-kill-company
23. Ricks, Thomas E., *The Gamble: General Petraeus and the Untold Story of the American Surge in Iraq* (New York: Penguin, 2009), p. 35
24. Interview with Task Force Ranger participant September 23, 2017
25. Interview with Task Force Ranger participant August 2, 2017
26. Interview with Task Force Ranger participant July 27, 2017
27. Kilcullen, David, *Out of the Mountains: The Coming Age of the Urban Guerrilla* (New York: Oxford University Press, 2013), p. 75
28. Ibid
29. http://www.longwarjournal.org/archives/2011/12/shabaab_leader_recou.php#
30. Duffield, Major Mark F., *Into the Beehive: The Somali Habr Gidr Clan As An Adaptive Enemy*; www.dtic.mil/dtic/tr/fulltext/u2/a374653.pdf

# NOTES

31. http://edition.cnn.com/2001/LAW/04/23/embassy.bombings.trial.01/index.html
32. http://www.weeklystandard.com/showstoppers/article/4846
33. https://www.washingtonpost.com/archive/politics/1993/10/31/the-words-behind-a-deadly-decision/061d5a21-d93a-4c7d-8ad5-4a0c10688595/?utm_term=.65ae1a4b6a57
34. Ibid
35. Senate Review
36. http://www.militaryhallofhonor.com/honoree-record.php?id=1973
37. Kragh, John F. and others, *Tragedy into Drama: An American History of Tourniquet Use in the Current War* (Fort Sam Houston: United States Army Institute of Surgical Research, 2013); www.dtic.mil/get-tr-doc/pdf?AD=ADA614535
38. Regimental Training Guidance
39. Couch, Sua Sponte
40. Eversmann, MOUT 2000 Conference
41. Adcock, Gene, *CCT – Eye of the Storm Volume 2: The GWOT Years* (Author House, 2012)
42. Senate Review

# REFERENCES

## INTERVIEWEES

John Belman, 75th Ranger Regiment
Tom DiTomasso, 75th Ranger Regiment
Mike Durant, 160th Special Operations Aviation Regiment (Airborne)
Matt Eversmann, 75th Ranger Regiment
Norman Hooten, 1st Special Forces Operational Detachment-Delta (Airborne)
Gerry Izzo, 160th Special Operations Aviation Regiment (Airborne)
Gary Keeney, 1st Special Forces Operational Detachment-Delta (Airborne)
Paul Leonard, 1st Special Forces Operational Detachment-Delta (Airborne)
Karl Maier, 160th Special Operations Aviation Regiment (Airborne)
Michael Moser, 1st Special Forces Operational Detachment-Delta (Airborne)
Jim Smith, 1st Special Forces Operational Detachment-Delta (Airborne)
Jeff Struecker, 75th Ranger Regiment
Kelly Venden, 1st Special Forces Operational Detachment-Delta (Airborne)

# REFERENCES

A number of additional interviewees chose to remain anonymous due to their continuing work in the field of special operations.

## BOOKS

Adcock, Gene, *CCT – Eye of the Storm Volume 2: The GWOT Years* (Author House, 2012)

Allard, Kenneth, *Somalia Operations: Lessons Learned* (Washington DC: National Defense University Press, 1995)

Baumann, Robert F. and Yates, Lawrence A. with Washington, Versalle F., *My Clan Against the World: US and Coalition Forces in Somalia 1992–1994* (Leavenworth: Washington Combat Studies Institute Press, 2003)

Bolger, Lieutenant General Daniel P., *Death Ground: Today's American Infantry in Battle* (Novato: Presidio Press, 1999)

Bolger, Lieutenant General Daniel P., *Savage Peace: Americans at War in the 1990s* (Novato: Presidio Press, 1995)

Bowden, Mark, *Black Hawk Down* (London: Bantam Press, 1999)

Boykin, Lieutenant General William G., *Never Surrender* (New York: Hachette, 2008)

Carney, Colonel John T. and Schemmer, Benjamin F., *No Room for Error: The Covert Operations of America's Special Tactics Units from Iran to Afghanistan* (New York: Ballantine Books, 2002)

Casper, Colonel Lawrence E., *Falcon Brigade: Combat and Command in Somalia and Haiti* (Boulder: Lynne Rienner Publishers, 2001)

Chun, Clayton K. S., *Gothic Serpent: Black Hawk Down Mogadishu 1993* (Oxford: Osprey, 2012)

DeKever, Andrew J. and Durant, Chief Warrant Officer 4 Michael J., *Here Rests in Honored Glory: Life Stories of Our Country's Medal of Honor Recipients* (Merriam Press Military, 2012)

DeLong, Kent and Tuckey, Steven, *Mogadishu! Heroism and Tragedy* (Westport: Praeger Publishers, 1994)

Durant, Chief Warrant Officer 4 Michael J., and Hartov, Steven, *In the Company of Heroes* (New York: GP Putnam's Sons, 2003)

Durant, Chief Warrant Officer 4 Michael J, Hartov, Steven & Johnson, Lieutenant Colonel Robert L., *The Night Stalkers: Top Secret Missions of the US Army's Special Operations Aviation Regiment* (New York: NAL Caliber, 2008)

Eversmann, Matt and Schilling, Dan, *The Battle of Mogadishu: Firsthand Accounts from the Men of Task Force Ranger* (New York: Presidio Press, 2004)

Galdorisi, George and Phillips, Thomas, *Leave No Man Behind: The Saga of Combat Search and Rescue* (St Paul: Zenith Press, 2009)

Kassinger, Jack, *Holding Hands with Heroes* (Pittsburgh: Dorrance Publishing, 2010)

Kilcullen, David, *Out of the Mountains: The Coming Age of the Urban Guerrilla* (New York: Oxford University Press, 2013)

McKnight, Lieutenant Colonel Danny, *Streets of Mogadishu* (Chester: Leading for Freedom, 2011)

Naylor, Sean, *Relentless Strike: The Secret History of Joint Special Operations Command* (New York: St Martins, 2015)

Peterson, Scott, *Me Against My Brother: At War in Somalia, Sudan, and Rwanda* (New York: Routledge, 2000)

Pushies, Fred J., *Night Stalkers: 160th Special Operations Aviation Regiment (Airborne)* (St Paul: Zenith Press, 2005)

Ricks, Thomas E., *The Gamble: General Petraeus and the Untold Story of the American Surge in Iraq* (New York: Penguin, 2009)

Rottman, Gordon L., *The Rocket Propelled Grenade* (Oxford: Osprey, 2010)

Smith, Michael, *Killer Elite: The Inside Story of America's Most Secret Special Operations Team* (London: Orion, 2006)

Struecker, Major Jeff, *The Road to Unafraid: How the Army's Top Ranger Faced Fear and Found Courage through Black Hawk Down and Beyond* (Nashville: Thomas Nelson, 2009,)

Thomas, Keni, *Get It On! What it Means to Lead the Way* (Brentwood: B&H Publishing Group, 2011)

Tucker, David and Lamb Christopher J., *United States Special Operations Forces* (New York: Columbia University Press, 2007)

Walker, Greg, *At the Hurricane's Eye: US Special Operations Forces from Vietnam to Desert Storm* (New York: Ivy Books, 1994)

# REFERENCES

Wasdin, Howard E. and Templin, Stephen, *SEAL Team Six* (New York: St Martin's, 2011)

Whetstone, Lieutenant Colonel Michael, *Madness in Mogadishu: Commanding the 10th Mountain Division's Quick Reaction Company during Black Hawk Down* (Mechanicsburg: Stackpole Books, 2015)

## REPORTS

Department of Defense, *Subject: After Action Report for TASK FORCE RANGER Operations in Support of UNOSOM II; 22 August–25 October 1993* (USSOCOM, 1994)
http://www.socom.smil.mil/socs-ho/aarll/somalia

DiTomasso, Captain Thomas, *The Battle of the Black Sea: Bravo Company, 3rd Ranger Battalion, 75th Ranger Regiment, 3–4 October 1993* (Fort Benning: Infantry Officer's Advanced Course, 1994)
www.benning.army.mil/library/content/Virtual/.../DiTomassoThomas%20CPT.pdf

Duffield, Major Mark F., *Into the Beehive: The Somali Habr Gidr Clan As An Adaptive Enemy*
www.dtic.mil/dtic/tr/fulltext/u2/a374653.pdf

Ecklund, Marshall V. and McNerney, Michael A., *Personnel Recovery Operations for Special Operations Forces in Urban Environments: Modeling Successful Overt and Clandestine Methods of Recovery* (California: Naval Postgraduate School Monterey, 2004)
https://calhoun.nps.edu/handle/10945/1159

Faust, Colonel James T., *Task Force Ranger in Somalia: Isaiah 6:8* (US Army War College, 1999)
http://www.lc-vans.lintcenter.org/wp.../08/TF-Ranger-Part-1-Paper-with-Prologue-pp-0-29.pdf

Karcher, Major Timothy M., *Understanding the Victory Disease, from the Little Bighorn, to Mogadishu, to the Future*
www.dtic.mil/get-tr-doc/pdf?AD=ADA416034

Kragh, John F. and others, *Tragedy into Drama: An American History of Tourniquet Use in the Current War* (Fort Sam Houston: United States Army Institute of Surgical Research, 2013) www.dtic.mil/get-tr-doc/pdf?AD=ADA614535

Lechner, Captain James O., *A Monograph of Combat Operations in Mogadishu, Somalia Conducted by Task Force Ranger* (Fort Benning: Infantry Officer's Advanced Course, 1994)

www.benning.army.mil/library/content/Virtual/.../LechnerJamesO%20%20CPT.pdf

Levin, C. and Warner, J., *Subject: Review of Circumstances Surrounding the Ranger Raid on October 3-4 1993 in Mogadishu, Somalia* (Washington: Senate Committee on Armed Services, 1995)

https://fas.org/irp/congress/1995_rpt/mogadishu.pdf

Marion, Forrest L., *Heroic Things: Air Force Special Tactics Personnel at Mogadishu, October 3–4, 1993* (Air Force Historical Foundation, 2013)

http://www.afhistory.org/air-power-history/2013-air-power-history-archive/

Perino, Captain Larry D., *The Battle of the Black Sea: Mogadishu Somalia* (Fort Benning: Infantry Officer's Advanced Course, 1994)

www.benning.army.mil/library/content/Virtual/.../PerinoLarryD%20%20CPT.pdf

Rysewyk, Captain Lee, *Experiences of Executive Officer from Bravo Company, 3d Battalion, 75th Ranger Regiment and Task Force Ranger during the Battle of the Black Sea on 3–4 October 1993, in Mogadishu, Somalia* (Fort Benning: Infantry Officer's Advanced Course, 1994)

www.benning.army.mil/library/content/Virtual/.../RysewykLee%20A.%20CPT.pdf

Sangvic, Major Roger N., *Battle of Mogadishu: Anatomy of a Failure* (Fort Leavenworth: School of Advanced Military Studies United States Army Command and General Staff College, 1999)

www.dtic.mil/get-tr-doc/pdf?AD=ADA366316

Smith, Captain Kurt, *Task Force Ranger in Somalia: 1st Special Forces Operational Detachment-Delta, 3–4 October 1993* (Fort Benning: Infantry Officer's Advanced Course, 1994)

www.benning.army.mil/library/content/Virtual/.../other/.../SmithKurt%20CPT.pdf

# REFERENCES

## ARTICLES

Atkinson, Rick, "Night of a Thousand Casualties" (The *Washington Post*, January 31, 1994)
https://www.washingtonpost.com/archive/politics/1994/01/31/night-of-a-thousand-casualties/1f0c97b1-1605-46e5-9466-ba3599120c25/?utm_term=.69a7c2b217aa

Butler Jr., Captain Frank, Hagmann, Lieutenant Colonel John H. and Richards, David T., "Tactical Management of Urban Warfare Casualties in Special Operations" (*Military Medicine*, 165, Supplement 1, 2000)
www.valorproject.org/uploads/Tact_Mgmt_Urban_Warfare.pdf

Ferry, Captain Charles P., "Mogadishu, October 1993: A Company XO's Notes on Lessons Learned" (*Infantry* Magazine, November-December 1994)
https://www.benning.army.mil/magazine/1994/1994_6/fa02.pdf

Grau, Lester W., "A Weapon For All Seasons: The Old But Effective RPG-7 Promises to Haunt the Battlefields of Tomorrow" (*Infantry* Magazine, May–August 1998)
http://fmso.leavenworth.army.mil/documents/weapon.htm

Hollis, Captain Mark A. B., "Platoon Under Fire: Mogadishu, October 1993" (*Infantry* Magazine, January-April 1998)
battleofmogadishu.com/Cms_Data/Contents/mog/Media/.../JAN_APR_98.pdf

Loeb, Vernon, "After Action Report" (The *Washington Post*, February 27, 2000) https://www.washingtonpost.com/archive/lifestyle/magazine/2000/02/27/after-action-report/3c474a43-ea21-4bf5-afc5-02820b8579e5/?utm_term=.9f97f4dbc593

## FILMS

*Frontline: Ambush in Mogadishu* (Public Broadcasting Service, September 1998) http://www.pbs.org/wgbh/pages/frontline/shows/ambush
*Return to Mogadishu: Remembering Black Hawk Down*

http://returntomogadishu.com

(This is a film produced with Jeff Struecker and Keni Thomas who returned to Mogadishu in 2013. They travel to the Bakara Market area including the location of the target building and the first crash site. It is particularly worthwhile as the viewer gets a glimpse of what the actual streets and buildings in the area look like, albeit 20 years after the battle.)

# INDEX

Abdi House  29–30
Abgaal  24, 68
Afghanistan  163, 275
African Union Mission in Somalia (AMISOM)  282, 283
AIAI *see* al-Itihad al-Islami
Aideed, Hussein Mohamed Farrah  281
Aideed, Mohamed Farah  13, 15, 22–23, 32, 34, 36
  and Atto  72–76
  and CIA  56–59, 61–62, 66, 68
  and death  250, 281
  and deception operations  45
  and Durant  247, 248–49
  and helicopters  263
  and hunt  37, 38, 40, 44, 246
  and isolation  47–48, 71–72
  and movie  291
  and technicals  157
  and UN  26
  and USA  30, 273–74
  *see also* Radio Aideed
aircraft, US:
  AC-130 Spectre  27, 38, 252–56
  Beechcraft 300/350; 60
  P-3 Orion  61
  RG-8 Schweizer  61
  *see also* helicopters
aircraft hangar  42–43, 46
AMISOM *see* African Union Mission in Somalia
ammunition  207–11, 298
Anderson, Steve  67
Aspin, Les  15, 32, 33, 38, 71
  and armored vehicles  258
  and Spectre  255
Atto, Osman  15, 23, 65, 72–76, 250, 289
Atwater, Sgt Chris  153–54
Authorized Weapons Storage Sites (AWSS)  24–25
Awale, Abdi Hassan  15, 29, 80, 82, 103
Aznan, Pvt Mat  223

Bakara Market  80–81
Bana, Eric  288
Barre, Siad  21, 22

Beckwith, Col Charlie  33
Belman, Sgt John  15, 50, 218, 257, 262, 296–97
   and equipment  217, 300
   and "Mogadishu Mile"  236, 238, 240
   and movie  293
   and rescue plan  223–24
   and Spectre  252–53
   and Super 61;  142–43, 146, 147, 148, 156–57, 158–59, 214
Benjamin, S Sgt Ray  15, 51, 96
Berendsen, Pvt 1C Anton  15, 85, 115–16
Bergamo, Chief WO Mark  49–50
Bin Laden, Usama  272–73, 275
*Black Hawk Down* (book/film)  53–55, 96, 125, 162, 286–93
Blackburn, Pvt Todd  15, 85, 106–11
body armor  299–300, 306
Boren, S Sgt Doug  118
Boutros-Ghali, Boutros  15, 23–24, 27, 30–31, 32
Boykin, Col William "Jerry"  15, 39, 70, 78, 283–84
   and SNA  206
   and Super 61;  131
   and Super 64;  167, 169, 176
Bray, S Sgt Jeff  15, 51, 104, 214, 215, 237
breaching  279–80
Briley, Chief WO Donovan  15, 127
British Army: SAS  31, 33, 261
Burns, S Sgt John  68
Busch, S Sgt Daniel  15, 129–30, 131, 134
Bush, George H. W.  23

Casper, Col Lawrence  219
casualties  240–45
Cavaco, Corp James  16, 184, 185, 194–95

Central Command (CENTCOM)  31–32
chalks  84–86
CIA (Central Intelligence Agency)  31, 32, 56–59, 61–62, 66, 282
   and Team Three  80, 81
civilians  70–71
clans  21, 24, 32; *see also* Abgaal; Hawiye Clan
Cleveland, S Sgt William  16, 170, 171
Clinton, Bill  24, 71, 249, 275
close quarter battle (CQR)  44
Colombia  33
combat leadership  266–69
Combat-Ready Clamp  277–78
Combat-Search-And-Rescue (CSAR) team  50–51, 217–18, 264–65
convoys  181–205
counterterrorism  262–63
Cugno, Maj Ron  166

David, Lt Col Bill  16, 28, 76, 221
Diemer, Specialist Dave  85
Direct Action Penetrators (DAPs)  263–65
DiTomasso, Lt Tom  16, 35–36, 40, 46, 270–71, 283
   and Bakara Market  81, 83
   and casualties  108, 218
   and convoy  189–90, 193, 203–4
   and Durant  180
   and equipment  217
   and leadership  266–67, 268
   and "Mogadishu Mile"  238–39
   and movie  287, 289
   and rescue plan  230, 233, 234
   and Salad  96, 99–102
   and SNA  208–9, 210–11
   and Spectre  252
   and Super 61;  125–26, 135–36, 137, 138–39, 143–44, 147, 148, 156–57, 207

# INDEX

and Super 64; 165–68, 169
Doody, 1Sgt Gary 203
Dowdy, S Sgt Ray 16, 147–48
Downing, Gen Wayne 16, 33, 37–38, 46, 249, 254–56
Durant, Chief WO Michael 16, 82, 92, 109, 306
   and capture 179–80, 245, 246–49
   and Salad 96–97, 98, 117
   and Super 61; 128, 136
   and Super 64; 161, 163–64, 170–71, 172–73, 176–77

Eastabrooks, Specialist David 198
equipment 276–81, 298–307
Ernst, Maj Gen Carl 16, 29, 56, 256
Escobar, Pablo 33
Ethiopia 21, 282
Eversmann, S Sgt Matt 16, 46, 109–10, 178, 285
   and convoy 181, 185, 186, 187, 188, 201
   and leadership 267–68
   and movie 287–88, 293
   and Salad 83, 84–85, 88–89, 102, 105, 107, 113–17
   and Super 61; 138–41

Fales, M Sgt Scott 16, 50–51, 143, 146, 149
famine 22
fast-roping 83–86, 96, 98–103
Faust, Lt Col James "Tommy" 16, 44–45, 59, 67, 69, 70, 77
   and casualties 245
   and Salad 80–81
Ferry, Capt Charles 222, 224
Field, S Sgt Tommy 16
Fillmore, Sgt 1C Earl 16, 150–51
first aid 43, 44, 280
food 24, 25, 44

Frank, Chief WO Ray 16, 164, 170–71
French forces 27, 28

Galentine, Sgt Scott 116, 290
Garrison, Maj Gen William "Bill" 12, 16, 39, 40, 41, 45
   and Aideed 71–72
   and armored vehicles 258
   and CIA 58–59
   and convoy 203
   and movie 291
   and Objective Flute 65–66
   and patrols 46
   and rescue plan 218–19
   and Salad 80–81, 88
   and SNA 63–64
   and Spectre 253
   and Super 64; 176
goats 44
Godane, Ahmed Abdi 271, 272
Goff, S Sgt Stan 52–53
Goffena, Chief WO Mike 16, 164, 165, 173–74
Good, Pvt 1C Marcus 16, 85, 106
Gordon, M Sgt Gary 16, 231, 244–45, 293
   and Super 64; 167–69, 170, 171, 174
Ground Reaction Force (GRF) 67–68, 104
   # 1; 180–97
   # 2; 197–205

Habr Gidr 22, 24–25, 27, 29, 32
   and jihadists 272
   and Mohamed 30–31
   and Objective Flute 64
Hale, M Sgt Jon 17
Hall, Sgt Mason 168
Harrell, Lt Col Gary 17, 34–35, 39, 50, 96, 170

Harris, 1Sgt Glenn  82
Harris, Adm Harry  59–60
Hartnett, Josh  287
Hawiye  21; *see also* Habr Gidr
helicopters  38, 44–45, 262–66
   AH-6J "Guns"  48–49, 67, 214–16
   Black Hawk  29–30
   Hueys  241–42
   MH-6 Little Bird  34, 61, 82–83, 89–90
   MH-60 Black Hawk  82–84, 89–104
   OH-58D Kiowa  60, 221–22
   Super 61;  123, 124–59, 180–82, 212–14, 228–31, 284
   Super 62;  164–76
   Super 63;  49–50
   Super 64;  161–62, 163–77, 226, 231–32, 244–45, 284
   Super 66;  209–10
   Super 68;  142–46
Hoar, Gen Joseph  17, 31–32, 33, 39, 42
   and armored vehicles  257, 258
   and government  273
   and Spectre  254
Hofstetter, Suzanne  248
Hollis, Lt Mark  222–23, 227
Hooten, Sgt 1C Norman  17, 34, 51–52, 276, 285
   and armored vehicles  260–61
   and Atto  76
   and *Black Hawk Down*  54–55, 287, 288–89
   and helicopters  262, 263
   and "Mogadishu Mile"  238, 239–40
   and rescue plan  223, 234–35
   and resupplies  209–10
   and rules of engagement  45
   and Salad  79, 82, 93, 103
   and Smith  212
   and SNA  207

   and Super 61;  127, 138, 141, 145–46, 149–50, 151, 152, 153, 154, 157–58, 213–14
   and Super 64;  175–76
   and Wolcott  228–29
Houston, Sgt Cornell  227, 228
Howcroft, James  56–57
Howe, Adm Jonathan  17, 26, 27, 30, 31, 32
   and Aideed  273–74
   and Durant  248–49
humanitarian aid  22–23, 24
HUMINT  32, 56–57

Indian forces  219
intelligence  29, 42; *see also* CIA; HUMINT; SIGINT
International Committee of the Red Cross (ICRC)  22, 243, 245, 248
Iraq  33, 261, 263–65, 268–69
Islamic Courts Union (ICU)  282
Italian forces  27, 68, 72, 219
Italy  62
al-Itihad al-Islami (AIAI)  281–82
Izzo, Chief WO Gerry  17, 76–77, 78, 211, 215
   and Blackburn  109
   and casualties  245
   and Durant  247
   and movie  288, 289, 292, 293
   and rescue plan  242–43
   and Salad  88, 96–97, 99, 103
   and Spectre  253
   and Super 61;  123, 129
   and Super 64;  161, 172

jihadists  80, 163, 272, 281–82
Jilao, Gen Ahmed  68
Johnston, Lt Gen Robert  47
Joint Special Operations Command (JSOC)  32, 33, 37–38, 282

# INDEX

Jollota, Chief WO Dan  17, 96, 142, 143–44, 232
Jones, Chief WO Keith  17, 133–34, 136
Jones, Chief WO Randy  17
Joyce, Sgt Casey  17, 85, 114, 188

Karcher, Maj Timothy  55
Kassinger, Jack  56
Kaufman, Chief WO Stu  49–50
Keeney, Sgt 1C Gary "Greedy"  17, 43, 44, 74–75, 301–2
  and convoy  182–84, 185, 188, 190–91, 192, 195–96, 204
  and movie  289
  and Salad  94, 120, 121
  and Super 61;  129
Khat  156–57
Kilcullen, David  271
Kowalewski, Pvt 1C Richard "Alphabet"  17, 181, 183–84
Kurth, Specialist Mike  122

Lamb, Sgt 1C Rick  230–31
Lechner, Lt James "Jim"  17, 47–49, 75–76, 89, 180
  and Super 61;  153–54
  and Super 64;  175
Leonard, Sgt 1C Paul  17, 34, 67–68, 70
  and Atto  74, 75
  and convoy  181–82, 184, 185, 186–87, 189, 191, 192, 194–95, 204–5
  and Salad  82, 91, 94–95, 120, 122
Lig Ligato Compound  64–66

McCain, John  32
McKnight, Lt Col Danny  18, 35–36, 37, 39, 51
  and *Black Hawk Down*  53–55, 290
  and Blackburn  107–8
  and convoy  190, 193, 200–1
  and Salad  87–88
  and Spectre  253–54
  and Super 61;  180–82
McKnight, Col David "Dave"  18, 56, 59, 62, 65, 249
McLaughlin, S Sgt Jeff  18, 85, 116
Maddox, Pvt John  192–93
Maier, Chief WO Karl  17, 60, 78, 216, 268
  and convoy  204
  and helicopters  263, 265–66
  and movie  293
  and RPGs  163
  and Salad  86, 89–91
  and Spectre  253
  and Super 61;  128–29, 132–34, 136
  and Super 64;  171–72, 244
Malaysian forces  218, 219, 220, 222–23, 224, 226–27, 229–30
  and casualties  243
marksmanship  279
Marsh, Dr John "Rob"  17, 44, 108
Martin, Pvt 1C James  224
Martin, M Sgt Tim "Griz"  17, 186, 187, 290
Matthews, Lt Col Tom  17, 39, 50, 96
  and Super 61;  127, 130, 134
  and Super 64;  164–65, 166
MEDEVACs  50, 211–12
medics  106–7, 148–49
  and equipment  277–78
  and training  280
Meyerowich, Capt Drew  18, 225
Military Compound  66–68
Miller, Capt Austin "Scottie"  18, 51–52, 81, 137–38, 194
  and Super 61;  212–13, 214
mines  219
Mitchell, Sgt Danny  87
Mobile Military Courts  21

349

Mogadishu  42–43, 62–63, 70–71
   and battle of (1993)  12–14, 283–85, 308–18
   *see also* National Street; Olympic Hotel; soccer stadium
"Mogadishu Mile"  235–40, 290–91
Mohamed, Sheikh Aden  30–31, 281
Mohammed, Ali Mahdi  22
Montgomery, Maj Gen Thomas  18, 25, 31, 40, 71–72, 219
   and armored vehicles  257–58
Moore, Specialist Jason  85
Moores, Lt Larry  18, 190, 197, 200–1, 239, 267
Moroccan forces  27–28
Moser, S Sgt Michael  18, 53, 93–94, 270, 276, 303–4
   and armored vehicles  260
   and helicopters  263
   and "Mogadishu Mile"  236
   and rescue plan  224, 229–30
   and resupplies  210
   and Salad  90, 91, 120
   and SNA  208
   and soccer stadium  241, 242
   and Super 61;  137–38, 144–45, 150, 152, 154

National Street  25, 112–13, 221–23
Nelson, Specialist Shawn  142, 291
Nigerian forces  179
night-vision devices  276
Niklaus, Chief WO Jeff  18, 110
Nixon, Maj Craig  40, 197

Oakley, Robert  20, 32
Objective Flute  64–68
Office of Military Support (OMS)  59–60
Ogaden War (1977)  21, 22
Olson, Capt Eric  221, 240

Olympic Hotel  80, 81, 83, 86, 90–91, 224
operational security (OPSEC)  46–47
operations:
   *Desert Storm* (1991)  33, 51, 256, 275
   *Gothic Serpent* (1993)  39
   *Iraqi Freedom* (2003–11)  263–65
   *Restore Hope* (1993)  23, 24

Pakistani forces  24–29, 30, 72, 243
   and rescue plan  219, 220, 222
   and soccer stadium  240–41, 242
Pamer, Pvt 1C Eugene  203
Perino, Lt Larry  18, 117–18, 153, 155–56
   and leadership  267
   and "Mogadishu Mile"  236
   and Smith  211–12
Pilla, Sgt Dominick  18, 112
Powell, S Sgt Bill  121–22
Powell, Gen Colin  18, 32–33, 254, 255
Pringle, Sgt Mike  67
prisoners of war  180–83; *see also* Durant

al-Qaeda  252, 271, 272–73, 281–82
Quick Reaction Force (QRF)  28–30, 36, 76–78, 201–5, 218–19

Radio Aideed  27, 68–70
radios  175–76, 231–32
Ramaglia, Sgt Randy  18, 127–28, 235
Ranger Assault Carry Kit (RACK)  276–77
Rierson, Sgt 1C Matt  18, 91, 92–93, 249–50
Rodriguez, Specialist Adalberto  85
Rodriguez, Maj Herb  18, 96, 142, 232
Rogers, Tech Sgt Pat  18, 51
Ruiz, Sgt Lorenzo  18, 187–88
Russia  21, 43, 66–68

# INDEX

Rwanda 275
Rysewyk, Capt Lee 18, 47, 63, 65–66, 230

safaris 44
Salad Elmi, Omar 18, 80–82, 103
Sangvic, Maj Roger 73
Schilling, Tech Sgt Dan 19, 51, 87–88, 119, 190, 193
Schnoor, M Sgt Dave 51
Schwarzkopf, Gen Norman 275
security 46
al-Shabaab 14, 272, 282
Shannon, Sgt Paul 168
Shughart, Herbert 275
Shughart, Sgt 1C Randy 19, 231, 244–45, 293
  and Super 64; 168–69, 170, 171, 174, 175–76
SIGINT 60
"signature flights" 44–45
Sizemore, Tom 290
Smith, Corp Jamie 19, 155–56, 207, 211–12
Smith, Sgt 1C Jim 19, 74
  and Super 61; 124–25, 126, 129–30, 131–32, 134
Smith, S Sgt Kurt 19, 36, 37, 40, 43
  and convoy 193
  and equipment 216–17, 300
  and intelligence 63
  and medical care 211–12
  and "Mogadishu Mile" 234–36
  and Objective Flute 65, 67
  and Radio Aideed 69
  and rescue plan 229
  and rules of engagement 45
  and Salad 92
  and Super 61; 129, 141–42, 145, 151–52
SNA see Somali National Alliance
sniper teams 124–26

SNM see Somali National Movement
Snodgrass, Specialist Kevin 85, 116
soccer stadium 240–42
SOCOM see Special Operations Command
Somali National Alliance (SNA) 24, 32, 63–64, 253
  and militia 179–203, 207
  and Salad 80–81, 98, 114–15
  and savagery 244–45
Somali National Movement (SNM) 21
Somalia 21, 281–83; see also Mogadishu
Spalding, Specialist Eric 192
Special Operation Forces (SOF) 274–75, 282
Special Operations Command (SOCOM) 32, 33
Stebbins, John "Stebby" 293
Steele, Capt Mike 19, 35–36, 39–40, 51, 52–55, 212
  and leadership 268–69
  and rescue plan 225
  and Super 61; 135, 152, 153–54, 156
Strous, Richard "Doc" 235
Struecker, Sgt Jeff 19, 87, 110–13, 215–16, 267
  and armored vehicles 259
  and casualties 241–42
  and convoy 190, 191, 195, 196–99, 201, 205
  and "Mogadishu Mile" 236–37
  and rescue plan 220–21, 222, 230
  and weaponry 298
supplies 207–11, 278

tanks 219, 220, 222, 292
techniques 276–81
Telscher, Sgt Jim 85
templates 269–71
terrorism 272
Thomas, Sgt Keni 19, 54, 98, 117, 152

tire burning 120–21
tourniquets 277–78, 280
training 43–44, 278–80
Twombly, Specialist Lance 142, 291

uniforms 43, 287, 305–6, 307
United Nations 29, 30–31, 42, 62, 72, 274
   Security Council Resolution 837 26–27, 36
United Nations Operations in Somalia (UNOSOM) 22–23, 68
United Nations Operations in Somalia II (UNOSOM II) 24, 27
United Somali Congress (USC) 21–22, 24
United States of America (USA) 21, 23, 30–33, 71–72, 273–75
UNOSOM *see* United Nations Operations in Somalia
US Army 39–42, 54–55
   1st Special Forces Operational Detachment-Delta 13, 33–40
   10th Mountain Dvn 28, 71, 201–5, 243
   2-14 Infantry Rgt 28
   2-25th Aviation Rgt 221–22
   75th Ranger Rgt 13, 35–37
   Task Force 160th Special Operations Aviation Rgt 13, 40, 45, 52, 65, 247–48
   Alpha (A) Company 35, 225
   Bravo (B) Company 35–36
   C-Company 226–27
   F-Troop 244
US Marines 24
US Navy: SEALS 23, 38, 57–58, 221, 282–83
USC *see* United Somali Congress

Van Arsdale, Lt Col Lee 19, 202, 221, 225

vehicles:
   and armored 256–62
   Condors 219–20, 222–23, 227–28
   Humvees 86–88, 110–13
   *see also* tanks
Venden, Sgt 1C Kelly 19, 34–35, 246, 259–60, 270, 302
Vietnam War (1955–75) 275
Vines, Col John 40
"Volkswagen" package 38–39

War on Terror 46–47, 252, 276
Warren, S Sgt Charlie 19, 146
Wasdin, Howard 121
water 207, 209–11
Watson, Sgt Sean "Tim" 19, 99
weaponry, Somali 30, 294–96
   AK47s 172–73
   "Dushka" machine gun 217
   RPGs 161–63, 169–70, 184, 230–31, 266
weaponry, US 85, 279–80, 292, 296–307
   CAR15 carbine 124
   M249 SAW 49, 67
   TOW missile 29
Whetstone, Capt Michael 19, 202–3, 204, 226, 227
White, Chief WO Paul 215
Wilkinson, Tech Sgt Timothy 19, 51, 146, 147–49, 158, 215
Williamson, Sgt Aaron 118
Wisner, Frank 255, 258
Wolcott, Chief WO Clifton 19, 127, 225, 228–29

Yacone, Capt Jim 19, 103, 169, 173–74, 272
Yurek, Sgt Ed 101, 135, 137, 142, 147

Zinni, Gen Anthony 251, 263